HIKING
THE PACIFIC
CREST TRAIL

SOUTHERN
CALIFORNIA

HIKING THE PACIFIC CREST TRAIL

SOUTHERN CALIFORNIA

SECTION HIKING FROM CAMPO
TO TUOLUMNE MEADOWS

SHAWNTÉ SALABERT

MOUNTAINEERS BOOKS

**MOUNTAINEERS
BOOKS**

Mountaineers Books is the publishing division of The Mountaineers, an organization founded in 1906 and dedicated to the exploration, preservation, and enjoyment of outdoor and wilderness areas.

1001 SW Klickitat Way, Suite 201, Seattle, WA 98134
800.553.4453, www.mountaineersbooks.org

Printed in China

Distributed in the United Kingdom by Cordee, www.cordee.co.uk

First edition, 2017

Copyeditor: Sarah Gorecki
Design and layout: Peggy Egerdahl
Cartographer: Pease Press Cartography

All photographs by author unless noted otherwise.
Cover photograph: Joshua tree in the Scodie Mountains
Frontispiece: Looking south along Bubbs Creek in Kings Canyon National Park

The background of the leg maps for this book were produced using the online map viewer CalTopo. For more information, visit caltopo.com.

Library of Congress Cataloging-in-Publication Data is on file for this title.

A NOTE ABOUT SAFETY

Safety is an important concern in all outdoor activities. No guidebook can alert you to every hazard or anticipate the limitations of every reader. Therefore, the descriptions of roads, trails, routes, and natural features in this book are not representations that a particular place or excursion will be safe for your party. When you follow any of the routes described in this book, you assume responsibility for your own safety. Under normal conditions, such excursions require the usual attention to traffic, road and trail conditions, weather, terrain, the capabilities of your party, and other factors. Keeping informed on current conditions and exercising common sense are the keys to a safe, enjoyable outing.

Mountaineers Books titles may be purchased for corporate, educational, or other promotional sales, and our authors are available for a wide range of events. For information on special discounts or booking an author, contact our customer service at 800-553-4453 or mbooks@mountaineersbooks.org.

ISBN (paperback): 978-1-59485-880-2
ISBN (ebook): 978-1-59485-881-9

CONTENTS

ACKNOWLEDGMENTS

I SAY WITH NO EXAGGERATION that the time I spent on the Pacific Crest Trail—and on this project itself—changed my life. I'll tell you the whole story over margaritas and mole enchiladas some time, friends, but the miles I walked and the process I experienced helped steer my proverbial ship back to center. Life is good.

To that end, I'm overflowing with gratitude. First and foremost, thanks to my wonderful mom, Rebecca Salabert-Jagiello, for not only her unconditional love, but also for setting me on an adventurous course from the very start by encouraging a younger me to "Dare to be different!" I did, and I do.

This book wouldn't exist if the inimitable Casey Schreiner of Modern Hiker (and guidebook) fame hadn't snuck some of my writing over to the folks at Mountaineers Books—I owe you for eternity, friend.

On that note, thanks to Kirsten Colton for initiating contact; to Kate Rogers for believing in me and acting as my Bacon of Reason; to Laura Shauger for her endless calm, patience, and insight; to fellow Wisconsinite Sarah Gorecki for her flawless copy editing; and to the entire Mountaineers Books team for its outstanding efforts.

I'm also greatly indebted to my fellow series authors—and friends—Tami "Doo-Dah" Asars (I'll dance with you at 13,000 feet anytime), Philip Kramer, and Eli Boschetto, without whom I'd have tossed myself off an invisible cliff long ago.

Limitless gratitude is extended to Michael Nieves, Andrea Litton, and Allysun Marshall at Sugaroo! for the endless support, understanding, caring, and cheerleading.

I enjoyed extraordinary trail company and other assistance from Alexis Owens, Alisa Le, Angela Chung (sage fount of inspiration), Bob Myers, Brady Houlberg, Brooke Black Just-Olesen (you were with me every step of the way, Scout), Dave Hansen, Dongwater, Gabe "Warrior" Miles, Hailey Cobb, Homer Tom, Jack Thompson (there is no more passionate desert enthusiast than he), Jayson "Fuck off" Lauden, Jim Clement at VVR, Justin Bruno (winner, Most Miles and Masochism), Laura Jones Martel, Katherine Yi, Kathleen "Katwalk" Cobb (one of the trail's biggest gifts), Katy McIlvaine, Kit Gillespie, Kolby "Condor" Kirk, Kris Kamrath, Kristina Rojdev, Legend (and Gypsy), Leighton "MacGyver" Cline, Mads Black Just-Olesen, Marc Weitz, Merrell, Michelle Faucheux, Mr. Burns, Niels Quist, Pamela "Pamellama" Zoolalian (our memories could fill another book!), Ray "Maverick" Chang, Rebecca Melrose, Rodney Newman, Sara Cline, Sarah Schuh Quist, Saveria Tilden (motivator and butt-saver), Scott "Devilfish" Matheson, Scott Turner (fellow guidebook author and highly overqualified research assistant), Suzanne Hall, Tiffani Bruno, Travis "Mr. Clean" Palovchik, the Vidette Meadows Trail Angels, and to all the nice folks who gave me a lift no matter how rank I smelled.

To Anna Glen, who graciously offered her time and world-class retouching skills: thank you a hundred times over. I promise I will never make you hike.

Exceptional thanks to everyone who kindly shared their knowledge: Anitra Kass and Jack Haskell of the PCTA; Trail Gorillas Dave Fleischman, Kevin Corcoran, Jim Richter, Jerry Stone, and Don Line; Tory Elmore of The Wildlands Conservancy; and every Forest Service, county park, state park, and national park ranger or representative who picked up the phone or listened with patience—bonus points to USFS's Jeannette Granger and SEKI's "Ranger Rick" Sanger.

A trail marker welcomes hikers after the Sand Fire swept through Soledad Canyon.

Utmost praise to Lon "Halfmile" Cooper and Matt "Double Tap" Parker—your kindness to hikers is unparalleled.

To all other friends and family (including my spectacular sister, Adrienne Salabert, and awesome stepdad, Mike Jagiello) who cheered me on throughout this process—they don't allow me enough words to expound here, but know that I felt your support and am indebted to you for life.

This book is for all of you, and for anyone who dreams of wandering free.

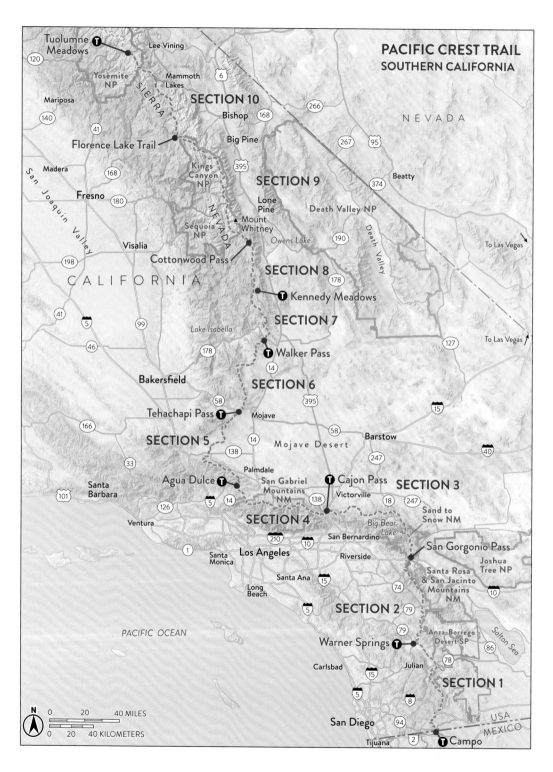

PACIFIC CREST TRAIL
SOUTHERN CALIFORNIA

Tuolumne Meadows 🆃
Lee Vining
120
Yosemite NP
Mariposa
SIERRA
Mammoth Lakes
SECTION 10
Bishop
140
41
Florence Lake Trail
Madera
168
NEVADA
Big Pine
395
Kings Canyon NP
SECTION 9
266
6
168
Fresno
180
Sequoia NP
Lone Pine
▲ Mount Whitney
Death Valley NP
Beatty
374
To Las Vegas
198
Visalia
Cottonwood Pass
Owens Lake
190
Death Valley
CALIFORNIA
SECTION 8
178
🆃 Kennedy Meadows
Lake Isabella
SECTION 7
Walker Pass 🆃
SECTION 6
127
To Las Vegas
5
99
178
Bakersfield
14
166
58
395
15
Tehachapi Pass 🆃
Mojave
SECTION 5
14
138
Mojave Desert
Barstow
247
40
33
Palmdale
San Gabriel Mountains NM
🆃 Cajon Pass
SECTION 3
Santa Barbara
Agua Dulce 🆃
Victorville
18
247
Sand to Snow NM
101
126
5
14
138
SECTION 4
Big Bear Lake
Ventura
1
Santa Monica
Los Angeles
210
10
San Bernardino
San Gorgonio Pass
Joshua Tree NP
Santa Ana
15
Riverside
Santa Rosa & San Jacinto Mountains NM
10
Long Beach
5
74
SECTION 2
79
PACIFIC OCEAN
79
Anza-Borrego Desert SP
Salton Sea
86
Warner Springs 🆃
Julian
78
Carlsbad
15
SECTION 1
5
8
N
0   20   40 MILES
0   20   40 KILOMETERS
San Diego
94
USA
MEXICO
Tijuana
2
🆃 Campo

INTRODUCTION

THE SIMPLE MAXIM, *"The trail provides,"* burns bright in the hearts of many backpackers who strike out toward adventure. But *what* does the trail provide—or more specifically, what does *this* trail provide? The Pacific Crest National Scenic Trail (PCT) offers a spectacular footpath tracing a mostly high route from the Southern California desert to the snowbound mountains of the Washington/Canada border. But it also provides so much more: the opportunity to experience peace, joy, love, reflection, accomplishment, inspiration, and transformation.

To help guide your exploration of this iconic trail, this book covers the incredibly varied ground between its sunny southern terminus in Campo and the iconic alpine beauty of Yosemite National Park's Tuolumne Meadows almost a thousand miles to the north. From the sweeping vistas of the high desert to the staggering beauty of the High Sierra, this segment of the PCT offers not only some of California's most mesmerizing scenery but also some of the trail's most challenging terrain. You'll sweat a lot, for sure, but every drop is worth the magic experienced while walking this enchanting—and possibly life-changing—path.

A BRIEF HISTORY OF THE PCT

No one knows exactly who first proposed a border-to-border trail through the western coastal states, but history favors a handful of people. Joseph T. Hazard, author and member of the Seattle-area Mountaineers, claimed that Bellingham (Washington State) educator Catherine Montgomery proposed the idea to him in 1926. Meanwhile, Fredrick W. Cleator, an overseer with the Forest Service, designed the Oregon Skyline Trail in the 1920s, now encompassed by today's PCT. Finally, Clinton C. Clarke, chairman of the Mountain League of Los Angeles, organized the PCT System Conference in 1932 to market the trail idea, earning him the moniker "Father of the PCT."

The PCT System Conference was a group of outdoor clubs and nonprofits led by Clarke and dedicated to creating one trail system made up of new and old trails that would extend from Mexico to Canada, cresting the mountainous states. Clarke inspired and planned the YMCA PCT relays—forty teams of young hikers between the ages of fourteen and eighteen who were the first to scout routes for the trail. In 1935, the teams, under the guidance of an outdoorsman named Warren Rogers, left Campo on the Mexico border and meticulously noted their route and adventures. Each subsequent summer, the teams picked up where they had left off, until they reached what is now Monument 78 on the Canada border on August 5, 1938. Their journey proved that, through combining trails, open country, and existing roads, a person could get from Mexico to Canada along a scenic alpine route. Much of the PCT still follows that same route.

In the 1960s, backpacking and hiking gained popularity, and in early 1965 President Lyndon B. Johnson sent a special message to Congress stressing the importance of environmental conservation and the development and protection of trail systems. Not long after, Secretary of the Interior Stewart L. Udall instructed the Bureau of Outdoor Recreation to head up a nationwide trail study. This study led to the National Trail System Act, enacted by Congress on October 2, 1968. The new law facilitated the development and operation of National Scenic Trails and National Historic Trails. As a result, the Appalachian Trail and the Pacific Crest Trail were the nation's first scenic trails.

A refreshing sign beckons in the hot, dry San Felipe Hills.

In 1970, the Pacific Crest National Scenic Trail Advisory Council was appointed, a mix of local recreationists, ranchers, tribal members, timber and mineral representatives, and members of conservation groups. At the council's second meeting, in 1971, it suggested a "Guide for Location, Design and Management," which was approved and published by the US secretary of agriculture. This document is still the official management plan used by various agencies. In January 1973, the advisory council, in agreement with the Bureau of Land Management, Forest Service, and other participating agencies, published the official route of the PCT in the *Federal Register*, another big step in creating the trail. In 1988, two monuments were placed at the southern and northern terminuses of the PCT, although the trail wasn't officially complete until 1993. The trail is primarily managed and maintained thanks to the stewardship of volunteers and employees of the Pacific Crest Trail Association (PCTA). Founded in 1977 as the Pacific Crest Trail Conference, the PCTA is a very active nonprofit that coordinates with the Forest Service, private landowners, and other agencies. One of the group's primary goals is to help you, the hiker or backpacker, experience the magic of walking this scenic and historic trail.

PCTA: YOU CAN HELP!

The Pacific Crest Trail Association (PCTA) needs you! Volunteers can help with trail construction, repairs, and other projects that keep the PCT passable and hikers safe. Become a member and help with critical trail needs, including trail maintenance, protection, and promotion, by donating an annual, monthly, or one-time gift. The PCTA website (www.pcta.org) alone is worth a mint in the information it provides.

SOUTHERN CALIFORNIA'S PCT: AN OVERVIEW

A hilltop monument marks the PCT's southern terminus in Campo, a stone's throw from the unsightly border fence separating the United States and Mexico. However, there's plenty of beauty ahead as the trail meanders through boulder-strewn hillsides and climbs to the pine-studded heights of the Laguna Mountains all within the first 40 miles, a surprise to anyone who imagines that Southern California is nothing but sand and tumbleweeds!

In fact, the trail here is full of incredible diversity. Yes, you'll hike through plenty of desert environments, but you'll also traverse multiple mountain ranges before landing in the High Sierra (technically in *Central* California, of course, but we had to keep the book's title concise). The PCT dips near—and sometimes, *through*—several small towns, but most of it is lightly traveled outside of the typical thru-hiking season and feels surprisingly remote. Still, the proximity to "civilization" means that it's fairly easy to access the trail from just about anywhere in Southern California.

From the Laguna Mountains, you pass through high desert cactus gardens, grassy pastures, and a riparian corridor, eventually traversing the forested (and often snow-covered) spine of the San Jacinto Mountains. A dizzying drop of more than 6000 feet deposits you into a world of wind turbines and refreshing desert waterways before you regain much of that elevation climbing through part of the Sand to Snow National Monument in the San Bernardino Mountains.

The infamous San Andreas Fault parallels the trail once you slip under bustling Interstate 15 at Cajon Pass. While earthquakes cause destruction in more populated areas, these same seismic forces helped shape the mountains you now traverse. Some of the more artistic flourishes are on display as you ascend past Mormon Rocks, travel above Devils Punchbowl, and land among the slanted fins of Vasquez Rocks. A brief stint through the overlooked, but surprisingly lush, Sierra Pelona deposits you in the hot, flat western reaches of the Mojave Desert. While trail realignment is planned to move this segment into the nearby Tehachapi Mountains, for now, the snaking Los Angeles Aqueduct and an ocean of churning wind turbines offer a unique backdrop for travelers.

The Sierra foothills beckon as you gain elevation from Tehachapi Pass to travel through the unexpectedly fertile Piute Mountains, then into the more arid Scodie Mountains before landing at Walker Pass. The peaks grow taller and the valleys deeper as you move toward Kennedy Meadows, where sagebrush flats and fragrant pine forest meet to form what's commonly revered as the "Gateway to the Sierra."

Leave the last of the desert (and civilization) behind as you slip past Cottonwood Pass to enter a land of true wilderness filled with powerful rivers, sparkling alpine lakes, blissful meadows, and snow-capped peaks—the High Sierra is nothing short of spectacular. Consider a detour to summit Mount Whitney, the highest peak in the Lower 48, then continue on to Forester Pass, the highest point on the entire PCT. From here, your journey proceeds through a stunning landscape of glacier-carved valleys and towering ridgelines, mostly following the path of the iconic John Muir Trail. Arriving at Yosemite National Park's Tuolumne Meadows is a bittersweet end to your journey, although a celebratory ice cream cone from the grill will tip the scales in favor of sweetness.

STATE MILEAGE AND ELEVATION GAIN AND LOSS

The PCT's total mileage in Southern California is 942.5 miles, give or take a few side trips or detours. Add a total elevation gain of 134,860 feet and a loss of 129,170 feet (rounded to the nearest 10), and this segment of the PCT makes for a superb fitness challenge.

HOW TO USE THIS GUIDE

This guidebook is designed for those who want to experience the PCT but don't have the time, resources, or motivation to hike for five months in one shot. This book breaks the Southern California trail into ten sections, south to north, which range from about 48 miles to 132 miles each. Each section is further divided into multiple legs spanning two landmarks; typically these are roads, passes, campsites, or water sources. The goal is not to tell you exactly how to hike, but rather to offer inspiration as you plan your time on the trail.

PCTA SECTION LETTER AND MILEAGE

The PCTA uses a widely recognized lettering system to identify PCT sections in each state. This book breaks the trail into manageable chunks lining up closely with the PCTA letters, which are included in the Section Overviews for reference.

The PCTA also counts overall PCT mileage from mile 0 at the Mexico border to mile 2668.98 at the Canada border. For hikers who are interested in such figures or are tackling multiple sections at once, this guide offers cumulative *state* mileage for each section, starting from mile 0 at the southern terminus.

The distances indicated in this guidebook were measured by GPS receiver and correlated with the 2015 Halfmile PCT mapset, currently the most accurate measurement of the PCT in *distance.* All waypoints and references in this guidebook are confirmed accurate; however, you may see small variances between my numbers and Halfmile's—and even your own, if you choose to track the trail—'tis the nature of fickle technology. Elevation measurements were also collected by GPS receiver and calculated using the CalTopo mapping program, resulting in more accurate topography and elevations than those in older trail maps and guides. The only elevation numbers *not* rounded to the nearest tenth are those for the High Sierra passes. Since every single source I consulted reported different numbers for these high points, I simply reported the elevation as noted on my GPS. While this is usually within a few feet of other sources, I cannot claim these numbers to be The One True Elevation, but they're pretty close.

Southern California's PCT Sections

Each of the state's ten sections begins with trail facts. The **distance** is the overall mileage for that section, calculated using a GPS unit as I hiked the trail and later correlated with paper maps and mapping software. **State distance** tells you how far along the Southern California PCT you've gone. **Elevation gain/loss** tallies the cumulative ups and downs over a section (rounded to the nearest 10 feet), so you'll know when you'll need to give your knees and your ticker a pep talk. Next comes the section's **high point** and **best time of year** to hike that particular span—in general, higher-elevation sections have a shorter optimal hiking season, opening up later in summer and getting first snowfall earlier in autumn. To help with your trip planning, each section also notes the corresponding **PCTA section letter**, as well as the **land managers** for the lands you'll be passing through and any **passes and permits** required. You'll find contact information for all agencies in the **appendixes** at the end of the book. Before

you head out, always check with the relevant land managers to get the latest on trail conditions, forest fires, detours, possible trailhead crime, and much more. Next up is a list of the **maps and apps** that you'll find useful (see sidebar), and of that section's trip **legs** between major landmarks.

To entice you, each section overview briefly describes what you'll find on trail—from wildflowers and wind turbines, to alpine lakes and high peaks, to cacti and coyote yelps—this portion of California's trail truly has something for every hiker! Next, you'll find **access** information for each section's starting and ending trailheads. **Notes** then offer a heads-up on what's coming. **Cities and services** close to trailheads can help you plan for resupplies or off-trail time. **Camping and other restrictions** explain where you'll have to skip putting your tent or building a campfire. Long stretches of trail without **water** are listed, so you're forewarned and don't end up parched. Good water sources are called out in trail descriptions with the ⬤ symbol; even if these water sources are seasonal, they're usually reliable in all but the driest summers or during extreme drought. **Hazards** mention a section's challenging river crossings or other potential dangers so you can plan a safe trip within your comfort zone. Finally, each section's opening details end with **suggested itineraries** from camp to camp, including daily mileage.

Section Legs

The leg descriptions come next within each section, starting with the landmark-to-landmark **distance** followed by the cumulative **elevation gain and loss** for that leg and its **high point**. The list of **connecting trails and roads** explains which major trails and roads you'll cross on that leg that could serve as alternate or emergency access points—this

doesn't mean you'll be near a trailhead when you reach one of these connectors, but the route will eventually lead back toward civilization.

Next comes the best part: reading the detailed **trail descriptions** for each leg and choosing where to go. The trail descriptions cover every mile of the PCT between Campo and Tuolumne Meadows. You'll find out what's around each bend—from water sources to camps—with enough left to your imagination so that your trip will be unique. **Maps** and **elevation profiles** for each section and each leg link up with the trail descriptions so you can easily find a place that's mentioned and see how much up and down it'll take to get there. Each leg ends with a list of **camp-to-camp mileages** so you can plan ahead or change your mind at the last

MAPS AND APPS

These are the most commonly used PCT maps and apps in Southern California:

Halfmile's maps (www.pctmap.net) are fantastic, free, up to date, and accurate. "Halfmile," a hiker with an appropriate trail name and amazing generosity, has mapped the entire PCT using GPS, including key waypoints. As the trail changes or detours happen, he's quick to update. Also fantastic are Halfmile's apps and Guthook's apps (www.atlasguides.com) for both Android and iOS smartphones. The apps use your phone's GPS technology to pinpoint your location and calculate trail distances to landmarks. Thankfully, these apps don't need cell service to work, and they include a battery-conservation setting.

Tom Harrison maps (tomharrisonmaps.com) are the gold standard for printed maps in California; some are now available for download via various mapping apps as well. These topographic maps are waterproof, tear resistant, and full color, and are especially impressive considering they're the handiwork of just one man (you guessed it, Tom Harrison) and his wife, Barbara, who have been mapmaking since 1976. The only downside is that the available maps do not cover all of the PCT segments detailed in this book.

US Forest Service (USFS) PCT maps (www.fs.usda.gov/main/pct/maps-publications) are large, easy to read, full color, waterproof, and topographic and include elevation profiles and historical notes. They're printed in conjunction with the PCTA and perhaps their best use is for planning because they provide a great overview.

Google Maps and Google Earth offer online mapping that uses shaded relief. The Google Earth satellite views of the trail are great for assessing the terrain of your chosen section. What's more, the PCTA website (www.pcta.org) links to PCT overlays that you can layer on top of Google Earth views.

MAP SYMBOLS

- - - - - - -	Featured PCT leg or segment	●—	Start/end of leg or segment	▭	National monument
··············	Alternate or recommended trail	T	Official trailhead	▭	Park or forest boundary
- - - - - -	Adjacent PCT leg or segment	T	Trailhead	▭	Boundary between forests or private inholdings
- - - - - -	Connecting trail	■	Point of interest	⊏⊐	Wilderness boundary
═══════	Divided highway	▲	Peak	▭	BLM or Indian reservation
──────	Highway	🗼	Fire lookout	⌐_⌐	County boundary
─────	Paved road	◪	Frontcountry campground	⌐_⌐	State boundary
- - - - - -	Unpaved road	▲	Camp	⌐ - ⌐	International boundary
+—+—+	Railroad tracks	🏓	Picnic area		
(5)(40)(210)	Interstate highway	ford —	Caution	🌊	Water
(6)(50)(395)	US highway	closed —	Restriction	〰	River or creek
(2)(94)(178)	State route	≍	Pass or gap	〰	Seasonal lake or stream
[24][1N23]	Forest or BLM road	-⋈-	Footbridge	៛	Spring
[S2]	County road	→l l←	Tunnel	◘	Water source
⊕ (N)	True north	——	Ski lift	〰	Fall
		↔	Gate		

minute, knowing that another snooze spot is just a mile or two ahead. Note that mileages do not reflect side trails or road walks to camps—these are simply point-to-point distances on the PCT itself; the trail description indicates additional mileage for off-trail campsites.

Camps

Pretty much anywhere flat along the PCT has likely been used as a camp. Some of these spots are suitable and sustainable Leave No Trace options, perhaps even named and signed, while others are too close to the trail or water sources. It's impossible to list every campsite along the PCT, but I've done my very best to include obvious, previously impacted locations near the trail. I do not describe camps that are in fragile areas, such as meadows or flood zones, even though they exist; practice good outdoor ethics and avoid such camps. More opportunities exist for those who are comfortable traveling off-trail, especially in the Sierra, where durable surfaces abound—consult a topo map and consider tucking yourself away for some sweet solitude.

Numbered camps are one-offs or trailside pullouts, often useful for solo travelers or small groups. These camps are numbered sequentially over an entire section and are called out on that section's maps and elevation profiles. **Named camps** are destination locations, generally with multiple sites and more visitors. Shoot for the named camps if you have a larger group or want more scenic, established sites. Some of the named camps are actually **car campgrounds**, managed by national forests, national parks, or private entities. Such campgrounds usually show up near trailheads and can be handy for PCT hikers (and any friends you've sweet-talked into meeting you with your favorite treats!). Unlike backcountry camps, most campgrounds charge a fee, and that's noted in the trail description.

Finally, be aware that not only may sites disappear in fires and floods, but also that land managers can remove campsites at any time—and

THE FIERY SUMMER OF 2016

The summer of 2016 was an exceptionally destructive one—between June and August, around twenty-six wildfires raged throughout California, exacerbated by continued drought. Of those, six caused closures in areas covered by this book. Several burned near, but not across the trail, and the closures were lifted soon after the fires moved out of the area. However, other impacts were more severe— the Sand Fire in Angeles National Forest, and the Pilot and Blue Cut fires, both in the San Bernardino National Forest, burned portions of the trail.

The Sand Fire directly affected only a small bit of trail on either side of Soledad Canyon Road (Legs 8 and 9 in Section 4), but the PCT was closed between Mill Creek Summit and Soledad Canyon Road shortly after the fire to control access to the burn area. The trail may continue to close periodically between Mill Creek Summit and Soledad Canyon Road as land managers complete recovery work—check with the Forest Service and PCTA for updates. The Blue Cut and Pilot fire burn zones nearly merged, creating a much wider swath of destruction. The latter burned just east of Silverwood Lake, mostly in the hills south of Summit Valley. A little less than 8 miles of trail were impacted in Leg 8 of Section 3, although the area is now open. The former covered a much larger area, around 18 miles beginning just east of Cajon Pass and ending near Gobblers Knob (the tail end of Leg 9 in Section 3 and a large portion of Leg 1 in Section 4); the trail is now open here, too.

Since all of these fires occurred as my fieldwork for this book was wrapping up, I was not able to completely re-hike those segments, so understand that what might have been a welcoming campsite in the past might now sit buried under a pile of debris. I did travel through some of the open portions of these three burn zones and what I can offer is this—yes, the denuded slopes and charred remnants can make for a somber hike. However, considering most of the affected terrain was covered in chaparral, not trees, it should rejuvenate quickly. A hike through these places offers not only the important reminder that fire safety is crucial in tinderbox California, but also a sense of optimism that comes from watching new growth sprout through the ashes. While there are many beautiful sights along the entire PCT, perhaps none gives me as much hope as the sight of spring wildflowers pushing through fire-blackened ground.

PCT LONG-DISTANCE PERMIT

If you intend to hike 500 or more continuous miles along the PCT, you'll want to secure a permit from the PCTA, especially important if you intend to start in Campo, where a permit limit is in place. This free and convenient permit comes with permission from federal land management agencies for travel and overnight stays along the PCT corridor. When requesting, be sure to include your start and ending locations along the PCT proper instead of the nearest city, national park or forest, or wilderness area.

The PCTA begins processing long-distance permit requests in early February and if approved, your permit will arrive via email. Each hiker must secure his or her own. Hikers younger than eighteen need a signed letter from a parent or guardian stating the dates and locations of their trip, and they must keep the letter with them at all times while on the PCT.

Note that if you intend to bring pets or stock, certain sensitive areas have restrictions. The PCT permit does not override any such restrictions.

they do. The national parks and forests may close areas for restoration, indicated by signs, in popular backcountry camps; it's important to respect such closures, which land managers usually institute once overuse poses a negative impact on the environment.

PLANNING AND PREPARATION

Before stepping foot on the trail, you'll need to decide on daily distances, consider nightly camps, and dream of adventure—for the planners among us, almost as much fun as seeing the trail in person! This guide, full of sneak-peek photos, informational sidebars, and helpful logistical details, will help prepare you to fulfill your own personal PCT journey.

NoBo or SoBo?

Most section hikers opt to hike the PCT in a northbound (NoBo) direction like their thru-hiking compadres, possibly because most of the available research materials (including this book) detail the trail in this direction. For thru-hikers, it's also easier to walk the California desert in spring, before the mercury rises and while there's still water to be found, and end in Washington by early fall, before significant snowfall begins. While SoBo trips tend to offer

more solitude, hikers must contend with snowbound Washington slopes stalling their progress and chance running out of water once they arrive at the trail's southern reaches.

Luckily, section hikers have a lot more flexibility when it comes to planning. Whether you head north or south is largely irrelevant along this rollercoaster segment since you're constantly gaining and losing altitude. Therefore, have a look at the included elevation profiles and let your knees be the directional judge.

Every Season is Hiking Season

I've hiked the trail in all four seasons, and believe me when I say that as a section hiker, there's no need to struggle through the sweltering Mojave Desert in May! The great news is that Southern California's generally mild climate allows for year-round trekking.

Avoid the desert in summer, when the mercury soars and water sources are depleted. This is a spectacular time to be in the mountains, however—both in the Peninsular and Transverse ranges of Southern California and farther north in the Sierra. Most thru-hikers aim to enter the latter in mid-June, but you'll likely encounter snow at high elevations and rivers will be swollen by snowmelt. Head out prepared for the elements or wait a few weeks until things calm down. Afternoon thunderstorms are always a possibility in the Sierra, especially in July during the summer monsoon period, which usually tapers off by mid-September. Come prepared: I once spent ten days in a row dodging relentless downpours and lightning in the Sierra high country.

Fall is a fantastic time to hike along nearly every segment of the trail—in fact, early fall in the Sierra is beautiful and quiet, if a tad bittersweet. Farther south, it's a treat to walk along riparian areas where cottonwood and sycamore trees offer autumnal color. Temperatures begin to calm in the desert by late October, and the mountains still haven't been dusted with snow.

Winter typically closes the high peaks to all but exceptionally experienced travelers. However, this is the perfect time to roam the desert, especially once rains replenish waterways. Low elevations are no stranger to cold temperatures, though—I woke up to frozen water bottles multiple times in the desert, and had to carve a snow platform for my tent in the Scodie Mountains.

Southern California's mountains come alive in spring as the snow melts, bringing grassy slopes, fields of wildflowers, and flowing creeks, especially in the underappreciated Sierra Pelona. The highest elevations (the Sierra, the area around Mount Baden-Powell in the San Gabriel Mountains, and the area around San Jacinto Peak in the San Jacinto Mountains) typically remain snowbound until early summer, except during times of extreme drought. If you choose to travel in these ranges when springtime or early summer snow is present, it's best to carry an ice axe and traction devices (i.e., crampons) and *know how to use them.* It's also imperative that you are able to navigate by map and compass when the trail is obscured by snow, and that you understand and are able to assess avalanche danger when traveling along or below steep slopes.

Permits and Passes

Section hikers do not need a PCT-specific permit, although if you're hiking 500 or more miles in one go, it saves time and hassle. For shorter hikes, follow the rules for permits and passes depending on what land management agency is in charge of the segment you're walking. In Southern California, that means the Forest Service and the National Park Service, along with Mount San Jacinto State Park, which requires a permit for hikers camping within the Mount San Jacinto State Wilderness.

Wilderness Use and Camping Permits

Most California wilderness areas are maintained by the Forest Service or the Bureau of Land Management (BLM); sometimes both share management duties. Permits aren't required in most wilderness areas south of the Sierra, but when they are, they are typically free. The only exceptions are reservations made via www.recreation.gov or when you're passing through Mount San Jacinto State Park and Wilderness, which charges a small fee for its wilderness camping permit. Each wilderness area is its own jurisdiction, and the land management agency in charge relies on you to help keep track of who's using what, when. This user information helps agencies apply for trail funding and also provides a record of where you are, essential for extracting you safely in case of a natural disaster such as a wildfire or landslide.

California Campfire Permits

You are required to carry a valid **California Campfire Permit** if you intend to channel your inner caveperson and make fire along your trek, whether that's starting a campfire (when allowed) or simply lighting a canister stove. These free permits are available

WILDERNESS AREA REGULATIONS

Wilderness use regulations vary slightly from area to area; it's best to check with the managing agencies before striking out. Most will review regulations when you pick up your permit (if one is required); these typically incorporate good Leave No Trace ethics but may also include specific guidelines for campfires, camping, party size, and bear-proof food storage.

at www.preventwildfireca.org and are valid for a year; simply watch a video, internalize its contents, pass a short quiz, and print out your permit.

Parking Permits

The **Adventure Pass** allows for parking at trailheads in the Cleveland, San Bernardino, and Angeles National Forests. An annual pass costs $30 and a day pass costs $5.

If you're a frequent visitor to national forests and parks, consider buying an **Interagency Annual Pass** ($80), which covers trailhead parking on Forest Service lands as well as those managed by the Bureau of Land Management, US Army Corps of Engineers, US Bureau of Reclamation, and US Fish and Wildlife Service; this pass also covers national park entrance fees. It's valid for a full year from the month you purchase it. If you've reached the lucky age of sixty-two, you're eligible for the annual **Interagency Senior Pass** (a bargain at $10), which covers all of the above. Additionally, if you have a permanent disability, you may qualify for a free **Interagency Access Pass**.

All passes are sold at Forest Service offices in California and at some retail stores, as well as online (see "Passes, Permits, Regulations" in Appendix 1). Throughout the book, I note where an Adventure Pass is required for parking; an Interagency Annual Pass is valid in these areas, too.

Trailhead Transportation Logistics

Getting to the trailhead or being picked up from one requires some forethought. This is possibly the most difficult part of section hiking, especially if you aren't trekking out and back or if you need a ride at a remote Forest Service road.

If hiking in a group, consider taking two separate cars to arrange a shuttle—meet at your endpoint, leave one car, then drive the other to the start. This can require several hours of driving, but it means a guaranteed ride at the end of a long trip. Don't forget to pack your waiting vehicle's keys!

If you're hoping to arrange rides to and from trailheads, research local online hiking forums and Facebook pages related to the PCT. This is a great way to meet fellow hiking enthusiasts who

PCT TRAIL NAMES

Nicknames are part of the PCT's unique subculture, even for section hikers. Your trail name becomes part of your persona; you become it. While some people opt to dub themselves, most hikers wait until the universe (or another hiker) presents them with a name based on a personality trait or some nebulous incident that occurs. You can choose whether or not to accept it, and of course, those who bestow the name should make an effort to avoid outright offense.

My trail name is "Rustic," given by a fellow hiker after a hilarious encounter at the KOA Campground in Acton. I named someone "MacGyver" for his genius engineering skills along the trail, and I met folks with names like Maverick, Wet Patch, Nightwalker, and Jurassic Crack. Sometimes, you'll bond with other hikers and never learn their real names, livelihoods, or histories, but none of that matters—learning about a person through a trail name is like getting to know someone on fast-forward.

might offer you a lift or even join your hike. Of course, there is certainly risk involved in accepting rides from strangers—trust your gut. I'm more likely to accept rides at trailheads or in small towns in the Eastern Sierra than anywhere else along the trail.

As for buses and trains, most public transit and private companies go to towns, not trailheads. However, you might consider calling a cab, using a shared ride app, or renting a car for your trip to the trail. For planning purposes, Appendix 3 lists transportation near several stops along the trail; always check ahead to make sure that a bus schedule and route meet your needs—they change frequently.

Resupplying Food and Other Necessities

As a section hiker, you can usually carry all that you need—but you don't have to! If hiking long distances, save yourself a little pack weight by planning ahead. Most backpackers need 1–2 pounds of food per day, which quickly adds up, especially if you're out for more than a week.

Most PCT hikers resupply in one of three ways: mail packages (usually to a post office or pre-arranged lodging near the trail), buy as they hike (from stores near trailheads), or talk a buddy into meeting them somewhere along the way with a resupply. Appendix 3 includes information on where you can send packages for later pickup.

Some places will hold your package for free, but some charge a fee, sometimes nominal, sometimes grand, depending on how remote the location and how much effort is required for them to receive mail. For longer trips, you might enlist a friend to mail your packages on agreed-upon dates. If you go this route, don't seal your packages before you leave—that way, you can ask your resupply guru to add a thing or two you might be missing on the trail—and leave room for surprises! Some hikers mail a "bounce box" up the trail, from resupply facility to resupply facility, with things like extra batteries, "town clothes," electronics chargers, prescription medicine, and so on. Post office hours vary, so always check ahead. You may also have to show photo ID to pick up a package.

If you buy as you hike, you might luck out with glorious fresh food or end up with enough instant ramen to satisfy an entire college dorm for a semester. While it might seem easier than preparing boxes ahead of time, it can also cost you time off the trail and some head scratching to figure out your nutritional needs for the coming stretch. People with stringent dietary restrictions may find the mail-ahead strategy a better (and necessary) option.

At some places—typically hostels and wilderness resorts—you might find a "hiker box" of freebies, anything from sunscreen to partially used fuel canisters to dehydrated meals, and you can cast off your own extras in return. However, it's best to use these boxes only as a backup.

Fueling the Machine

Replenishing electrolytes and downing plenty of calories is important while backpacking, and food will account for a lot of your pack weight—typically 1–2 pounds per day. Dehydrated and freeze-dried foods can help you consume more calories for less weight, but whether you purchase prepackaged food or prepare your own, it has to be something you like or your hiker hunger will go unsatisfied. For this reason, I accept the weight penalty of bringing along a giant bag of Swedish Fish candy on long trips.

Whether you prefer your own recipes or buy premade, a test run is a good idea: try out a few meals before your trip to make sure everything agrees with your palate (and stomach) and that the portion sizes are correct. For longer trips, remember that variety is key to avoid developing aversions to once-favorite foods. *It's not you, instant mashed potatoes; it's me.*

COME ON BABY, LIGHT MY STOVE

Some backpackers simply boil water, while others inspire awe with their trail creations. Temperature, wind, elevation, and fuel bottle weight can all affect stove performance and efficiency. If you want to be scientific about how much fuel you'll need, first weigh a full fuel bottle or canister on a small scale. Next, cook one of the meals you intend to bring, using your camp stove. Then weigh the container again and subtract the result from the "before" weight. Finally, multiply the difference by how many meals you'll prepare on the trail. If you plan on cooking moderately elaborate meals, a loose requirement is 15 grams of fuel per person per day. Spend some time doing calculations with your own stove.

If you need to resupply stove fuel during your hike, know that it's never okay to mail flammable substances—*ever*. If you use white gas or compressed fuels like isobutane, research ahead of time where you can buy it along the way, typically in trailhead towns or resorts.

On trail, keep snacks handy and make sure your lunch isn't buried in your pack. At camp, it should go without saying: never cook in your tent. Aromas attract wildlife, and you risk fire and carbon monoxide poisoning. Cook outside and enjoy the beauty of nature, in your raingear if you have to, doing your best to ward off interloping insects.

GEAR AND CLOTHING

On long backpacking trips, a lighter pack makes for a happier hiker. While you can't avoid packing the pounds when heavy water carries are involved, you *can* cast a crucial eye to everything else hoisted on your back.

As a rule of thumb, your pack weight should not exceed 25–30 percent of your body weight, even for hikes of less than a week. To figure out what makes the cut, make two columns on a sheet of paper: "Need" and "Want." Be realistic and pragmatic when listing your pack's contents. A shelter of some sort is imperative for most people on most trips, but a fifth pair of socks is overkill. Ditch most, if not all of the "Wants," and treat yourself to a luxury item or two, like an inflatable pillow or a book.

Boots and Socks

Having happy feet on trail is paramount, and a lightweight sensibility makes sense since it's been said that 1 pound on your feet equals an extra 5 on your back. Almost all long-distance backpackers use trail running shoes these days; trail runners are lightweight, extremely breathable, and feature tread designed to handle a variety of trail conditions. Because your legs probably won't fatigue as quickly while wearing them, you can also put in greater distances each day. They are, however, much less durable than hiking boots, usually aren't waterproof, and typically don't have ankle support. Ultimately, choose the right footwear for *your* feet.

Socks are a big part of the comfort picture. As with clothing, certain natural and synthetic fibers are moisture-wicking, but cotton is a no-go. Contemporary wool blends are soft, keeping your feet comfortable in a wide range of temperatures. Some

people opt for lightweight liners underneath their socks, but I find that a single pair of "toe socks" works best to keep me blister-free.

Trekking Poles

Trekking poles provide extra stability on steep or uneven terrain—a bonus in these times of lightweight boots and trail running shoes, which offer less. Extend them on downhills to give your

TIPS FOR LIGHTENING YOUR LOAD

- Use tiny travel containers—never carry a full tube or bottle of anything.
- Minimize stuff sacks and pouches—let things wiggle around loose in your pack.
- Pare down your first-aid kit to the realistic "what-ifs" and those items used most frequently.
- Remove the cardboard core from your TP. Women, use a designated "pee rag" to dab, and reserve TP for poop duty.
- Everything should have more than one purpose. A piece of cord serves as clothesline, shoelace, or tent guyline; a clothes-filled stuff sack becomes a pillow; a compass sighting mirror is a personal mirror and emergency signaling device.
- Wrap duct tape around a trekking pole or water bottle to use in case of emergency repairs.
- Carry one set of clothes for hiking and one set for sleeping. Bring two pairs of socks and undies; wash one while wearing the other.
- Replace hard-sided water bottles with the grocery-store variety, which are surprisingly durable, lightweight, and easy to refill.

A hiker stands dwarfed by a magnificent manzanita near Lake Morena.

knees relief and shorten them going uphill to help with upward momentum. Bonus: they make great splints and tarp supports, too.

Electronic Devices

While we often hike to "get away from it all," people still tote their portable electronics into the backcountry. Many people trek with digital cameras, smartphones, personal locator beacons, and GPS units. Regarding the latter, remember that nothing is as failproof as dialing in your navigation skills with map and compass. Batteries die; hopefully your brain doesn't.

Speaking of batteries, mail extras ahead in your resupply packages, or plan to recharge at populated trailheads, then toss your charger into your bounce box. Putting your smartphone in airplane mode when not in use can often buy several days of battery power. Solar panel systems add weight to your pack and can perform poorly; many people now opt for small battery packs instead.

ON THE TRAIL

You planned and packed, and now it's time to hit the dirt! Keep the following best practices in mind to ensure you experience miles of smiles during your journey.

Wilderness Ethics and Multiuse Trails

The PCT passes through different federal lands used by many people and user groups. Being aware of a few simple principles can ensure a good experience for everyone.

Plan ahead and be prepared. Pack thoughtfully, research weather conditions, know sunrise and sunset times, create a bailout plan, and follow wilderness or other land use guidelines.

Travel and camp on durable surfaces. Avoid camping on vegetation, in meadows, or in fragile alpine areas. Avoid widening the path; navigating mud, water, and ruts in the trail can be frustrating, but you can handle it, champ.

Dispose of waste properly. To bury human waste, dig catholes 6 inches deep and at least 200 feet away from water sources. Pack out *all* toilet paper—it will not decompose in our dry climate, which leads to animals excavating disgusting piles of poo-encrusted paper. Don't use rocks to hide waste piles and don't pee on vegetation—animals will destroy it to taste the salt residue.

THE MOUNTAINEERS' TEN ESSENTIALS

If you've planned correctly, odds are that you'll already have the Ten Essentials even if you don't know what they are. These items can save the day should something unforeseen happen:

1. Navigation (map and compass)
2. Sun protection (sunglasses and sunscreen)
3. Insulation (extra clothing)
4. Illumination (headlamp or flashlight)
5. First-aid supplies
6. Fire materials (fire starter and matches or lighter)
7. Repair kit and tools including a knife or multitool
8. Nutrition (extra food)
9. Hydration (extra water)
10. Emergency shelter

Pack out everything, including uneaten food, peels, and trash.

Leave what you find. Take only memories; your pack will be heavy enough, trust me!

Minimize fire hazards. If you must have a fire, only use existing fire rings in areas where fires are permitted, *when* fires are permitted—land managers announce restrictions every summer. Keep fires small and use only downed, dead wood smaller than your forearm. Don't leave any trash in fire pits, and make sure your fire is completely extinguished and its ashes cool to the touch before you go to bed or leave camp.

Respect wildlife. Don't feed animals, use bear-resistant containers where required, and don't interrupt our furry friends for a photo op. Quiet observation and appreciation is key to awesome wildlife encounters.

Be considerate of other visitors. If you listen to music, leave the portable speakers at home and pop in some earbuds. If hiking in a group, walk single file when passing others. Grant uphill hikers the right-of-way.

Horses are permitted on the entire length of the PCT, although particularly steep hillsides, precarious terrain, or washouts may be challenging or inadvisable for them. Step to the downhill side of the trail and let our hoofed friends pass. Sure, horse patties can be irritating underfoot, but volunteer equestrian groups support trail maintenance—they pack in tools, food, and gear to remote backcountry trail crews and are sometimes involved in search-and-rescue efforts.

Mountain bikes and motorized vehicles are prohibited on the PCT. Ongoing pressure from the mountain-biking community in recent years has sparked debate about allowing bikes on the trail. The Forest Service, however, continues to uphold its 1988 order closing the PCT to mountain bikes to protect the recreation experience of the trail's primary users (hikers and equestrians).

Fishing can be a fun diversion in the Sierra, and some lakes, creeks, and rivers along the route are popular with anglers. If you choose to try your hand at reeling in dinner, nab a permit and follow the California Department of Fish and Wildlife regulations (see "Passes, Permits, Regulations" in Appendix 1). If you do get a bite, avoid attracting curious critters by cleaning and cooking the fish away from camp.

Staying Found

Most of the time, the PCT is fairly easy to follow, with blazes and posts marking the way. However, some signs are misleading (or missing), some trail turns are not second nature, and some stretches follow reroutes or ephemeral paths through shifting sands and floodplains. Fog, snow, and other inclement weather can also throw you off. If it feels wrong, it most likely is! Stop and reassess your surroundings, map, and direction. If for some reason you get lost or find yourself in an uncomfortable situation, here are a few tips that may help.

Always let someone know where you're going and when you plan to return home. Leave your itinerary and possibly a map marked with your route with a friend, including a list of the land management agencies and contact numbers for the areas you'll be passing through. Specify a date and time to contact rangers should you not return, but be sure to give yourself a buffer for weather or unforeseen circumstances.

Stay put if lost or injured! It's easier to locate a fixed target than a moving one. Use the waiting time to gather firewood, filter water, examine your food situation, and pen a bestselling autobiography.

Don't panic. Relax your mind with positive, constructive thoughts, and settle into a daily routine that will help ease the situation.

Use your cell phone, satellite phone, or personal locator beacon for help. Almost everyone takes a cell phone into the backcountry these days, but reception can be very spotty. Satellite phones have become cheaper and smaller, making them a better option if you travel frequently in remote areas. Additionally, personal locator beacons such as SPOT messenger devices connect to private satellite networks and alert emergency personnel if you trigger an SOS. They are less expensive to use than satellite phones.

Staying Safe and Crime-Free

Thankfully, most criminals are lazy, and committing crimes on trails is usually too much effort. That said, staying vigilant and keeping a healthy level of awareness is always a good idea.

Never leave valuables in your vehicle. Before setting off, remove anything and everything that might appear interesting to nefarious types. Even if it's empty, a closed sunglasses case might look like it contains an expensive pair of designer specs; a smartphone charger might make a prowler think the phone is still in the car.

Be alert. When you arrive at a trailhead, look for anything or anyone that seems out of place— for example, someone shining a flashlight into empty car windows. If you feel nervous about something you see, consider waiting in your car, leaving, or choosing a different trailhead for entry.

Trust your instincts. If you sense that someone you meet has bad intentions, allow yourself to be guarded and "antisocial" if necessary.

Never tell anyone you meet where you're planning to spend the night, especially if you're alone. Be vague—"I'm just hiking until I get tired."

Never mention your party size. If you're hiking alone, using "we" statements might confuse a would-be criminal. Shouting "Hurry up, guys!"

BLAZES OF GLORY

Navigating along the PCT is fairly straightforward thanks to trail blazes and signs on trees and signposts, all the way from Mexico to Canada. Most blazes feature the PCT emblem in black, white, and teal coloring, with the wording "Pacific Crest Trail, National Scenic Trail" and an image of a mountain and a tree. In other places, you'll find attractive wooden signs reading "Pacific Crest Trail," or 4x4 posts embossed with the emblem. Perhaps most common in Southern California are less exciting brown Carsonite posts with a small PCT logo sticker affixed; they may not be pretty, but they do the trick. Thanks to those who have traveled this path before us, we can rest assured that, in a roundabout way, we will be right behind them.

behind you may deter someone who thinks you're an easy solo target.

Avoid hiking with headphones. Listen to the sweet birdsong, squeaking pikas, and whistling marmots instead. Paying attention to your surroundings will help you hear someone or something coming.

Trail Angels

Whether they are former hikers hoping to give back to the trail, or friendly locals who want to help trekkers, "trail angels" are ubiquitous in Southern California. Some people open their homes to thru-hikers, some offer rides, and some show up at trailheads with anything from root beer floats to fresh fruit and hamburgers. I have not included much about trail angel "hostels" in this book because they are typically only used by thru-hikers and their availability and services change over time. If you do encounter trail angels—or their much-debated water caches—treat it as a nice surprise, rather than something that is expected. I've always offered gas money or a small donation to these folks; while it's rarely been accepted, I know it's appreciated.

Treating Water

Although I know some hardy individuals who refuse to filter their water at springs or in the Sierra, remember that it takes only one bad swig to ruin your entire trip. Animals graze nearly the entire run of the PCT in Southern California, and they leave behind some unpleasant gifts. Even if water looks clear and clean, it may contain tasteless protozoa such as *Cryptosporidium* and *Giardia*. These waterborne pathogens cause flulike symptoms, including vomiting and diarrhea, lasting one to six weeks or in some cases, up to a year.

Water-treatment devices range from UV-light pens that prevent bacteria and viruses from reproducing to carbon or ceramic filters that eliminate bacteria and unpleasant tastes. Almost all are lightweight, portable, and extremely effective. Or, opt to use **water-treatment tablets or drops**,

WATER MATH

The Southern California segment of the PCT is notoriously dry, especially so when an extended drought hits the state and snowpack dwindles. It's not uncommon to travel anywhere from 20–30 miles between reliable water sources. As such, it's important to prepare yourself for heavy loads and carefully research all potential water sources before setting out—Facebook groups and the PCT Water Report (pctwater.com) are usually the most up-to-date information channels.

Do not rely on water caches being available—these are typically seasonal and can disappear within hours after a large group of hikers passes through. Rather, carry what you need—many people can get by on a cool day with 1 liter per 5 miles, but the need increases as the mercury rises (or as your body dictates). "Camel up" when you arrive at a source—that is, drink a half liter to a liter while hanging around, then pack what you need to get to the next source. Take even more if you're "dry camping"—you'll need the extra water to cook with and drink in camp. If you choose to leave a cache for yourself (which is discouraged, but possibly necessary to pass through a long, dry stretch safely), mark the bottles with your arrival date, secure them out of sight from the trail or nearby roads, and carry the containers out when you leave.

Finally, a few notes about water etiquette—if you *do* stumble across a cache, take only what you need to get by and do not use that precious liquid to wash your stinky body or clothes. In fact, never wash yourself or things in *any* water source, including spring troughs—they might look inviting, but those are not bathtubs!

Don't rely on water caches in the desert; instead, treat them as a nice surprise.

usually made with iodine or chlorine dioxide. You can also **boil water**—that's the only 100 percent effective way to kill waterborne pathogens, but doing this will quickly deplete your fuel supply.

If you're using a filter, remember to back-flush it occasionally, especially when pulling water from murky and silty sources. For example, I carry a Sawyer MINI filter, and a Smartwater bottle fitted with a sport cap does the trick to flush out debris.

Potty Talk

Although you'll find vault toilets sprinkled along the route at trailheads, picnic areas, and established campgrounds, most of the time you'll need to cop a squat when making a deposit.

Find a spot that's at least **100 feet from camps or the trail** and at least **200 feet from water**.

Dig a hole no more than 6 inches deep. If you dig too deep, the bacteria won't be able to properly break down the waste.

Dispose of toilet paper in a small baggie and take it with you; I rinse out and save zip-top food bags from trail mix, lentils, etc. for this purpose.

I reserve the more opaque bags for used tampons and poopy TP.

Cover up the waste completely after stirring some dirt in your dung to ensure that it will decompose efficiently.

Apply a squirt of hand sanitizer to your palms and fingers, rub vigorously, and you're good to go.

Hazards

While most trail time is full of the good kind of adventure, you may encounter hazardous challenges along the way that will test your mettle.

No Bridge over Troubled Water

Arriving at an intact bridge over raging waters is always cause for relief. Unfortunately, not every wily waterway along the PCT features a handy man-made walkway. When crossing swift water, a little know-how goes a long way.

Cross early. Cross creeks in the morning, when water levels are at their lowest.

Cross with others. If hiking solo, make some trail friends (or wait for some to appear) and cross

A hiker appreciates some much-needed ventilation.

Log crossings can be hazardous. Crossing on a downed log might seem like the best bet for keeping your shoes dry, but inspect the log closely. Is the bark completely intact? If not, it could peel off when you step onto it. Is it slippery with water or moss? If you fell off, would you be sent sailing toward a waterfall or sustain serious injuries? If yes, find a different option. As you cross, focus your gaze on the log or opposite riverbank.

Wear well-fitting camp shoes to aid your footing. Once across, dry your feet completely before putting your hiking shoes back on, or you may end up with blisters.

Slides (Not the Fun Kind)

In October 2015, heavy rains caused massive mudslides that stranded motorists and washed out the PCT in several spots between the Sierra Pelona and the Piute Mountains near Tehachapi Pass. While these areas have been repaired, this isn't the last time the trail will see movement. Slides are a real danger in places that have been denuded by wildfires and along steep scree slopes where there is little vegetation around to hold everything in place.

Should you encounter any type of slide, attempt to cross only if you think the ground is stable enough. Slides can be a result of years of soil erosion, water runoff, or seismic activity, and the soil and debris often shifts when you step on it. Probe the debris with your trekking poles or a long stick to ensure that it's stable. Carefully kick in steps as you would in solid snow, and keep your weight centered above your feet as you move. Move as quickly as you can to clear the area.

Flash Floods

Although the desert floor might appear as if it's never met with a single drop of water, looks are often deceiving. Upon closer inspection, you might notice channels carved in the sand, along with mud deposits, uprooted vegetation, debris piles, and other indicators of flash flood activity.

It might seem an unlikely occurrence in a region with minimal rainfall, but flash floods *do* happen in Southern California. If you're traveling through any of the desert canyons described in this book, be sure to check the forecast before

together. If the river is high, you may want to link arms and choreograph your movements.

Look for straight, shallow, wide, and gentle water. Throw a stick into questionable sections to determine the speed and direction of the current.

Watch for hidden debris. Keep a close eye out for small logs or downed trees underwater, which can trap your feet as you cross.

Don't cross if it's above your knees. Any higher than this, and the current can suck you downstream. If the water is flat, however, you can probably bend this rule of thumb.

Unbuckle your pack's waist belt. Your pack might shift slightly as you walk, but having an easy exit strategy could save your life if you go for an unexpected swim.

Maintain at least two points of contact. Use trekking poles or find a big stick to help you balance.

leaving home—not just for the area you'll hike through, but also for areas upstream. Never camp in a wash or in a place that shows obvious flash flood damage. If a flash flood occurs during your trip, do not attempt to cross the floodwaters—be prepared to seek higher ground and stay put until they recede.

Wildfires
It used to be that "fire season" began in Southern California with the arrival of autumn's infamous Santa Ana winds, but with the "new normal" of extended drought, wildfires have become a year-round occurrence. The PCT is affected every single year by fires, and as you'll learn, both short- and long-term closures present unique challenges for those attempting long hikes on the trail.

While on trail, if you encounter or hear about a wildfire anywhere in your vicinity, head out to a road via the nearest safe route. Wildfires spread incredibly fast, so don't assume that because a fire's burning in the distance, you're safe. Wildfire updates are posted on the land management agency and PCTA websites to help you stay on top of new developments and trail closures.

Respect existing closures. These areas are off-limits to users for a reason, usually because the trail is destroyed or for rehabilitation purposes. Soil is often unstable after a burn, which means mudslides, debris flows, and trail washouts are more likely. In addition, burned, dead trees (snags) can fall across the trail or a campsite. The PCTA works in concert with the Forest Service and other crews to help reopen trails as quickly as possible, but the area needs to be safe before land managers give the go-ahead.

Even when these places reopen, hazards remain—move quickly and never camp underneath snags as they may fall without warning; watch your footing on loose, debris-covered slopes; and avoid stumbling into "ash pits" that develop at the base of burnt trees.

Forest Service Roads
Even for short expeditions, you may find yourself beginning on, ending on, or simply using unpaved Forest Service roads. Erosion from small creeks, storm events, flash floods, and poor maintenance can break down the road grade or even wash it out completely.

Always call ahead to check on current road conditions. If possible, **take a high-clearance vehicle** to the trailhead to make the bumps and potholes less noticeable. Drive slowly. Gravel and dirt roads, especially in wet weather, can become very slick. Use extreme caution in passing, especially where roadways are narrow. Even if you see no other cars, stay to the right side of the road—vehicles may appear when you least expect them.

Hunting Season
California's hunting seasons vary from year to year by region, depending on the health of the population being hunted and other factors, but it's a good idea to wear bright orange in the backcountry throughout the fall. For complete hunting regulations and seasonal openings, visit the California Department of Fish and Wildlife online (see "Passes, Permits, Regulations" in Appendix 1).

Critter Cautions
You'll undoubtedly encounter some wildlife on your PCT journey. Most pose little threat, but it's best to practice good etiquette to ensure safety for both human and animal.

Bear Necessities
Some folks hike all the way from Mexico to Canada without seeing a single bear, while others trek for a week and spot several; your bear-viewing karma is up to fate and luck. Whether they're black, brown, or cinnamon-colored, the only type you'll see in California are black bears, despite the grizzly decorating our flag. Beginning in its foothills, the Sierra teems with ursine inhabitants, but you'll find them wandering the San Bernardino and San Gabriel Mountains as well. From late spring through midsummer, bear sightings are more common in the morning or early evening hours. In fall, bears work very hard to fatten themselves up on seasonal berries and juicy grubs as they prepare for the long winter.

Bears prefer to be left alone to forage, feed, and raise their young. In many places along the PCT,

First light on the descent from Fuller Ridge

Cook meals at least 300 feet from your sleeping area, and don't nosh inside your tent.

Hang all food and any scented toiletries (toothpaste, lip balm, sunscreen), or use a bear canister where required. Food storage rules are in place to keep our bears alive; the discomfort of carrying a canister is a small price to pay for preserving their population. As the saying goes, "A fed bear is a dead bear."

Empty your pack pockets each night to ensure that no leftover food or wrappers are left behind. Move your pack away from your tent, in case it smells of food or garbage. Do not sleep with food in your tent.

Watch for signs. Prints in the mud and scat piles are good indications, but also watch for smaller, easier-to-miss signals such as scratched trees. Bears looking for grubs will overturn and occasionally shred logs. In berry patches, bears will pull bushes downward, breaking branches and sending bits of berry, brush, and leaves to the ground.

Animal carcasses of any kind are bad news as they attract predators. If you find one, leave the area immediately.

If a bear is aggressive, it's likely feeling threatened and defending its cubs or food source. Startled bears will also act out in agitation. If a bear is jaw popping, huffing, vocalizing, or aggressively slamming its paws to the ground, it's trying to tell you that you've crossed the line. Avoid eye contact, which bears perceive as a challenge. Never turn your back on the bear, but if it's safe to do so, slowly back up. Talk calmly and quietly so the bear can identify you as a human. Occasionally, a bear will bluff charge (charge, stop short, and run away) to try to intimidate you. Stand your ground and avoid eye contact; don't take even a half step backward. If a black bear does attack, fight back with all you've got.

Here, Kitty

While the odds of seeing a cougar (mountain lion) are higher in California than along the rest of the PCT, your overall chance of spotting these solitary, secretive creatures is quite slim.

Look for prints in loose soil or mud. The sheer size of an adult cougar print, roughly the width of

except in national parks, they are hunted and are therefore extremely wary of people. Hikers will be lucky to snap a shot of a bear's hind end as it bounds off into the forest. Nonetheless, it pays to play it safe when traveling in bear country.

Make noise, especially where the trail is overgrown or you're hiking around blind corners. Clap, sing, and talk loudly to avoid surprising a foraging bear family.

an adult hand, makes it easy to identify. The cats' recessed toenails cause a lack of nail marks, and the paw pad beneath the "toes" has two distinctive lobes at the top and three at the base.

If a cougar does become curious about you, there are a few things to keep in mind:

Maintain eye contact. In fact, wage an all-out staring contest. Cougars rely on being stealthy and hidden. Staring a cat down tells it you're aware of its presence.

Never run! Fast movement may trigger a cougar's instinctive urge to chase.

Get big and go crazy. Wave your trekking poles or pull your jacket up over your head to make yourself look larger. Shout, bark, scream—do whatever it takes to make yourself a formidable enemy.

Keep children close. Don't let the wee ones (or trail dogs) run ahead. If you see a cougar, pick up small children and pups, and keep them high by holding them or placing them on a stump to make them appear larger. Cougars usually target the easiest prey.

Back away slowly if it's safe to do so, using care not to trip. Don't turn your back on the animal.

If a cougar does attack, fight back and fight dirty. Those who have survived cougar attacks have duked it out. Throw rocks and punches— right hooks, haymakers, fingers in eyeballs—it's all fair game.

Far less unnerving to hikers, bobcats are medium-sized cats that make their home along much of California's PCT. While these wildcats are usually solitary and rarely seen, quiet hikers may occasionally catch a glimpse of one on forest edges or in meadows, where rabbits and rodents are often found. Attacks on humans are extremely rare, but if you do encounter an aggressive bobcat, take the same actions as you would for a curious cougar.

Canine Companions

Perhaps one of the most haunting sounds along the PCT is the strange yip-yowl of coyotes breaking through the quiet night air. While these canines are ubiquitous in Southern California, they are also fairly benign—I've sauntered past several in my urban neighborhood without so much as a blink. However, they can become

aggressive if you're walking with small dogs or children. If this happens, many of the same tips for cougar encounters may prevent things from escalating.

Hoofed Wonders

Bighorn sheep are relatively common in California's alpine and high desert environments. While they're not as easy to spot as deer, you'll gasp in shock once you do see them, usually scaling a sheer cliff face in mesmerizing fashion. While seemingly docile, they may behave aggressively, especially in fall when rams stage intense mating rituals to entice nearby ewes. Always give them plenty of space and never try to shoo one off the trail.

You're far more likely to encounter wandering cows since you'll traverse numerous parcels of public and private land open to grazing. Although they might seem like gentle giants, cows (especially bulls) can become aggressive—I have been menaced by bovines, and know several hikers who have been charged. You're most likely to see large herds in the Warner Springs area since you're walking through ranchland—give them a wide berth, even if that means walking quite a distance off-trail.

Leashed pups are allowed on portions of the PCT.

Ssssnakes

California is home to several varieties of slithering denizens, including gopher snakes, king snakes, garter snakes, and the most feared, rattlesnakes.

Rattlesnakes usually offer a warning tail shake to let you know they're nearby although an alarming increase in the absence of rattles has been documented over the past few years in Southern California. However, most rattlers usually try to hide or blend into the rocks and warm soil since they are food for many birds of prey. Like most creatures, they're rarely aggressive unless they feel threatened. Take these precautions to minimize your chances of an encounter:

Use extra caution when traveling through downed wood, scree fields, rocky outcroppings, and areas with dense undergrowth. Avoid sticking hands and feet into crevices.

Keep dogs on a short leash in snake country, and avoid letting them sniff and explore under bushes and rocks.

Rattlesnakes are common, if unwanted, trail companions.

Use trekking poles. Snakes are sensitive to vibration and might feel you before they hear you.

Learn what a mad rattlesnake sounds like! YouTube is full of examples of rattling rattlers, usually being antagonized by someone. Their rattle sounds a lot like dried grass rustling in a breeze.

Back away slowly if you hear a rattle, and don't make any sudden movements. Keep your distance!

Snake bites are rare, but if someone is bitten, contact emergency personnel immediately. Keep your hiking companion calm and remove any restrictive clothing such as jewelry, watches, socks, and the like. Immobilize the bitten limb, keeping it below the heart. Cleanse the wound, but don't flush it with water. Cover the affected area with a dry dressing and avoid ice. If possible, place a lightly constricting band, with a finger's worth of wiggle room for blood flow, above the bite to help prevent the spread of venom. Do not attempt to "extract" the venom.

Winged Terrors

Mosquitos, gnats, black flies, ticks, and horseflies are some of the annoying biting, burrowing, buzzing bugs you may have to battle on the PCT. Thankfully, walking at a good clip tends to discourage most of them from landing or attaching. A little know-how in the biting battalion department is often key to avoiding looking like you have the mumps.

Invest in a good insect repellent or wear a loose-fitting long-sleeved shirt and pants and carry a headnet. The most common and effective repellents contain DEET. This pesticide makes some folks nervous, but the US Environmental Protection Agency has given it a thumbs-up and human-health complications are rare. Unless you plan on bathing in it or have extreme sensitivities, you should be fine. Some products are almost 100 percent DEET, but I prefer a repellent in the 30 percent range—enough to prevent most bites while not burning holes in my clothes.

A relatively new bug repellent, picaridin, has an almost undetectable odor and is less greasy and sticky than DEET. Manufacturers claim that it works as well, but some people are skeptical. A wide variety of herbal products make for gentler, but somewhat less effective, mosquito repellents.

A backpack and its owner enjoy views of Devils Crags in Kings Canyon National Park.

You're most likely to encounter **ticks** in grassy areas. There are typically 80 to 100 cases of Lyme disease reported in California per year, so your odds of a journey-ending tick bite are reasonably low, although it's certainly possible. Using insect repellent, wearing long, light-colored pants and a long-sleeved shirt, and frequently checking clothing and skin are the best ways to prevent a tick from latching on.

To combat ticks and mosquitos, you might consider treating your clothing and gear with a chemical called permethrin. One application is usually effective for up to six weeks and through six washings. This insecticide is so effective that several outdoor clothing lines bake it right into their garments.

Bee stings and horsefly bites can cause severe allergic reactions. If you get stung or bitten and develop hives, wheezing, or swelling of the lips, throat, or tongue, seek help immediately. It's always a good idea to carry antihistamine tablets even if you don't think you're allergic—these can buy a little time if you develop an unexpected reaction. Also, keep a close eye out for signs of infection at the bite site, such as weeping or discoloration, which might require a doctor's care.

Now, Go Hike!

Since every single ounce counts on the trail, you likely won't be carrying this guide with you. Then again, you might just photocopy the pages you need and tuck them in with your maps to peruse each evening. Or perhaps invest in a lightweight e-reader and download the book, along with other reading material, to keep you entertained and informed. Some of today's e-readers have battery lives of up to eight weeks and weigh less than 7.5 ounces, although I find a smartphone works just as well if you bring a solar charger and don't mind squinting.

With a little planning, a bit of know-how, and some get-up-and-go, you'll soon be on your way to enjoying the spectacular Pacific Crest Trail and its grand landscapes. As you wander amid fragrant fields of wildflowers, stroll through impressive cactus gardens, and marvel at glaciated peaks, know that these places and this path will become woven into your mind, heart, and soul for the rest of your life. Now, get out of here—your journey awaits!

CAMPO TO WARNER SPRINGS

IF YOU DON'T HAVE, say, five months to spare, but want a taste of the excitement thru-hikers feel when they take those first steps heading north on their journey from the Mexican border to Canada, plant yourself at the trail's southern terminus in Campo and get ready for a host of iconic Southern California delights.

This section ventures through what's often unfairly considered some of the trail's most brutal terrain, but that's only because most thru-hikers start in late spring when the thermostat rockets toward the triple digits. Instead, consider hiking during late winter or early spring, when the water sources are flowing and you can't go ten feet without dancing around bunches of vibrant wildflowers underfoot.

Even if you head out during a less blossomy season, there's plenty of scenery to keep your eyes (and camera) busy. Although most people think "desert" when they imagine the southernmost PCT, the landscape is surprisingly diverse. While you'll definitely encounter just about every prickly plant known to man, you'll also stroll through sun-dappled oak glades, make your way along chaparral-clothed hillsides, traverse some epic boulder fields, dip into refreshingly shady canyons, and even pass through a fragrant high-elevation pine forest as you make your way through the Laguna Mountain Recreation Area.

No matter what time of year you venture out, research water conditions—check the PCTA website, read the PCT Water Report, visit the PCT listserv, and chat with local rangers to get a read on which sources are running. While this section is notoriously short on reliable places to tank up, with a bit of careful planning and a large carrying capacity, you'll stay refreshed from the rolling hills of Campo to the pastoral fields of Warner Springs.

DISTANCE 109.5 miles

STATE DISTANCE 0–109.5 miles

ELEVATION GAIN/LOSS +11,060/-10,920 feet

HIGH POINT 6063 feet

BEST TIME OF YEAR Oct–Apr for low elevations, June–Sept for high elevations

PCTA SECTION LETTER A

LAND MANAGERS Bureau of Land Management (El Centro Field Office), Cleveland National Forest (Descanso Ranger District, Hauser Wilderness, Laguna Mountain Recreation Area), Lake Morena County Park, Anza-Borrego Desert State Park

PASSES AND PERMITS A permit is required to camp outside of developed campgrounds in the Cleveland National Forest. Adventure Pass may be required to park at certain trailheads within the Cleveland National Forest. California Campfire Permit.

MAPS AND APPS
- Halfmile's CA Section A
- USFS PCT Map #1 Southern California
- USGS Topo Quads: Campo, Potrero, Morena Reservoir, Cameron Corners, Mount Laguna, Monument Peak, Cuyamaca Peak, Julian, Earthquake Valley, Tubb Canyon, Ranchita, Hot Springs Mountain, Warner Springs
- Halfmile's PCT app
- Guthook's PCT app

Opposite: Begin your journey at the PCT's iconic southern terminus monument.

LEGS

ACCESS

Campo

From San Diego, head east on Interstate 8 toward El Centro. Take exit 51 (Buckman Springs Road) and turn right onto the road. In approximately 10 miles, turn right onto Campo Road (CA Highway 94 westbound), then make a left onto Forest Gate Road in 1.5 miles. In 1 mile, Forest Gate Road bends left, but you'll turn right to continue straight down an unnamed dirt road that parallels the PCT. From here, the southern terminus monument and metal border fence are visible on top of a small hill 0.6 mile ahead. As strange as it seems, you can drive right up to the monument itself, but you won't be able to park there. Most hikers are dropped off or use public transportation (a public bus stops infrequently at the intersection of CA 94 and Forest Gate Road—check with the San Diego Metropolitan Transit System for route information, cost, and schedule).

Warner Springs

From San Diego, head north on Interstate 15 toward Escondido. Take exit 17 for Scripps Poway Parkway and turn right. In 8.6 miles, turn left onto CA Highway 67 northbound, which eventually becomes Main Street, then Julian Road (CA Highway 78 eastbound). After it becomes Julian Road, travel about 14.4 miles, then turn left to join CA Highway 79 northbound. You'll reach the trailhead in just under 14 miles; parking is available along the north side of the road across from the fire station.

NOTES

Cities and Services

The tiny town of Campo, centered about 1.4 miles north of the southern terminus, has a small market and a post office. The community of Warner Springs at the northern trailhead doesn't have much in the way of services aside from a post office, although the community center often offers up varied services to hikers during the thru-hiking season.

Camping and Fire Restrictions

Camping outside of established campgrounds is prohibited in the Laguna Mountain Recreation Area and Lake Morena County Park. Fires are allowed only in designated fire rings. Check for seasonal fire restrictions in Cleveland National Forest before heading out.

Water

With few exceptions, reliable year-round water is scarce throughout this entire section—plan for dry camps and heavy water carries, and do not rely on caches. The longest likely waterless stretches are the 20 miles between the southern terminus and Lake Morena County Park, the 8.9 miles between the Sunrise Trailhead Connector and Rodriguez Spur Truck Trail, and the 32.7 miles between Rodriguez Spur Truck Trail and Barrel Spring.

Hazards

Plan your trips for cooler times of day (or year); hikers have experienced heat-related illnesses—and in one sad case, have died—on the exhausting climbs up from Hauser Canyon and through the San Felipe Hills. On the opposite end of the spectrum, snow can accumulate in the upper reaches of the Laguna Mountain Recreation Area, causing road closures and unsafe trail conditions. In low-lying

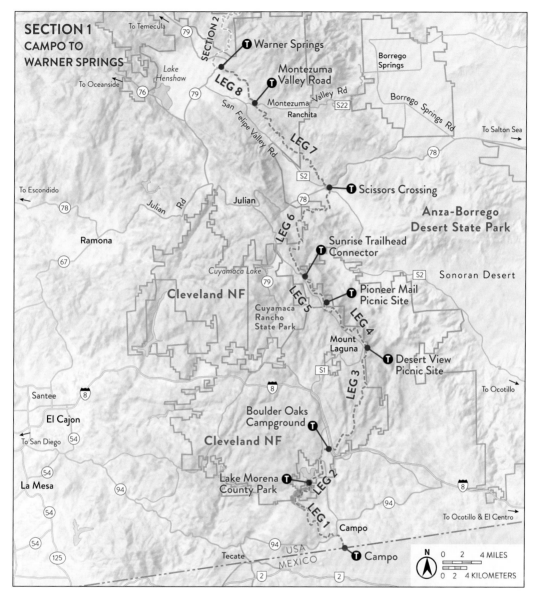

SECTION 1
CAMPO TO
WARNER SPRINGS

To Temecula
79
SECTION 2
Warner Springs
Borrego
Springs
Lake
Henshaw
LEG 8
Montezuma
Valley Road
To Oceanside
76
79
Montezuma   Valley Rd
Ranchita
San Felipe Valley Rd
S22
Borrego Springs Rd
To Salton Sea
78
LEG 7
To Escondido
78
S2
Scissors Crossing
Julian Rd
Julian
78
Anza-Borrego
Desert State Park
LEG 6
S2
Sonoran Desert
Ramona
Cuyamaca Lake
79
Sunrise Trailhead
Connector
67
LEG 5
Pioneer Mail
Picnic Site
Cleveland NF
Cuyamaca
Rancho
State Park
LEG 4
Mount
Laguna
Desert View
Picnic Site
Santee
8
S1
LEG 3
To Ocotillo
El Cajon
8
To San Diego
54
Boulder Oaks
Campground
Cleveland NF
54
La Mesa
94
LEG 2
54
Lake Morena
County Park
8
54
LEG 1
To Ocotillo & El Centro
94
Campo
125
94
USA
Campo
N
MEXICO
Tecate
2
2
0   2   4 MILES
0   2   4 KILOMETERS

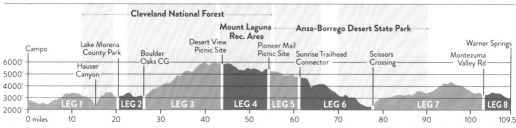

········ Cleveland National Forest ········
Mount Laguna ······· Anza-Borrego Desert State Park ·······
Rec. Area

Campo
Lake Morena
County Park
Desert View
Picnic Site
Pioneer Mail
Picnic Site
Warner Springs
6000'
Boulder
Oaks CG
Sunrise Trailhead
Connector
Scissors
Crossing
Montezuma
Valley Rd
Hauser
Canyon
5000'
4000'
3000'
2000'
LEG 1   LEG 2   LEG 3   LEG 4   LEG 5   LEG 6   LEG 7   LEG 8
0 miles   10   20   30   40   50   60   70   80   90   100   109.5

areas, heavy winds can cause dust storms. Rattle-snake sightings are common during the warmer months, typically beginning in early spring.

Other

The Border Patrol is active throughout the first leg of this section, which sees traffic from undocumented immigrants, especially at night. While it's rare to encounter anyone besides fellow PCT hikers and Border Patrol agents (and their noisy helicopters), it's best to stick to the trail and camp in established spots for the first 20 miles. Pets are not allowed on trails in Anza-Borrego Desert State Park.

SUGGESTED ITINERARIES

Camps are either viewable from the trail or located within a few tenths of a mile from the noted location unless otherwise specified in leg descriptions.

9 DAYS

		Miles
Day 1	Campo to Hauser Camp	15.4
Day 2	Hauser Camp to Boulder Oaks Campground	10.6
Day 3	Boulder Oaks Campground to Morris Meadow Camp	12.6
Day 4	Morris Meadow Camp to Laguna Campground	8.8
Day 5	Laguna Campground to Camp 3	16.3
Day 6	Camp 3 to Camp 6	9.7
Day 7	Camp 6 to Camp 12	14.7
Day 8	Camp 12 to Barrel Spring Camp	13.0
Day 9	Barrel Spring Camp to Warner Springs	8.4

8 DAYS

Day 1	Campo to Hauser Camp	15.4
Day 2	Hauser Camp to Boulder Oaks Campground	10.6
Day 3	Boulder Oaks Campground to Burnt Rancheria Campground	15.1
Day 4	Burnt Rancheria Campground to Camp 2	14.8
Day 5	Camp 2 to Camp 4	12.5
Day 6	Camp 4 to Camp 9	16.8
Day 7	Camp 9 to Barrel Spring Camp	15.9
Day 8	Barrel Spring Camp to Warner Springs	8.4

7 DAYS

Day 1	Campo to Hauser Camp	15.4
Day 2	Hauser Camp to Yellow Rose Camp	14.6
Day 3	Yellow Rose Camp to Burnt Rancheria Campground	11.1
Day 4	Burnt Rancheria Campground to Sunrise Camp (via Sunrise Trailhead Connector)	18.4
Day 5	Sunrise Camp to Camp 6	13.9
Day 6	Camp 6 to Camp 13	20.8
Day 7	Camp 13 to Warner Springs	15.3

1 CAMPO TO LAKE MORENA COUNTY PARK

DISTANCE
20 miles

ELEVATION GAIN/LOSS
+3160/-2990 feet

HIGH POINT
3520 feet

CONNECTING TRAILS AND ROADS
Forest Gate Road, State Highway 94, South Boundary Road, Hauser Creek Road, Lake Morena County Park Interpretive Nature Trail, Lake Shore Drive

ON THE TRAIL

The southern terminus of the Pacific Crest Trail is located within arm's reach of the border with Mexico on a dusty lump backed by a double-duty international security system of corrugated metal panels and rusted barbed wire fencing. On top of such staggering beauty, Border Patrol agents cruise the nearby dirt roads, and their helicopters whip up the air overhead. You'd be forgiven for thinking this is a lackluster start for one of the world's most famous scenic trails, but all you have to do is turn around and look north toward rolling green hills, pastoral farmlands, and jagged boulder fields, and you'll know you're in the right place.

Plan to arrive with enough water to last the entire way to Lake Morena County Park—other than a faucet just over 1 mile ahead and a market deeper into Campo, you're facing a parched 20 miles. Hydration concerns aside, don't forget to snap a photo next to the iconic monument (a collection of wooden posts located on top of the hill) and peek around behind to find the register. Write something profound, then go ahead and place your right foot in front of your left, your left in front of your right—and begin hiking the Pacific Crest Trail!

While the majority of the PCT is incredibly well marked, the path headed down from the monument isn't completely obvious—you're surrounded by a spiderweb of dirt roads and use trails (unofficial footpaths carved by both people and animals). To find your route, stroll down to the northwest to spot a lone oak standing at the edge of the road; sometimes there's a sign here, sometimes there's not, but there's always a trail just to the right—*your* trail. Ambling along the soft path, you'll soon cross a dirt road and continue walking through a healthy dose of shoulder-high chamise; you'll become close friends with this prolific shrub if you walk any length of the chaparral-dominated trail in Southern California.

Next, cross unpaved **Forest Gate Road** at 0.6 mile, bend to the west, then cross it again a few minutes later. Despite the whir of nearby farm machinery, this area is peaceful and very pretty in the spring when vibrant grasses and wildflowers dominate the boulder-specked landscape. Your last glimpse of (rural) civilization comes at 1.2 miles when you pass the **Juvenile Ranch Facility** across the road to your right. If you're thirsty, pop over and look for a water spigot **O** located behind the facility's sign. You also have the option of departing the PCT here to walk north up the road for just over 1.5 miles to hit a small market where you can buy water and basic provisions.

At just about 1.4 miles, you'll leave the road and head northwest into the hills. Now surrounded by boulders, oaks, cottonwoods, ceanothus, and yucca, you'll hear birds chirp, bees buzz, and despite a string of power lines rudely encroaching on your views, you're finally (mostly) surrounded by nature! The only thing that may shake you from that sweet hiking reverie is a meeting with paved **State Highway 94** just under 1 mile ahead—carefully scan for traffic, then zip across to pick up the trail on the other side.

Wind your way alongside typically dry **Campo Creek**, which you'll cross on a small wooden

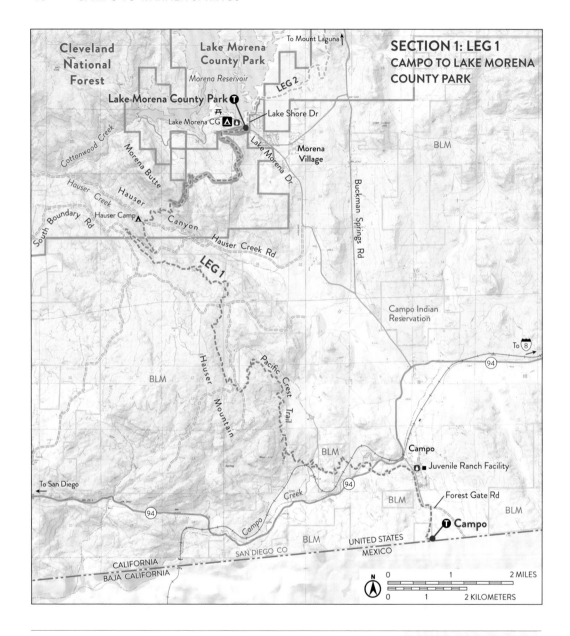

SECTION 1: LEG 1
CAMPO TO LAKE MORENA
COUNTY PARK

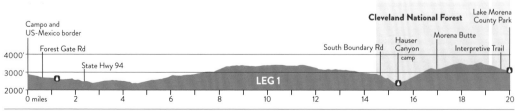

bridge at 2.6 miles. The area is shaded by cottonwoods and looks like a forest gnome paradise in spring when poppies, chaparral pea, and wild peonies intersperse with moss-covered rocks. Even the railroad tracks you'll cross just under 0.5 mile later are picturesque, with long views to the north and south.

At 4.4 miles, round a gully that holds a seasonal creek—don't count on any water here unless you're passing through during a very wet season. While the scenery is pleasantly distracting, don't overlook the massive amount of poison oak lingering around the area, or you'll end up itching all the way to Lake Morena.

Enjoy these last lazy meanders through thickets of manzanita and intermittent shade before you start a measured, but noticeable ascent of the sunny, boulder-filled eastern slopes of rambling **Hauser Mountain**. As with most climbs, the higher you get, the better the views—here, mostly to oak-dotted ranchland to the east and the borderlands to the south, with the occasional grazing cow thrown in for good measure.

Once the climb is over, you'll level out on a windswept plateau that offers a host of oceanic-appearing grasses, lumpy boulder formations, and even more epic views. You'll also likely spot lasting damage from the 2006 Horse Fire and 2010 Cowboy Fire, both sparked by illegal campfires. At 8.8 miles, head through a pipe gate (a metal barrier commonly found in areas where livestock grazing occurs), cross a dirt road, then do it again just down the way. Enjoy the herby scent of California sagebrush, also known as "cowboy cologne" (or "hiker deodorant," if you're feeling a bit ripe), while peering down into a wide, spring-fed semi-flat area bisected by a dirt road and filled with grassy patches and occasional oaks. Peeking out just beyond all of this to the north is peach-colored Morena Butte—you'll get up close and personal with this behemoth soon enough.

You'll reach yet another dirt road at 10.9 miles; continue across and lengthen those poles to begin weaving your way downhill. You're now looking down into deep **Hauser Canyon** and straight across to the face of Morena Butte. If it looked impressive before, it looks absolutely imposing

A TOUGH CLIMB

The climb out of Hauser Canyon is serious business—you face over 1000 feet of elevation gain in about 1.5 miles. Dehydrated, overheated, and underprepared hikers are rescued near here *every single year*; sadly, one hiker died after making the grueling climb in 2014. Consider timing your ascent for a cooler time of day, make sure you're hydrated, and ensure that you eat enough to keep your motor running.

now, once you spot the trail zigzagging sharply up its flanks and realize that you have to plunge *all* the way down to the canyon floor before climbing *all* the way back up. If you arrive during the golden hour before sunset, the light dancing on the butte will charge your batteries (metaphorically, at least).

At the 14-mile mark, the trail makes an abrupt hairpin turn to the east as it joins up with wide, unpaved **South Boundary Road**. Continue straight for 0.7 mile until you reach a single-track trail that descends to the left; here, the trail barrels down rather suddenly and steeply until your knees quiver with gratitude as you finally reach the canyon bottom at 15.4 miles, home to seasonal **Hauser Creek ⬦**, its namesake road, and a small sycamore-shaded campsite just to the west of the trail crossing with room for a few tents (**Hauser Camp**). You may find water here if you arrive during spring in a wet year, but don't count on it. Another option is to walk just over 1.5 miles west on **Hauser Creek Road** to its intersection with **Cottonwood Creek ⬦**, which has a slightly more reliable flow.

Now it's time to power back up! This side of the canyon is fairly shadeless and the grade is constant, but if you take it slow and focus on the beauty unfolding around you, it won't seem as taxing. The dirt and rocks underfoot mirror the butte's vibrant granite, a small army of wildflowers adorns the slopes in spring, and the views across and down the canyon are worth every fleck of sweat. About

Morena Butte features a collection of intriguing rock formations, offering a fun side trip from the trail.

17 miles in, you'll crest the shoulder and reach an intersection with a signed use trail on your left that ascends steeply toward **Morena Butte**'s triple summit. If you're in the mood for expansive vistas, pop off here for a steep, mile-long ascent to the nearest high point. If not, continue around, scoring views of the butte's massive back side.

Undulate through granite slabs, boulders, manzanita, ribbonwood, and yucca, passing several intersections with use trails—keep the PCT markers in sight and you'll stay on track. Morena Reservoir ("Lake Morena") creeps into view far below; however, during dry years, these early sightings may be of a sad, dry meadow surrounded by hills (including the prominent, pointy Los Pinos Mountain to the northwest). Snag the best views past the 18.7-mile mark as you descend granite slabs.

You'll reach a junction with the **Lake Morena County Park Interpretive Nature Trail** on your left at 19.9 miles—descend here for a shortcut to the park or continue straight for another 0.1 mile to reach a parking area at the intersection of **Lake Shore Drive** and **Lake Morena Drive**. To reach restrooms, showers, picnic tables, fire rings, water **0**, and a potential home for the evening (**Lake Morena Campground**), swing left onto Lake Morena Drive to enter **Lake Morena County Park**. There's a shared backpacker-only site available year-round for a few bucks per person; you can also nab your own or spring for one of the park's ten rustic cabins. If you're already sick of dehydrated food, wander back down Lake Morena Drive to reach a small market and deli less than 0.5 mile down from the park entrance, where you can stock up on basic provisions, grab some fishing gear, and feast upon tasty burgers and shakes.

CAMP-TO-CAMP MILEAGE

Campo to Hauser Camp. 15.4
**Hauser Camp to Lake Morena
     Campground** 4.6

2 LAKE MORENA COUNTY PARK TO BOULDER OAKS CAMPGROUND

DISTANCE
6 miles

ELEVATION GAIN/LOSS
+820/-710 feet

HIGH POINT
3465 feet

CONNECTING ROADS
Lake Morena Drive, Lake Shore Drive

ON THE TRAIL

While this short but sweet leg kicks off in a quiet residential area, you quickly bid adieu to houses and street signs and disappear into a grassy bit of rolling, boulder-filled pastoral bliss. Begin at the parking lot on the south side of the intersection of **Lake Morena Drive** and **Lake Shore Drive**, and head straight up the latter with **Lake Morena County Park** to your left; if you need a bathroom break, water **⓿**, or campsite, it's easy enough to dip into the park here to find what you seek.

Strolling along, enjoy the sweet sounds of playing children, barking dogs, humming RV motors, crowing roosters, and possibly even some gobbling wild turkeys if you're lucky (unless you're poultry averse). In 0.2 mile, hang a left onto single-track marked with a brown PCT post. Travel under leafy oaks, stepping over any number of horseshoe imprints in the soft soil—don't be surprised if you have equestrian company on this stretch of the trail and remember to give our hoofed friends the right-of-way.

Just shy of 0.1 mile later, the path splits—bank right to walk through a gate that guards a pretty and peaceful section of trail filled with tall grasses, scrub oak, and towering tufts of sagebrush whose yellow flowers provide a burst of color against the beige surroundings in late summer and fall. Plenty of use trails cross this area—stick to the most obvious path, and at 0.6 mile, head right at

another split, this time walking through a pipe gate. As you move farther away from the sounds of the park-adjacent community of Morena Village, the ground turns sandy underfoot (gaiters suggested) as you begin a gentle ascent into a mixture of boulders, chamise, scrub oak, manzanita, and prickly pear. Cross several unpaved roads, the most prominent at 1.2 miles, after which the boulders grow even larger, providing ample hiding places for all of the adorable chipmunks scurrying around.

Views begin to open up as you continue your ascent—you start to catch glimpses down to Interstate 8 to the east and back out to Morena Reservoir, which will either be full of water or appear as a very un-lakelike grassy field, depending on when you visit. My favorite viewpoint comes

HIKERS AND HUNTERS

You spend most of this leg—and a large chunk of this first section of the PCT—inside the Cleveland National Forest. Hunting is legal and very popular in much of this area (and throughout the mountains of Southern California), with targets including mule deer, California quail, and wild pig. The exact dates of each hunting season vary by year and can be found on the California Department of Fish and Wildlife website; while a few animals are pursued year-round, autumn is the most common season. One camouflage-sporting person I met said that while any good hunter will never shoot anything they're not 110 percent sure is their intended target, it's still a smart idea for trekkers to stay on trail, leave the camouflage behind, and wear red (good for hunters because it doesn't scare the deer) or blaze orange (good for hikers because it's the universal color of "I am not a deer!").

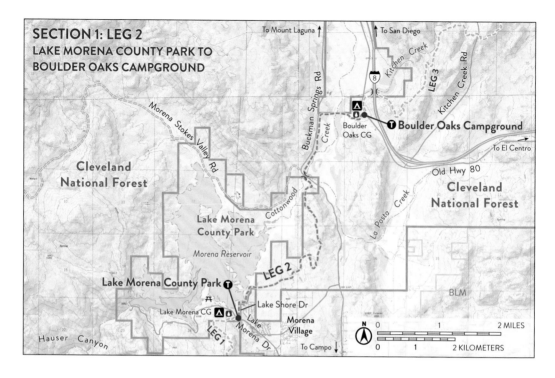

SECTION 1: LEG 2
LAKE MORENA COUNTY PARK TO
BOULDER OAKS CAMPGROUND

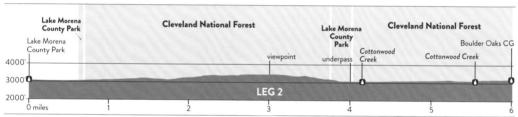

around the 3.2-mile mark, where you'll find a large granite hump to your right. From here, you can see the squiggle of unpaved Morena Stokes Valley Road snaking along far below to the east, but you won't spot your next objective, paved Buckman Springs Road (or rather, a spot where the trail crosses *under* it) until you head downhill in earnest, which happens just ahead. Stomp through loose sand and piles of horse-made fertilizer, dropping down into a shady glen where you'll proceed to dip under a bridge around the 4-mile mark. The occasional zoom of cars overhead and ubiquitous graffiti mar what would be an otherwise pretty riparian area, so quickly make your way to the far side of the underpass, look for a trail marker

ahead, and proceed toward **Cottonwood Creek** 0.1 mile up, which may provide refreshment (and a wade) in wetter months.

A wooden sign indicates that it's a scant 2 miles to Boulder Oaks Campground, and these miles will whip by quickly as you amble through the relative flatness leading up toward the obvious line of distant cottonwoods whose leaves glow like a bright yellow beacon in late fall—or a bright green one in spring and early summer. As you stroll along, you're flanked on the left by **Buckman Springs Road** and on the right by a lazy field studded with scattered oaks, sagebrush, cholla, and occasionally the pretty, but potentially toxic, Datura, also known as jimsonweed.

The path to Boulder Oaks Campground is paved with . . . boulders—not quite the flat desert many people envision!

Around 4.9 miles, pass a rusty barbed wire fence to get through a narrow area with barely enough room to stretch your arms between competing fence lines and No Trespassing signs. While this bit isn't the most welcoming, you'll reconvene with your old buddy **Cottonwood Creek** at 5.5 miles. The bird-filled oasis is a welcome sight—even if the water's run dry (which it's apt to do in summer); the sudden burst of bright cottonwoods and willows provides a pleasant stop before you hit the relative bustle of **Boulder Oaks Campground** 0.4 mile ahead. Once there, pop through a pipe gate and head left on a dusty unpaved road toward a PCT marker, passing horse corrals (and probably horses), reaching a dirt parking lot at 6 miles; your route ends at the trail marker plunked on the north side of the lot. From here, vault toilets are within sight, and a water spigot provides refreshment on the east side of the parking lot—although you may walk away with a sad face and empty water bottles if you come through when the water is off, an occasional occurrence.

Speaking of access, the campground is open generally between mid-June and the beginning of March; it then closes for several months to give

endangered arroyo toads some much needed privacy during their annual courtship, during which the males entice females with a sexy whistle. While this may be the first time your camping plans are interrupted by catcalling amphibians, it may not be the last since they live (and love) in small riparian pockets across the mountains of Southern California.

CAMP-TO-CAMP MILEAGE

Lake Morena County Park to Boulder Oaks Campground 6.0

ACCESS INFO

An Adventure Pass or day use fee (cash or check only, paid in the "iron ranger" located near an informational sign) is currently required to park in the PCT trailhead parking lot inside Boulder Oaks Campground. There is also some parking available alongside Old Highway 80 in a turnout just north of the campground entrance.

3 BOULDER OAKS CAMPGROUND TO DESERT VIEW PICNIC SITE

DISTANCE 16.6 miles

ELEVATION GAIN/LOSS
+3930/-1170 feet

HIGH POINT 6063 feet

CONNECTING TRAILS AND ROADS
Old Highway 80, Kitchen Creek Road,
Fred Canyon Road, Thing Valley Road,
Burnt Rancheria Connector, Desert View
Interpretive Nature Trail

ON THE TRAIL

If you think the southernmost portion of California is nothing but tumbleweeds and beach bums, think again—you'll watch the landscape change dramatically on this leg as you ascend through oak-studded chaparral into mountainous pine forest, with epic views out to the spectacular desert beyond.

Your trip starts at the north end of the parking lot for the **Boulder Oaks Campground**, a fine, semi-shaded spot to pitch a tent the night before if you don't mind dust swirls and incessant noise from the nearby road and interstate. Bring cash or a check for the iron ranger if you're setting stakes here, display an Adventure Pass if you're using the trailhead parking lot, and check to make sure the place is actually open—they typically close from the beginning of March to mid-June to allow the endangered arroyo toad to cuddle in private. This is also a great place to tank up on water ⬥ at any number of campground spigots (unless they're unceremoniously turned off, which sometimes happens) before hitting what can be a very dry section of trail. When you're ready to boogie, hang a right and walk down the campground's main (dirt) road, curving left onto the trail just before reaching **Old Highway 80**.

Pretend the hum of traffic is just the sound of some distant raging river as you make your way along and then across the road at 0.2 mile; there's no crosswalk, so dash carefully. Once safely across, the trail parallels seasonal **Kitchen Creek** ⬥ (like most water sources in the area, often dry in summer, fall, and during drought conditions), lined with arroyo willow, sagebrush, and Fremont's cottonwoods, whose heart-shaped leaves blaze golden yellow in fall. Enjoy the shade because it's the last you'll see for a while as you start heading uphill into the sunny Laguna Mountains.

At 0.6 mile, pass under bustling **Interstate 8** and start gaining ground with a couple of quick manzanita-lined switchbacks. Sweating your way upward, you'll begin traversing a steep slope, clothed year-round with cacti and chaparral and dotted with colorful wildflowers in spring. Here, the highway becomes a distant memory and geology takes center stage, from the deep canyon below to the array of colorful granite studding the trail.

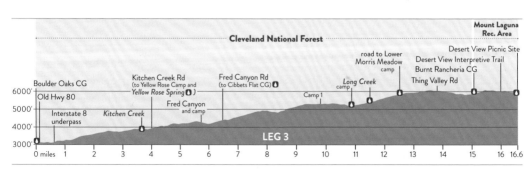

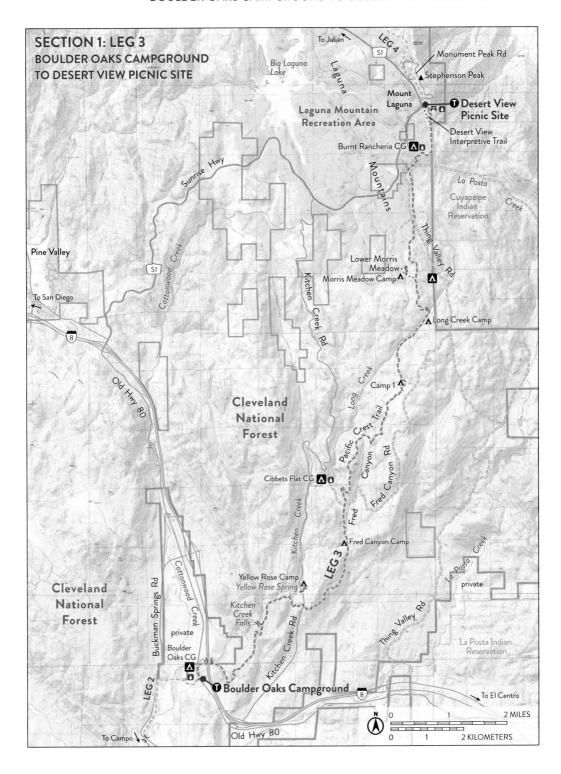

SECTION 1: LEG 3
BOULDER OAKS CAMPGROUND
TO DESERT VIEW PICNIC SITE

To Julian
LEG 4
S1
Monument Peak Rd
Stephenson Peak
Big Laguna
Lake
Laguna
Mount
Laguna
Desert View
Picnic Site
Laguna Mountain
Recreation Area
Desert View
Interpretive Trail
Burnt Rancheria CG
Mountains
La Posta
Creek
Cuyapaipe
Indian
Reservation
Sunrise Hwy
21
Pine Valley
S1
Thing Valley Rd
Lower Morris
Meadow
Morris Meadow Camp
Cottonwood Creek
Kitchen Creek Rd
To San Diego
8
Long Creek Camp
Old Hwy 80
Long Creek
Camp 1
Cleveland
National
Forest
Pacific Crest Trail
Fred Canyon
Fred Canyon Rd
Cibbets Flat CG
Kitchen Creek
La Posta Creek
private
Fred Canyon Camp
LEG 3
Yellow Rose Camp
Yellow Rose Spring
Buckman Springs Rd
Cottonwood Creek
Kitchen
Creek
Falls
Kitchen Creek Rd
Thing Valley Rd
La Posta Indian
Reservation
Cleveland
National
Forest
private
Boulder
Oaks CG
Boulder Oaks Campground
8
LEG 2
To El Centro
N
0   1   2 MILES
To Campo
Old Hwy 80
0   1   2 KILOMETERS

Superhero photo opportunities abound on several large outcroppings.

Hike another 0.5 mile or so to be within scrambling distance of **Kitchen Creek 0**, whose flow is most reliable in late winter and early spring. There are about a hundred feet between you and the creek bed; while you can forge your own path, there *is* a faint use trail that cuts through the brush. If you're so inclined during the wetter months, walk up the creek about 0.2 mile to find secluded **Kitchen Creek Falls**. The rock is slippery here due to water erosion, so mind your step.

Once you're back on the main drag, keep winding through the canyon, passing through a metal pipe gate at 3.6 miles. Just past this point, you'll once again meet up with **Kitchen Creek 0**, where you'll have direct access to its flow at a brief crossing—a much easier refill point than the deeper canyon you just passed through.

A little farther up, you'll cross moderately traveled, paved **Kitchen Creek Road** at 4 miles, where a trailhead dirt patch offers room for a few creatively parked cars. If you're still thirsty (or tired), hop off trail and turn left, heading 0.4 mile north on the road to find seasonal **Yellow Rose Spring 0**, located in a small grassy flat with room for several tents (**Yellow Rose Camp**).

Once you're ready to forge on, turn right on the road and look for a trail marker on your left to continue the journey, now earning completely different views to the east—on a clear day, you can see all the way into Mexico! You're once again traversing steep slopes dotted with occasional funky rock formations (and possibly rattlesnakes), heading gently uphill, which won't feel quite so gentle on a hot day.

At 5.5 miles, you'll reach a saddle and suddenly descend into the mountains at the entrance to **Fred Canyon**, where at 5.8 miles you'll find a shady respite in a small grove of coast live oaks that offers a few small campsites (**Fred Canyon Camp**). The usually dry stream here *might* be running, though it's doubtful. Even if you're not planning on spending the night, this is a peaceful place for lunch or a bit of R & R.

Leaving your new happy place behind, begin a slow climb out of the canyon bottom to reach a dirt flat about 0.5 mile out, where you'll encounter a rather alarming sign that warns of

Fall color and late afternoon magic above Lower Morris Meadow

"unexploded military ordinance." A Marine helicopter crashed here in 2009, leaving munitions scattered around the area. Suffice it to say, this isn't the best place to take a bathroom break unless you want to get up close and personal with the phrase "fire in the hole."

Just ahead at 6.5 miles, you'll reach an intersection with **Fred Canyon Road**. A small wooden sign points you toward **Cibbets Flat Campground**, 0.8 mile west via the dirt road, where you'll find year-round camping, water **O**, and pit toilets. If you can resist the temptation, keep going straight on the PCT, beginning yet *another* hot, shadeless climb that shortly offers you an aerial view of the campground below. If you look even farther out to the west, you'll also spot some white specks in the distance—this is the Mount Laguna Observatory, and you're headed that way!

At about 8 miles in, you'll start heading downhill, but the thrill is short-lived when you start blazing upward again. A dirt road appears on your right about a mile later, but keep straight, eventually descending into a shady nook at 9.9 miles. This little paradise features a gorgeous, huge coast live oak and makes a perfect campsite if you already have all the water you need for the night (**Camp 1**).

From here, continue upward, then descend into lovely **Long Canyon** a mile later. In the fall, it's filled with the bright colors of transitioning black oaks; in the spring, you're surrounded by vibrant green foliage. You'll also spot your very first conifers of the hike, with many more to follow! Traveling alongside seasonal **Long Creek O**, you'll have the best luck tanking up in the late winter and early spring, and you'll find some scattered campsites nestled in the trees around 10.9 miles (**Long Creek Camp**).

Ford the creek at 11.5 miles, then switchback up through intermittent pines, crossing a dirt road at 12.5 miles. When you cross this road again a few minutes later, you have the option of hopping off trail here, descending about 0.3 mile to **Lower Morris Meadow**, where you'll find a spring **O** and ample room for a scenic night under the stars (**Morris Meadow Camp**). If you can time it right, visit this area during sunset, when the mountains morph into pastel shapes and the meadow takes on a golden glow.

MOUNT LAGUNA

Mount Laguna is a quiet mountain community with a post office, general store, visitor center, outfitter, two restaurants, and a handful of rustic lodging options. If you need an Adventure Pass, you can buy one at the general store. The town sits within the Laguna Mountain Recreation Area, which begins just south of Burnt Rancheria Campground and extends to Kwaaymii Point in the north; in between these spots, camping is allowed only in established campgrounds.

When you've had your fill of the gorgeousness (which might take a while), continue on trail through an increasingly dense pine forest filled with majestic Jeffrey pines. I highly encourage you to become a tree hugger here—literally—if only to press your nose into the bark and enjoy a scent that reminds me of sugar cookies, and calls up vanilla or butterscotch for others. Now that you're probably hungry, keep moving along, but make sure you pay attention in this area—the trail crosses several dirt roads (including prominent **Thing Valley Road** just shy of 14 miles) as you draw closer to the town of Mount Laguna, so you'll need to keep a lookout for trail markers as you pass through this pleasantly flat segment.

At about 14.5 miles, you'll start angling out of the tree cover and onto the more sparsely forested east-facing slopes above the Cuyapaipe Indian Reservation, where you start earning epic views of the desert below. Heading slightly uphill, you'll pass a signed junction at 15.1 miles that offers a side trip to "civilization." Although unmarked save for a small tent icon, this is the turnoff for **Burnt Rancheria Campground O**, generally open mid-April (depending on weather) through October. This is a bustling site during the summer months, popular because it offers group camping for PCT hikers, but don't come expecting flowing faucets (or showers) in the winter—they're turned off when the season ends; same goes for the spigot and horse trough **O** along the trail another 0.5 mile down.

Not to fear if your tanks are running low—you're almost to the finish line! Stay straight to pass the unmarked **Desert View Interpretive Nature Trail** at 16 miles, curve to the left and look up 0.6 mile later to see picnic tables above you—look for a use trail heading uphill, which will deposit you at the **Desert View Picnic Site**, where you'll find parking (Adventure Pass required), restrooms, a seasonal water fountain, and a year-round water spigot ⬤. You're also spitting distance to **Mount Laguna**'s main drag, **Sunrise Highway** (County Highway S1), so pop out here to hunt down a cold beverage if you're feeling thirsty.

CAMP-TO-CAMP MILEAGE

Boulder Oaks Campground to
    Yellow Rose Camp 4.0
Yellow Rose Camp to Fred Canyon Camp 1.8
Fred Canyon Camp to Cibbets Flat
    Campground 0.7
Cibbets Flat Campground to Camp 1 . . . . 3.4
Camp 1 to Long Creek Camp 1.0
Long Creek Camp to Morris Meadow Camp . . 1.7
Morris Meadow Camp to Burnt Rancheria
    Campground 2.5

4 DESERT VIEW PICNIC SITE TO PIONEER MAIL PICNIC SITE

DISTANCE 10 miles

ELEVATION GAIN/LOSS
+1300/-1970 feet

HIGH POINT 6014 feet

CONNECTING TRAILS AND ROADS
Monument Peak Road, Big Laguna Trail, Noble Canyon Trail

ON THE TRAIL

This vista-packed segment of trail offers an introduction to some of the most dramatic scenery outside the Sierra as you weave along pine-studded cliffs thousands of feet above the stunning pale peaks and valleys of Anza-Borrego Desert State Park. Don't leave your camera at home!

Before setting off from the **Desert View Picnic Site**, make sure you're carrying all the water you'll need, unless you don't mind leaving the trail later to top off; there's a seasonal water fountain near the restrooms, as well as a year-round pump spigot ⬤ located just uphill from the far end of the parking area (Adventure Pass required). Head downhill past the information kiosk located next to the bathroom, through an array of picnic tables, and look for a narrow but obvious rutted trail that dead-ends a nanosecond later at an unmarked intersection with the PCT. Head left, making a lazy climb through a shady array of Jeffrey pine and black oak, earning some teaser views to the west through breaks in the sparse woodland.

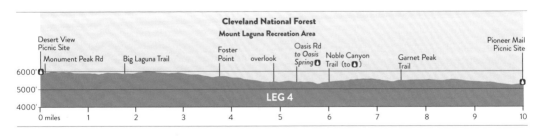

Hikers head north toward impressive Garnet Peak.

Within minutes, cross paved **Monument Peak Road** (your first of two quick encounters); if you're already tired of trail life, hang a left to walk into the hamlet of Mount Laguna, where you'll find a small assortment of food, sundries, and lodging—but if not, carry on. Continuing on, you'll notice a big white orb perched on a hill up to your right—this alien craft is actually an Air Force communications facility located on top of Stephenson Peak. As you wind through tightly knit manzanita thickets, you'll come across an intersection with the **Big Laguna Trail** on your left at 1.7 miles— this will take you back to Sunrise Highway, the main drag running through Mount Laguna. Just ahead, keep your eyes peeled around the 2.1-mile mark for a faint use trail located at a bend in the trail. Flanked by brown PCT markers, this path will take you up to a saddle between **Hayes Peak** and **Monument Peak** to the east if you'd like to add some peakbagging to your day.

From here on out, the slopes are exceedingly shadeless, but the tradeoff for increased UV

SNOW IN SOCAL?!

Despite the wildly incorrect (and shockingly widespread) notion that the first 700 miles of the PCT are composed just of hot, dry, flat "desert," hikers ascend to the pine-studded heights of the Laguna Mountains within the first 40-ish miles of the trail, which may be coated in frost—or more. The first significant winter snowfall usually occurs in early November, and snow can continue falling well into late spring. Make sure you have adequate clothing and shelter to be self-sufficient in possible winter weather in this area and across Southern California's mountain ranges.

exposure is that suddenly the whole Laguna Mountain Recreation Area is yours for the taking, including great views to the redundantly named, but somewhat mesmerizing Flathead Flats just

PEAKBAGGING

Monument Peak and Hayes Peak are located a quick hop off of the PCT. To make the side trip, scoot up the short use path mentioned in the text, likely bushwhacking through overgrown chaparral. Once at the saddle, you'll turn right on the firebreak for Monument, left for Hayes. The latter involves a bit more scrambling, but its summit isn't crowded with the man-made eyesores that mark the top of Monument Peak. Regardless, both offer spectacular views down into the flats of Vallecito Valley and the desert peaks beyond.

below. Even better, you're about to be knocked out with stunning views to the north and east—but first, you'll continue across a saddle to a broad plateau filled with a haunting skeleton crew of burned bushes, then down through an eerie swath of charred forest, the result of the devastating 2003 Cedar Fire, a human-caused catastrophe that remains one of the largest, deadliest, and costliest wildfires in California history.

At 3.7 miles, you'll reach a signed spur trail to **Foster Point**, a perfect perch just a short jog uphill from the PCT, where you'll find a stone pedestal featuring a directional plate pointing to every prominent peak on the skyline, including, on a clear day, the faraway twin behemoths of San Gorgonio Mountain and San Jacinto Peak.

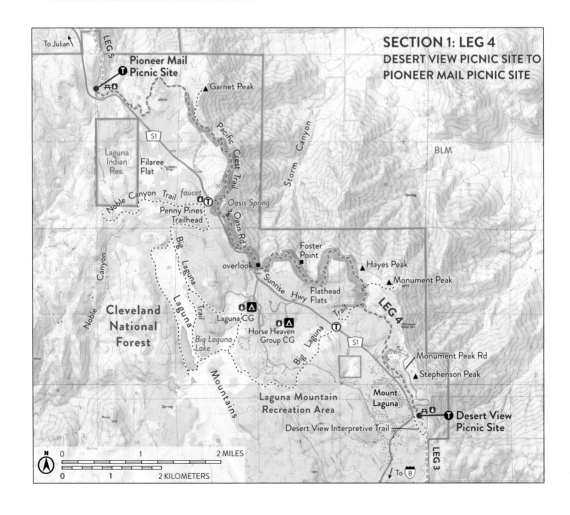

Make a side trip to Foster Point for stunning views across Vallecito Valley.

Make sure you also look down—the deep gash you're hovering over is **Storm Canyon**, which melts into wide, flat Vallecito Valley (yes, that's "Little Valley Valley" for those following along at home), home to the Campbell Ranch and a wealth of cultural history. On that note, long before European, Mexican, and American travelers arrived in the area, Vallecito Valley was known as "Hawi" by the indigenous Kumeyaay people who took advantage of the area's seasonal springs and wetlands, enjoying a rare oasis in the parched Colorado Desert.

Don't worry about leaving the views behind at Foster Point—after a brief dip through burn-scarred slopes, you'll round Storm Canyon, and at 4.8 miles, will pass under a hexagonal **overlook** perched next to a small parking area on **Sunrise Highway**. Pop up a short set of stairs to check out some interpretive displays, and if you're feeling sleepy, this is the best way to access the only legal place to pitch your tent on this section

of trail—**Laguna Campground 🄾**, a sprawling year-round site where you can enjoy flush toilets, showers, and drinking water; **Horse Heaven Group Campground 🄾** is located next door if you're bringing the whole neighborhood. The campground entrance is located 0.2 mile south on the west side of the highway; be very careful crossing the road—cars whip past here fast enough to create hiker pancakes in an instant.

From here, the trail clings for a bit to a very steep, very exposed slope that is absolutely no fun to navigate when icy or if the infamous Santa Ana winds kick in—I almost took an express trip to the bottom of the canyon one particularly blustery day. This bit is over quickly, though, and around the leg's halfway point you'll make a few quick switchbacks downhill—the old roadbed (**Oasis Road**) jutting off from the second turn will lead you to **Oasis Spring 🄾**, an out-of-the-way source that adds a full mile to your hike; consider skipping it since you'll have another opportunity to refill in the near future.

53

Just ahead at 6 miles, you'll hit a Y-intersection on your left; if you're running low on water, pick the left fork to hop on the **Noble Canyon Trail**. Walk a few minutes down this path to the narrow pullout that serves as a parking lot for the Penny Pines Trailhead on Sunrise Highway, then carefully cross the road (remember: hiker pancakes!). Once you go through a gate and pass an information board, you'll spot a spigot **◊** (informally known as the "GATR faucet" on account of the trail's former incarnation as a road leading to a former Air Force Ground to Air Transmit Receive site) and a horse trough. Drink out of the latter only in times of desperation since the much cleaner faucet water is typically accessible year-round. This whole side trip adds a scant 0.2 mile to your day, so it's worth the detour if you're parched.

From here, you start to lose your Vallecito Valley views, but you'll also enjoy a different type of beauty—rambling cliff-edge boulder formations to your right and the sweeping expanse of Filaree Flat to your left. The steep, reddish prow of Garnet Peak also makes itself known, looming straight ahead along your path. Walk through patches of manzanita, ceanothus, yucca, and the occasional Jeffrey pine to reach a four-way junction at 7.5 miles—to the left, a rough dirt road winds back to Sunrise Highway, and to the right, a spur trail ascends to the top of **Garnet Peak**, adding about 1 mile round-trip

if you're in the mood for more jaw-dropping vistas.

Even if you don't make the summit jaunt, you still earn views—both to the burned flats to the west and eventually out to Cottonwood Canyon and distant desert peaks to the north. One of the most interesting sights, though, is across the canyon to the flanks of Garnet Mountain, where the old Sunrise Highway, decommissioned due to rockfall danger, seems to cling precipitously to the steep face.

By 9.4 miles, you'll have dropped down through yet another burn area to a grassy low point just beneath Sunset Highway, where you'll pass through a few stock fences—make sure you do a tick check when you're done. A few minutes ahead, you'll start to spot a few picnic tables up to your left—this is part of the **Pioneer Mail Picnic Site**. To finish, keep heading straight to reach a humongous gravel parking lot at the 10-mile mark; like most trailheads in the Laguna Mountains, an Adventure Pass is required to park here. This is a great place to enjoy a picnic, with ample tables, fire rings, and vault toilets. There's also water sometimes in the concrete trough located just beyond the information kiosk; try the spigot **◊** for a less algae-ridden experience.

CAMP-TO-CAMP MILEAGE

**Desert View Picnic Site to Laguna
  Campground** 4.8

5 PIONEER MAIL PICNIC SITE TO SUNRISE TRAILHEAD CONNECTOR

DISTANCE 6.9 miles

ELEVATION GAIN/LOSS
+1310/-1590 feet

HIGH POINT 5525 feet

CONNECTING TRAIL
Sunrise Trailhead Connector

ON THE TRAIL

If I were forced to choose only one segment of the trail to hike in the Laguna Mountains, this would be my pick, hands down. Featuring a heaping dose of fascinating history mixed with some of the most jaw-dropping views in the southernmost reaches of SoCal, this short, but staggeringly sweet hike packs quite the punch.

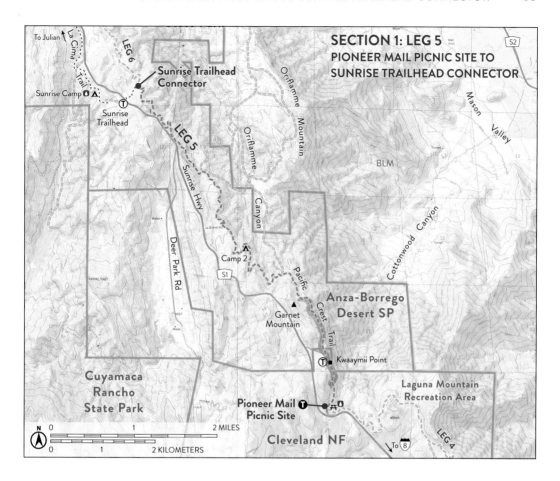

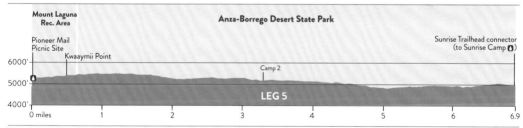

Your starting point is the **Pioneer Mail Picnic Site**, a strangely unimpressive spot considering the epic landscape you're about to explore. Park in the large gravel parking lot (Adventure Pass required), make a quick visit to the vault toilet (you won't see another until the end of your trip), and perhaps grab a quick bite at one of the many picnic tables before hitting the dirt. The trail begins at the eastern side of the parking lot at the large information sign that explains the trailhead's name as a dedication to those who served on the Birch Overland Pioneer Mail Trail. The service began in 1857, and it took the first mule team thirty-eight days to travel between San Antonio and San Diego—think about that next time you complain about slow internet service!

As soon as you walk behind the sign, you'll spot a circular concrete trough **❶**. While this often has water inside, it's most certainly non-potable and almost always a bit mangy, so plan to arrive fully tanked up for the day or deploy your filter. From here, start your trek along a short stretch of crumbled roadbed—a decommissioned segment of **Sunrise Highway** blasted straight into the cliffs. Rerouted in 1975 for safety reasons, this precipitous route dangles thousands of feet above the striking gorge of **Cottonwood Canyon** and the desert flatlands of Mason Valley beyond. As you round the bend to start heading north, the views of both open up spectacularly. The vibrant metamorphic rocks skirting the precipice are studded with all kinds of makeshift plaques and memorials (and some rather uninspired graffiti, unfortunately)—this is **Kwaaymii Point**, a popular destination for day-trippers, so you'll likely be surrounded by plenty of folks enjoying the view, launching gliders, or possibly even memorializing a loved one.

Don't soak up *all* the views just yet—you have plenty more to go! At 0.7 mile, continue across Kwaaymii Point's tiny parking area (an alternate starting point accessed via Sunrise Highway just north of Pioneer Mail), rejoining the trail on the

GREAT SOUTHERN OVERLAND STAGE ROUTE

Looking northeast across the flat, seasonally green expanse of Mason Valley, you'll notice what looks like a farmstead or ranch plopped down in the middle. This is the Butterfield Ranch Resort, an RV campground located along the historic Great Southern Overland Stage Route (now the less enthusiastically named County Highway S2), a once-popular travel corridor used by the likes of the Kumeyaay and other indigenous people, old-timey mailmen, military travelers, prospectors, settlers, and even Mark Twain, who apparently didn't enjoy the bumpy ride from Missouri.

other side. Here, you'll stay straight to pass a use trail on your right, soon encountering the marked boundary of **Anza-Borrego Desert State Park**. Now outside the Laguna Mountain Recreation Area, you're free to enjoy dispersed camping (although the steep slopes will conspire to make this nearly impossible).

For a short while, the landscape makes an abrupt shift from colorful rocky outcroppings to beautiful, green, rolling hills dotted with large boulder jumbles and sheathed in manzanita. However, almost as soon as you step into this pastoral wonderland, you'll suddenly find yourself past it, tiptoeing across a thin ribbon of trail carved into the steep, rocky escarpment of **Garnet Mountain** (not to be confused with nearby Garnet Peak). This section might give pause if you're afraid of heights, but the dramatic views are completely worth any stomach knots. However, suffice it to say that unless you're looking to join the hawks coasting on thermals, you might skip this hike on days when the Santa Ana winds are howling.

Just before the 2-mile mark, the trail completely mellows out into lazy folds of chaparral speckled with occasional boulders. If you've been focusing on your feet this whole way while trying to scurry past the steep stuff, now is the time to pause, pull out your camera, and plan to deplete your stock of superlatives—if you thought the views were outstanding before, they're *phenomenal* now. The desert is fully unfolded below you, a scooped-out bowl of purple, pink, and beige surrounded by peaks near (Oriflamme Mountain to your north) and far (the often snowcapped San Jacinto Peak, over a hundred miles away). Unless you're traveling in spring during thru-hiking season, you're likely to have this stretch of scenery all to yourself, so enjoy the solitude.

At 2.1 miles, you'll hit one of the area's many jeep roads—cross the sandy track and continue up toward a metal trail marker. Just under a mile later, the terrain becomes rockier as you head downhill; the only viable camping is located just ahead at 3.3 miles (**Camp 2**), situated on and around a boulder-strewn hill up to your left. The trail makes a hairpin turn around the hill, so you can access a handful of scattered sites (enough for a few tents)

The old Sunrise Highway route (and now PCT) is blasted straight into steep cliffs.

from either side. It's an incredibly beautiful (if breezy) place to pitch a tent, although it can be a bit tricky to find a perfectly flat spot.

As you make your way downhill through the rolling boulder fields, your view shifts toward Oriflamme Canyon, a once-bustling trade route for indigenous people, pioneers, mail delivery, and the military that now serves as a recreation corridor for all manner of wheeled enthusiasts. At 5 miles, you'll cross one of the many sandy unpaved roads that lead down into the canyon as you make your way back uphill.

At just under 6 miles, you'll find yourself staring up at Sunrise Highway as you're suddenly dropped back into a world of speeding cars and billowing exhaust fumes. Try not to let it get you down—instead, enjoy the abundant chaparral (including agave, chemise, and sagebrush) and power upward to snag one last epic view of the expansive desert

and its jagged skyline. If your trip ends here and you're ready to leave those vistas (and the PCT) behind, hang a left at 6.9 miles onto a short connector trail marked "Sunrise Highway"; when you reach the road around 0.25 mile ahead, cross carefully to reach the Sunrise Trailhead.

The trailhead features a gigantic gravel parking lot and a vault toilet along with access to a concrete water trough ⬤ a few minutes' walk up the signed La Cima Trail at the northwestern corner of the lot; bring a filter if you plan on drinking from this non-potable source. You can also camp here if you'd like, although the ground is pretty lumpy and scattered with cow patties—and possibly even the patty-makers themselves (**Sunrise Camp**).

CAMP-TO-CAMP MILEAGE

Pioneer Mail Picnic Site to Camp 2 . . . . 3.3
Camp 2 to Sunrise Camp 3.6

6 SUNRISE TRAILHEAD CONNECTOR TO SCISSORS CROSSING

DISTANCE 17.8 miles

ELEVATION GAIN/LOSS
+1540/-4280 feet

HIGH POINT 4993 feet

CONNECTING TRAILS AND ROADS
Sunrise Trailhead Connector, Mason Valley
Truck Trail, Chariot Canyon Road, Rodriguez
Spur Truck Trail, County Highway S2, State
Highway 78

ON THE TRAIL

Enjoy the aerial views and hopeful breeze during
this first segment because you'll soon drop down to
the hot desert floor below. Also make sure you take
steps to avoid ending up glowing with sunburn at
the end (shade is scant), and tank up—your first
reliable water source is almost 9 miles ahead. Heading north from the **Sunrise Trailhead Connector**,
Oriflamme Mountain—your constant companion
during the last leg—looms large directly to the

east. Waltz through the sunny chaparral (mostly
chamise and manzanita) as you weave your way
along a ridge, scoring views to much sandier portions of **Anza-Borrego Desert State Park**, whose
borders you'll stay within for most of this leg.

Undulate along until you hit an unpaved
road 2.9 miles in—this is the **Mason Valley
Truck Trail**. If you went left, you'd pick up
the southbound **California Riding and Hiking
Trail (CRHT)** and would reach the Pedro Fages
Monument trailhead 1.4 miles southwest on Sunrise Highway. However, you'll hang a right, then
make a quick left to join up with the CRHT for
a short bit as it wiggles ever downward. There *is*
a fire tank located on the right just a hair farther
if you continue on Mason Valley Truck Trail, but
it's almost always empty, so it's likely not worth
your time to check for water.

Although you've left Oriflamme behind, a
new peak has taken its place over to the northeast—Chariot Mountain, whose flanks you'll
ascend soon enough (yes, that trail you see
climbing across Chariot Canyon is, in fact, the

SUNRISE TRAILHEAD

Sunrise Trailhead is located 0.25 mile
southwest of the PCT via a short
connector trail that ends at Sunrise
Highway. Cross carefully to reach a
large dirt parking area on the far side,
where you'll find vault toilets and not
much else. Pick up the La Cima Trail
from the northwest corner and walk a few
minutes down to find a water trough; 🛑
be sure to filter, since this area is party
town for cattle. Camping is available
nearby (**Sunrise Camp**), although you'll
probably need to clear away some cow
patties before setting down your tent.

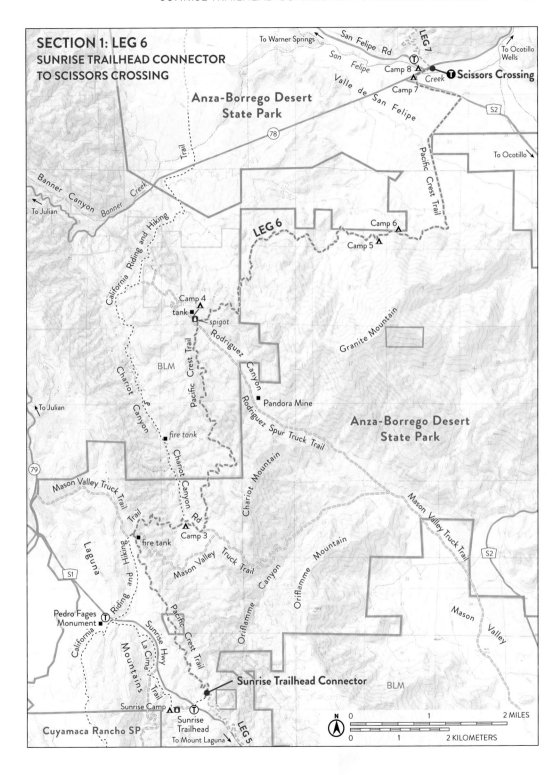

SECTION 1: LEG 6
SUNRISE TRAILHEAD CONNECTOR
TO SCISSORS CROSSING

PCT—sorry!). But first, wiggle steeply downhill, keeping your eyes peeled for a dirt clearing on the right at 4.2 miles, which makes for a sort of unappealing campsite (**Camp 3**), with room for several tents. The upside is that you can occasionally find water nearby, although it may not be worth the effort. If you want to try, make a left onto the CRHT to head north into the canyon and find a seasonal trickle about 0.8 mile up from the PCT. If that's dry, continue farther up to check out a fire tank at 1.2 miles, and as a last resort, a spring tucked among some oaks on your right 0.2 mile past that. All in all, a lot of extra hiking for possible crushing disappointment.

Just after that dusty campsite, hit unpaved **Chariot Canyon Road** on the floor of **Chariot Canyon** itself. Leave your new buddy, the CRHT, behind as it heads left, and join the road to head right and begin a steep uphill climb. Keep in mind that people do use these unpaved roads for wheeled travel, so pop your earbuds out and remain alert in this area. Luckily, this section is short, and

you leave the road to rejoin the trail at 4.6 miles, beginning a lengthy traverse beneath **Chariot Mountain**. The scenery doesn't change much, which can make this segment seem tedious, but I think it's beautiful to see the earth's bends and folds across the canyon.

Eventually you round a gully and pop onto a ridgeline that offers several glimpses to what's ahead (and below) at a saddle around 6.5 miles. While Chariot Canyon remains to your left, Rodriguez Canyon now comes into sight down to your right. The unpaved road you see snaking through it is the Rodriguez Spur Truck Trail, and the solitary structure below is the Pandora Mine. **Granite Mountain** rises above to the northwest, and the San Felipe Hills play peek-a-boo to your north; you'll get much better views of the latter once you hit the road itself.

Dance along the rocky trail until you reach the head of **Rodriguez Canyon**, where things suddenly flatten out and become nearly pastoral. Ignore a side trail on your left and instead

Rodriguez Spur Truck Trail boasts a unique trail sign.

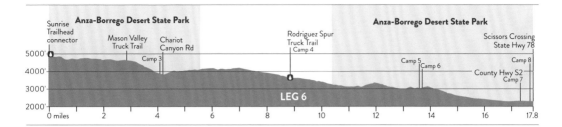

continue toward a gate ahead at 8.9 miles that straddles **Rodriguez Spur Truck Trail** (a rather rustic street sign above your head confirms this intersection). If you turn left here, you'll find a spigot 🄾 just ahead tucked into some bushes on the right that provides water from a tank just up the way, and if you continue south just past the tank, you'll find a mediocre campsite (**Camp 4**) also on the right. Many people camp in a large dirt clearing directly across from the gate you passed through, but it's located right on the road; while the views from here are fantastic, the proximity to wheeled vehicles is not.

To continue on the trail, hang a right from the gate and keep your eyes peeled for a trail marker and single-track descending almost immediately to your left under some power lines. Much like the first half of this trek, you can see the trail stretch out endlessly in front of you as you sidle along mostly north-facing slopes below Granite Mountain. Manzanita and chamise mix with adorably named, but bloodthirsty, teddy bear cholla and beavertail cactus. You'll be forgiven for running into some of the pointier desert denizens as you admire the flat Valle de San Felipe stretched out below and the San Felipe Hills rising across—if you continue northwards, you'll grunt your way up them in the next leg.

For now, head mostly downhill along the narrow, shadeless trail, with the occasional short gain to keep some pep in your step. The landscape here definitely embraces the high desert vibe, with beautiful boulders, hedgehog cactus, yucca, and agave all enhancing the atmospherics, even though you occasionally pass though sections of burned out wasteland, remnants of the 2012 Banner Fire. You'll begin to notice the slope angle mellow out, and not only can you see a few scattered buildings

below, you'll also notice the glint of cars driving along State Highway 78 in the distance, your eventual endpoint! Until then, appreciate the quietude of your current surroundings.

Around 13.6 miles, you'll round a prominent gully, which provides some of the best shade on this part of the trip. There are also a few decent campsites here (**Camp 5**), tucked off to the right via a short use trail. After a short uphill, you'll find another small spot (**Camp 6**) located on a lumpy ridge to your left, guarded by one bedraggled juniper—not much wind protection, but you do get some magnificent views.

Coast down a few switchbacks, pop down through some low hills, then begin a beeline toward your final destination, leaving the boulders behind to cross dry, flat **Valle de San Felipe**. It might feel a little apocalyptic here, especially if you're alone; if you want company, keep your eyes trained to the ground to see if you can spot a tarantula making its own slow trek across the desert floor.

In 16.1 miles, you'll pass through a gate and continue along a fence, eventually turning to parallel paved **County Highway S2**, historically known as the Great Southern Overland Stagecoach Route. There's a popular RV campground located a few miles south down this road—they often post a small sign along the trail here to entice you with visions of ice cream and showers, so hop off the trail and hang a right if you're seeking refreshment.

Otherwise, continue along the trail, now paralleling the road, eventually passing through a metal gate to cross Highway S2 at 17.5 miles. You're now in what most people consider the general **Scissors Crossing** area, where Highway S2 and **San Felipe Road** both intersect State Highway 78. You can

Clouds roll across the Volcan Mountains as a double rainbow appears over Valle de San Felipe and the San Felipe Hills.

find a few places to plop down a tent (**Camp 7**) in this in-between area, but it's a less-than-desirable place due to the traffic and garbage strewn about. Some hikers also choose to camp near the highway underpass and **San Felipe Creek** watershed just ahead, despite the general creepiness and the sign warning of flash flood danger. This is, however, a good place to catch some shade before the next

leg if there's no threat of storms (or unsavory characters).

Despite all of the trash littering the place, you can tell that it was probably very pretty before the encroachment of man, with the cottonwood-lined creek passing through. You'll finally reach the ultimate man-made invasion at 17.8 miles, when you come up to very busy **State Highway 78**, ending this leg right next to a heavily graffitied mileage sign. Not the prettiest place to finish, but it'll do. If you want another camping option, carefully cross the road (cars drive *very* fast here), and look west of San Felipe Road to find some clearings (**Camp 8**). However, I recommend you skip this idea and instead look for a cozy bed in Julian or continue north into the San Felipe Hills for a less sketchy night's sleep.

JULIAN

Many hikers catch rides from Scissors Crossing into the town of Julian, about 12 miles west along State Highway 78—use good judgment if you choose to hitch. Known for its apple orchards (and apple pies), this picturesque town sits snuggled into pine-forested hills, a world away from the desiccated flats below. While it doesn't offer big box stores or giant supermarkets, you can eat a tasty meal, snooze at a bed-and-breakfast, and pick up a few supplies for the next leg of your trip.

CAMP-TO-CAMP MILEAGE

Sunrise Trailhead Connector to Camp 3 . . . . . 4.2
Camp 3 to Camp 4 . . . . 4.7
Camp 4 to Camp 5 . . . . 4.7
Camp 5 to Camp 6 . . . . 0.3
Camp 6 to Camp 7 . . . . 3.6
Camp 7 to Camp 8 . . . . 0.3

7 | SCISSORS CROSSING TO MONTEZUMA VALLEY ROAD

DISTANCE 23.9 miles

ELEVATION GAIN/LOSS
+3670/-2480 feet

HIGH POINT 4413 feet

CONNECTING ROADS
State Highway 78, Montezuma Valley Road

ON THE TRAIL

If you hiked the previous leg, you no doubt gazed across to the imposing **San Felipe Hills** and felt a sense of gentle dread build inside upon realizing your gain-intensive fate. However, standing on the shoulder of State Highway 78, you can see only a small portion of the hills, so it should feel a lot less daunting once you actually set out.

Before hoisting your pack, ensure you have enough water to last the blistering 23.8 miles to Barrel Spring, the only natural water source on this leg. Although trail angels generally maintain a cache tucked off-trail about 14 miles in, it's never a good idea to rely on these, especially if traveling outside of the normal thru-hiker season. This leg is notoriously hot and sunny until the very end—shade is difficult to find, so grab it when you can. On the upside, brisk winds often rip through the area, which might help with temperature regulation as long as you're not whipped off the trail.

Now that I've imbued you with a sense of gentle dread, I want to mitigate it by sharing that this was actually one of my favorite segments of trail when I first hiked through! With that comforting thought in mind, carefully cross **State Highway 78** where the PCT intersects just east of **San Felipe Road** (and the actual **Scissors Crossing** itself), then continue across into **Anza-Borrego Desert State Park**, through the beginnings of what will become a really spectacular high desert garden as you ascend. Hiking in early spring is an exceptional treat: brittlebush bursts forth with yellow blooms, barrel and hedgehog cacti sprout lush fuchsia toppers, and towering ocotillo shows off with vibrant red petals. Fragrant sage, "fuzzy" teddy bear cholla, and the floral crowns of fishhook cacti also join the show.

While you'll likely become enamored with the profuse plant life, don't forget to cast a glance back to the south, where Granite Mountain towers over

ALTERNATE START

While there is a small, rough turnout on the north side of Highway 78, it's not a great idea to leave your car here overnight. Instead, head west on the highway, then take the first right onto San Felipe Road where you'll find a massive unpaved parking lot on the right side just a few minutes up. Look for faint use trails on the northeast side of the parking area to make your way to the trail above, about 0.3 mile past the official start of this leg. Hang a left to continue north.

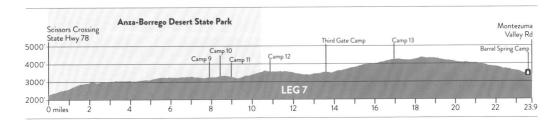

The southernmost San Felipe Hills host a dense concentration of cacti, especially beautiful during early spring.

the flats of Valle de San Felipe. Even though you'll feel the ascent (especially with the massive water haul), it's not as bad as you might have imagined from the outset. As you maneuver through the landscape's squiggles, you'll pass several washes in the first few miles—while these sandy flats seem like an inviting place to crash, they're not safe campsites since they can flood during a rain event. Also avoid throwing your gear down at any number of rough bivy sites gouged out directly next to the trail in this first stretch—this not only flouts Leave No Trace practice, but is also a source of consternation for state park officials tasked with preserving the park's landscapes for all users. Trust me—there are better spots farther along this leg.

Around 4 miles in, you'll start to notice the effects of the 2012 Vallecito Lightning Complex Fire, a series of blazes that scorched almost 23,000 acres, affecting nearly half of this leg. Even though some charred tree skeletons remain, it's impressive to realize how quickly things can bounce back after fire—chaparral, especially chamise, becomes more frequent as you move north. Around this point in the trail, you'll also start earning views east to Grapevine Mountain, northeast to Pinyon Ridge rising above Grapevine Canyon, then west to the Volcan Mountains, often swaddled in billowy clouds.

You'll encounter the first "legitimate" campsite around 7.9 miles, with room in a juniper-ringed clearing on your right for a few tents (**Camp 9**). Continue on to find a few more sites to your left just past a metal gate along a large ridge at 8.6 miles (**Camp 10**). Neither of these spots offers much in the way of ambiance, but they'll do if you're too tired to continue. Another opportunity presents

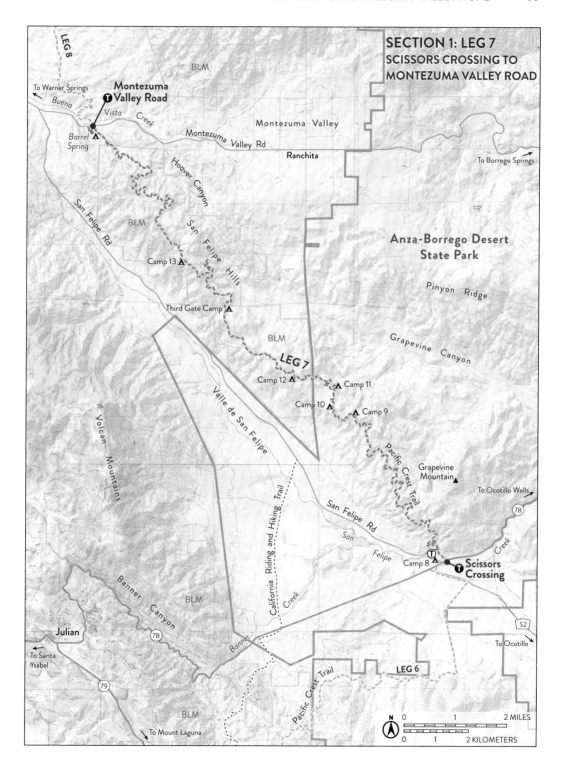

SECTION 1: LEG 7
SCISSORS CROSSING TO
MONTEZUMA VALLEY ROAD

LEG 8

To Warner Springs

Montezuma
Valley Road

Buena

Vista   Creek

Barrel
Spring

BLM

Montezuma   Valley

Montezuma   Valley Rd

Ranchita

To Borrego Springs

Anza-Borrego Desert
State Park

Hoover Canyon

San Felipe Rd

BLM

San   Felipe   Hills

Pinyon   Ridge

Camp 13

Third Gate Camp

BLM

Grapevine   Canyon

LEG 7

Camp 12

Camp 11

Camp 10

Camp 9

Valle de San Felipe

Volcan Mountains

California Riding and Hiking Trail

Grapevine
Mountain

Pacific Crest Trail

To Ocotillo Wells

78

San Felipe Rd

San

Felipe

Creek

Creek

Camp 8

Scissors
Crossing

Banner   Canyon

BLM

S2

Julian

78

To Santa
Ysabel

Banner

To Ocotillo

79

Pacific Crest Trail

LEG 6

BLM

To Mount Laguna

N   0   1   2 MILES

0   1   2 KILOMETERS

VOLCAN MOUNTAINS

The nearby Volcan Mountains are lush and green, standing in stark contrast to the arid San Felipe Hills you traverse throughout this leg. This anomaly is created by a "rain shadow" that causes precipitation to linger over the range but dissipate before it can travel any farther. When the Cleveland National Forest was tasked with building the trail through this area, one of their proposed options was to run it through the Volcan Mountains. However, private landowners opposed that plan, so it was scrapped in favor of this routing, which caused the least amount of conflict with locals who feared negative impacts from the trail and its users.

zone coated in chamise and dotted with scrub oak, ceanothus, chia, and sugarbush.

Pass through a third pipe gate at 13.7 miles, known to thru-hikers as the legendary "Third Gate." This is home to multiple shady campsites tucked into the brush on the left side of the trail (**Third Gate Camp**), and a cache located on private property 0.3 mile off trail (marked by a rustic "Water" sign pointing the way). As mentioned earlier, the latter is a volunteer effort and can end at any time; it's better to carry what you need from the beginning of this leg, rather than count on the stash being stocked. The trail continues left at the fork here, resuming the somewhat maddening squiggle along the hillside. Let the amazing views provide emotional comfort.

A fourth metal gate is located around 16.3 miles; from here, head toward an obvious ridgeline ahead, which you'll reach in just over 0.5 mile. Follow a use trail on your left to find my favorite campsite

itself just a bit farther, when you drop down into a huge dry creek bed at 9.2 miles—although there's space for a veritable tent village, choose spots located up and away from the watershed (**Camp 11**). It can rain—and *does* flood—in the desert!

After that enjoyable coast down to the flats, you immediately regain much of that lost elevation switchbacking up the other side of the creek bed. The views improve with each huff and puff, and you eventually wiggle out of the state park and into BLM land to hit another pipe gate at 10.8 miles, guarding a long ridge to the left. Here, you'll find sweeping vistas and room for several tents, although make sure to really hammer in your stakes so they don't rip out in a wicked gust (**Camp 12**).

From here, begin winding around the seemingly interminable gullies carved into west-facing slopes. The monotony can become grating, although there are a few positives: sweet views of the Volcan Mountains and the San Felipe Creek watershed down below, plus respite from howling wind whenever you step into a gully. While the landscape might feel repetitive, it does eventually morph from high desert into a full-blown chaparral

Teddy bear cholla looks *fuzzy, but you definitely don't want to hug it!*

in this area with room for multiple tents, and stunning sunset (and sunrise) views (**Camp 13**). Morning offers the spellbinding sight of fog rolling over peaks, through canyons, and across distant Lake Henshaw if visibility allows; strolling mule deer only add to the magic.

After rounding a big gully, dip inland, passing a small cave on the left side of the trail (known as "Billy Goat's Cave") at 18.5 miles. Slip inside the cramped space for a shady rest before finishing the uphill portion of this leg with views across to the San Ysidro Mountains to the northeast and to the wide, relatively flat expanse of Montezuma Valley far below. Do a little jig, because now it's time to go down!

After grumbling your way around an especially lengthy branch of **Hoover Canyon**, bounce along past bright clusters of bush poppies, moving through several shabby pipe gates. Twittering birds fight for dominance over the growing din of traffic on Montezuma Valley Road as you suddenly drop down into tree cover. Curve around to find piped **Barrel Spring** ⚪ spilling into a trough on the left side of the trail in a shady oak glen at 23.8 miles.

Rejoice as you chug life-sustaining *agua*, and perhaps even consider setting up shop here for the night (**Barrel Spring Camp**). Note that while some signs mark the fringes of this area as private property, there are also others legitimizing this as an easement for "Barrel Springs Trailcamp."

To finish, pick up the trail past the trough and pass through one final gate to reach a dirt parking area and paved **Montezuma Valley Road** 0.1 mile past the spring. The small town of Ranchita (4 miles east along the road) offers a small general store along with an excellent (and strange) photo op, which awaits at the quaint market if you choose to make this side trip.

CAMP-TO-CAMP MILEAGE

Scissors Crossing to Camp 9. . . . . 7.9
Camp 9 to Camp 10 . . . . 0.7
Camp 10 to Camp 11. 0.6
Camp 11 to Camp 12 . . . . 1.6
Camp 12 to Third Gate Camp 2.9
Third Gate Camp to Camp 13 . . . . 3.2
Camp 13 to Barrel Spring Camp. 6.9

8 MONTEZUMA VALLEY ROAD TO WARNER SPRINGS

DISTANCE 8.3 miles

ELEVATION GAIN/LOSS +1200/-1600 feet

HIGH POINT 3570 feet

CONNECTING TRAILS AND ROADS Montezuma Valley Road, California Riding and Hiking Trail, State Highway 79

ON THE TRAIL

If you hiked the previous leg through the hot, dry San Felipe Hills, this next segment will come as a welcome surprise as you meander through the lush pastoral landscape leading up to Warner Springs.

My *Lord of the Rings*–loving hiking companion had no problem envisioning any number of elfin creatures taking up residence here.

If you're not stringing together a longer hike, it's fairly easy to set up a car shuttle, with ample parking on both ends—find a large dirt parking area on the south side of **Montezuma Valley Road**, whereas a smaller pullout exists on the north side of State Highway 79 near this leg's endpoint. While there are a few natural water sources along the way, you can also duck back 0.1 mile to **Barrel Spring** ⚪ just south on the trail to tank up. One last note: the entirety of this leg technically runs through private property, so while you'll spot tempting bedtime locales near both San Ysidro Creek and Cañada Verde, it's best to continue

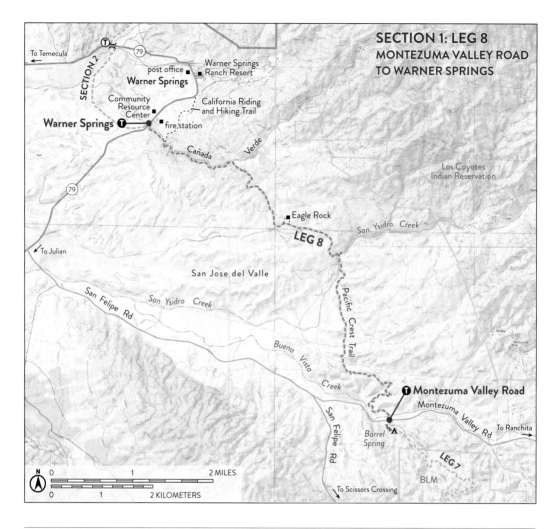

SECTION 1: LEG 8
MONTEZUMA VALLEY ROAD
TO WARNER SPRINGS

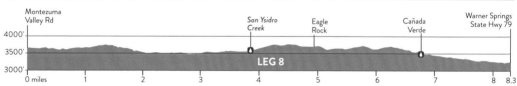

north through the end of this leg and into the next to reach "legal" campsites.

To begin, cross the moderately busy road and head north, angling left to stay on the trail as it passes a rough dirt road and meanders along the perpetually dry watershed of **Buena Vista Creek**. The terrain is mixed, with scattered oaks,

sagebrush, and plentiful chaparral, including sugarbush, chamise, ceanothus, and mountain mahogany. If you're hiking in spring, a smattering of wildflowers, including apricot mallow and Indian paintbrush, provide some extra color.

Wiggle around the hillsides for a bit, cresting a ridge around 1.3 miles that offers sweeping views

Give any bovines you encounter a wide berth.

to the vibrant grasslands of San Jose del Valle below, as well as northwest toward the Palomar Mountains; a sharp eye will spot the white dome of the Palomar Observatory perched up high. After gawking for a bit, sail down toward the green stuff (and possibly orange stuff, if coming through when California poppies are in bloom), then head uphill on the other side. This becomes a familiar pattern—down-up-down-up—as you navigate a series of potentially cow-filled pastures and small rises. Our hoofed friends create many social paths, so scan for PCT markers posted at regular intervals to stay on track. Also watch for the path-makers themselves and prepare to *moooove* over to give any wandering bovines a wide berth—having grown up in Wisconsin, I generally enjoy their

THE CUPEÑO PEOPLE

As you begin to parallel San Ysidro Creek, look for a flattish rock on the right with a prominent hole gouged into it. This is a mortero, used long ago by indigenous people to pulverize acorns into flour, which was then leached of tannins and baked into bread; you'll see evidence of these grinding stones scattered around Southern California and into the Sierra. Here, the mortero was likely left by one of the Cupeño people who knew this place as "Kupa," a name that changed to Warner's Ranch after their land was invaded by Spaniards in the late 18th century and transferred to rancher Juan José Warner in 1844. After a failed revolt and later legal battles, the Cupeño lost any land rights and were forced to relocate to the Pala Indian Reservation, the displacement referred to as the Cupeño Trail of Tears.

A rare lonesome shot of Eagle Rock, waiting for another hiker to mount its shoulders for a photo op

company, but was forced to rethink my position after one cranky (and surprisingly spry) cow began an angry advance toward my hiking companion and me. I was later told that since they're used to humans feeding them, cows sometimes approach hikers seeking snacks, but that didn't make it any less unnerving.

Continue dodging cow patties and their makers a bit longer until the scenery switches from sunny, grassy pastures to a shady oak-studded riparian zone. You're now hiking just above small, but pretty, **San Ysidro Creek ⓪**, which often reduces to a trickle in the absence of rain and dries up completely by summer. Cross the creek at 3.8 miles and top off your water bottles—this is the most reliable flow on this leg. From here, ascend to score more views to the Palomar Mountains.

After cresting the rise, it's time to dip down into another grassy wonderland; if you need to relieve

WARNER SPRINGS

Warner Springs is a quiet ranching community built around a natural hot spring. Services are very limited, mostly focused around the Warner Springs Community Resource Center near the trail's southern crossing of Highway 79, with a small store and lots of dusty people lounging around during thru-hiking season. They often let hikers camp on their lawn during this time; ask permission before pitching your tent. Farther into town you'll find a post office and the Warner Springs Ranch Resort, a former literal celebrity hot spot now undergoing a multiyear renovation.

yourself after imbibing that tasty creek water, take care of it before descending since you're about to lose all opportunity to do so covertly. From the lumpy field below, a rock formation looms in the distance—it doesn't look like much now, but this is one of the most popular day hiking destinations in the area. To see what all the fuss is about, look for a use trail on your right at around 4.9 miles that curves around to the front of the iconic, unmistakable **Eagle Rock** formation. Indulge your inner child and scramble up its back side to perch on top and pretend you're riding this magnificent bird.

After posing, hop down and back onto the trail, eventually heading up toward a chaparral-clad ridgeline featuring a small bit of shade, courtesy of a few stately Engelmann oaks. You once again spot a lush, green area below—this is the gorgeous **Cañada Verde 0**, whose seasonal waters are accessed via several use trails located on your right beginning around 6.7 miles. Even if the waterway is dry, this oak- and sycamore-shaded canyon makes for a pretty and peaceful hike.

Soon enough the sounds of civilization creep in as you near the small town of **Warner Springs**. Pass through a pair of trail gates, the second of which sports a map of the area. There's also a marker here noting the **California Riding and Hiking Trail**, which departs to the right. Otherwise, hang a right after reaching a fenced-off underpass, pop up next to a fire station, and cross the pavement to end this leg on the north side of **State Highway 79** at the 8.3-mile mark. If you're thirsty, check to see if water is available at the fire station or walk east just a short way to reach the hiker-friendly **Warner Springs Community Resource Center**.

CAMP-TO-CAMP MILEAGE

This leg traverses private property—there are no viable campsites.

WARNER SPRINGS TO SAN GORGONIO PASS

IF YOU WANT TO SNAG a grand tour of Southern California's diverse landscapes without gassing up your car (aside from whatever your tank requires to deposit you at the trailhead), check out this century miler for a rollercoaster snapshot of the southland's most intriguing terrain.

After a brief wander through the pastoral expanse of rolling Warner Springs Ranch, you'll make close acquaintance with burbling Agua Caliente Creek, whose seasonal flow you'll cross a handful of times under a leafy canopy of oak, cottonwood, and sycamore. Winding along this shady riparian corridor, you'll wonder how willows, prickly pears, and pines can all occupy the same square footage. Soon you'll switch things up and ascend the chaparral-clad slopes. En route, your nose will dance with the herby scent of "cowboy cologne" sagebrush while weaving through massive boulder fields, which tempt hikers with tantalizing off-trail scrambling opportunities.

Next up on your sampler platter is the northwestern corner of Anza-Borrego Desert State Park, where you'll earn sweeping views from the shoulder of Combs Peak, revel in the refreshing waters of the Tule Spring oasis, and become distracted by the stunning high desert cactus gardens on display.

Continue your ultimate SoCal experience with a trip across the pine-forested spine of the rocky Desert Divide—your gateway to the often snowcapped high peaks of the San Jacinto Mountains. Rest for a bit in the charming, artsy haven of Idyllwild, then take an optional side trip to San Jacinto Peak itself for spectacular views of both the desert and the jagged San Bernardino Mountains (the next stop on your northbound PCT pilgrimage). Finally, make a shockingly rapid descent of almost 7000 feet through a whirlwind of ecosystems to sunbaked San Gorgonio Pass. Variety truly is the spice of life!

DISTANCE 100 miles

STATE DISTANCE 109.5–209.5 miles

ELEVATION GAIN/LOSS +14,030/-15,740 feet

HIGH POINT 9058 feet

BEST TIME OF YEAR Nov–Apr for low elevations, June–Sept for high elevations

PCTA SECTION LETTER B

LAND MANAGERS Cleveland National Forest (Palomar Ranger District), Anza-Borrego Desert State Park, San Bernardino National Forest (San Jacinto Ranger District, San Jacinto Wilderness, Santa Rosa and San Jacinto Mountains National Monument), Mount San Jacinto State Park (Mount San Jacinto State Wilderness)

PASSES AND PERMITS A wilderness permit is required for day and overnight trips in the San Jacinto and Mount San Jacinto state wilderness areas; the latter is not covered by a long-distance PCT permit. Adventure Pass may be required to park at certain trailheads within the San Bernardino National Forest. California Campfire Permit.

Opposite: *Keep an eye out for gnomes as you walk through the lush Mount San Jacinto State Wilderness.*

MAPS AND APPS

- Halfmile's CA Section B
- USFS PCT Map #1 Southern California
- USGS Topo Quads: Warner Springs, Hot Springs Mountain, Bucksnort Mountain, Butterfly Peak, Palm View Peak, Idyllwild, San Jacinto Peak, White Water
- Halfmile's PCT app
- Guthook's PCT app

LEGS

1. Warner Springs to Chihuahua Valley Road
2. Chihuahua Valley Road to Table Mountain Truck Trail
3. Table Mountain Truck Trail to State Highway 74
4. State Highway 74 to Cedar Springs Trail
5. Cedar Springs Trail to Saddle Junction
6. Saddle Junction to Fuller Ridge Trailhead
7. Fuller Ridge Trailhead to San Gorgonio Pass

ACCESS

Warner Springs

From San Diego, head north on Interstate 15 toward Escondido. Take exit 17 for Scripps Poway Parkway and turn right. In 8.6 miles, turn left onto CA 67 northbound, which eventually becomes Main Street, then Julian Road (CA 78 eastbound).

After it becomes Julian Road, travel about 14.4 miles, then turn left to join Highway 79 north. You'll reach the trailhead in just under 14 miles; parking is available along the north side of the road across from the fire station.

San Gorgonio Pass

Because this section ends under a freeway underpass that is distinctly lacking in parking opportunities, your best options are to begin at the trail's intersection with Snow Creek Road in the previous leg, have someone drop you off where the trail crosses Tamarack Road on the north side of the Interstate 10 underpass, or park at Cottonwood Trailhead just under 2 miles north. For the latter, head west from Los Angeles on I-10 toward San Bernardino. Take exit 110 (Haugen-Lehmann Way) and turn left onto the road. After 0.8 mile, take a right onto Cottonwood Road and drive for approximately 1.2 miles until you reach a large dirt parking lot on your right; pick up the PCT from the southeast corner of the parking lot.

NOTES

Cities and Services

The small community of Warner Springs at the southern trailhead doesn't have much in the way of services aside from a post office, although the community center often offers up varied services to hikers during the thru-hiking season. Cabazon, located 4.5 miles west of the northern trailhead, offers a post office, gas station, dining options, casino, and an outlet mall; for more variety, head 11 miles southeast to the much larger Palm Springs.

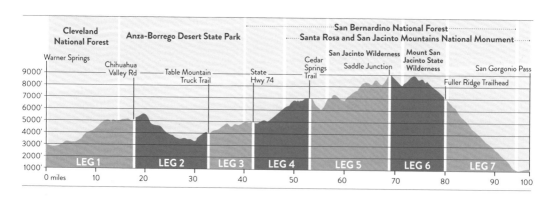

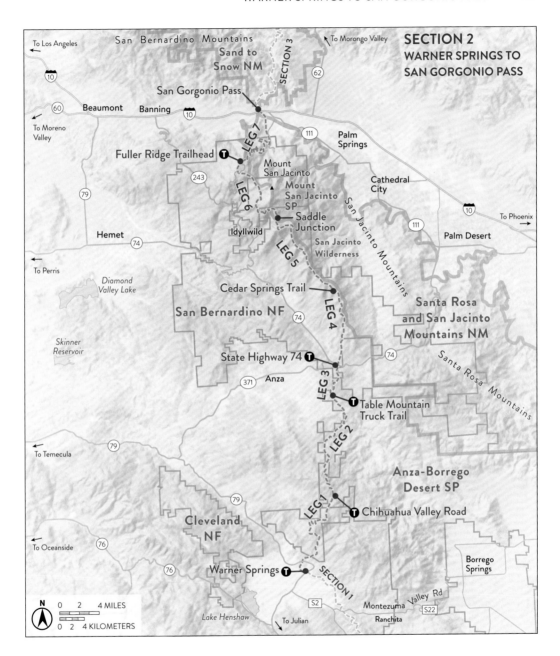

Camping and Fire Restrictions

Camping in the San Jacinto Wilderness and Mount San Jacinto State Wilderness requires a wilderness permit and is restricted to designated sites. Camp at least 200 feet from water. Campfires are not allowed in San Jacinto Wilderness and Mount San Jacinto State Wilderness areas. In other areas, fires are only allowed in designated fire rings. Check for seasonal fire restrictions in Cleveland and San Bernardino National Forests before heading out.

Beavertail cacti sport beautiful spring blooms.

SUGGESTED ITINERARIES

Camps are either viewable from the trail or located within a few tenths of a mile from the noted location unless otherwise specified in leg descriptions. Itineraries reflect PCT miles only, with the hope that the Mountain Fire closure will be lifted by this book's publication.

8 DAYS

		Miles
Day 1	Warner Springs to Camp 1	14.3
Day 2	Camp 1 to Camp 3	14.5
Day 3	Camp 3 to Camp 6	17.6
Day 4	Camp 6 to Apache Camp	13.3
Day 5	Apache Camp to Strawberry Trail Camp	14.1
Day 6	Strawberry Trail Camp to Fuller Ridge Camp	7.2
Day 7	Fuller Ridge Camp to Camp 21	10.7
Day 8	Camp 21 to San Gorgonio Pass	8.3

7 DAYS

Day 1	Warner Springs to Camp 1	14.3
Day 2	Camp 1 to Camp 4	16.3
Day 3	Camp 4 to Camp 6	15.8
Day 4	Camp 6 to Apache Camp	13.3
Day 5	Apache Camp to Strawberry Trail Camp	14.1
Day 6	Strawberry Trail Camp to Camp 20	13.9
Day 7	Camp 20 to Fuller Ridge	12.3

6 DAYS

Day 1	Warner Springs to Camp 1	14.3
Day 2	Camp 1 to Camp 4	16.3
Day 3	Camp 4 to Live Oak Camp	18.2
Day 4	Live Oak Camp to Camp 12	21.2
Day 5	Camp 12 to Camp 20	17.7
Day 6	Camp 20 to Fuller Ridge	12.3

Water

Water is scarce along this entire section, especially during a drought year or in late season; consult with rangers regarding availability and trail conditions before setting out. The longest likely waterless stretches are the 17.4 miles between the spur to Lost Valley Spring and the one to Tule Spring, the 18.9 miles between the guzzler south of Nance Canyon and the spur to Live Oak Spring, and the 19.5 miles between a tributary of the North Fork San Jacinto River and the faucet on Snow Canyon Road.

Hazards

This section sees extreme temperatures—the low elevation desert can easily reach the triple digits in the warmer months, and the high elevations, especially north-facing slopes, often retain snow into early summer. Fuller Ridge can be dangerous when covered in snow and ice—traction devices and an ice axe may be required to safely maneuver

around the steep drop-offs in this area. Hikers have become disoriented and lost (and in some cases, have died) in the high elevations of the San Jacinto Mountains, not just when the area is blanketed in snow or fog, but also on occasion while navigating the latticework of trails and access roads around the Tahquitz Valley area—bring a map and compass, and know how to use them.

Other

Pets are not allowed in the Mount San Jacinto State Wilderness or on trails in Anza-Borrego Desert State Park. A 10.7-mile section of the PCT between Fobes Saddle and Tahquitz Creek has been closed for several years due to extreme damage from the 2013 Mountain Fire—until this section is rebuilt, hikers must either skip ahead to Idyllwild to rejoin the trail or take a lengthy detour. Sources tell me the trail might reopen by late 2017.

1 WARNER SPRINGS TO CHIHUAHUA VALLEY ROAD

DISTANCE 17.8 miles

ELEVATION GAIN/LOSS
+3680/-1670 feet

HIGH POINT 5236 feet

CONNECTING TRAILS AND ROADS
State Highway 79, Lost Valley Road spur, Chihuahua Valley Road

ON THE TRAIL

The start of this leg might conjure up words like "pastoral" and "bucolic" as you saunter through the oak-studded pastures of **Warner Springs Ranch**, but soon you'll come up with much grander appellations to describe the canyons, peaks, and boulder fields you'll encounter on this rollercoaster journey across the far northeastern corner of the Cleveland National Forest.

State Highway 79 forms a sideways horseshoe around the quiet community of **Warner Springs**; park at a dirt turnout across from the local fire station where the PCT crosses the highway's southern portion and look for a metal pipe gate on the north side of the road to enter Warner Springs Ranch. The trail angles down to the left for a mellow amble through seasonally green fields sprinkled with live oaks; though it may look inviting, this area is private land and camping is not allowed. The route is well marked and pretty obvious, but if you're not paying attention, you may find yourself accidentally following one of the many informal paths that cross the rolling hills alongside one of the cattle, creators of said paths.

As you *mooove* along, you'll reach a second pipe gate at 1.2 miles; bid adieu to your new bovine pals and secure the gate as you transition out of the pasture and into the shady **Agua Caliente Creek** drainage, which is almost always dry here. Lulled

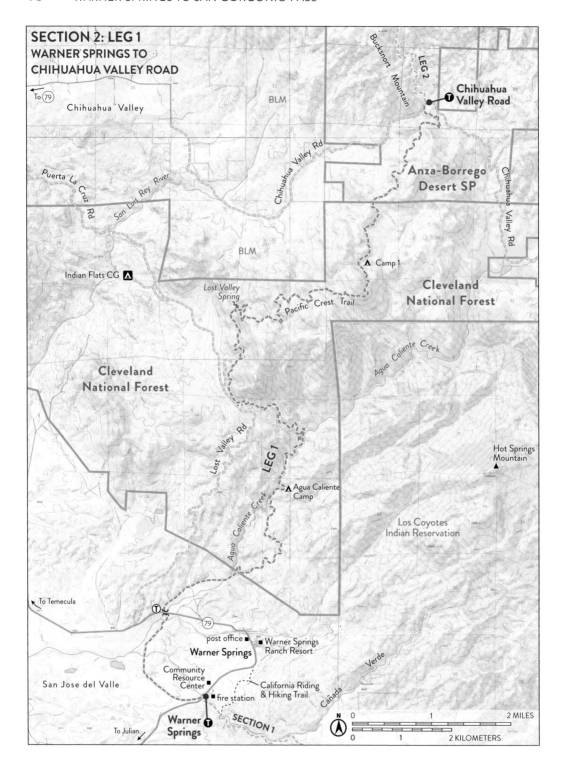

SECTION 2: LEG 1
WARNER SPRINGS TO
CHIHUAHUA VALLEY ROAD

To (79)

Chihuahua Valley

Bucksnort Mountain

LEG 2

Chihuahua Valley Road

BLM

Chihuahua Valley Rd

Puerta La Cruz Rd

San Luis Rey River

Anza-Borrego Desert SP

Chihuahua Valley Rd

BLM

Indian Flats CG

Lost Valley Spring

Camp 1

Cleveland National Forest

Pacific Crest Trail

Agua Caliente Creek

Cleveland National Forest

Lost Valley Rd

LEG 1

Agua Caliente Creek

Agua Caliente Camp

Hot Springs Mountain

Los Coyotes Indian Reservation

To Temecula

79

Verde

post office
Warner Springs
Warner Springs Ranch Resort

San Jose del Valle

Community Resource Center

California Riding & Hiking Trail

fire station

Cañada

To Julian

Warner Springs

SECTION 1

N   0   1   2 MILES

0   1   2 KILOMETERS

by the serene surroundings, you might be startled to stumble across a ropes course a few minutes later; lest you consider staging an impromptu team-building retreat, signs will remind you that unsanctioned use is not allowed. Hang left to follow a dirt road for a moment, then make another left as the trail circles a neglected private campground, complete with horse corrals, water troughs, picnic tables, a tire swing, and somewhat creepy giant hooks used to hang food out of critters' reach.

At 1.9 miles, you'll reach your second encounter with State Highway 79, which you'll cross by slipping under a bridge and heading up past a wooden gate. For those cattle-averse folks who wish to skip the first section, there are several places to park alongside the road to make this your alternate start point.

The trail continues gently from here through hilly terrain marked with oaks, grasses, and the occasional cactus, and the (seasonally dry) creek bed becomes a constant presence down to your right. In the spring, especially, your senses come alive with the scent of sage, the sound of rustling cottonwoods, the sights of rainbow-hued wildflowers, and just a bit farther down the trail, finally, the taste of cool, refreshing water. As you walk the soft, sandy trail, take note of the mountains occupying your views to the northeast—the prominent peak is Hot Springs Mountain, and you'll get a chance to scope its pointy summit from several different vantage points throughout this leg.

Just under 3 miles in, you'll pass a small clearing hosting a shed and a tall bench; while you might be tempted to curl up here for the evening, you'll need to keep trucking since this is private property. Just a few minutes down the trail, you'll come to your first crossing of **Agua Caliente Creek**—while there may be a moderate flow here during wetter months, count on this being dry by summer; more reliable sources can be found ahead, so hang tight. Before then, though, you'll leave the canyon behind for a short while as you gently switchback up slopes carpeted in chamise, manzanita, ceanothus, and ribbonwood and dotted with the occasional wild cucumber, beavertail cactus, and a smattering of wildflowers including everlasting and baby blue eyes. While you might miss the shady cover down below, your efforts are rewarded with sudden southwestern views out to wide, flat San Jose del Valle, sparkling Lake Henshaw, and the eastern slopes of the Palomar Mountains, including the range's namesake peak.

Almost as soon as you've gone up, it's time to drop back down to reach another easy crossing of **Agua Caliente Creek** at 5.2 miles—this one typically holds water year-round, so it's a great place to tank up, but keep an eye out for nearby poison oak. Willow, oak, sycamore, succulents, and plenty of grasses fringe the sandy path—check for free-loading ticks after you pass through. Cross the creek once more to reach a large shady glade at 5.5 miles, complete with fallen logs, boulders, and plenty of flat spots, which makes a perfect location for a small army of tents (**Agua Caliente Camp**). If you're not spending the night, this is still a great place to take a snack break and enjoy the serene surroundings, complete with a pretty seasonal array of miner's lettuce, scarlet buglers, goldfields, and wild pea likely attended to by a fluttering butterfly contingent.

You have a few more opportunities to get your feet wet before transitioning into more arid terrain. Cross the creek three more times after the campsite,

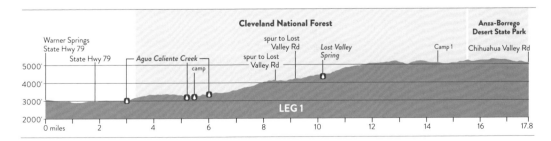

Secluded campsites await in this field of large, pink dinosaur eggs . . . I mean, boulders.

your final visit occurring at the 6-mile mark  while hopping across scattered rocks. Keep in mind that your next opportunity for refreshment is at an off-trail spring just over 4 miles ahead. However, consider yourself warned: the water there is routinely algae-inhabited, sulfuric, and generally unpleasant.

While you might not see much water from here on out, you can still hear it burbling along for a while as you ascend the slopes above the creek. In certain spots along this segment of trail, you can stand in one place to see willows, Coulter pines, oaks, wildflowers, grasses, chaparral, and cacti all at once! As you make your way up, the landscape unfolds in green waves, and your views to the southwest expand—see if you can spot the fire lookout tower perched on top of distant Palomar Mountain. One of the things you'll spot a bit more easily is a road snaking down below—this is **Lost Valley Road** (sometimes called Lost Creek Road), and you can reach this lightly traveled route via a set of spur trails descending at both 8.4 miles and 9.1 miles. If you've had enough of the wilds, you can depart the PCT at the second spur, then continue north on the road for about 1.7 miles (the road here is also

named on different maps as Puerta La Cruz Road and Indian Flats Road, just to keep it confusing) to the entrance for **Indian Flats Campground**. Although you'll find some vault toilets here, you won't find any water.

Speaking of the wet stuff, from that second spur, the path curves to the right on a rough, untraveled portion of Lost Valley Road and reaches a Y-intersection at 10.1 miles. To continue on, head up to the right, but if you want to fill up your reservoir, head toward a concrete post and a sign that reads simply "Water," then descend on a well-defined tread to find **Lost Valley Spring**  jutting out of the right side of the slope about 0.2 mile down. Although it can run dry, there's often water here, even if the trough smells sulfuric and is coated in a stomach-turning mixture of algae and gnats. Bring a good filter, something to mask the taste, and a dose of internal fortitude. If you're continuing on past this leg's endpoint at Chihuahua Valley Road, the next reliable water source is 17.7 miles ahead, 0.25 mile off trail at Tule Spring—plan accordingly!

Moving on, you'll keep climbing at a moderate grade, seeing more boulders not just on the trail itself but also covering the surrounding hillsides to the northwest. The rocks get blockier and bigger the farther you go, and you'll find your head on a constant swivel between taking in their enormity and enjoying the sudden pockets of Coulter pines on slopes near and far. Once you hit the 12-mile mark, you'll also add the beautifully named Bucksnort Mountain to your list of distractions—that's the reddish formation looming above Chihuahua Valley to the north.

You'll enjoy more views of Hot Springs Mountain—perhaps the best yet—as you skirt steep slopes behind a large hump to emerge at 13.8 miles into a fascinating landscape of large, nearly oval boulders strewn across an undulating sandbox like a bunch of pink dinosaur eggs. The best place to drop into the boulder field is just past a saddle at 14.3 miles—scout around for a bit to find several sandy spots that generally fit one tent each, then settle in to watch the granite blobs change color with the setting sun (**Camp 1**).

From here, it's smooth sailing on easy trail to your endpoint. Skirt even more boulders on a soft, sandy path that crests a saddle about 1 mile after

> ## WATER ALERT!
>
> A Chihuahua Valley homeowner has long offered his water tank for thirsty hikers; you'll know whether he's still serving as hydration trail angel if you see wooden signs pointing down a spur trail before Chihuahua Valley Road toward refreshment and shade.

camp, which marks your transition back to westward views. Bucksnort Mountain and Chihuahua Valley now seem almost close enough to touch, and you can spot the latter's namesake road cutting a path down below. Enjoy the easy descent from here, strolling through thick chaparral (and colorful bluebells and Indian paintbrush in the spring) until you reach unpaved **Chihuahua Valley Road** (called Lost Valley Road on some maps) at 17.8 miles; parking is available along the road.

CAMP-TO-CAMP MILEAGE
Warner Springs to Agua Caliente Camp 5.5
Agua Caliente Camp to Camp 1 . . . . 8.8

2 CHIHUAHUA VALLEY ROAD TO TABLE MOUNTAIN TRUCK TRAIL

DISTANCE 15.8 miles

ELEVATION GAIN/LOSS
+2470/-3440 feet

HIGH POINT 5646 feet

CONNECTING ROADS
Chihuahua Valley Road, Tule Canyon Road, Coyote Canyon Road, Table Mountain Truck Trail

ON THE TRAIL
From the lofty shoulder of Combs Peak to the green oasis of Tule Spring to the cactus-sprinkled

high desert hills beyond, this tour of a remote snippet of **Anza-Borrego Desert State Park** doesn't disappoint. Whether it's the gorgeous scenery, the epic views, or the general downhill hiking—or more likely, a combo of all three—this is one of my favorite desert segments!

Before you start the climb up from the **Chihuahua Valley Road** trailhead, make sure you have enough water to keep you happy for just about 10 miles until you hit a reliable spring. Have a sip, slap on some sunblock, and high five any other hikers in range, then charge up a steady incline as you ascend the eastern slopes of **Bucksnort Mountain**. You're headed up toward its highpoint, Combs Peak, whose tippy top you'll spot as you

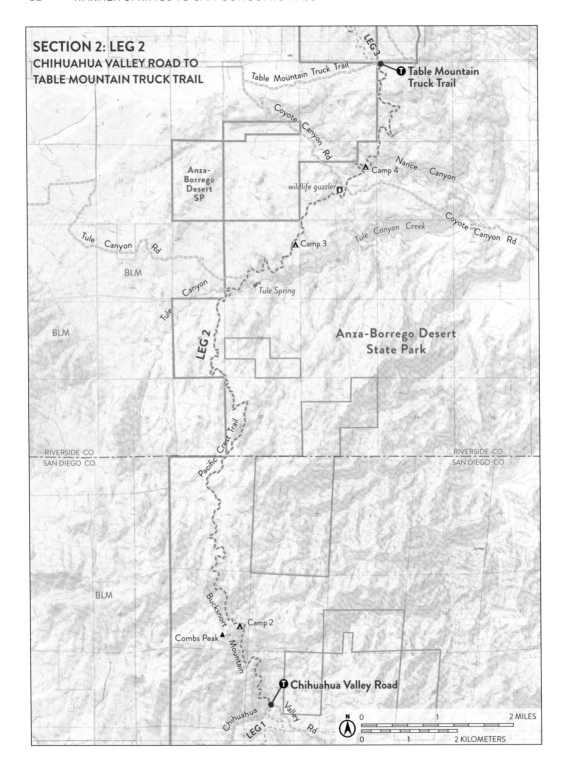

SECTION 2: LEG 2
CHIHUAHUA VALLEY ROAD TO TABLE MOUNTAIN TRUCK TRAIL

LEG 3

Table Mountain Truck Trail

Table Mountain Truck Trail

Coyote Canyon Rd

Nance Canyon

Anza-Borrego Desert SP

Camp 4

wildlife guzzler

Coyote Canyon Rd

Tule Canyon Creek

Tule Canyon Rd

BLM

Tule Canyon

Camp 3

Tule Spring

BLM

LEG 2

Anza-Borrego Desert State Park

Pacific Crest Trail

RIVERSIDE CO
SAN DIEGO CO

RIVERSIDE CO
SAN DIEGO CO

BLM

Bucksnort Mountain

Camp 2

Combs Peak

Chihuahua Valley Road

Chihuahua Valley Rd

LEG 1

N

0   1   2 MILES

0   1   2 KILOMETERS

make your way up on rocky tread flanked by copious amounts of chamise and manzanita.

The theme for this first part of the trip is *Views, Views, Views!*, and while you'll score some good ones as you gaze upon the earth's many folds, including the Santa Rosa Mountains to the northeast, the best are yet to come once you hit a large saddle at 1.9 miles. Combs Peak now looms directly above you to the west, and to your north, the whole world seems to open up with an absolutely epic (yes, the word is warranted) vista that includes the massive Anza Valley and Terwilliger Valley far below, sweeping over to the distant Desert Divide, and up to the snowy heights of San Jacinto Peak and San Gorgonio Mountain, the towering twin guardians of San Gorgonio Pass.

It'll be hard to break away from the majesty, but if you decide you want to spend more time here, there are a few clearings on the south side of the ridge that make fine, if windy, campsites (**Camp 2**). You'll notice that this area is a bit charred—the lightning-sparked Coyote Fire swept through in 2003, destroying a stand of Coulter pines that used to decorate the saddle. Just past here, you'll also spot a use trail headed straight up toward the summit of **Combs Peak**, a 0.6-mile roundtrip scramble up a loose slope that offers up even more grand views.

While you may be reluctant to leave, rest assured that spectacular stuff lies ahead. You'll see a clear path angle across the slopes in front of you—it's all downhill from here (literally) for quite some time. Lengthen your trekking poles and enjoy an easy coast on a narrow tread lined by manzanita, white sage, chamise, and yucca, along with bush poppies, Indian paintbrush, desert lavender, and other floral beauties in the spring season. While it's easy to float on autopilot here, marveling at

The scenery is prickly, but beautiful.

the stunning scenery, the trail is very uneven and rocky in spots, so be careful not to lose focus and turn your ankle.

The trail drops down (with a few occasional bits of uphill to jog you from complacency), crossing a sandy flat and meandering around a host of small hills. A few scattered homes dotting the hillsides steal away some of nature's thunder, but occasional tunnels of shady ribbonwood will draw you back in. You'll go through a less-than-scenic pipe gate at 7.1 miles. Go around another gate just beyond

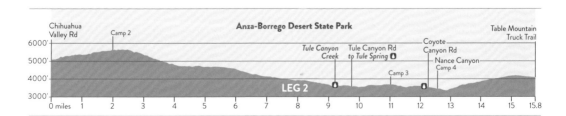

Enjoy expansive views on the descent from the shoulder of Combs Peak.

it, the one made of just about every fencing material known to man. Keep heading straight under intruding power lines and continue enjoying the much finer sights of the distant mountains.

Sadly, you eventually lose those gargantuan views, but you also start to notice a bright green patch in the distance—a sure sign of water in this arid landscape. To get there, you'll need to first pass through another pipe gate at 8.9 miles, drop down to cross often-dry **Tule Canyon Creek** just beyond (some water will be present during a wet season), then cross a grassy flat toward the chlorophyll explosion that marks the wettest

WATER ALERT!

The next possible water past Tule Spring is from a wildlife guzzler **0** 2.5 miles ahead. However, since this is not always full (and is often disgusting), your next reliable source on trail, if continuing past this leg, is 18.9 miles past the guzzler at **Live Oak Spring 0** or **Tunnel Spring 0**; both require a side trip. There is also a café at the intersection of State Highway 74 and State Highway 371 about 1 mile north of the trail, which means a carry of about 16.2 miles, including the side trip to the spring and the off-trail miles.

part of **Tule Canyon**. You'll hit unpaved **Tule Canyon Road** at 9.7 miles and can head right to leave the trail and descend 0.25 mile to refreshing **Tule Spring 0**. Here, you'll realize that the bright green you saw earlier is a shimmering pocket of cottonwoods, providing much needed shade as you seek out the spring's pump and hose on the left side of the road to tank up.

After you've sprawled out for a nice nap in the grassy canyon, haul that water (and yourself) back up the steep road to the trail intersection and continue heading northeast. There's a bit of climbing involved here, but let yourself be distracted by the views back down into Tule Canyon and the sudden explosion of cacti on the rocky slopes around you. Within minutes you've gone from a wet oasis to a beautiful high desert environment studded with yucca, juniper, buckhorn cholla, and beavertail, hedgehog, and barrel cacti. If you time it right to catch the desert bloom in early spring—especially around sunrise and sunset—you'll wish you had a hundred cameras to capture the magic.

Watch out for prickly things as you continue up, passing one solitary pinyon pine clinging to the trail's edge along the way. You'll reach a flatter area 11 miles in, where some intrepid folks have cleared out small tent spots far back from either side of the trail, but you'll need to be very careful that the area is not expecting rain, since there are a lot of dry channels that cross the flats (**Camp 3**); while it's certainly possible to set up camp here, due to the possibility of flash flooding I'd suggest moving along unless you're exhausted.

At 12.1 miles, you'll reach a strange looking broken concrete slab on your left—this is a wildlife guzzler **O**, a small tank that collects rainwater to provide a watering hole for passing animals—and humans, in your case. To collect the wet stuff, you'll need either a filter with a hose or something else you can dip down into the tank if it's not filled to the brim; be careful not to step on the unstable concrete itself as you filter. Be warned that the tank can often sit empty—or might serve as community swimming pool for area reptiles.

From here, turn the corner and head down through deep sand to reach unpaved **Coyote Canyon Road** at 12.3 miles. Head straight across, winding your way down toward **Nance Canyon**, where you'll see plenty more pinyons and cottonwoods. You'll cross the canyon itself at 12.8 miles; if you're looking for a nice place to bed down, head downstream to find sandy spots on a bench above the usually dry streambed (**Camp 4**). It goes without saying that you need to check the weather reports if camping here to avoid being washed away in a downpour; also be very careful to practice good Leave No Trace techniques to avoid contaminating the water supply.

Hopefully your legs haven't been lulled to sleep by the moderate terrain—it's time to get your climb on as you move up the canyon wall. If you pace yourself and avoid this stretch at high noon, it's not a big deal—and can even be downright enjoyable if you choose to ascend at sunrise. Still surrounded by high desert vegetation, you'll weave around giant boulders while trying to avoid brushing against any number of cholla threatening your calves with their barbed spines—they call this stuff "jumping" cholla for a reason! If you're wondering where to take a bathroom break along the steep slopes, you'll find respite at around 13.7 miles in the form of a broad, much more gently sloped area to your left, where you can enjoy sunrise from any number of rocky thrones.

Continuing on, you'll round a gully at 15.1 miles to pop over a ridge at the southern end of **Table Mountain**. Unpaved **Table Mountain Truck Trail** now comes into view, although you'll wind around quite a bit through the tall chaparral before actually hitting the dirt road at 15.8 miles. There's no reliable place to park nearby, so you'll want to arrange for a pickup, backtrack your route, or continue hiking on the PCT (hint: the last option is the most fun).

CAMP-TO-CAMP MILEAGE

Chihuahua Valley Road to Camp 2 . . . . 1.9
Camp 2 to Camp 3 . . . . 9.1
Camp 3 to Camp 4 . . . . 1.8

3 TABLE MOUNTAIN TRUCK TRAIL TO STATE HIGHWAY 74

DISTANCE 8.8 miles

ELEVATION GAIN/LOSS
+2110/-1270 feet

HIGH POINT 5072 feet

CONNECTING ROADS
Table Mountain Truck Trail, State Highway 74

ON THE TRAIL

Enjoy one last hurrah in **Anza-Borrego Desert State Park** as you transition up, up, up through sandy, chaparral-clad slopes toward cooler air and plentiful pine trees, scoring expansive valley views and ogling a host of captivating peaks and canyons along the way. Bring all the water you need to stay hydrated on this sunny section since there are no natural sources the entire way.

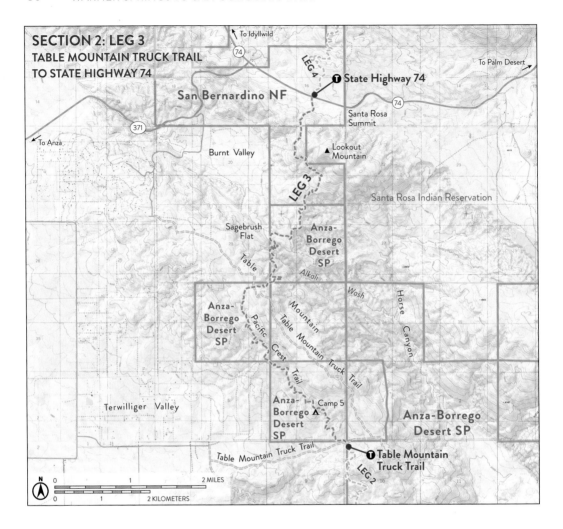

SECTION 2: LEG 3
TABLE MOUNTAIN TRUCK TRAIL
TO STATE HIGHWAY 74

WATER ALERT!

There are no natural water sources along this leg. While local trail angels sometimes leave water jugs out for passing trekkers during the thru-hiking season, don't rely on their generosity—arrive with all you need to make it either to the end of this leg, plus 1 mile down to Paradise Valley Café at the intersection of State Highway 74 and State Highway 371, or 15.3 miles ahead into the next section, when you have the option of departing to either **Live Oak Spring** or **Tunnel Spring**.

Begin your trip north of **Table Mountain Truck Trail** on a sandy path lined with cholla, yucca, beavertail cacti, and low chaparral. The tread remains incredibly soft for much of today's hike, so although the climb along the southwestern slopes of **Table Mountain** is modest, your calves may beg to differ. Pretty soon, though, you'll earn distracting views over rural Terwilliger Valley and out to distant peaks, including Bucksnort Mountain, whose folds you might have traveled a day or two earlier.

As you ascend, the action on the slopes starts to compete with the vistas—large boulders begin to pop up around the trail, which is now flanked by manzanita, ribbonwood, white sage, and an array

While the PCT doesn't pass through them, the Santa Rosa Mountains make a guest appearance in the distance.

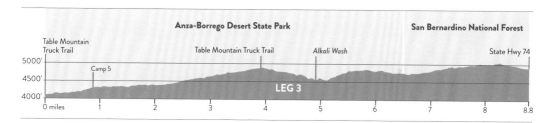

of seasonal wildflowers—baby blue eyes, Indian paintbrush, desert lavender, and bush poppies are common sights in this area. If you're really digging both the views *and* the rocks, then you'll love the boulder-strewn outcropping you reach on the left at 0.9 mile—there's plenty of room here for several tents, and while it's a dry camp, you'll find a bit of shade and wind protection among the bulging formations (**Camp 5**). Sunset is especially magical here—I've made one-night trips to this spot because I love it so much!

The trail continues to undulate and your views remain pretty much the same as you wiggle along Table Mountain's lower reaches; this segment can feel a little monotonous and even a bit annoying

when you start to encounter houses perched on the hills below you. Take solace in the fact that things are going to get a whole lot more interesting pretty soon! In the meantime, keep your eyes peeled for horned lizards racing around. You'll know them by the crown of spikes perched on their heads, their round bodies, and their general prehistoric visage. Many people think these are toads or frogs, due to their shape and size, but I think they look a lot more like tiny dragons. You be the judge.

Change course at 3.5 miles to head inland through a small scrub oak flat to meet Table Mountain Truck Trail once again 0.4 mile ahead. Once you cross the dirt road, the terrain pulls out all the stops as you're suddenly staring down a massive formation dominating the eastern horizon—the twin hulks of Santa Rosa Mountain and Toro Peak. What looks like a huge plateau jutting from those slopes is actually Vandeventer Flat, which sits inside the Santa Rosa Indian Reservation, nestled at the foot of the Santa Rosa and San Jacinto Mountains.

The drama unfolds the deeper you wander. You'll see San Jacinto Peak and the Desert Divide to the north—this will be your route if you choose to continue this adventure past State Highway 74. Horse Canyon forms an impressive gash to the southeast and you'll suddenly realize it's not the only rip in the earth—you'll need to make a demoralizing descent to the head of **Alkali Wash**, which you reach at 4.9 miles, only to slog your way back up a set of switchbacks. Let the spectacular scenery distract from the cruelty.

Once you hit the last switchback and catch your breath, you'll earn a bit of reprieve as the trail flattens out for a bit. At 5.9 miles, you'll start making your way across a ridge that might hold the best views yet since you can scan both east and west plus straight ahead to attractive **Lookout**

Mountain; look carefully and you'll see the trail jog across its slopes.

You'll reach that final traverse at 7.1 miles; in this gentle uphill stretch, you get full-on views down to grassy Burnt Valley below. Just 1 mile ahead, you'll reach a saddle where you earn a sweeping look at the San Jacinto Mountains and where State Highway 74 comes into sharp relief—if it's been a hot day, *you'll* feel sharp relief when you start heading downhill in earnest. In just a short bit, you'll cross a dirt road under power lines, then come upon paved **State Highway 74** just northwest of Santa Rosa Summit at 8.8 miles. Be very careful when you cross here—drivers routinely blaze past en route to their mountain vacations, and it would be unfortunate to end your trip squished into the blacktop. Parking is available in a large lot on the north side of the road, accessed by walking just a few minutes farther along the trail or hopping on a gravel driveway to the right.

CAMP-TO CAMP MILEAGE
Table Mountain Truck Trail to Camp 5. . . . . . . 0.9

4 STATE HIGHWAY 74 TO CEDAR SPRINGS TRAIL

DISTANCE 10.7 miles

ELEVATION GAIN/LOSS
+2840/-980 feet

HIGH POINT 6850 feet

CONNECTING TRAILS AND ROADS
State Highway 74, Cedar Springs Trail

ON THE TRAIL
If you love pines and peaks, this gateway to the higher elevations of the San Jacinto Mountains will tickle your fancy with a walk along the range's southern section on the incredible Desert Divide,

a view-packed, rocky ridgeline route. From this lofty perch, you'll spy Lookout Mountain, Thomas Mountain, Pine Meadow, Garner Valley, and Lake Hemet to the west, and the greater Palm Springs area and Coachella Valley to the northeast. With aerials like this, you'll feel like you're truly traveling the Pacific Crest!

Although a trail departing the parking lot on the north side of **State Highway 74** quickly meets up with the PCT, purists will want to start on the highway shoulder just southwest of the lot. The mileages on the sign posted near the start are slightly off, so ignore those and keep in mind that the only place you'll find water on this segment is on either side of a trail junction 6.5 miles ahead (plus a detour of up to 1 mile depending on which

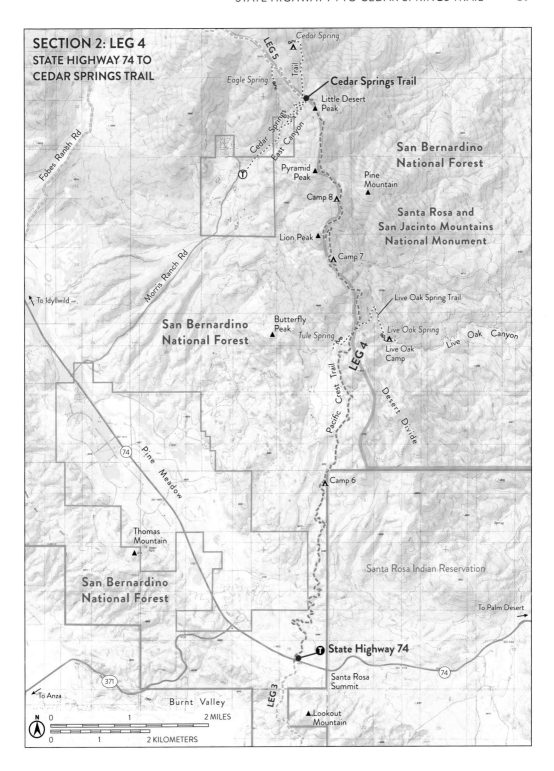

SECTION 2: LEG 4
STATE HIGHWAY 74 TO
CEDAR SPRINGS TRAIL

Pines begin to appear as you start climbing along the Desert Divide.

of the two available watering holes you choose). Just beyond this sign, there's an informational display about the trail plus a plaque memorializing Andy Elam, a hiker who was murdered in the parking lot here back in 1989, a case that remains unsolved to this day.

The trail winds easily along a gently undulating landscape filled with ribbonwood, manzanita, and the occasional paddle cactus. When you hit the 0.5-mile mark, a surprise awaits—the boulder-strewn Desert Divide suddenly comes into sight, its peak-filled ridge rising up from the lazy waves of green as if to announce, "It's time for the *real* mountains to begin."

Before you get there, though, you have some work to do. The sandy path ascends through blocky, peach-colored boulders, offering fantastic views toward Lookout Mountain, Thomas Mountain, Pine Meadow, Garner Valley, and Lake Hemet. As you're walking, you'll notice a deep gash down below—this is **Penrod Canyon**,

and you'll descend to cross its usually dry bottom at 3.5 miles. The trail levels out for a bit, which makes it easy to enjoy the soft pine needles underfoot and their scent lingering in the air. If you want to take it all in for a bit longer, look to the right of the trail at 4 miles to see a shady opening underneath a glade of oaks that will hold a few small tents (**Camp 6**).

Almost as soon as you leave this cozy nook, you lose the tree cover and emerge back into the chaparral and sun—it's now time to head up onto the Desert Divide in earnest. As you climb up from the canyon, the trail hugs the rugged slopes, and your westward views resume. At 5.5 miles, you'll cross a gravelly unpaved road, heading toward a trail marker ahead. The view of Butterfly Peak just a hop-skip to the northwest is captivating, but the tread is very rocky and clings to much steeper slopes now, so watch your footing—I saw a friend almost sail off the edge one particularly blustery day.

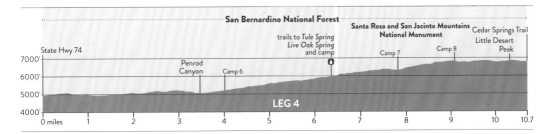

At 6.4 miles you'll reach a pipe gate, and just beyond, an intersection with the **Live Oak Spring Trail**, which descends 1 mile to Live Oak Canyon; watch out for grabby cacti as you head down. At the bottom you'll find a large dirt area studded with—*wait for it*—live oaks, which makes an absolutely spectacular camp (**Live Oak Camp**). The aptly named **Live Oak Spring ⬤** is just past here, with a pipe gushing refreshing water into a round trough. This point also marks your entry into the massive **Santa Rosa and San Jacinto Mountains National Monument**, whose boundary you'll stay within all the way to San Gorgonio Pass at the end of this section.

Once past this trail junction, you'll pop over to the Divide's east-facing slopes for a whole different set of vistas, including back down into Live Oak Canyon and out to the faraway Coachella Valley. Hiking among scrub oak, cacti, and handfuls of desert mallow, you'll also see a lot of downed trees littering the landscape, the result of

WATER ALERT!

Another refill option is **Tunnel Spring ⬤**, 0.3 mile down a steep, unmarked, but obvious jeep trail on the opposite side of the PCT from the Live Oak Spring Trail. Turn right once you come to a fork in the trail near a large manzanita and keep your eyes peeled for a metal trough in a clearing. The water sometimes tastes of sulfur, the trough is almost always coated in algae, and the walk back up the eroded path can feel grueling with a full tank, but the mileage is quite a bit less than the trip to **Live Oak Spring ⬤**.

damaging windstorms. Your other constant companion is an eyesore, a barbed wire fence running alongside the trail for quite a ways, marking one of the many private property boundaries scattered across these hills.

As you enjoy the expansive views out to the east, make sure you also look to the northwest to spot the boulder-strewn hump of Lion Peak looming above the trail ahead. Before you reach it, though, you'll come upon a clearing located under some shady oaks on your right at 7.8 miles—there's room here for a few tents (**Camp 7**).

After two switchbacks, you'll ascend through colorful granite to reach a saddle on the shoulder of **Lion Peak**, where you're able to snag spectacular views to the east and west; you'll be forgiven for wanting to linger. From here, your route traverses across the highest reaches of the Divide; make sure to turn back from time to time to check out Lion Peak, even more impressive from this side.

You'll reach another saddle at 9.1 miles, with room to stash one tent under the protection of some oaks to your left (**Camp 8**), where you switch back to westward views and look north toward appropriately named, pointy Pyramid Peak and the boulder-topped Pine Mountain farther down the trail. Along with squawking crows and a million zippy little western fence lizards, you might also start to see dogs taking their owners out for a morning stroll, since this section of trail is popular with local residents.

At 9.5 miles, you reach the base of **Pyramid Peak**, and for almost the entire rest of this leg you're back to peering out dreamily to the northeast; the sights are absolutely stellar as the desert hills below you begin to unfold in waves of beige and mauve and Palm Springs comes into view.

OPTIONS, OPTIONS

The Cedar Springs Trail offers two points of departure. The northbound branch descends to **Cedar Spring ⓞ**, with space to camp nearby. The southbound trail switchbacks down 2.5 miles to reach bucolic East Canyon and paved Morris Ranch Road, where there's a dirt parking area located just south of the Cedar Springs Trailhead.

You have one more peak to skirt (or really, to *summit*, since you pass within arm's reach of its high point)—**Little Desert Peak** at 10.4 miles,

which affords you one last splashy look at the big desert far below. After you've inhaled as much splendor as you can take, wind downhill back toward the western side of the divide to hit this leg's end at the **Cedar Springs Trail** junction at 10.7 miles. There's a makeshift bench stretched across the roots of a friendly oak here, offering a perfect place to sprawl out and enjoy a bite to eat, a little nap, or a bit of reflection on just how much you love the mountains.

CAMP-TO-CAMP MILEAGE
State Highway 74 to Camp 6 .... 4.0
Camp 6 to Live Oak Camp 2.4
Live Oak Camp to Camp 7................. 1.4
Camp 7 to Camp 8 .... 1.3

5 CEDAR SPRINGS TRAIL TO SADDLE JUNCTION

DISTANCE 16.8 miles

ELEVATION GAIN/LOSS
+4770/-3430 feet

HIGH POINT 8612 feet

CONNECTING TRAILS
Cedar Springs Trail, Fobes Ranch Trail,
Little Tahquitz Valley Trail,
Caramba Trail, Willow Creek Trail,
Devils Slide Trail

ON THE TRAIL
The Mountain Fire ripped through the San Jacinto Mountains in July 2013, scorching nearly 30,000 acres before it was finally doused. Around 30 miles of the PCT were closed, and some of this leg was still off-limits as of this writing. While the PCTA and other entities have worked tirelessly for several years to repair the trail, it was further damaged during post-burn storms, which caused delays. I haven't been able to scout the closed portion, so this write-up constitutes a general overview, mixed with a detailed description of the open areas. Before setting out, check with the PCTA and San

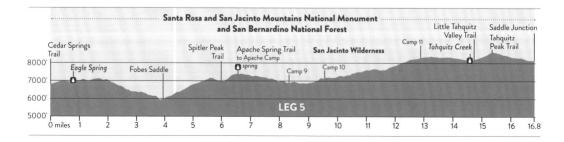

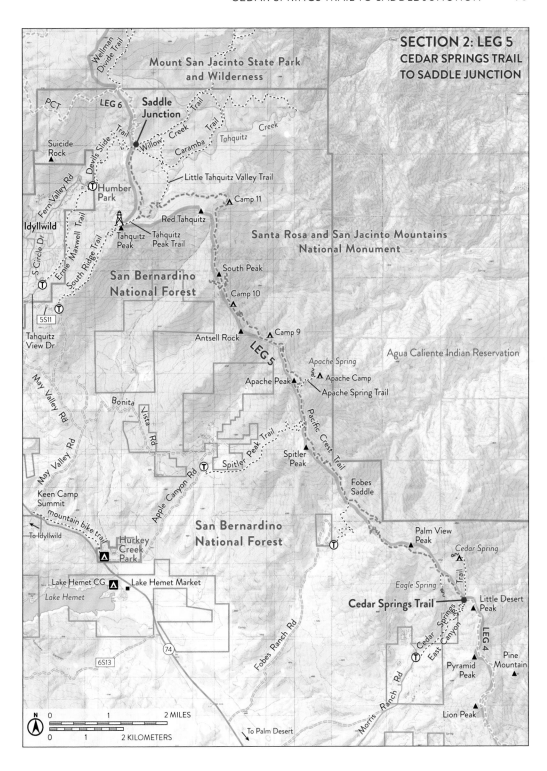

SECTION 2: LEG 5
CEDAR SPRINGS TRAIL TO SADDLE JUNCTION

Mount San Jacinto State Park and Wilderness

Wellman Divide Trail

PCT

LEG 6

Saddle Junction

Suicide Rock

Devils Slide Trail

Willow Creek Trail

Caramba Trail

Tahquitz Creek

Creek

Little Tahquitz Valley Trail

Fern Valley Rd

Humber Park

Camp 11

Idyllwild

Ernie Maxwell Trail

S Circle Dr

Red Tahquitz

Tahquitz Peak

Tahquitz Peak Trail

Santa Rosa and San Jacinto Mountains National Monument

San Bernardino National Forest

South Ridge Trail

South Peak

Camp 10

5S11

Tahquitz View Dr

Antsell Rock

Camp 9

LEG 5

Agua Caliente Indian Reservation

Apache Spring

Apache Camp

Apache Peak

Apache Spring Trail

May Valley Rd

Bonita

Vista Rd

Spitler Peak Trail

Pacific Crest Trail

Spitler Peak

May Valley Rd

Apple Canyon Rd

Fobes Saddle

Keen Camp Summit

mountain bike trail

To Idyllwild

Hurkey Creek Park

San Bernardino National Forest

Palm View Peak

Cedar Spring

Lake Hemet CG

Lake Hemet Market

Lake Hemet

Eagle Spring

Cedar Springs Trail

Cedar Spring Trail

Little Desert Peak

LEG 4

74

Fobes Ranch Rd

Cedar Springs

East Canyon

Pyramid Peak

Pine Mountain

6S13

Morris Ranch Rd

Lion Peak

To Palm Desert

N

0   1   2 MILES

0   1   2 KILOMETERS

ALTERNATE ROUTE

There is no great alternate for skirting the Mountain Fire closure, which currently begins at Fobes Saddle and ends at Tahquitz Creek, 10.7 miles north. If you wish to connect the dots with continuous steps, depart the PCT at Fobes Saddle via the Fobes Ranch Trail, which descends 1.6 miles to **Fobes Ranch Road**. Head southwest along this road to reach **State Highway 74** in 4 miles.

Make a right onto Highway 74 and continue along the shoulder to pass by the **Lake Hemet Market** 2.8 miles ahead; here you'll find groceries, a café, camping, and water **O**. Continuing along Highway 74, **Hurkey Creek Park O** appears on the right 0.5 mile later—again, with camping and water. The shoulder disappears after this, so it's best to pick up an unnamed trail heading northwest from the campground, walking parallel to the highway until reaching unpaved **May Valley Road** (Forest Service Road 5S05) 1.7 miles ahead near **Keen Camp Summit**. Make a right and begin walking uphill until hitting a Y-intersection—**Bonita Vista Road** is the right branch, but you want to stay left, eventually reaching a sign for the **South Ridge Trail** on your right about 2.7 miles after turning onto May Valley Road. You now begin ascending the steep, mostly shadeless south ridge of Tahquitz Peak. Pass the "official" South Ridge trailhead (accessible via rough **Forest Service Road 5S11**) 1.5 miles up this route and continue zigzagging until deposited at a junction with the **Tahquitz Peak Trail** 3.4 miles after leaving the road. Head right to tag the peak, or left to rejoin the PCT less than 0.5 mile ahead.

Bernardino National Forest to see what portion of the trail is accessible; as of November 2016, the trail was open to Fobes Saddle but closed beyond that until Tahquitz Creek.

This route travels along the Desert Divide, a stunning, peak-studded ridgeline that forms the spine of the San Jacinto Mountains, and on this leg, the western boundary of the **Santa Rosa and San Jacinto Mountains National Monument**. Begin at a junction with the **Cedar Springs Trail**, which descends on the right to reach **Cedar Spring O** and camping 1 mile to the north; a left branch switchbacks down approximately 2.5 miles to reach paved Morris Ranch Road, which has trailhead parking. You, however, continue straight uphill to intersect a trail on your left at 0.75 mile, which descends steeply to **Eagle Spring O**. Your route continues along the ridgeline, skirts below **Palm View Peak**, then heads down via a set of tight switchbacks and a north-facing traverse to reach **Fobes Saddle** at 3.9 miles, currently the eastern boundary of the Mountain Fire closure. If the closure is still in effect when you come through, you'll need to either retrace your steps or

depart the PCT via the **Fobes Ranch Trail**, which descends 1.6 miles to reach a small parking area on unpaved Fobes Ranch Road—see the Alternate Route sidebar for more detail.

If the trail is open when you come through, it's back uphill to round the eastern slopes of **Spitler Peak**, then down (sense a pattern here?) to reach a saddle at 6 miles where the **Spitler Peak Trail** heads down 4.8 miles to reach Apple Canyon Road, which also leads to Highway 74. After this, it's back up to meet the **Apache Spring Trail** just over 0.5 mile ahead, which descends to the right to reach **Apache Spring O** and camping in a steep 0.5 mile (**Apache Camp**). You may also find campsites located along a few saddles north of this point; since the area was still closed as I completed my fieldwork, it's unclear whether they are still viable post-fire—as such, they're listed in the camp-to-camp mileages in italic (**Camps 9, 10,** and **11**).

Curve around to the east of **Apache Peak**, then do the same around **Antsell Rock** and **South Peak**. The trail eventually bends west to hop across seasonal **Tahquitz Creek O** at 14.6 miles, the northern boundary of the trail closure as of this writing. Just up from here, reach a junction with the **Little Tahquitz Valley Trail**; the PCT turns left, climbing through fragrant conifers on slippery decomposing granite, and you score views of Red Tahquitz to the east. Just a short bit ahead, you'll reach a sandy flat and a spur trail to **Tahquitz Peak** at 15.4 miles; it's absolutely worth the short climb for the incredible views from the peak's historic fire lookout tower.

You're in the home stretch now, especially since the rest of this leg is primarily downhill. The path carves through a thick carpeting of chinquapin bushes, with fantastic views of Marion Mountain and Jean Peak. Tree cover eventually resumes, and you land at **Saddle Junction** at 16.8 miles. Here, a network of trails radiates from the flat: the **Caramba Trail** veers off to your right, the **Willow Creek Trail** banks to the northeast, and the **Devils Slide Trail** descends on your left to reach Idyllwild's Humber Park in 2.6 miles. There you'll find a large paved parking lot (Adventure Pass required),

The Tahquitz Peak fire lookout is a must-see destination, located only a half mile off trail.

THE DEMON OF THE DESERT DIVIDE

While unlimited peakbagging opportunities exist along the PCT in the San Jacinto Mountains, including San Jacinto Peak itself, my can't-miss suggestion is Tahquitz Peak, located less than 0.5 mile off trail. First, it offers the opportunity to visit a historic fire lookout. The small wooden tower was built in 1937 and still houses volunteers who scan the horizon for smoke; they'll let you inside if you swing by during visiting hours. Second, the views are unbeatable—you can see the length of the Desert Divide to the south, a smattering of lakes to the west (including Lake Hemet and Diamond Valley Lake), Lily Rock (also known as Tahquitz Rock), Marion Mountain and Jean Peak to the north, and even southeast to the shimmering Salton Sea on a clear day.

Finally, there's the fascinating history of the peak's name itself, which comes from a story passed down by the Cahuilla people indigenous to the area. Tahquitz was a good shaman gone bad, banished to the mountain to atone for his transgressions against the tribe. Various tales have emerged over the years, but the gist is that if he's having a bad day, Tahquitz might choose to wreak any number of havocs upon the mountain (and its visitors). Even more reason to tread lightly and practice good Leave No Trace principles!

IDLE A WHILE

Shhh . . . don't tell all of the other mountain towns in Southern California, but Idyllwild is my favorite. The adorable hamlet has plenty of eateries and shops, a post office, laundromat, vibrant arts scene, and a plethora of cozy cabins for rent. Those with tighter budgets might consider staying instead at one of the many campgrounds in the area, the nearest located in Mount San Jacinto State Park. Many hikers are tempted to extend their stay in this forested paradise, whether because of weather delays or simply because they fall in love with the, yes, idyllic surrounds.

vault toilets, garbage, picnicking options, and a route to Idyllwild. If you don't have a car available, it's possible to pick up the Ernie Maxwell Trail near the park's entrance, following it 2.6 miles to the Tahquitz View Drive trailhead in town.

CAMP-TO-CAMP MILEAGE

Cedar Springs Trail to Apache Camp 6.6
Apache Camp to *Camp 9* 1.7
Camp 9* to *Camp 10 .... 1.3
Camp 10* to *Camp 11 .... 3.2

6 SADDLE JUNCTION TO FULLER RIDGE TRAILHEAD

DISTANCE 11.1 miles

ELEVATION GAIN/LOSS
+2870/-3240 feet

HIGH POINT 9058 feet

CONNECTING TRAILS
Devils Slide Trail, Caramba Trail, Willow Creek Trail, Wellman Divide Trail, Deer Springs Trail, Marion Mountain Trail, Seven Pines Trail

ON THE TRAIL

If you're looking for that Eastern Sierra experience, but don't want to actually *drive* there, this spectacular leg will do the trick. You'll quickly understand why it seems everyone has a piece of the pie up here as you travel through portions of the **Santa Rosa and San Jacinto Mountains National Monument, San Jacinto Wilderness**, and **Mount San Jacinto State Wilderness** (part of—*wait for it*—**Mount San Jacinto State Park**).

Begin at **Saddle Junction**, a forested flat that acts as hub for a number of trails—the **Devils Slide Trail** descends to your left, the **Caramba Trail** parallels to the near right, and the **Willow Creek Trail** juts off to the northeast. Unless you're hoping to descend to the cozy mountain burg of Idyllwild or have your eye on a detour, head north to stay on the PCT, marked toward Round Valley and San Jacinto Peak.

ALL ACCESS PASS

Alternate trailhead parking is available at Humber Park (Adventure Pass required), where you ascend the popular 2.6-mile Devils Slide Trail to this leg's start at Saddle Junction. Parking is also available at the Marion Mountain, Deer Springs, and Fuller Ridge trailheads, although the latter requires high-clearance vehicle, 4WD capacity, or patience and nerves of steel to navigate the often rutted-out, unpaved Black Mountain Truck Trail.

Alpine scenery in this area hints at what you'll experience farther north in the Sierra.

The area's beauty unfolds immediately as you walk through thick conifer forest studded with bright green manzanita and giant boulders. Campsites abound, beginning just 0.1 mile in at a shaded clearing on your left with room for several tents (**Camp 12**). From here, head up a series of switchbacks that serve as a reminder that you're huffing through thinner air—take it easy and enjoy views down to leafy Humber Park and over to Lily Rock, colloquially known as

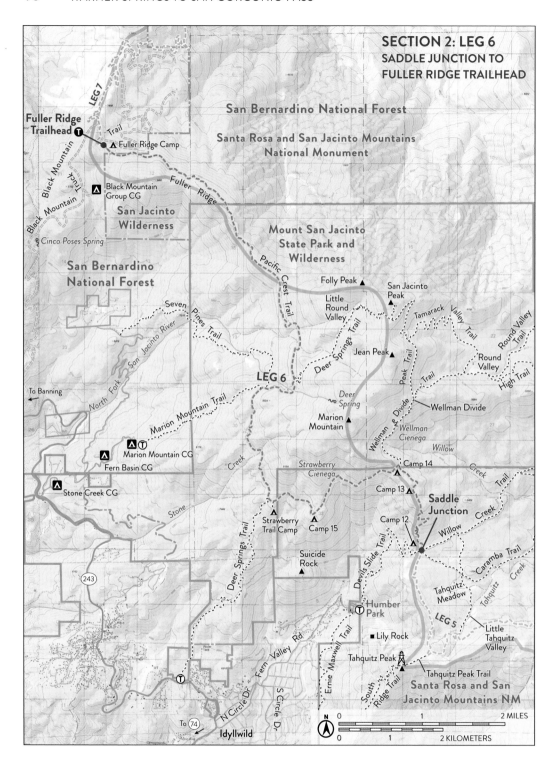

SECTION 2: LEG 6
SADDLE JUNCTION TO
FULLER RIDGE TRAILHEAD

LEG 7

Fuller Ridge
Trailhead

Trail   ▲ Fuller Ridge Camp

Black Mountain Truck Trail

Black Mountain

San Bernardino National Forest

Santa Rosa and San Jacinto Mountains
National Monument

▲ Black Mountain
Group CG

Fuller Ridge

San Jacinto
Wilderness

Cinco Poses Spring

San Bernardino
National Forest

Mount San Jacinto
State Park and
Wilderness

Pacific Crest Trail

Folly Peak ▲

San Jacinto
Peak ▲

Little
Round
Valley

Tamarack Valley Trail

Round Valley Trail

Seven Pines Trail

San Jacinto River

Deer Springs Trail

Jean Peak ▲

Peak Trail

Trail

Round
Valley

High Trail

To Banning

North Fork

LEG 6

Deer
Spring

Wellman & Divide

Wellman Divide

Marion Mountain Trail

Marion
Mountain ▲

Wellman
Cienega

Willow

Creek

Creek

▲Ⓣ Marion Mountain CG

Strawberry
Cienega

▲ Camp 14

Trail

▲ Fern Basin CG

▲ Stone Creek CG

Stone

▲ Strawberry
Trail Camp

▲ Camp 15

Camp 13 ▲

Saddle
Junction

Camp 12
▲

Willow

Creek

Caramba Trail

243

Deer Springs Trail

Suicide
Rock ▲

Devils Slide Trail

Tahquitz
Meadow

Tahquitz Creek

Ⓣ

Ⓣ Humber
Park

LEG 5

Little
Tahquitz
Valley

Fern Valley Rd

■ Lily Rock

Ernie Maxwell Trail

Tahquitz Peak ▲

Tahquitz Peak Trail

Ⓣ

South Ridge Trail

Santa Rosa and San
Jacinto Mountains NM

N Circle Dr

S Circle Dr

To 74

Idyllwild

N   0   1   2 MILES

0   1   2 KILOMETERS

Tahquitz Rock, a mecca for Southern California climbers.

The next camping option appears at 1.4 miles in another clearing to the left (**Camp 13**). From here, grunt out a bit more uphill to reach a junction with the **Wellman Divide Trail**. That route heads past a spring at Wellman Cienega north toward Wellman Divide, offering the option to tag San Jacinto Peak, the highest point in the San Jacinto Mountains and a veritable rite of passage for regional hikers. Otherwise, turn left and head toward Strawberry Cienega and the Deer Springs Trail, now contouring just south of Marion Mountain.

A third camping option appears 0.5 mile past the last one—look for a boulder-strewn clearing in a small depression down to your left (**Camp 14**). From here, the views open up to include Tahquitz Peak to the south along with the slightly closer Suicide Rock. The latter's morbid name comes from a Cahuilla legend of two rather tragic Shakespearean-style lovers driven to jump to their deaths when the tribe's chief forbade their passions. I thought dating in Los Angeles was hard!

Continue contouring along steepening slopes guarded by buckthorn, a spiky shrub that my hiking companion posited as "made from the souls of tortured porcupines." Ferns provide softer cover as you move along, and you swing around a gully at 2.7 miles positively teeming with them, marking the seasonal trickle of **Strawberry Cienega** ⦿. From here, reach a wide, flat area just over 0.5 mile ahead, where you'll find a few campsites tucked behind bushes and boulders, mostly on the left side (**Camp 15**).

Around 3.8 miles, a pair of wooden signs flanks the path indicating the boundary between the San Jacinto Wilderness and Mount San Jacinto State Park and Wilderness, which you're entering.

Camping is allowed only in designated sites and you must obtain a permit in advance. About 0.1 mile ahead, encounter the only sanctioned campsite along the PCT in this area—signed **Strawberry Trail Camp**, a very pretty spot studded with boulders and trees. There are a few sites scattered to the left along with a portable toilet.

Head downhill for 0.1 mile to reach a path joining from the left—this is the **Deer Springs Trail**, which ascends 4 miles from Idyllwild. The trails merge for a while headed north (signed for Little Round Valley and Mount San Jacinto) as you continue uphill. The area is stunning, offering views to the east, including anvil-shaped Diamond Valley Lake sparkling in the distance. Pass a seep at 4.4 miles that might be nothing more than a dark splotch buzzing with bees, then ascend a series of fern-filled switchbacks. The foliage is extremely lush through this next bit, and you might wonder how you ended up in the Pacific Northwest (or in the Jurassic Period).

Pass seasonal **Stone Creek** ⦿ 0.3 mile past the seep, then pick up some more elevation as you ascend to a signed trail junction at 5.7 miles. Here, the **Marion Mountain Trail** swings in from the left, offering a nearly 3-mile descent to the Marion Mountain Campground northwest of Idyllwild. Another sign beckons just ahead, where the somewhat rough **Seven Pines Trail** descends steeply; instead, stay to the right toward Little Round Valley and San Jacinto Peak.

More quad grinding brings you to a patch of corn lilies at 6.1 miles marking the flow from **Deer Springs** ⦿ above, whose waters roll downhill to help form the **North Fork San Jacinto River**. Like most water sources in the area, this may be dry by early summer. A final junction appears less than 0.25 mile ahead where the PCT and Deer Springs

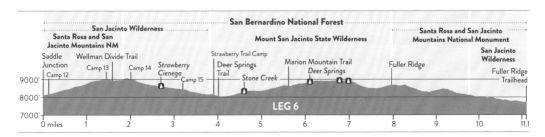

Looking back along craggy Fuller Ridge toward San Jacinto Peak

PEAKBAGGING

San Jacinto Peak (often called Mount San Jacinto) is one of Southern California's crown jewels. It boasts the distinction of having one of the steepest escarpments in the country, with its northern aspect rising well over 9000 feet above the desert below. Many people tag the peak from the east, after riding a tram up from Palm Springs, but you can instead depart the PCT at the Wellman Divide Trail, picking up the Peak Trail to head north to the summit, then descend via the Deer Springs Trail, which rejoins the PCT 4.5 miles past the Wellman Divide Trail junction. The entire side trip is approximately 6.1 miles total. Check the weather before embarking on your summit bid—snow lingers in these mountains well into early summer, and hikers have become lost, injured, and have even died in harsh conditions.

Trail part ways—your path to the left is signed for Fuller Ridge. The beauty continues with more westward views along slopes studded with large boulders, vibrant manzanita, and stately white firs. Ascend a granite staircase, then switchback down while earning views of Folly Peak just above. At 6.8 miles, round a gully that holds another feeder for the **North Fork San Jacinto River 🌢**; this provides the most reliable water on this leg. If you're continuing to the end of this section at San Gorgonio Pass, fill your bottles here since the next

sure source is nearly 20 miles away at a water spigot located near Snow Creek.

Less than 0.25 mile ahead, pass a smaller and less reliable feeder creek 🌢. A set of short, slippery switchbacks on decomposed granite squiggle down a stubby ridgeline, and you'll have to regain all of that elevation as you work up toward **Fuller Ridge** just shy of the 8-mile mark. If you're coming through in summer and early fall, you'll wonder what all the fuss is about, but if snowy conditions exist, it's best to have an ice axe and traction devices (and know how to use them) from here. The ridgeline traverses steep territory and one slip could spell an early end to your hike (or life).

The ridgeline itself is a steep, rocky jumble, and the trail weaves every which way. The upside is that the views are stellar—including the San Bernardino Mountains to the north, the Coachella Valley and Little San Bernardino Mountains to the northeast, and back to San Jacinto Peak rising majestically to the southeast. Eventually dip back into thicker forest, passing the State Park Wilderness boundary at 9.8 miles—you're now free to enjoy dispersed camping, although the steep slopes make it impossible. An opportunity for sleep arises at the end of this leg once you descend to a large dirt lot at the **Fuller Ridge Trailhead** at 11.1 miles. Find good tent spots (along with a picnic table and fire grill but no water) to the right of

the trail, just past the parking area (**Fuller Ridge Camp**). A spur road just before the camping area leads north to unpaved Black Mountain Truck Trail, which offers seasonal access from nearby State Highway 243 via a winding, sometimes rough route—high-clearance vehicles recommended. If you're desperately thirsty, descend this road for about 2.5 miles to reach a water spigot fed by nearby Cinco Poses Spring, passing the Black Mountain Group Campground along the way.

CAMP-TO-CAMP MILEAGE

Saddle Junction to Camp 12	0.1
Camp 12 to Camp 13	1.3
Camp 13 to Camp 14	0.5
Camp 14 to Camp 15	1.4
Camp 15 to Strawberry Trail Camp	0.6
Strawberry Trail Camp to Fuller Ridge Camp	7.2

7 FULLER RIDGE TRAILHEAD TO SAN GORGONIO PASS

DISTANCE 19 miles

ELEVATION GAIN/LOSS +460/-6860 feet

HIGH POINT 7743 feet

CONNECTING ROADS Black Mountain Truck Trail, Falls Creek Road, Snow Creek Road

ON THE TRAIL

Extend those trekking poles because you're about to lose nearly *seven thousand* feet of elevation as you descend from forested heights to the desert floor. Most of the trek is shadeless, so come prepared with sunblock, protective gear, and possibly even a reflective umbrella to keep the oppressive sun at bay—especially important as you lose

elevation and descend into the virtual frying pan of San Gorgonio Pass. Finally, ensure you have enough water to get you there safely—the only reliable source on this leg is a faucet installed in Snow Canyon over 15 miles ahead.

Begin at the far (west) end of the large dirt parking area located at the **Fuller Ridge Trailhead**, picking up the slightly faint trail just to the left of an obvious campsite. Head downhill, reaching unpaved **Black Mountain Truck Trail** in less than 0.25 mile; this offers seasonal trailhead access for those with high-clearance or 4WD vehicles. While the scenery is quite pretty throughout most of this leg, be sure to appreciate the shady conifer forest you're currently strolling through because it will be gone soon enough. Pines, firs, and cedars all mix together here, offering a shocking contrast as soon as you catch the first glimpse of the desert below. This segment is especially beautiful in early morning—in fact, begin as early as possible to get

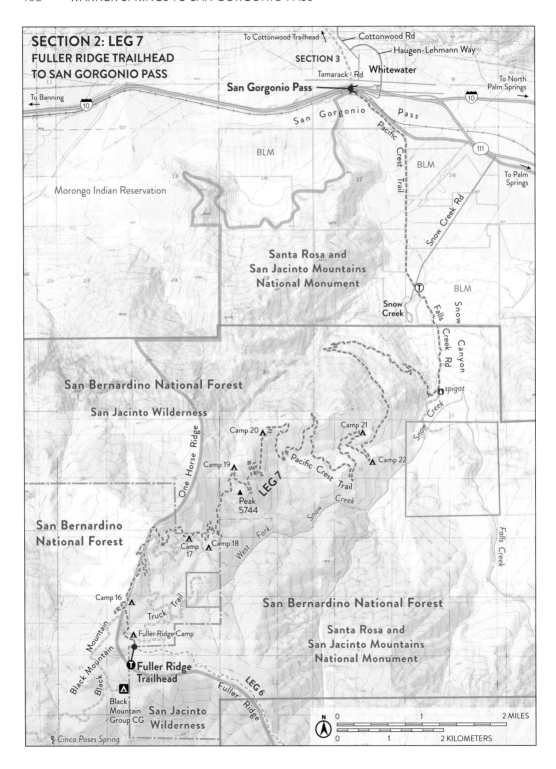

SECTION 2: LEG 7
FULLER RIDGE TRAILHEAD
TO SAN GORGONIO PASS

To Cottonwood Trailhead
Cottonwood Rd
Haugen-Lehmann Way

SECTION 3

Tamarack Rd   **Whitewater**

San Gorgonio Pass

To Banning

To North Palm Springs

BLM

Morongo Indian Reservation

San Gorgonio Pass

Pacific Crest Trail

BLM

To Palm Springs

Santa Rosa and
San Jacinto Mountains
National Monument

Snow Creek Rd

Snow
Creek

spigot

Snow Canyon

Falls Creek Rd

BLM

San Bernardino National Forest

San Jacinto Wilderness

Camp 20

Camp 21

One Horse Ridge

Camp 19

Pacific Crest Trail

Camp 22

LEG 7

Peak
5744

Snow   Creek

Snow Creek

Falls Creek

West Fork

San Bernardino
National Forest

Camp
17   Camp 18

San Bernardino National Forest

Santa Rosa and
San Jacinto Mountains
National Monument

Camp 16

Truck   Trail

Black Mountain

Fuller Ridge Camp

Fuller Ridge
Trailhead

Black

Black
Mountain
Group CG

San Jacinto
Wilderness

LEG 6

Fuller Ridge

Cinco Poses Spring

N   0   1   2 MILES
     0   1   2 KILOMETERS

A wide-brimmed hat or umbrella is useful along the sunlit descent to Snow Creek.

mileage under your belt before the mercury starts to rise.

Several campsites exist along the way, the first coming at 0.8 mile as you curve around a saddle, with a few spots hidden up to the right (**Camp 16**). From here, the views widen to include the San Bernardino Mountains to the north, topped by San Gorgonio Mountain. You also see the San Gabriel Mountains to the northwest along with their high point, Mount San Antonio ("Mount Baldy"). If you're continuing north on the PCT, you'll walk through both of these ranges. Of course, with that

realization comes the sobering reality that all of today's elevation loss is for naught since you'll have to sweat your way right back up the other side of the pass. Cue the sad trombone.

The forest thins as ground cover kicks in, with scratchy buckthorn, rabbitbrush, and holly-leaf cherry lining the path. Weave around boulders, earning views to the Coachella Valley and Little San Bernardino Mountains to the northeast, with impressive San Jacinto Peak towering behind to the southeast. It's hard not to feel at least a little bit awestruck, as it seems

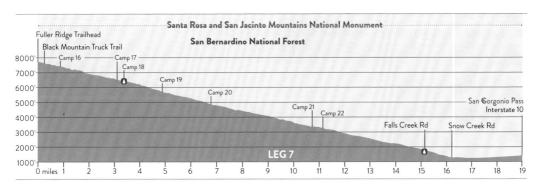

like half of Southern California spreads out below!

Just over the 2-mile mark, reach an unpaved road, then look for the obvious single-track trail continuing to the left. The foliage continues to transition—manzanita and scrub oak now make an appearance, and wildflowers may add some color to the landscape in spring. Squiggle down to reach a sandy, manzanita-filled flat at 3.1 miles, with small clearings tucked back on either side of the trail (**Camp 17**). For something more private, look for a faint use trail jutting off of a hairpin turn 0.3 mile ahead. It leads to at least one flat spot (**Camp 18**) and also offers the opportunity to scout for water at a feeder branch of the nearby **West Fork Snow Creek ◐**; this seasonal source can disappear by early summer.

Thank you, Desert Water Agency!

Take a moment to appreciate the shade because you won't experience it again until standing underneath Interstate 10 many miles ahead. The trail enters an old burn zone below **One Horse Ridge**, which abruptly spells the end of all tree cover. The change is quite sudden, with buckthorn, manzanita, and holly-leaf cherry now the dominant foliage. The upside is that you have unobstructed views for the rest of this leg, so try to marvel at the scenery rather than grumble in shadeless misery.

Descend to an obvious ridge at around 4.9 miles with at least two campsites (**Camp 19**), then continue around **Peak 5744** to begin a series of exceptionally flat, lengthy, and seemingly illogical switchbacks. Although you can just about see this leg's endpoint, it will take you an excruciatingly long time to get there as you double back on your steps countless times, making what feels like no progress at all. Adding frustration is the unfortunate reality that the sandy slopes can't seem to hold the tread in place, with hikers exacerbating the problem by sliding down to cut switchbacks. On top of that, the trail is often exceptionally overgrown with yerba santa, scrub oak, and sharp thickets of buckthorn. Patience is a virtue, friends.

Make your way down to another ridgeline at 6.7 miles, where you'll find not only a few scattered campsites (**Camp 20**), but also whiplash-inducing views of both San Gorgonio Mountain and San Jacinto Peak. That should put some pep in your step as you continue the lazy descent. The foliage eventually thins out and the scenery changes slightly to include excellent sightlines into the wide alluvial spread of Snow Canyon—you'll end up there, though it'll take quite some time. You can also spot the large canyon carved by the Whitewater River just across San Gorgonio Pass to the northeast—you'll also end up there if you decide to hike the next section of trail!

The farther you descend, the larger the boulders become—both a blessing and a curse as the impressive formations sometimes offer shade but also become giant sun reflectors. Keep an ear and eye out for rattlesnakes since this is some of their favorite terrain. Continue cooking as you pass a post at 10.4 miles with "200" carved into the wood—this marks your distance from Mexico on the PCT! Of course, the other side featuring the distance to Canada bears a much larger number. Ahead at 10.7 miles, a use trail banks to the left, leading to a sandy clearing with room for several tents (**Camp 21**). Another camping option comes 0.5 mile ahead, on the right side of a breezy saddle (**Camp 22**).

The small village of Snow Creek and the obvious north-south line of Snow Creek Road come into sharper relief the closer you get as you eventually curve around to the northwest. A few more switchbacks place you on a southwest course, and you eventually drop into **Snow Canyon** itself, crossing both a rusty pipe and a much newer one to reach a water spigot ⓦ and paved **Falls Creek Road** at 15.2 miles. The spigot is provided courtesy the Desert Water Agency, and you're now on their property—fill your tanks and move on since camping is prohibited. The trail is now the road itself—make a left and walk on the asphalt toward **Snow Creek** (the town) and away from Snow Creek (the seasonal waterway). Be sure to glance back up toward San Jacinto Peak—it's probably hard to believe that you were hiking in pine forest at the start of this trip!

Skirt a locked gate, then continue slightly uphill on the road, staying straight to intercept **Snow Creek Road** at 16.3 miles. While the nearby community is private, you can park on the road's shoulder just north of the trail junction. In fact, if you're ending your trip at San Gorgonio Pass, this is the logical place to leave a car (and possibly even end your journey) since there's no parking near the leg's actual endpoint under the freeway overpass. If you want to see the last bit of trail here, or if you're continuing into the next section, cross the road and rejoin the trail. The sandy tread is fairly indistinct from here, washed away by rain, whipped by wind, or scoured by off-road vehicles—a series of posts helps mark the route.

Ground cover is all but gone, with only sparse pockets of sage and cholla for lizards to scurry around. You have a front row seat to the San Bernardino Mountains ahead as you make your way toward busy Interstate 10 and an active set of railroad tracks—noise from both, along with power lines buzzing overhead, creates an unpleasant man-made symphony. Cross an unpaved road around 17.8 miles, then traverse the sandy wash that marks the course of the **San Gorgonio River**; you'll see water (or damp ground) here only after heavy rains. Continue searching for trail markers as you parallel below the railroad tracks, eventually ducking under them to land beneath **Interstate 10** in **San Gorgonio Pass** at the 19-mile mark. While this shady nook provides respite from the relentless sun, it's also extremely creepy here if you're alone—you'll probably want to hightail it north into the next section or turn back toward your car at Snow Creek to avoid running into any unsavory characters lounging on the wrong side of the tracks.

CAMP-TO-CAMP MILEAGE

Fuller Ridge Trailhead to Camp 16	0.8
Camp 16 to Camp 17	2.3
Camp 17 to Camp 18	0.3
Camp 18 to Camp 19	1.5
Camp 19 to Camp 20	1.8
Camp 20 to Camp 21	4.0
Camp 21 to Camp 22	0.5

SAN GORGONIO PASS TO CAJON PASS

VENTURE FROM SAND to snow to surprising rock formations on this journey across the diverse environments of the San Bernardino Mountains, with more natural water sources than you've seen in the previous two sections combined. Before ascending to the range's higher reaches, there's a generous swath of cactus-studded desert terrain to navigate, so slather on sunscreen as you begin the trek into Whitewater Canyon—and make sure to wipe it all off before dunking your sunbaked body into its namesake river.

From here, begin a long, sweaty uphill march along burbling Mission Creek, letting the receding desert floor, cool waters, and eventual smattering of pine trees lift your spirits, if not your feet. Towering cedars steal the show as you approach the outskirts of twin mountain towns Big Bear Lake and Big Bear City, both wonderful places to take in that crisp alpine air (possibly on snowshoes, depending on your timing) while stocking up on provisions—and perhaps even sleep.

Enjoy the pine duff and cool breezes while they last. After a gentle meander along the ridgeline north of Big Bear Lake, descend into the Deep Creek drainage, where you lose the shady tree cover, but occasionally gain the opportunity to fling your weary body into the creek's refreshing waters—*au naturel* at the Deep Creek Hot Springs, if you so choose. From here, travel along the ephemeral West Fork Mojave River, past scenic, man-made Silverwood Lake, and end skipping along rocky fins within spitting distance of milkshakes and cold sodas. Not bad for notoriously dry Southern California!

Opposite: *San Gorgonio Mountain is the crown jewel of the San Bernardino Mountains.*

DISTANCE 132.4 miles

STATE DISTANCE 209.5–341.9 miles

ELEVATION GAIN/LOSS +15,780/-14,060 feet

HIGH POINT 8760 feet

BEST TIME OF YEAR Oct–Apr for low elevations, June–Oct for high elevations

PCTA SECTION LETTER C

LAND MANAGERS Bureau of Land Management (Palm Springs–South Coast Field Office, Barstow Field Office, San Gorgonio Wilderness, Sand to Snow National Monument), San Bernardino National Forest (Mountaintop Ranger District, Front Country Ranger District, San Gorgonio Wilderness, Sand to Snow National Monument), Silverwood Lake State Recreation Area

PASSES AND PERMITS A wilderness permit is required for day and overnight trips in the San Gorgonio Wilderness. Adventure Pass may be required to park at certain trailheads within the San Bernardino National Forest. California Campfire Permit.

MAPS AND APPS
- Halfmile's CA Section C
- USFS PCT Map #1 Southern California and Map #2 Transverse Ranges
- USGS Topo Quads: White Water, Catclaw Flat, Onyx Peak, Moonridge, Big Bear City, Fawnskin, Butler Peak, Lake Arrowhead, Silverwood Lake, Cajon
- Halfmile's PCT app
- Guthook's PCT app

LEGS

1. San Gorgonio Pass to Whitewater Canyon
2. Whitewater Canyon to Mission Springs Trail Camp
3. Mission Springs Trail Camp to Onyx Summit
4. Onyx Summit to State Highway 18
5. State Highway 18 to Holcomb Valley Road
6. Holcomb Valley Road to Bench Trail Camp
7. Bench Trail Camp to Deep Creek Hot Springs
8. Deep Creek Hot Springs to Cleghorn Road
9. Cleghorn Road to Cajon Pass

ACCESS

San Gorgonio Pass

Because this section begins under a freeway underpass that is distinctly lacking in parking opportunities, your best options are to begin at the trail's intersection with Snow Creek Road in the previous leg, have someone drop you off where the trail crosses Tamarack Road on the north side of the Interstate 10 underpass, or park at Cottonwood Trailhead just under 2 miles north. For Cottonwood Trailhead, head west from Los Angeles on I-10 toward San Bernardino. Take exit 110 (Haugen-Lehmann Way) and turn left onto the road. After 0.8 mile, take a right onto Cottonwood Road and drive for approximately 1.2 miles until you reach a large dirt parking lot on your right; pick up the PCT from the southeast corner of the parking lot.

Cajon Pass

From Los Angeles, head west on I-10 toward San Bernardino and take exit 58A for I-15 north, toward Barstow and Las Vegas. In about 14.9 miles, take exit 131 to head east on State Highway 138 toward Palmdale and Silverwood Lake. Turn right onto CA 138 eastbound, and in just under 200 feet, turn right onto Wagon Train Road. The trailhead is located just over 0.5 mile ahead at the end of the road.

NOTES

Cities and Services

Cabazon is a town 4.5 miles west of the southern trailhead that offers a post office, gas station, dining options, casino, and an outlet mall; for more services, head 11 miles southeast to much larger Palm Springs. Near the northern trailhead, you'll find a hotel, fast food, and gas stations; for more amenities, travel roughly 16 miles north to Hesperia or south to Fontana.

Camping and Fire Restrictions

Camp at least 200 feet from water in the San Bernardino National Forest. Campfires are not allowed in the San Gorgonio Wilderness or at

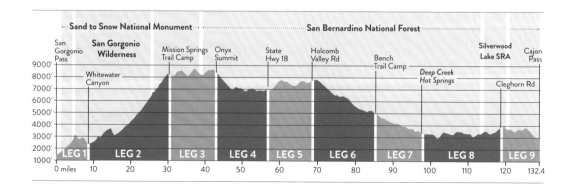

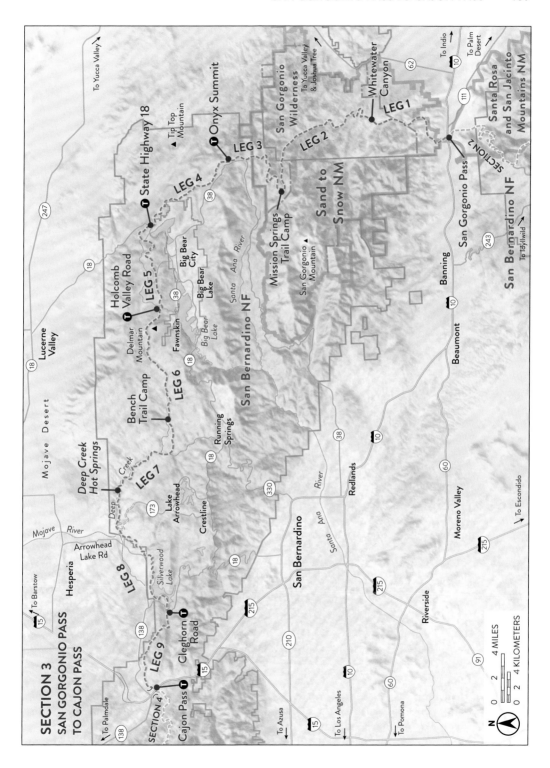

SECTION 3
SAN GORGONIO PASS
TO CAJON PASS

This section offers a diverse array of scenery, from desert waterways to mountain views.

Whitewater Preserve. In other areas, fires are allowed only in designated fire rings, while seasonal fire restrictions may exist in San Bernardino National Forest.

Water

While water is more plentiful in this section than in those previous, many of the sources are seasonal—check before heading out to ensure springs and smaller waterways are still flowing (or plan for longer water carries). The longest likely waterless stretches are the 9.1 miles between this section's beginning and the spur trail to Whitewater Preserve, the 16.2 miles between Mission Spring Trail Camp and Arrastre Trail Camp, the 10 miles between the final Arrastre Creek crossing and Doble Trail Camp, the 10.7 miles between Caribou Creek and Little Bear Springs Trail Camp, and the last 9 miles of this section.

Hazards

The first and final thirds of this section are quite exposed, with little ground cover, which magnifies the sun's presence—opportunities for shade are limited, so bring your own. In late

SUGGESTED ITINERARIES

Camps are either viewable from the trail or located within a few tenths of a mile from the noted location unless otherwise specified in leg descriptions.

10 DAYS

		Miles
Day 1	San Gorgonio Pass to Whitewater Preserve	9.1
Day 2	Whitewater Preserve to Camp 4	13.5
Day 3	Camp 4 to Coon Creek Cabin	14.3
Day 4	Coon Creek Cabin to Camp 7	13.0
Day 5	Camp 7 to Doble Trail Camp	9.2
Day 6	Doble Trail Camp to Little Bear Spring Trail Camp	16.8
Day 7	Little Bear Spring Trail Camp to Bench Trail Camp	9.3
Day 8	Bench Trail Camp to Camp 16	20.0
Day 9	Camp 16 to New Mesa and Mesa Campgrounds	14.1
Day 10	New Mesa and Mesa Campgrounds to Cajon Pass	13.1

9 DAYS

Day 1	San Gorgonio Pass to Whitewater Preserve	9.1
Day 2	Whitewater Preserve to Camp 5	16.9
Day 3	Camp 5 to Coon Creek Cabin	10.9
Day 4	Coon Creek Cabin to Camp 7	13.0
Day 5	Camp 7 to Camp 10	17.2
Day 6	Camp 10 to Bench Trail Camp	18.1
Day 7	Bench Trail Camp to Camp 16	20.0
Day 8	Camp 16 to New Mesa and Mesa Campgrounds	14.1
Day 9	New Mesa and Mesa Campgrounds to Cajon Pass	13.1

8 DAYS

Day 1	San Gorgonio Pass to Camp 1	16.7
Day 2	Camp 1 to Mission Springs Trail Camp	13.7
Day 3	Mission Springs Trail Camp to Camp 7	19.5
Day 4	Camp 7 to Camp 10	17.2
Day 5	Camp 10 to Bench Trail Camp	18.1
Day 6	Bench Trail Camp to Camp 16	20.0
Day 7	Camp 16 to New Mesa and Mesa Campgrounds	14.1
Day 8	New Mesa and Mesa Campgrounds to Cajon Pass	13.1

fall, winter, and early spring, snow can accumulate in the higher elevations near Big Bear, and snow chains may be required if driving to trailheads in the area. Rattlesnake sightings are common in lower elevation areas during the warmer months, typically beginning in early spring. Black bears are present in small numbers in the upper elevations of the San Bernardino National Forest. While a bear canister isn't required, you'd be smart to at least hang your food. Grazing cattle frequent the land west and southwest of Whitewater Preserve—keep your distance if you should encounter any bovine inhabitants.

1 SAN GORGONIO PASS TO WHITEWATER CANYON

DISTANCE 9.1 miles

ELEVATION GAIN/LOSS
+2610/-1640 feet

HIGH POINT 3222 feet

CONNECTING TRAILS AND ROADS
Tamarack Road, Clay Road, Boulder Drive,
Cottonwood Road, Canyon View Loop Trail

ON THE TRAIL

While this leg has a less-than-scenic start at a highway underpass, it makes up for that initial indiscretion with surprising solitude, beautiful desert vistas, and the option to visit a refreshing riparian paradise at the end. Start with lots of sunscreen, water, and motivation—the only camping and refill opportunity on this leg is at the lovely Whitewater Preserve, a (worthy) 0.5-mile side trip past your endpoint.

Begin under what just might be the most congested highway in the entire United States—**Interstate 10**. While the underpass provides much-needed shade on a hot day, it's less than aesthetically pleasing and can be downright creepy if you arrive here solo—all the motivation needed to strike north, crossing paved **Tamarack Road** less than 0.1 mile in. The first 2 miles of your hike skirt the small community of **Whitewater**—private property abounds, so be sure to stay on the trail, which is intermittently marked by wooden posts.

Continue through low desert scrub to cross no less than ten unpaved roads in fairly regular intervals, some named, some not. However, a few serve as landmarks for your progress through this area. **Clay Road**, which you cross just over 1 mile in, features a trail register. Write something philosophical, then continue 0.25 mile past that (and past another dirt road) to cross **Boulder Drive**, where a gate blocks access to the south.

Cross four more dirt paths after this, the last one being **Cottonwood Road** at 1.5 miles; parallel this until passing to the south of the unpaved parking area at the **Cottonwood Trailhead** just 0.5 mile later. This offers an alternate start point for this leg (and section) if leaving a car behind since there's no parking near the Interstate 10 underpass.

Now well into the **Sand to Snow National Monument**, leave behind the relatively flat topography and make your way toward a series of wind turbine-topped foothills. The relentless spiderweb of unpaved roads continues as you cross a pair almost immediately past the parking area, dip down into a wash, and cross several more dirt paths in rapid succession, the largest being an access road to the nearby wind farm. PCT markers guide you through the dusty chaos. At 2.6 miles, you reach a complicated-looking system featuring a metal pipe gate and a wooden stock pen along with a large mileage sign that reads "Welcome To Section C." Pass through to the right and keep your eyes peeled for cows throughout the rest of this leg—cattle grazing used to occur in the area, and some bovine inhabitants continue to roam the

ALTERNATE START

If you're not a purist and would rather skip the admittedly creepy freeway underpass, you can start at the Cottonwood Trailhead. Exit Interstate 10 at Haugen-Lehmann Way, turn left off the freeway, then make the first left onto Tamarack Road and the second right onto Cottonwood Drive. About 1 mile up, the paved road turns to gravel, and about in 0.5 mile, you'll find the unsigned Cottonwood Trailhead and parking area on the right side; the PCT is the obvious track that runs just south.

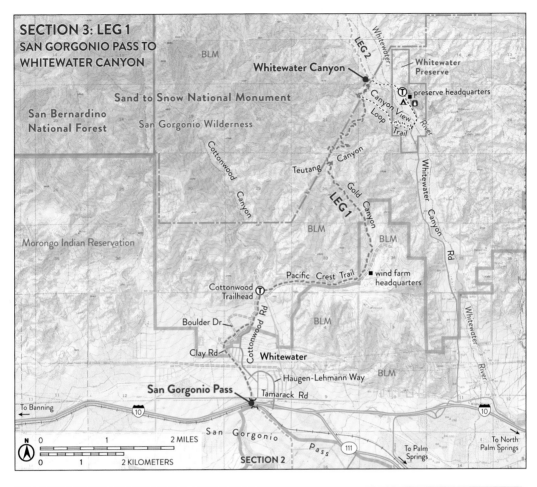

SECTION 3: LEG 1
SAN GORGONIO PASS TO WHITEWATER CANYON

LEG 2

Whitewater

BLM

Whitewater Canyon

Whitewater Preserve

preserve headquarters

Sand to Snow National Monument

Canyon View Loop Trail

San Bernardino National Forest

San Gorgonio Wilderness

Cottonwood Canyon

Canyon

Teutang Canyon

Gold Canyon

LEG 1

Whitewater River

BLM

BLM

Whitewater Canyon Rd

Morongo Indian Reservation

Pacific Crest Trail

wind farm headquarters

Cottonwood Trailhead

Cottonwood Rd

BLM

Boulder Dr

Whitewater River

Clay Rd

Whitewater

Haugen-Lehmann Way

BLM

San Gorgonio Pass

Tamarack Rd

To Banning

10

10

N

San Gorgonio

To North Palm Springs

0   1   2 MILES

0   1   2 KILOMETERS

Pass

111

To Palm Springs

SECTION 2

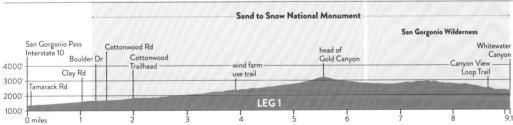

Sand to Snow National Monument

San Gorgonio Wilderness

San Gorgonio Pass Interstate 10

Cottonwood Rd

head of Gold Canyon

Whitewater Canyon

Boulder Dr

Cottonwood Trailhead

Canyon View Loop Trail

4000'

Clay Rd

wind farm use trail

3000'

Tamarack Rd

2000'

LEG 1

1000'

0 miles   1   2   3   4   5   6   7   8   9.1

land, occasionally harassing hikers. If you see any, especially bulls, be sure to *mooooove* over and give our hoofed pals their space.

Head up a gentle hill, then descend to cross the access road. Here, walk along a typically dry streambed that still manages to breathe life into the surroundings—butterflies flutter around pockets of creosote, rabbitbrush, prickly pear, and arroyo willow, with the latter offering small patches of shade. Re-cross the road as the grade steepens, with the nearby wind farm coming into view as you ascend. A rock-lined use trail departs to the right at 3.9 miles—while this leads to the wind farm's headquarters, only detour if you notice

The impressive Whitewater Canyon features a year-round waterway, a bit of a desert anomaly.

FROM SAND TO SNOW

In February 2016, President Obama added to his conservation legacy by designating not one, but *three* new national monuments in California—Mojave Trails, Castle Mountains, and Sand to Snow. These lands link together vital wildlife habitat and preserve a spectacular array of ecological and cultural landscapes. The PCT travels through about 30 miles of Sand to Snow National Monument, beginning about 1 mile north of San Gorgonio Pass, through Whitewater Canyon and into the Mission Creek drainage. If you're wondering about the name, it'll become clear as you progress through this leg and the next, as you stand slack-jawed on a sandy plateau, looking skyward to the snowbound heights of Mount San Gorgonio and beyond.

signs welcoming hikers or if considering a career in alternative energy.

Continue dodging cow patties and possibly even bullets (I interrupted target shooting practice when I rolled through) as you curve north into **Gold Canyon**. The area is fairly shadeless, with only the occasional large bush offering respite. Cross a dirt road at 4.3 miles, pick up the trail again, then briefly join the road before it curves to the right and your path stays straight. Less than 1 mile ahead you pass through a mangled barbed wire fence and the realization dawns that you have to climb to the canyon's head. Mutter obscene things under your breath as you trudge up steep, loose switchbacks until you turn around at the top to realize you've been gifted with incredible views of San Jacinto Peak to the south. You also score a peek of the massive slash of Whitewater Canyon and its telltale fanglomerate cliffs in the distance—the closer you get, the more impressive it becomes.

It's now a downhill wiggle on somewhat crumbly trail to dip into **Teutang Canyon**. Here, another barbed wire fence guards the border of the **San Gorgonio Wilderness**, marked with a sign at 6.2 miles. The trail undulates along a series of breezy ridges and sandy ravines that offer deeper views into the rock-walled canyon. Cross a large, barren plateau marked by cairns and a large wooden trail marker, and marvel at the expanding views—suddenly this leg's unattractive start is nothing but a dusty memory. Whitewater Canyon opens up to reveal its true size, which is to say, massive. The Whitewater River snakes through the wide watershed, its serpentine squiggle surrounded by sun-bleached rocks and towering cliffs sometimes dotted with bighorn sheep. The best views come at 8.2 miles once you reach a junction with the **Canyon View Loop Trail** on your right—the panorama is spectacular.

Tear yourself away and stay straight to join the Canyon View Loop Trail and descend a set of switchbacks angling down a deep gully. At 9.1 miles, you'll reach the bottom, where the PCT and Canyon View Loop Trail diverge, the latter splitting right to reach **Whitewater Preserve** in 0.5 mile. This junction marks the end of this leg. Even if continuing north on the PCT, the side trip is well worth it. The preserve, a former fish hatchery, is part of The Wildlands Conservancy, the largest nonprofit preserve collection on the west coast. Not only is the landscape beautiful, but the rangers here are also very friendly to PCT hikers, making this a great place to cool your heels. You'll find picnic tables, camping, water spigots **O**, and glorious flush toilets, along with a lovely ranger station and trout ponds (including a wading pool to relieve your tired tootsies). Ample parking is available and rangers can help coordinate access outside of operating hours if you want to get an early start. This is a fee-free facility, but considering it's run completely on private contributions, I strongly suggest you leave a few dollars in the donation box.

CAMP-TO-CAMP MILEAGE

San Gorgonio Pass to Whitewater Preserve . . . 9.1

2 WHITEWATER CANYON TO MISSION SPRINGS TRAIL CAMP

DISTANCE 21.3 miles

ELEVATION GAIN/LOSS
+6710/-1080 feet

HIGH POINT 7946 feet

CONNECTING TRAILS AND ROADS
Canyon View Loop Trail, West Fork Trail, Mission Creek Road

ON THE TRAIL

Do you crave solitude, sand, mountain views, and . . . desert waterways? That's not a typo—this leg offers not one, but *two* refreshing riparian corridors for your enjoyment! The price of admission is a somewhat lengthy, often hot, and mostly uphill journey—but there are plenty of places to cool off (and feel awestruck) along the way.

Begin at the PCT's divergence from the Canyon View Loop Trail, which splits right for a 0.5-mile side trip to **Whitewater Preserve**, part of The Wildlands Conservancy's extensive holdings. The car-accessible space, a former fish hatchery, offers water **O**, flush toilets, a picnic area, interpretive displays, and overnight camping. It's situated along the Whitewater River, a desert anomaly that draws visitors to frolic in its cooling waters—you'll get your chance soon enough. Although this leg ends high in the pines, the first half can get quite toasty—start early in the morning, both to avoid being cooked in the relatively shadeless surrounds

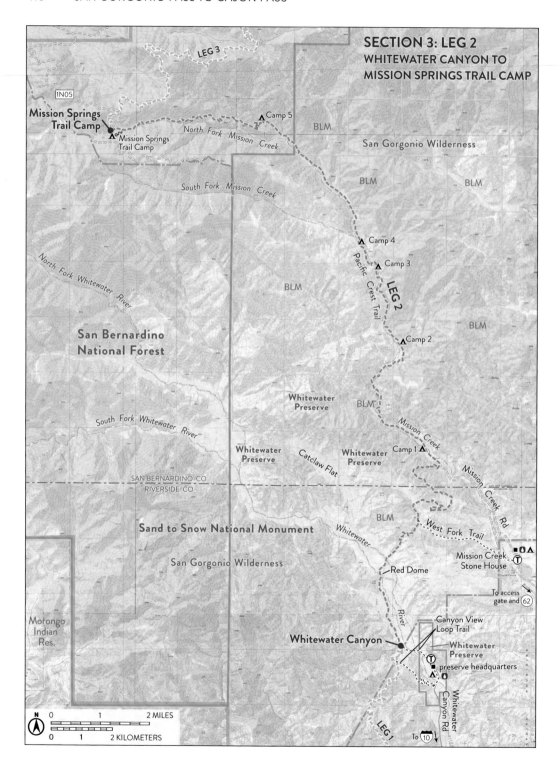

SECTION 3: LEG 2
WHITEWATER CANYON TO
MISSION SPRINGS TRAIL CAMP

LEG 3

1N05

Mission Springs
Trail Camp

Mission Springs
Trail Camp

North Fork Mission Creek

Camp 5

BLM

San Gorgonio Wilderness

South Fork Mission Creek

BLM

BLM

Camp 4

North Fork Whitewater River

Pacific Crest Trail

LEG 2

Camp 3

BLM

BLM

Camp 2

San Bernardino
National Forest

South Fork Whitewater River

Whitewater
Preserve

BLM

Mission Creek

Whitewater
Preserve

Catclaw Flat

Whitewater
Preserve

Camp 1

SAN BERNARDINO CO.
RIVERSIDE CO.

Mission Creek Rd

Sand to Snow National Monument

BLM

West Fork Trail

Whitewater

Mission Creek
Stone House

San Gorgonio Wilderness

Red Dome

To access
gate and 62

River

Morongo
Indian
Res.

Whitewater Canyon

Canyon View
Loop Trail

Whitewater
Preserve

preserve headquarters

Whitewater
Canyon Rd

LEG 1

To 10

N   0   1   2 MILES
     0   1   2 KILOMETERS

and for the amazing morning light that casts an ethereal glow on the resident cacti.

To begin, head north on the sandy trail into the **San Gorgonio Wilderness**, passing a large red outcropping of iron-rich basalt along the trail at 1.6 miles—this marks **Red Dome,** a popular turn-around spot for day hikers. Unless hiking in prime thru-hiker season, you're bound to have the trail mostly to yourself from here on out—a great thing if you crave solitude, a potentially nerve-wracking thing if you let your imagination dwell on all of the fresh mountain lion tracks crossing the sand. Cross a channel of the **Whitewater River ◑** just beyond and scan for trail markers that serve as guideposts across the area since the trail is sometimes erased by high waters caused by heavy rainfall and rapid snowmelt. Reach the other end of the wide river drainage just before the 2-mile mark—collect enough water here to keep dehydration at bay as you make the hot journey to Mission Creek.

From this point, leave behind the whitewashed gravel of Whitewater River's watershed and enter a completely different world. The ground shifts from soft sand to rocky soil, with an explosion of prickly pear threatening your tender ankles as you begin heading uphill. Climb a set of steep, crumbly switchbacks to crest the canyon mouth at 2.8 miles. The views are great, especially back out across Whitewater Canyon, but they'll become exponentially better in a short bit. Head downhill, reaching an intersection with the **West Fork Trail** (signed for the Mission Creek Stone House) at 3.2 miles. The structure sits 2 miles east in the Mission Creek Preserve, also part of The Wildlands Conservancy holdings. Unless detouring, continue straight, watching as a large

peak creeps into view to the northwest across Catclaw Flat—this is San Gorgonio Mountain, or "Ol' Greyback," the tallest peak south of the Sierra at a cloud-kissing 11,503 feet. It's absolutely stunning when dusted in snow. Take some pictures here—but know that the views are going to get *even better!*

The trail meanders across the gently sloping desert floor, passing through chamise and plenty of clothes-shredding catclaw—if you don't know it by sight, you'll know it by feel. Just when the trail seems to dead-end, it curves around to climb a canyon, topping out on a ridge around 4.6 miles. Here are those jaw-dropping views I promised earlier, encompassing the serpentine trail you just hiked, along with a sizeable swath of Whitewater Canyon, while both Mount San Gorgonio and San Jacinto Peak (to the south) tower above their surroundings. Once you finish gaping at the 360-degree views, continue to undulate along the ridgeline. The Mission Creek watershed eventually creeps into view, especially pretty after spring rains and in autumn, when its riparian foliage glows with color.

Descend a series of switchbacks to reach the canyon floor and an intersection with unpaved **Mission Creek Road** on your right at 7.2 miles. Unless coming through in summertime when it often disappears underground, it's likely you'll hear the creek before reaching it less than 0.5 mile ahead. A few campsites sit on the near side of the first crossing of **Mission Creek ◑ (Camp 1)**, but this is also a lovely spot to simply take a break, surrounded by shade—*glorious shade!*—thanks to a smattering of willows, cottonwoods, and a stately sycamore.

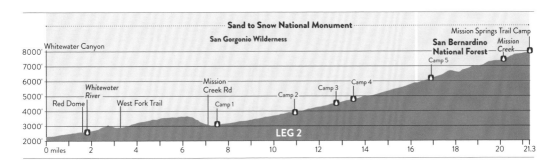

The Whitewater River provides a cool oasis for wildlife . . . and hikers.

You'll spend much of the rest of this leg making a gradual ascent along Mission Creek, crossing its typically modest flow too many times to mention in this text (on a trip in late August, I soaked my trail runners crossing *twenty* times!). I'll mention only the most notable crossings and leave you to discover the rest on your own. As with the Whitewater River traverse, the trail in this canyon sometimes disappears and can be rerouted after floodwaters scour it away. Look for giant (and I mean *giant*) rock cairns and wooden posts to mark the way, noticeable on either side of water crossings.

Cholla and prickly pear still stab at your legs, but not as much as before—the foliage transitions to less violent chaparral as you ascend. Creekside willows and cottonwoods offer pockets of shade, and granite pinches in the canyon feel like a dreamy burst of air conditioning on a hot day. As you cross, re-cross, and re-re-cross the creek, look for signs of animal visitors—this is a major wildlife corridor, offering travel between the desert and the higher reaches of the San Bernardino Mountains. Look for signs of coyotes, mountain lions, bobcats, sheep, and even black bears—sadly, the latter have

slowly expanded their range in the quest for dwindling food and water; I saw no less than a dozen piles of nut-filled bear scat decorating the trail.

If you want to bed down with these ursine nomads, several opportunities abound along Mission Creek. At 10.9 miles, a lone cottonwood tree marks a handful of spots perched on a sandy shelf above the creek ◑ (**Camp 2**). Another few sites appear after a creek crossing at 12.8 miles ◑ (**Camp 3**), but these are somewhat subpar. There's a much larger spot ahead at 13.5 miles (**Camp 4**), with room for plenty of tents just before the largest crossing ◑ yet—this time, on logs. Cattails add to the swampy ambiance.

Just after this, continue to follow the **North Fork Mission Creek,** while the **South Fork** veers off to the west. At 16.2 miles, a sign announces the **San Bernardino National Forest,** and things begin to change once again, as most of the desert denizens are replaced with yerba santa, manzanita, rabbitbrush, scrub oak, and ceanothus. Veer away from Mission Creek to dip into a small gully whose seasonal stream ◑ offers water for those camped on the shady shelf at 16.9 miles (**Camp 5**). Even if you're not staying the night, this is a lovely place to rest under a pair of large oak trees, unless it is breezy, in which case their acorns may turn into painful little missiles. Tend to any head wounds before tackling the remainder of this leg. Beginning with a switchbacked ascent out of the gully, the terrain steepens considerably as the canyon walls close in, with a few somewhat maddening elevation losses to round out your efforts.

Pass through an old burn scar and hunt for the trail as it occasionally disappears under mudflows, flood debris, and crumbling rock. The consolation for your efforts is the appearance of pine trees studding the slopes above; you'll walk under their fragrant boughs soon enough—although closer inspection reveals that many were damaged (and killed) in the 2015 Lake Fire, a massive blaze that stole some of the beauty from this segment of trail. Be especially cautious to avoid lingering under dead trees ("snags") and watch your feet while navigating the messy landscape.

A final visit to **Mission Creek** occurs at a pair of crossings just over 20 miles in. From here, it's a little bit more up and down to arrive at the small dirt parking lot resting below **Mission Springs Trail Camp** at 21.3 miles. Pop uphill between wooden barriers to find a pair of picnic tables and fire rings, a horse corral, and plenty of room to stake your sleeping claim. Water is available via two springs, both accessed via use

WILD WATERS

While the Whitewater River has certainly seen its share of floods, the North Fork Mission Creek runs through a much narrower canyon, and the floodwaters here run much more intensely. Do not attempt a hike through the area if storms are predicted nearby—one look at the wrecked canyon walls, towering debris piles, and frequently washed-out trail should squash any desire to test yourself against Mother Nature's watery will.

trails departing on either side of the tables. Head right (west) to cross a gully and walk uphill to spot a pipe sticking out of a patch of ferns, or head left (east) to pass a horse corral, then wrap around it to land at a dripping cave whose waters collect in a small basin.

CAMP-TO-CAMP MILEAGE

Whitewater Canyon to Camp 1 . . . . 7.6
Camp 1 to Camp 2 . . . . 3.3
Camp 2 to Camp 3 . . . . 1.9
Camp 3 to Camp 4 . . . . 0.7
Camp 4 to Camp 5 . . . . 3.4
Camp 5 to Mission Springs Trail Camp 4.4

3 MISSION SPRINGS TRAIL CAMP TO ONYX SUMMIT

DISTANCE 12.2 miles

ELEVATION GAIN/LOSS
+2670/-2070 feet

HIGH POINT 8760 feet

CONNECTING ROADS
Forest Service Road 1N05, Forest Service Road 1N02, Forest Service Road 1N01

ON THE TRAIL

Even though the 2015 Lake Fire affected the beginning of this leg, the burn zone becomes a distant memory as you move along pine-studded ridgelines offering spectacular views. Begin at the dirt parking area for **Mission Springs Trail Camp**, where two springs provide the only water available on this leg; the next possible source is at Arrastre Trail Camp, 16.3 miles away. Once you are sufficiently stocked, look for trail markers leading

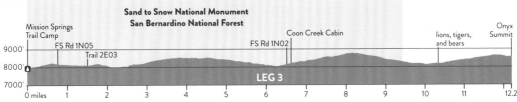

up an unpaved access road, then across **Forest Service Road 1N05** to hit actual trail tread.

While much of this trail segment feels remote, you also cross a dizzying array of unpaved roads, including a second crossing of Forest Service Road 1N05 at 0.7 mile. Leave the dust behind for a short bit while maneuvering around large boulders, manzanita, rabbitbrush, and striking tufts of Parish's buckwheat,

which wouldn't seem out of place on the ocean floor. Hop across another unpaved path (**Trail 2E03**) at 1.5 miles, and move uphill into burn-scarred forest. While the blackened snags add a spooky vibe, they're soon replaced by healthier specimens along with a seemingly endless parade of mountain mahogany; look for the latter's telltale fuzzy tendrils glowing in the late summer sun while in fruit.

Opposite: *The ascent from Coon Creek Cabin offers fantastic views of San Gorgonio Mountain.*

ACCESS ISSUE

The 2015 Lake Fire ravaged a beautiful swath of the San Bernardino National Forest, destroying many beloved trails and roads. A portion of the PCT was closed for a year afterward, and many of the Forest Service roads in this area remain closed as of this writing, including all of the ones mentioned here. Therefore, although it's technically possible to drive to the beginning trailhead with a high-clearance vehicle, you'll have to wait to make that trip until the Forest Service reopens access roads.

Meander along gently rolling terrain before popping onto steeper slopes offering views straight down into the canyon carved by **Heart Bar Creek** and out to the wide, flat expanse of creatively named Big Meadows. Even better, your vantage point offers an unobstructed look at San Gorgonio Mountain sneaking up behind Ten Thousand Foot Ridge to the southwest. You'll have more opportunities to soak in the sights farther ahead, so make your way around an obvious ridge at 3.5 miles, peering down into the canyon formed by ephemeral Coon Creek. Pines now dominate the slopes, much healthier than the ones you saw in the earlier burn zone, and their duff creates a soft (if sometimes slippery) tread. While the trees obscure some of the views, it won't matter when a striking slash of sparkly white rock steals your attention—this is actually a form of marble, and you dance along its eye-catching gravel for a few minutes.

At 4.8 miles, emerge onto a saddle where the trail morphs into a wide gravelly road. Here, look down into a deep gully and peek out to the North Fork Mission Creek watershed you traveled through in the previous leg. Farther south, San Jacinto Peak caps the skyline above San Gorgonio Pass. Around 0.5 mile after joining it, depart the road and stay right to continue along the breezy ridgeline, eventually descending back across north-facing slopes to reach a dirt road and clearing. Keep right to rejoin the trail just ahead next to the **Coon Creek**

Jumpoff, a stunning vantage point that might induce a little vertigo for those averse to heights.

Reach a much larger unpaved road just a moment later—this time, it's **Forest Service Road 1N02** at 6.5 miles. The trail continues straight, but you might want to hang a right here to visit the historic **Coon Creek Cabin**, a bare bones, but lovely log building erected as a retreat by a local named Charles Tayles. It now acts as a different kind of lodging, serving as a reservation-only group campground run by the Forest Service, complete with a vault toilet, picnic tables, garbage receptacles, and fire rings. There is a parking area here, although your vehicle should be up for the challenge of driving along the lumpy road. My Honda Civic made it, albeit with a few close calls.

The trail continues uphill along a few lazy switchbacks, each offering even more spectacular views into the **San Bernardino National Forest** high country. San Gorgonio Mountain and San Jacinto Peak stay in view, as does the Coachella Valley far below. Pinyon and Jeffrey pines dot the slopes, mingling with large boulders, white firs, mountain mahogany, and a smattering of colorful wildflowers in spring. The spellbinding vistas disappear once you crest a ridgeline, but you'll have one more opportunity to soak in some grandeur near the end of this leg.

Before that happens, coast downhill to cross yet another unpaved road, then squiggle into a gully. You're deposited at the hairpin bend of *another* dirt road at 9.4 miles—make a right to continue downhill, now traveling through private property for much of the remainder of this leg. Be sure to stay on trail—or the dirt paths that serve as the "trail." You meet up with another dirt road marked by a large wooden gateway just under 1 mile ahead; make a left onto the road, then a quick right to rejoin the trail. As you ascend past a chain-link fence, don't be startled if a lion slinks over to greet you—this fence guards a compound housing large cats and other animals trained to appear in films and on TV, a strange, fascinating, and disturbing sight all at once.

If the incessant road crossings haven't done it already, the sound of traffic on nearby State Highway 38 might snap you out of any remaining forested reverie. The trail reverts back to single-track at 11.1 miles as you head uphill to the right; the tread here is often obscured by shrubbery, so look for a post marked "Go Right" to point the way. Things become a bit more peaceful as you snag one last, longing glance at majestic San Gorgonio Mountain and impressive Ten Thousand Foot Ridge. Arrive at a final unpaved road at 12.2 miles, a spur from **Forest Service Road 1N01** (Pipes Road) that marks the end of this leg. While the PCT continues straight ahead, it's possible to depart to the left to hit a large parking area at **Onyx Summit** a moment later. This gap sits alongside Highway 38, one of the main arteries offering access to the twin towns of Big Bear Lake and Big Bear City.

CAMP-TO-CAMP MILEAGE
**Mission Springs Trail Camp to
  Coon Creek Cabin**. 6.5

4 ONYX SUMMIT TO STATE HIGHWAY 18

DISTANCE 14 miles

ELEVATION GAIN/LOSS
+1380/-3090 feet

HIGH POINT 8694 feet

CONNECTING ROADS
Forest Service Road 1N01, Forest Service Road 2N01, Forest Service Road 2N02, State Highway 18

ON THE TRAIL
Even though you can hear cars whizzing nearby, focus instead on the sound of birdsong as you skip through a fragrant forest at the start of this leg, beginning where a brief connector trail links the PCT to **Onyx Summit** and its large parking area along **State Highway 38**. Cross a small section of chunky pink quartzite, ascending just enough to catch glimpses to San Gorgonio Mountain down to the southwest and far out to sometimes wet, sometimes dry Baldwin Lake to the northwest.

In just over 1 mile, cross unpaved **Forest Service Road 1N01** (Pipes Road), and if you need a nap, look to your left to find several flat spots scattered under the trees (**Camp 6**). The trail is very rocky underfoot, so be careful not to turn an ankle while enjoying the towering lodgepole pines all around. You're technically heading uphill, but the grade is pretty mellow—still, it's nice to sit for a spell on any number of the tree stumps dotting the ground. In fact, every time I hike in this area, I feel an urge to plop down and read a book.

A coniferous canopy offers wonderful shade.

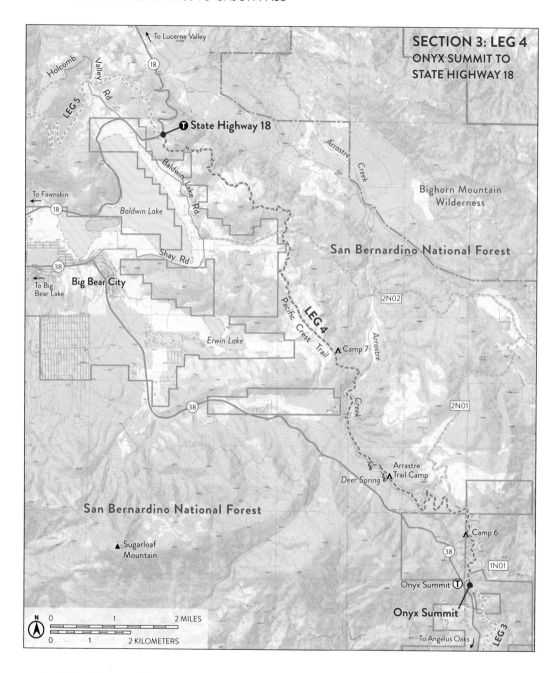

At 3.2 miles, you'll cross unpaved **Forest Service Road 2N01**, soon walking along **Arrastre Creek**, whose waters will be easier to collect up ahead. Western fence lizards dart along the path, perhaps seeking out the limited sunbathing spots in this thick, shady forest. The only thing that might break the spell is a ringing cell phone—yes, you may have service here, but try to avoid the temptation and remain one with nature.

You'll reach **Arrastre Trail Camp** at 4.1 miles, and as its name implies, it is literally right on the trail—okay, just to the right of the trail, if you want to be specific about it. It's a really nice spot, complete with picnic tables and a fire ring with improvised seating. There's also a spigot **◐** and a trough, although both may be dry; if so, try your luck at **Deer Spring ◐**, located a short scramble up the hill across from the camp (and Arrastre Creek). If that's dry, continue up the trail about 0.1 mile to cross the creek and hope for better luck. If all three sources are a strikeout, your best bet is a spring **◐**, located on the left side of the trail 0.5 mile up from camp, dripping out of a small, cave-like depression on the hillside.

Continue through the canyon, crossing a small wooden footbridge and possibly even some seasonal flows across the trail itself. The sun begins to cut through as the forest cover thins, making room for sage, beavertail cactus, and Indian paintbrush to mingle with pines and black oaks, whose leaves brighten the trail in autumn. You'll cross a few unpaved roads in this area (and even join one for a bit)—if you're ever confused at an intersection, look around until you see a trail marker, then proceed. Make another crossing of **Arrastre Creek ◐** at 5.8 miles, then ascend a bit on sunny slopes, passing a slash of grey quartzite not unlike the pink version you saw earlier in this leg. Just after this area, start a few lazy switchbacks toward the canyon bottom, where you'll spot not only sage and pine, but also mountain mahogany, cottonwoods, and willows lining your last crossing of **Arrastre Creek ◐** at 6.4 miles.

When you've filled your tanks, it's time to make a steady, shadeless climb to gain a ridgeline. Once on top, you'll find some pines—and now, giant junipers—that offer some respite. If you want something

Make new friends (and keep the old) around the fire at Arrastre Trail Camp.

longer than a quick break, you'll find a few campsites (**Camp 7**) scattered around on the right side around 7.3 miles. Shortly after these, you'll briefly join yet another unpaved road, then quickly depart it on the left to walk along the west side of the

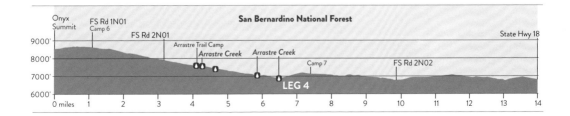

The trail is full of surprises; here, the author relaxes on one of them.

ridgeline. Here, you earn views down to the meadowy flat of Erwin Lake and homes just beyond.

Soon you'll duck back to the east side, and after a rather sudden exit from tree cover, you're greeted by the sight of a deep valley far below to your right created by your old friend Arrastre Creek and a ridgeline including Tip Top Mountain beyond. The walking here is pretty easy, so you can turn on autopilot for a bit as you enjoy the sights. Eventually pass several unpaved roads and use trails, continuing straight through each until you reach a T-intersection at 9.5 miles, where you'll hang right to stay on the PCT. Even though the trail is generally well marked through here, you'll definitely want a good headlamp if you decide to pass through at night.

Believe it or not (mega-sarcasm intended), you'll hit *another* unpaved road at 9.8 miles—this one is **Forest Service Road 2N02**. Head across, the sound of nearby target shooting perhaps adding a little pep to your step. Head uphill on soft tread, through juniper and pinyon pines, eventually catching glimpses of the Mojave Desert out to the northeast; once you cross an unpaved road at 11.5 miles, these views grow exponentially better at the same time you realize the slopes you're traveling have started sprouting yucca in seeming solidarity. You might also feel some solidarity with the desert below if it's a hot day because you lose shade until you reach pockets

BIG BEAR

What is commonly called "Big Bear" is actually the area covered by the resort town of Big Bear Lake and more residential Big Bear City. Food and lodging are available in both; Big Bear City is a bit closer to the trail, but Big Bear Lake has more variety. While there are buses in town, there are no public transportation options where the PCT hits State Highway 18. If they haven't prearranged a ride, most hikers try their hand at a hitch, although this can be difficult due to the speed of passing traffic and the fact that you're on the wrong side of the road to head into town!

of pinyon pine about 1.5 miles from this leg's end. Curve around the eastern slopes for one last view of Ernie Lake, then pop back around to see giant Baldwin Lake (or what's left of it in a drought year) and **State Highway 18** ahead. You'll reach the latter at 14 miles, dumping out at a massive parking lot on the south side of the road. This is where

you'll end your leg, a short ride away from tasty food, cold beverages, and soft pillows in Big Bear.

CAMP-TO-CAMP MILEAGE
Onyx Summit to Camp 6 . . . . 1.1
Camp 6 to Arrastre Trail Camp 3.0
Arrastre Trail Camp to Camp 7 . . . . 3.2

5 STATE HIGHWAY 18 TO HOLCOMB VALLEY ROAD

DISTANCE 12.5 miles

ELEVATION GAIN/LOSS
+2100/-1380 feet

HIGH POINT 7808 feet

CONNECTING TRAILS AND ROADS
State Highway 18, Holcomb Valley Road, Forest Service Road 3N69, Van Dusen Canyon Road, Cougar Crest Trail

ON THE TRAIL
Begin in a large parking area on the southeast side of **State Highway 18** and when the coast is clear, dart across to the other side, picking up the trail through a metal gate. Almost immediately, you're greeted with the lingering fragrance of pinyon pines—but you'll also find pockets of sage, yucca, beavertail cactus, Indian paintbrush, and desert mallow dotted along the rocky path. Enjoy intermittent views out to the dusty Antelope Valley to the north, gently ambling along mostly north-facing slopes until you cross an unnamed, unpaved road at 1.3 miles, then reach the paved eastern branch of **Holcomb Valley Road** at 2 miles. This is not the road you are looking for, so continue across on your way.

Look to the slopes in front of you to see Doble Mine perched on the hillside above. Just ahead at 2.5 miles, you'll reach an intersection with a use trail on your left, which leads down to **Doble Trail Camp**. Here, you'll find a solar toilet, fire ring,

picnic table, horse corral, trough, and a spigot ○ that is turned off in the colder months; inquire with rangers ahead of time to find out if it's on when you pass through. This isn't the most scenic spot to set up camp, but it'll do.

From here, ascend what I like to call The Path of the Twisted Ankle, a section of softball-sized chunky rock that will test even the strongest of tendons as you ascend. The upside is that as you make uphill progress, you earn views of the desert to the north, and to large, sometimes dry Baldwin Lake. This section boasts the biggest elevation gain for the rest of this leg, so pace yourself and enjoy walking through increasingly thicker tree cover filled with not just pinyon pines but also incense cedar, especially after you cross unpaved **Forest Service**

EASY ACCESS

Several access points exist throughout this leg (Holcomb Valley Road, Van Dusen Canyon Road, and Cougar Crest Trail) that will take you to (or near) the north shore of Big Bear Lake. It's important to note that this side of the lake is mostly residential and you'll still need to make your way around to Big Bear City or the resort town of Big Bear Lake if you want to shop for groceries or score a bed for the night.

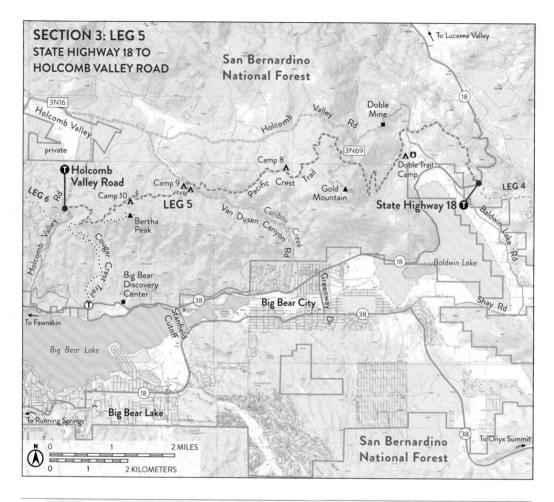

SECTION 3: LEG 5
STATE HIGHWAY 18 TO
HOLCOMB VALLEY ROAD

Road 3N69 at 4.7 miles to begin curving around **Gold Mountain** to the south.

Make your way back around to the north-facing slopes and saunter along gentle, duff-softened tread. The tree cover offers that awesome tucked-in-the-forest feeling, but you also get occasional sightings of the desert far below. Soon enough, you head a bit more inland through some forested flats

around 6.8 miles, and you'll start to spot possible shady campsites (**Camp 8**) tucked under the trees on the right. Round a gully and look down below you to see Van Dusen Canyon Road carving a path; you'll cross it soon enough. You'll also start seeing the green line of willows marking **Caribou Creek**'s path just north of the road; you'll reach it at 8.9 miles. This source can dry up in summer

Earn final views toward the San Bernardino Mountains' tall peaks as you gaze across Big Bear Lake.

heat, but whether there's water or not, there's a small camp located in some sandy clearings on your left just before crossing the creek on a small footbridge, and an even larger camp on your right just after the bridge (**Camp 9**).

Just ahead is **Van Dusen Canyon Road** at 9 miles. If you filled up at the creek, your pack will feel exponentially heavier as you start heading uphill again, but at least it's shady (many thanks to Jeffrey pine, incense cedar, and scrub oak) and things flatten out again soon enough. If you passed on creekside camping, but are feeling a bit sleepy, you'll find several small, decent camps beginning at 10.5 miles (**Camp 10**)—first on the left, near the completely obliterated remnants of a picnic table, then just ahead on your right under a big cedar, and finally again on your left near another ghost of picnic tables past.

Quite suddenly, you score a panoramic view of Holcomb Valley, a green flat ringed with hillsides denuded by mining activities. Your own surroundings start to change here as well, with manzanita, mountain mahogany, and an assortment of

wildflowers studding the white rock. You get an entirely different vantage point soon enough as you reach an unpaved road at 11.2 miles, signed on the left for Bertha Peak; unless you want to pay her a visit, continue straight toward a large cedar and look out to the south for increasingly great views across Big Bear Lake, including the town itself, plus a line of peaks in the distant San Gorgonio Wilderness, from left to right: San Gorgonio Mountain, Jepson Peak, Charlton Peak, and then the many high points forming the spine of lengthy San Bernardino Mountain.

The vistas get even better as you approach the **Cougar Crest Trail** junction, which you'll reach at 11.6 miles. You might see day hikers here since this path drops just under 2.5 miles to State Highway 38 on the north shore of Big Bear Lake and links up to the popular Big Bear Discovery Center just up the road. Unless you've had enough of this hiking stuff, make a hairpin turn to the right and begin the final descent toward your endpoint. Pass another unpaved road at 11.9 miles, and look for markers to make sure you stay on your route; it

129

can get a little confusing with all of the unmarked intersecting paths in this area. Wind down through boulders, manzanita, and cedars to reach the western branch of **Holcomb Valley Road** (Forest Route 2N09 or Polique Canyon Road on some maps) at 12.5 miles. Unfortunately, there is no parking available here, so you'll either have to make a left and walk south 2.3 miles toward Big Bear Lake or head straight across to start the next leg. You know which one I'd pick.

CAMP-TO-CAMP MILEAGE

State Highway 18 to Doble Trail Camp 2.5
Doble Trail Camp to Camp 8............... 4.3
Camp 8 to Camp 9 .... 2.1
Camp 9 to Camp 10 .... 1.6

6 HOLCOMB VALLEY ROAD TO BENCH TRAIL CAMP

DISTANCE 16.1 miles

ELEVATION GAIN/LOSS
+1150/-3500 feet

HIGH POINT 7894 feet

CONNECTING ROADS
Holcomb Valley Road, Forest Service Road 3N12, Forest Service Road 3N14, Crab Flats Road

ON THE TRAIL

Begin this leg at the PCT's junction with Holcomb Valley Road, surrounded by a perfectly Southern Californian assortment of fragrant Jeffrey pines, mountain mahogany, Indian paintbrush, sagebrush, and black oaks. If you're not too busy admiring the beautiful, shady surrounds, be sure to glance over to your left to spot shimmering Big Bear Lake and the San Bernardino Mountain ridge dominating to the south. Make a gentle ascent on soft tread to reach a broad forested saddle at 1.4 miles that holds a few clearings for tents (**Camp 11**) to the right of the trail. From here, snag views down to the green flats of Holcomb Valley before curving around the northern slopes of **Delamar Mountain** to reach unpaved **Forest Service Road 3N12** at 2.6 miles.

Cross another dirt road just ahead and make sure to look back wistfully at the beautiful, shade-giving pines since you're about to spend some significant time in the sun courtesy of the charred remnants of the 2007 Butler 2 Fire, an extremely destructive blaze that scorched over 14,000 acres. You have ground cover in the way of sparse chaparral (and blowdowns), but not much else. On a hot, sunny day, this segment might sap your energy, especially as you have to duck into deep folds that add mileage, but the silver lining is that as you traverse these crumbly, denuded north-facing slopes, you have unobstructed views down to the green path carved by Holcomb Valley and out to Lake Arrowhead and the distant San Gabriel Mountains peeking out to the west.

Salvation arrives at 6.8 miles when you drop down into a valley that offers a perfect rest stop,

WATER ALERT!

If you're thirsty and can't wait for the spigot **O** at **Little Bear Springs Trail Camp** 6.8 miles into this leg, it's possible to detour just under 1 mile south along Forest Service Road 3N12 to reach **Delamar Spring O**. There's no telling whether it will be running or not, so most hikers just keep on trucking.

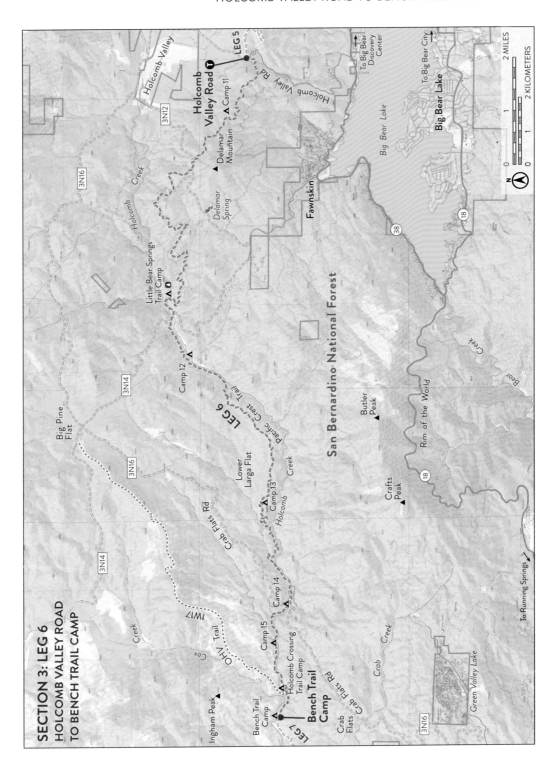

SECTION 3: LEG 6
HOLCOMB VALLEY ROAD
TO BENCH TRAIL CAMP

Fire is an unfortunate reality along Southern California's PCT. Learn to appreciate the unique beauty of nature's post-burn reclamation.

whether you want to pause for a few minutes or overnight. Here, you'll find a solar toilet on your left, then walk ahead just a bit farther to arrive at **Little Bear Springs Trail Camp** via a use trail on your right. Here you'll find a fire ring, picnic table, horse corral, trough, and a spigot ⬤. The burn definitely stole the charm from this spot, but you'll still find a few decent places to lay your head.

Continue descending to parallel Holcomb Creek, whose refreshment you'll reach very soon. Until then, pay attention—you'll reach unpaved **Forest Service Road 3N14** (Coxey Truck Trail) at 7.3 miles. Hang a right to join it momentarily, then quickly depart to cross a pipe gate onto single-track on the left. This is your first access point for **Holcomb Creek** ⬤, which may run dry in summer, although you can

typically find pools along the way even if this is the case. You're still in the burn area now, but you're also in a riparian zone filled with large boulders and a smattering of pinyon pines, willows, Indian paintbrush, snow plant, thistle, rabbitbrush, and ceanothus.

Your first water crossing ⬤ occurs at 8.1 miles. There's a small selection of shady campsites (**Camp 12**) on the left above the stream before popping across. The water here draws in all manner of wildlife—I've seen chipmunks, western fence lizards, and blue jays, but this area also serves as a stomping ground for bigger creatures like bobcats, mule deer, and mountain lions. Try not to focus on the latter as you weave up through large boulders, eventually leaving the creek behind to get high and dry. The ground you're crossing is full of sand, sage, and manzanita, and not much else. Well, except for rattlesnakes—not to alarm you, but I've seen more of these guys sunbathing in this section of the PCT than anywhere else, including the deserts south and north of here.

Stomp your way along to clear any slithery residents from your path, cross an unpaved road just after the 10-mile mark, and continue through the barren surrounds of **Lower Larga Flat**, scoring views out to the north, where uniquely rounded boulder formations summon visions of Joshua Tree National Park (if you've never been, perhaps this will inspire you to schedule a visit). Rejoice at 11.3 miles when you reach a high point on the left offering a bit of shade and a small camping area (**Camp 13**). From here, you descend with gusto down a soft, sandy, somewhat slippery path, motivated by scattered wildflowers in late spring, some oak-provided shade, and the sound of Holcomb Creek burbling below. You'll cross an intermittent stream that might be dry, but more reliable liquid finally appears when you reach an incredibly beautiful crossing of **Holcomb Creek** at 13.5 miles. While winged pests attempt to threaten your happiness, swat them away and enjoy the bucolic surrounds as the cold water cascades over rounded boulders under the shade of willows, cottonwoods, and pines.

It may be difficult to tear yourself away, but you won't be gone from the water for long. Hop across stones, then head uphill to reach paved **Crab Flats Road** 0.1 mile up. You'll be near the creek for a while here, so water is never that far away—unless you're traveling through in late summer or during a drought year. If you'd like to stay for a bit, find a small camping area (**Camp 14**) at 13.8 miles on your right, with easy access to the wet stuff; one or two more sandy spots await just ahead. Cross the creek once more, making a short ascent,

then dip back down to find a huge sandy area on your left at 14.6 miles offering plentiful soft camping (**Camp 15**) and water access. I once saw someone string a hammock down here—it's pretty idyllic.

Cross a side trickle, then head back up on the sunny slopes only to drop right back down at 15.2 miles for yet another creek crossing. If you're getting sleepy, there are two more bedtime options ahead. The first comes about 0.3 mile after your last creek crossing, when you see a use trail leading off to the right; this path leads to **Holcomb Crossing Trail Camp**, a pine-shaded spot offering plentiful camping, a few fire rings, and access to relatively nearby **Holcomb Creek**.

Not too long after this, you'll cross a rough road (**OHV Trail 1W17**) that heads right toward Big Pine Flat, but you'll continue straight up through intermittent pines and scrub oak to reach a side trail on your right at 16.1 miles leading to **Bench Trail Camp**. There's not much here other than wide open space and nearby access to **Holcomb Creek**, but if relative solitude is what you seek, this shady outpost is a great answer unless you come through on a summer weekend, when you might have to play nice and share.

CAMP-TO-CAMP MILEAGE

Holcomb Valley Road to Camp 11 . . . . 1.4
Camp 11 to Little Bear Springs Trail Camp . . . 5.4
Little Bear Springs Trail Camp to Camp 12 . . . 1.3
Camp 12 to Camp 13 . . . . 3.2
Camp 13 to Camp 14 . . . . 2.5
Camp 14 to Camp 15 . . . . 0.8
Camp 15 to Holcomb Crossing Trail Camp . . . 0.9
Holcomb Crossing Trail Camp to Bench
    Trail Camp 0.6

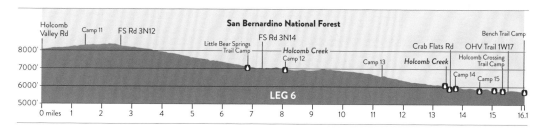

7 BENCH TRAIL CAMP TO DEEP CREEK HOT SPRINGS

DISTANCE 13.3 miles

ELEVATION GAIN/LOSS
+1720/-3380 feet

HIGH POINT 5328 feet

CONNECTING TRAILS AND ROADS
Splinters Cabin Connector, Devils Hole
OHV Trail 2W01

ON THE TRAIL

You've had a good run of camping opportunities to this point, but I'm sorry to say that it gets a lot trickier throughout this leg and the next due to a stretch of somewhat inhospitable landscape and the narrow canyon that hosts Deep Creek, where you'll spend the bulk of your time. Apologies in advance—you're in for some long days. The good news is that the general trend is downhill, so as long as your knees don't wobble, tacking on some extra mileage shouldn't be too much of an issue.

As you head uphill from the **Bench Trail Camp** junction, the San Gabriel Mountains loom to the west, closer than they were earlier in this

NO BEDS AT THE INN

The next possible campsite past **Bench Trail Camp** is located an exhausting 20 miles ahead. While you'll see plenty of obvious sites at the first bridge spanning Deep Creek and at the end of this leg near Deep Creek Hot Springs, along with several rough bivy spots scratched into deeper gullies, none of these are actually legit spots since camping is not allowed within 1 mile of the creek. You risk incurring the wrath of the Forest Service if you plant your tent in any of these places.

section, but still plenty far away (for now). Enjoy some dappled shade, reaching your first water access (after the camp) 1.2 miles in when you pass a spring **O** on the left side; however, this may run dry in the heat of summer. The tree cover becomes sparse, and the footing, looser as you continue through remnants of the 2003 Old Fire (an arson-caused blaze that resulted in five deaths, destroyed 1000 homes, and burned over 91,000 acres) and the smaller 2007 Slide Fire.

Soon enough, the outlook improves, with green hills to the west and several giant gouges opening in the earth in front of you. While you can't see it yet, the yawning chasm directly in front guards **Deep Creek O**, and you'll reach its refreshing waters at 3.8 miles after descending through a lush band of greenery on a few quick switchbacks. Actually, you'll reach a bridge spanning the creek; if you want to access the water itself, hop on a use trail to the right to descend to its banks. This is a wonderful place to fill your tanks, enjoy a refreshing swim, or fish for rainbow or brown trout—Deep Creek is actually a designated Wild Trout Water! The area is full of obvious tent sites, although sadly, it's not legal to camp within 1 mile of Deep Creek. Regardless, this is a beautiful place to spend some time.

After you cross the bridge over Deep Creek, the trail continues to the right, but you can make a left to head about 0.1 mile up a small connector trail to reach **Splinters Cabin Day Use Area**, which offers an alternate access point to this leg if coming from Lake Arrowhead (and equipped with a high-clearance vehicle). Here, you'll find a parking area (Adventure Pass required), garbage receptacles, vault toilets, and a small pavilion filled with picnic tables. The latter marks the remnants of the "Cabin" itself, originally built in 1922 by Le Roy Raymond and christened as a sort of joke related to his wife's commentary on his carpentry skills. Otherwise, enjoy the sound of frogs and crickets (less so, the sound of buzzing mosquitos) as you continue your trek on the other side, now changing direction to head north. The

entire remainder of this leg is spent traversing the slopes above (and sometimes next to) Deep Creek. Shade grows more intermittent and the trail underfoot grows thinner and crumblier—I actually slipped in this section, pulling a butt muscle in the process, and let me tell you, when added to some hot-weather induced chafing, my buns weren't particularly happy this day. Speaking of heat—you're going to want to slather on the sunblock and toss on a hat, because shade becomes infrequent, with chaparral becoming the dominant vegetation from here on out.

Deep Creek teases from below as you traverse the sunny, dry slopes above.

The farther you go, the better views you get both up and down canyon, where you can watch the creek course below the steep walls. There are a lot of little use trails (human and animal)

WATER ALERT!

The Forest Service warns that the hot springs here may contain not just massive quantities of fecal coliform bacteria (this is what happens when you poop too close to waterways), but also *Naegleria fowleri*, a gnarly "brain-eating" amoeba that can cause primary amebic meningoencephalitis, a potentially fatal attack on the central nervous system. While it's long been recommended to avoid drinking water directly from the hot springs and to keep your head above water (the amoeba enters through your nostrils), many longtime hot spring–goers brush off the threat and happily submerge themselves in the warm pools; I've never heard of anyone contracting the amoeba here and my own brain is wonderfully intact (I think). Perhaps a more pertinent warning is that several people have died in recent years after jumping into the relatively shallow waters from nearby cliffs—play it smart.

angling down the precipitous slopes toward tantalizing swimming and fishing holes, but your first easy access comes at 6.6 miles, when you reach a junction with unpaved **Devils Hole OHV Trail 2W01**. You'll notice a few benches here, a short path to the right that offers easy access to **Deep Creek ⊙**, and an interpretive sign about the arroyo toad, which hops around Southern California's riparian areas, burrowing into sandy soil. Figures estimate that these once-prolific amphibians have lost about 75 percent of their habitat due to a range of factors including drought, fires, mining, off-road vehicle use, water control measures, and general human encroachment, and they are now classified as an endangered species.

Once you've had a rest and paid your respects to our amphibian friends, cross the road and continue up along the slopes. There are a few moderate climbs and descents, but overall, the trail remains fairly level. You'll round a gully over a bridge at 7.8 miles, with a bench on the near side offering a pleasant rest spot. If you've spent the last few miles staring at your feet, you may be somewhat shocked to look up and notice that the canyon walls are much sandier—and even sunnier than before. The high and dry route takes you frustratingly far above the tempting blue pools below.

If you're going crazy in the sun, rejoice when you enter a shady gully at 11 miles; this is home to seasonal **Willow Creek** ⊙, which usually runs dry by summer. Even if there's no water here, giant boulders, willows, and sycamores make this a heavenly grotto in which to take a lengthy break before plunging back onto the sunny slopes beyond. In another mile, you start to notice use trails descending to the canyon bottom; while all will take you to Deep Creek, wait until you reach an obvious spot at 13.3 miles that offers access to popular **Deep Creek Hot Springs** ⊙ and its myriad pools—any of the regulars will happily list out the names and temperatures of each if you so desire.

One important note: Deep Creek Hot Springs is traditionally considered a clothing optional area. While you're in no way required to doff your duds to enjoy the water, don't take offense when others do. Even on a weekday, even on the hottest afternoon, you will see plenty of people—clothed and otherwise—scattered around this area, picnicking,

listening to music, teetering across a slackline, swimming, and soaking in the small rock pools created along the creek's edge. Most of these folks come in via a short hike through private property on the north side of the creek, although you'll see plenty of your smelly PCT brethren in late spring. The hot springs become party central on weekends, with drug and alcohol use being fairly common—sadly, despite regulars' efforts, so is littering (including ubiquitous toilet paper blooms). For that reason, you may want to gather water back upstream or farther ahead on the trail. While it's quite obvious that many people camp here overnight, it's technically not allowed; your next possible camping is 6.7 miles ahead—so enjoy a nice soak, then be on your way.

CAMP-TO-CAMP MILEAGE
There are no viable campsites on this leg.

8 DEEP CREEK HOT SPRINGS TO CLEGHORN ROAD

DISTANCE 21 miles

ELEVATION GAIN/LOSS
+2760/-2910 feet

HIGH POINT 3711 feet

CONNECTING TRAILS AND ROADS
State Highway 173, Mojave River Forks Connector Trail, Forest Service Road 2N33, Cleghorn Road

ON THE TRAIL
Say goodbye to all of your new, possibly naked, friends at **Deep Creek Hot Springs** ⊙ and continue on your way along equally exposed slopes. The tread thins out and gets a bit mushy in here as you begin your descent, but a pair of trekking poles will help you navigate the sketchier bits. At 1.3 miles, dip into a sharp gully where you'll

find a seasonal stream ⊙, which may be reduced to stagnant pools in summer. It's possible to walk a bit farther back, steering clear of the plentiful poison oak, to find a small waterfall that may offer better opportunity to slake your thirst.

Just ahead, you'll notice a small, colorful bridge spanning Deep Creek. Continue down a few switchbacks along even messier tread that at times feels like a mere *suggestion* of trail to reach this rainbow-painted pathway at 2 miles and commence a switch to the opposite slopes. The desert suddenly feels closer, especially on a hot day—even more so if a rattlesnake crosses your path. Slithering intrusions aside, you'll eventually notice some graffiti down in the creek bed below, where the relics of past mining activity combine with more modern intrusions. Around 4.3 miles, you'll round a curve to find that the canyon suddenly bursts open—you're now looking over the **Mojave River Forks**

ALTERNATE ROUTE

Mojave River Forks Reservoir marks the spot where Deep Creek joins the West Fork Mojave River. During times of high rainfall, water here may actually flood the trail, requiring a 2.9-mile detour—it's not advised to walk through the area when this happens since quicksand may develop. From the PCT atop the spillway, pick up a paved access road that will take you across the dam. From here, you'll make a left onto Arrowhead Lake Road and another left onto State Highway 173. The PCT appears just as the road turns from paved to unpaved; you'll make a right to continue your trek.

Reservoir, usually dry, but on rare occasion wet enough that the trail below is submerged—see the sidebar for an alternate route to avoid floating downstream.

Whether you're looking at dry sand (most likely) or standing water (less likely), you'll also notice a concrete spillway and neighboring dam; head down some switchbacks to reach the former—but perhaps take some photos first since it's a pretty awesome sight. You'll cross the spillway at 5.1 miles, picking up the trail on the opposite side. Keep your eyes peeled for trail markers leading across the bottom of the dam and then across to the willows edging what is now technically the **West Fork Mojave River O**, which you'll wade across at 5.6 miles.

Continue along the opposite bank, likely feeling sunny and sweaty in contrast to the lush, cottonwood-enabled shade just below. You'll reach

State Highway 173 at 6.3 miles, unpaved to the left of the trail, paved to the right. You continue straight to begin a lengthy traverse of the winding chaparral-clad slopes above wide, flat Summit Valley. If your legs can do no more, look to your right around 6.7 miles to spot a use trail leading to a small dirt clearing that will fit about two tents **(Camp 16)**. I speak from personal experience—even though the spot itself isn't much to write home about, watching the sunrise here is a pretty sweet deal.

From here, waste no time gaining elevation. The uphill provides for views not just back to the spillway and dam but also west toward the San Gabriel Mountains, which are especially pretty if clouds have settled in the pass between their eastern end and the San Bernardino Mountains (the range you're navigating). At 8.2 miles, you'll round

PILOT FIRE

The Pilot Fire sparked in August 2016, burning just over 8000 acres in the San Bernardino National Forest. The PCT was affected between its eastern junction with State Highway 173 and just before the eastern state park boundary, although the trail was closed well into the Deep Creek drainage during active firefighting. Although the PCT was quickly reopened in this area, the landscape was completely charred in some places, a stark contrast to the thick chaparral that previously dominated these slopes. Some campsites are less attractive now, stripped of their vegetative surrounds, but the upside is that you'll have an unobstructed view for sunset and sunrise.

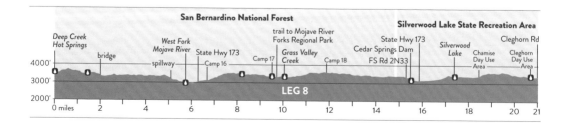

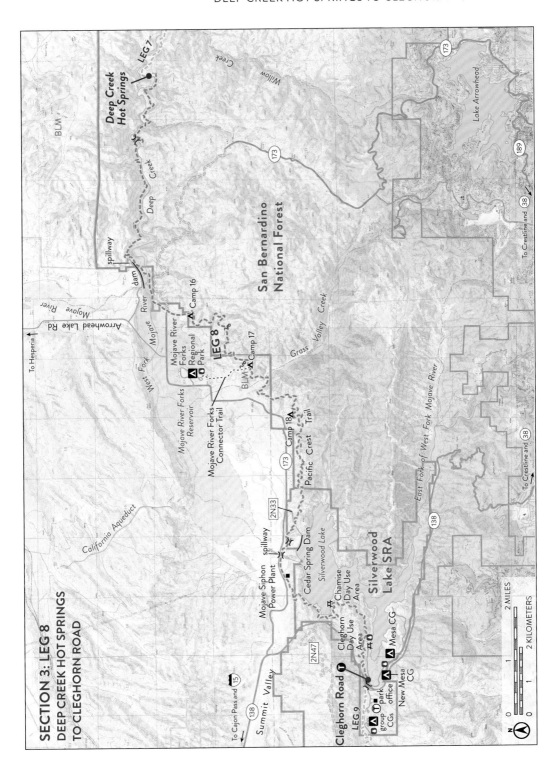

SECTION 3: LEG 8
DEEP CREEK HOT SPRINGS
TO CLEGHORN ROAD

A view of the Mojave River Dam awaits as you exit Deep Creek's narrow canyon walls.

a gully that used to sprout with plant life from a spring seep 🄾 on your left; the 2016 Pilot Fire stripped the area of its vegetation, but rest assured that where there's water, there will once again be greenery. If this seep is dry or stagnant, continue ahead to find another spot on your right at 9.4 miles. The spring 🄾 here used to flow from a bit of tubing, but that was destroyed in the fire—time will tell if it's replaced. If you'd like to snooze, there is a bivy spot on the right just before you hit the spring (**Camp 17**).

Just 0.2 mile ahead, you'll reach a junction with a trail that descends about 0.75 mile to **Mojave River Forks Regional Park**, where you'll find water 🄾, bathrooms, showers, picnic tables, fire rings, and camping. Although it didn't burn the campground itself, the fire exposed all of the animal trails in this area, so it can be difficult to stay on the correct path—aim for a large, green tank in the distance since the campground is located just northeast of this landmark. Unless you feel like parting with your hard-earned cash, continue on, where you'll hop onto an unpaved road for a bit. At 10 miles, you'll cross the seasonal flow of **Grass Valley Creek** 🄾, which may dry up in the summer. Leave the road just ahead to continue heading uphill.

If the spillway and dam didn't provide enough human impact for you, the buzz of power lines overhead and the sound of cars below will really bring it home that there are dwindling options for the kind of solitude you enjoyed in the higher mountains. Cross an unpaved road at 10.7 miles, then intersect a use trail on the right about 1.2 miles ahead to find room for one tent (**Camp 18**) in a small clearing perched high above Summit Valley. Wiggle around the hillsides for a bit more, crossing a boundary marker sign at 14.5 miles—you are now leaving the **San Bernardino National Forest** (and Pilot Fire burn scar) behind for the remainder of this leg and entering **Silverwood Lake State Recreation Area**. Dispersed camping is not allowed within its boundary, so stick to official campgrounds here if you want to overnight.

Rabbits and horned lizards cross your path as cows graze in the valley below. Pop across paved **Forest Service Road 2N33** at 15.2 miles and turn a corner to look upon a wall of rocks and boulders—this is the **Cedar Springs Dam**; you'll walk beneath it to cross a concrete bridge over its outflow. It's possible to collect water ⬤ here, but it can get pretty scummy. This next bit can be a little confusing; make sure to keep your eyes

peeled for trail markers. You'll pass through an unattractive area featuring some large metal cylinders then cross a paved road near some massive junipers to walk along **State Highway 173** past the **Mojave Siphon Power Plant** and the Cedar Springs Dam's spillway. Rejoin the trail on the left side at 16.4 miles after taking the obligatory photo of this giant waterslide.

Follow along some less-than-scenic barbed wire fencing and the power plant's driveway, obeying the No Trespassing signs posted along the route. Cross several unpaved roads in the next 0.5 mile, gaining a bit of elevation under a shade-giving smattering of scrub oak. Once you crest the hill ahead, you're in for a treat—**Silverwood Lake** sits

A LONG JOURNEY

Silverwood Lake is a man-made reservoir created in 1971 by damming the waters of the West Fork Mojave River. It is part of California's lengthy (and contentious) water management history, and is named after W. E. Silverwood, a local advocate for the California State Water Project, which was created to bring wet stuff from the north down to Southern California. The water you're looking at traveled to this point via the California Aqueduct; if you continue on the PCT, you'll eventually walk right next to the water that will soon become Silverwood Lake!

pretty below, surrounded by a picturesque array of peaks. Snap some shots, then wind downhill to walk along the water's edge, passing a sweet little beach ◑ via a use trail on your left at 17.4 miles that makes a perfect rest spot (and a great opportunity to top off your water supply). Just after this, make a left to join an unpaved road, then quickly depart it to continue your lakeside walk.

You'll eventually dip slightly inland for a bit, passing a use trail on your left at 18.3 miles that descends to the **Chamise Day Use Area**, where you'll find vault toilets, picnic tables, and garbage receptacles—but no water. Continue through scrub oak and chamise to reach an unpaved road at 20.7 miles; if you turn left here, you'll drop down to the **Cleghorn Day Use Area**, another day use spot that features similar amenities to Chamise, but with the bonus of drinking water access ◑. Continue on the trail to join a paved bicycle path and cross a short bridge that might offer another opportunity for water collection. If you want to bed down for the night, make a left here on the paved road to wind around to the **New Mesa**

and **Mesa Campgrounds**, which offer drive-up and "hike and bike" sites; otherwise stay right to continue on the bike path. You end this leg at the 21-mile mark, standing at the trail's meeting with paved **Cleghorn Road** near a gate, PCT marker, and sign for **State Highway 138** hovering almost directly above. If you continue west on Cleghorn Road, you'll reach the park's office, which also offers bathrooms, water ◑, and paved parking—although if you're planning to use this as one end of a car shuttle for a multiday hike, you'll want to prearrange overnight parking with a ranger, so you don't end up with a hefty ticket.

CAMP-TO-CAMP MILEAGE

Deep Creek Hot Springs to Camp 16	6.7
Camp 16 to Camp 17	2.7
Camp 17 to Mojave River Forks Regional Park	0.2
Mojave River Forks Regional Park to Camp 18	2.3
Camp 18 to New Mesa and Mesa Campgrounds	8.9

9 CLEGHORN ROAD TO CAJON PASS

DISTANCE 12.9 miles

ELEVATION GAIN/LOSS
+2410/-2750 feet

HIGH POINT 4163 feet

CONNECTING ROADS
Cleghorn Road, Wagon Train Road

ON THE TRAIL

Although this leg begins at an unappealing chain link fence near an off-ramp for **State Highway 138**, I promise it'll make up for the less than appealing start by the time you reach the end. Begin by walking along the right side of paved **Cleghorn**

Road and under the freeway, looking for a brown sign just ahead on the right side of the road; as you approach, you'll see that it points toward Interstate 15 and Guffy Campground (albeit with incorrect mileage)—pick up the trail and head on your way.

A small drainage to the left has a few willows in it, but otherwise, you're mostly surrounded by manzanita, chaparral, and the sweet, sweet sound of traffic all around. You're walking parallel to the western chunk of **Silverwood Lake State Recreation Area**, so you might also hear some happy campers partying in the group sites down below. Cross an unpaved road to pass through a small area with picnic tables, grills, a horse corral, and possibly even a portable toilet, then shortly after, you'll hit a paved road that leads down to the campgrounds on your left. Flirt with the road

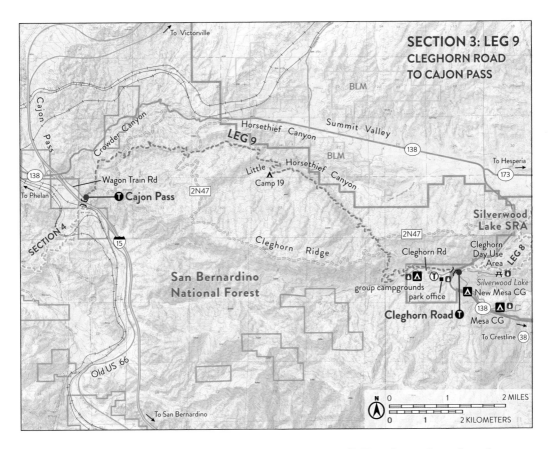

for a moment, then pass one last junction on your left at 0.8 mile—this is your final chance to visit the nearby campgrounds to use a toilet or grab

WATER ALERT!

If you need to tank up on water, head up Cleghorn Road 0.2 mile to reach the Silverwood Lake State Recreation Area's park office where you'll find restrooms (with flush toilets!) and water during regular business hours. You can also walk along the trail for a bit to find a few group campground access points within the first mile. Other than this, there are no reliable water sources along this leg. If you're traveling through on a warm day, be extra cautious and carry a little extra.

some water . From here, it's up along the sunny slopes to leave behind the park grounds and enter the **San Bernardino National Forest** at 1.1 miles; you'll know you're there by a small sign and a gentle whiff of solitude.

Shade options are few and far between on this leg, so take them while you can—gullies, in particular, tend to offer some cooler nooks under pockets of scrub oak and sycamore, although they may also threaten any exposed skin with poison oak—learn to identify this three-leaved menace in any season. Around 2.2 miles, you'll finish ascending above the flats bisected by Cleghorn Road, and this spot offers a nice vantage point back to Silverwood Lake, especially pretty in the early morning, when the surrounding peaks stand in silhouette. Once you've soaked in the views, head north along steeper slopes to pass through a pipe gate and

Walk along narrow ridgelines to score incredible views across Cajon Pass into the San Gabriel Mountains.

join unpaved **Forest Service Road 2N47** at 3.3 miles—you're now walking along lofty **Cleghorn Ridge**. Enjoy a few last views out to the lake, then make a left to rejoin the trail just before the unpaved road splits ahead.

Wander into a gully at 4.1 miles to come through a dense thicket of willows guarding

BLUE CUT FIRE

The Blue Cut Fire made a devastating run through the Cajon Pass area in August 2016, burning over 36,000 acres. Many homes and buildings were destroyed, railroad lines were affected, and about 20 miles of the PCT and its viewshed were burned to some extent between this leg and the next. As of this writing, the trail was open throughout the entire burn area, if a bit bleak in the fire's immediate aftermath. Still, I have no doubt that Mother Nature will work her magic within the next few years to begin restoring the once abundant chaparral to its former glory.

a seasonal flow $\mathbf{O}$ that dries up in the warmer months. Keep an ear and eye out for rattlesnakes sunning on the chunky boulders shoved into the slopes here, although you're more likely to see western fence lizards darting around in the sun. Immediately below you sits Little Horsethief Canyon, with (not so little) Horsethief Canyon cutting through wide Summit Valley just beyond that. There are a million folds in the earth here, and you will seemingly duck into all of them, most noticeably when you make an obvious turn at about 6 miles to descend into **Little Horsethief Canyon**. This flattish, boulder-dotted area is not the prettiest, especially once it browns out in the summer months, but it offers the only camping option in this leg at 6.6 miles, when you pass a pair of unattractive dirt clearings on either side of the trail (**Camp 19**).

After you finish your detour around the canyon, it's back out and up to the north-facing slopes. The effects of the 2016 Blue Cut Fire become apparent as you continue ahead since you're now walking through a portion of its eastern boundary. While chamise and manzanita still make an appearance, you'll also encounter plenty

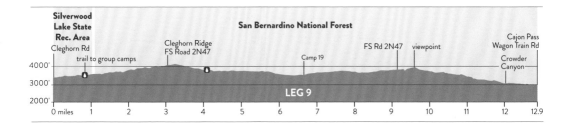

of devegetated slopes, with the burn scar becoming more prominent as you near this leg's end. Still, there's magic ahead.

Pop across a small ridgeline, then continue through remaining patches of chamise and manzanita. At 9.1 miles, hop back onto **Forest Service Road 2N47** for a moment to cross straight under the looming power transformers and look for the brown trail marker ahead. Just as you're wondering when the monotony will end, *boom!*—0.3 mile ahead you round a corner to face not just the towering San Gabriel Mountains across Cajon Pass, but also an incredibly dramatic cliff guarding a steep drop-off. This should put some pep in your step as you finish the last bit of noticeable uphill.

Once you top out, the views are spectacular. Forget about Interstate 15 down below—the landscape here is absolutely captivating as you descend to walk along a series of squiggly, distinct ridgelines, each offering amazing photo opportunities—proof that this leg wasn't just full of chaparral (or its remnants) and dust. Eventually you drop down from the most dramatic portions to cross a series of unpaved roads beginning at 11.4 miles. You can hear the highway below, a strangely welcome sign on a hot day that you're getting closer to milkshakes—I mean, to this leg's end.

Around 12.1 miles, dip down into **Crowder Canyon**. Once the canyon narrows, it not only becomes more beautiful, but also shadier. Rest underneath the towering rock walls, and possibly even score some water if you come through during a wet period. It's hard to believe you're so close to a major freeway, but it's only a short jog ahead

FRIES WITH THAT?

For many hikers, the end of this leg (and this section) is pure magic, not because it's particularly pretty or peaceful (hello, Interstate 15), but because it's within walking distance of not just a gas station and a hotel but also (more importantly) a McDonald's, whose calorie-dense presence is announced here on a trail mileage sign. When the restaurant was damaged in the Blue Cut Fire, worried hikers wondered if this would be the end of trail-necessitated gluttony as they knew it, but as of this writing, repair work is underway. Thus, if Hiker Hunger calls (or if you want to tank up on water before the 22.5 mile dry stretch ahead), take a right here to end up on Wagon Train Road, a parking-friendly frontage road that leads to as many french fries and milkshakes as your stomach and budget allow.

to reach this leg's end at 12.9 miles, where the trail passes **Wagon Train Road** to the right, just before making a left to duck under **Interstate 15** at **Cajon Pass** to begin the next leg. You can't miss the famous mileage sign pointing out that while the next leg's end, Guffy Campground, is still quite a long ways to go, the nearest McDonald's is only 0.4 mile away. Choose wisely.

CAMP-TO-CAMP MILEAGE
Cleghorn Road to Camp 19 . . . . 6.6

CAJON PASS TO AGUA DULCE

THIS SECTION LIFTS you away from the Vegas-bound traffic on Interstate 15 into the fresh alpine air of the San Bernardino and Angeles National Forests, then down to the edge of the Mojave Desert via a rollercoaster romp across the crest of the San Gabriel Mountains. Despite its proximity to Los Angeles, only small pieces of this section see much traffic outside of PCT hikers, so you'll likely have the incredible peak-packed views (mostly) to yourself as you trek the forested heights.

Bookend your trip with two sets of freaky rock formations created by seismic activity along the infamous San Andreas Fault (and its neighbors), starting with the tilted sandstone fins of the Mormon Rocks and ending with the similarly slanted Vasquez Rocks, which have served as backdrop to a number of films and TV shows, including *Star Trek*, *Planet of the Apes*, and *Battlestar Galactica*. In between these geologic wonders, you'll gain (and eventually lose) some impressive elevation, wandering through fragrant chaparral before ascending into a mixed conifer forest, which includes a small grove of ancient limber pines near Mount Baden-Powell, the section's high point.

Although the first 22.5 miles of this section are waterless, you'll have plenty of opportunities to fill up after that—from the hiker-friendly town of Wrightwood to the numerous campgrounds and springs you'll pass along the way. However, many of these sources peter out by late summer, possibly earlier in a drought year. Like many portions of Southern California, this section sees a lot of fire activity. As a result, you'll not only notice a landscape in constant transition, but you'll also likely encounter an affectionately named nemesis: poodle-dog bush. This burn area resident makes your skin itch with a fury, so prepare to dance around it to avoid scratching your way up the trail.

DISTANCE 112.6 miles

STATE DISTANCE 341.9–454.5 miles

ELEVATION GAIN/LOSS +17,680/-18,200 feet

HIGH POINT 9226 feet

BEST TIME OF YEAR May–Nov

PCTA SECTION LETTER D

LAND MANAGERS San Bernardino National Forest (Front Country Ranger District, San Gabriel Mountains National Monument), Angeles National Forest (Los Angeles River Ranger District, San Gabriel River Ranger District, Santa Clara/Mojave Rivers Ranger District, Sheep Mountain Wilderness, Pleasant View Ridge Wilderness, San Gabriel Mountains National Monument), Devil's Punchbowl Natural Area, Vasquez Rocks Natural Area Park

PASSES AND PERMITS Adventure Pass may be required to park at certain trailheads within the San Bernardino and Angeles National Forests. California Campfire Permit.

MAPS AND APPS
- Halfmile's CA Section D
- USFS PCT Map #2 Transverse Ranges
- USGS Topo Quads: Cajon, Telegraph Peak, Mount San Antonio, Mescal Creek, Crystal Lake, Valyermo, Juniper Hills, Waterman Mountain, Pacifico Mountain, Acton, Agua Dulce
- Halfmile's PCT app
- Guthook's PCT app

Opposite: *A high perch along Blue Ridge offers spectacular views into the Sheep Mountain Wilderness.*

LEGS

1. Cajon Pass to Guffy Campground
2. Guffy Campground to Vincent Gap
3. Vincent Gap to Islip Saddle
4. Islip Saddle to Burkhart Trail
5. Burkhart Trail to Three Points Trailhead
6. Three Points Trailhead to Mill Creek Summit
7. Mill Creek Summit to Messenger Flats Campground
8. Messenger Flats Campground to Acton
9. Acton to Agua Dulce

ACCESS

Cajon Pass

From Los Angeles, head west on Interstate 10 toward San Bernardino and take exit 58A for Interstate 15 northbound toward Barstow and Las Vegas. In about 14.9 miles, take exit 131 to head east on CA 138 toward Palmdale and Silverwood Lake. Turn right onto CA 138 eastbound, and in just under 200 feet, turn right onto Wagon Train Road. The trailhead is located just over 0.5 mile down at the end of the road.

Agua Dulce

From Los Angeles, head north on Interstate 5 to State Highway 14 north (toward Palmdale and Lancaster). Continue on this road for 14.3 miles, exiting at Agua Dulce Canyon Road (exit 15). Head north for 1.8 miles, where you'll turn left to stay on the road (if you continue straight

here, the road becomes Escondido Canyon Road, and you'll soon see Vasquez Rocks Natural Area on your right). This section formally ends at the intersection of Agua Dulce Canyon Road and Darling Road, but you'll have an easier time finding parking outside of Vasquez Rocks Natural Area Park on Escondido Canyon Road; overnight parking is not allowed inside the park.

NOTES

Cities and Services

Near the southern trailhead, find a hotel, fast food, and gas stations; for more amenities, travel roughly 16 miles north to Hesperia or south to Fontana. The northern trailhead is located on the main drag of Agua Dulce, a small town that boasts a grocery store, several restaurants, and a post office.

Camping and Fire Restrictions

Camping is not allowed in Vasquez Rocks Natural Area Park without a group camping reservation or permission from rangers. Fires are allowed only in designated fire rings. Check for seasonal fire restrictions in San Bernardino and Angeles National Forests before heading out.

Water

The longest likely waterless stretches are the 22.5 miles between Cajon Pass and Guffy Campground, the 8.1 miles between the Lamel Spring turnoff and Little Jimmy Spring, the 8 miles between North Fork Ranger Station and Soledad

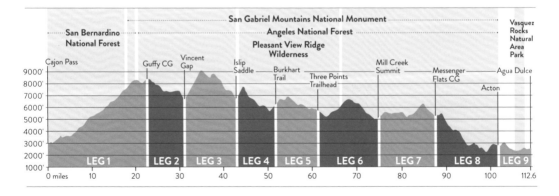

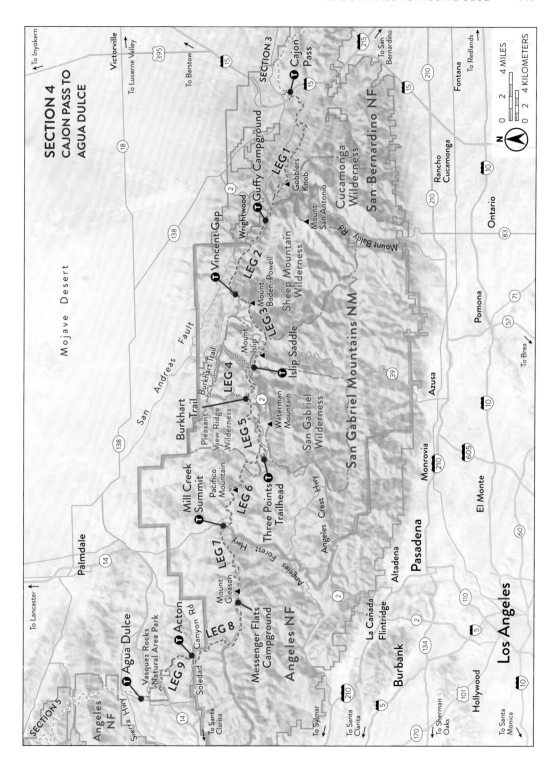

SECTION 4
CAJON PASS TO
AGUA DULCE

SUGGESTED ITINERARIES

Camps are either viewable from the trail or within a few tenths of a mile from the noted location unless otherwise specified in leg descriptions. Mileages here include the long-standing Endangered Species Detour as described in Leg 4, with an alternate itinerary if you choose the road walk option.

10 DAYS

		Miles
Day 1	Cajon Pass to Gobblers Knob Camp	15.3
Day 2	Gobblers Knob Camp to Blue Ridge Campground	10.1
Day 3	Blue Ridge Campground to Camp 4	12.2
Day 4	Camp 4 to South Fork Campground	11.7
Day 5	South Fork Campground to Little Rock Camp	15.3
Day 6	Little Rock Camp to Sulphur Springs Campground	12.8
Day 7	Sulphur Springs Campground to Camp 11	14.1
Day 8	Camp 11 to Messenger Flats Campground	9.7
Day 9	Messenger Flats Campground to Acton and North Los Angeles KOA	13.8
Day 10	Acton and North Los Angeles KOA to Agua Dulce	10.3

9 DAYS

Day 1	Cajon Pass to Gobblers Knob Camp	15.3
Day 2	Gobblers Knob Camp to Jackson Flat Group Campground	14.3
Day 3	Jackson Flat Group Campground to Little Jimmy Trail Camp	12.4
Day 4	Little Jimmy Trail Camp to Holcomb Canyon Camp	9.8
Day 5	Holcomb Canyon Camp to Cooper Canyon Trail Camp	14.2
Day 6	Cooper Canyon Trail Camp to Camp 8	16.5
Day 7	Camp 8 to Messenger Flats Campground	18.7
Day 8	Messenger Flats Campground to Acton and North Los Angeles KOA	13.8
Day 9	Acton and North Los Angeles KOA to Agua Dulce	10.3

8 DAYS

Day 1	Cajon Pass to Camp 1	19.8
Day 2	Camp 1 to Camp 3	15.3
Day 3	Camp 3 to South Fork Campground	14.2
Day 4	South Fork Campground to Cooper Canyon Trail Camp	16.7
Day 5	Cooper Canyon Trail Camp to Camp 8	16.5
Day 6	Camp 8 to Messenger Flats Campground	18.7
Day 7	Messenger Flats Campground to Acton and North Los Angeles KOA	13.8
Day 8	Acton and North Los Angeles KOA to Agua Dulce	10.3

8 DAYS (ROAD WALK OPTION)

Day 1	Cajon Pass to Gobblers Knob Camp	15.3
Day 2	Gobblers Knob Camp to Blue Ridge Campground	10.1
Day 3	Blue Ridge Campground to Little Jimmy Trail Camp	16.6
Day 4	Little Jimmy Trail Camp to Cooper Canyon Trail Camp	12.3
Day 5	Cooper Canyon Trail Camp to Camp 8	16.5
Day 6	Camp 8 to Messenger Flats Campground	18.7
Day 7	Messenger Flats Campground to Acton and North Los Angeles KOA	13.8
Day 8	Acton and North Los Angeles KOA to Agua Dulce	10.3

The tough climb from Cajon Pass rewards hikers with mountain magic.

Canyon Road (detouring to the KOA), and the 8.6 miles between Soledad Canyon Road and Vasquez Rocks Natural Area Park.

Hazards

In early season, snow may be present in higher elevations, especially on north-facing slopes; those around Mount Baden-Powell are especially steep, and serious accidents have occurred in this area. Tire chains may be required on mountain roads in winter. In late season (or during a low rainfall year), springs and creeks may run dry—check with rangers for current trail and water conditions before heading out. Black bears are present in small numbers in the upper elevations of the Angeles National Forest. While a bear canister isn't required, you'd be smart to at least hang your food. The trail crosses busy Angeles Crest Highway in many places—be especially careful in these spots.

Other

This section has a long history of fire activity, resulting in a proliferation of the skin-irritating (though adorably named) poodle-dog bush in former burn areas; although trail crews have worked hard to eradicate the plant, take care to avoid touching it.

1 CAJON PASS TO GUFFY CAMPGROUND

DISTANCE 22.5 miles

ELEVATION GAIN/LOSS
+6970/-1760 feet

HIGH POINT 8386 feet

CONNECTING TRAILS AND ROADS
Wagon Train Road, Swarthout Canyon
Road, Forest Service Road 3N28,
Forest Service Road 3N31,
North Backbone Trail, Acorn Trail,
Blue Ridge Truck Trail

ON THE TRAIL

Have you ever considered a side career moonlighting as a camel? Well, here's your chance to live out that dream! After leaving the roadside conveniences at **Cajon Pass**, your next reliable water source is 22.5 miles ahead at Guffy Campground, so load up on the clear stuff before heading out. It's a lengthy, waterless hike, but as long as you head out early, taking it slow and steady, you'll find yourself focusing more on the intriguing scenery than on the annoying hump on your back.

While it now hosts Vegas-bound Angelenos, Cajon Pass has long served as an important corridor, first to the indigenous Serrano, Paiute, and Cahuilla people, then to various ranchers, miners,

and settlers who passed through on the Mormon Trail, Santa Fe Trail, and other footpaths. In 1885, the California Southern Railroad wound its way through, and later, a segment of famed Route 66 did the same. The echoes of history ring loudly, although you might only hear the sound of honking horns as you pass through.

From this leg's start near the end of **Wagon Train Road**, you'll immediately notice the burn scar from the 2016 Blue Cut Fire, discussed in more detail in the previous leg. Except for a few patches of tenacious greenery, the charred echoes of that blaze follow you throughout much of this leg, finally receding about 15 miles in. Still, I think the expansive views and unique rock formations make this a worthy trek, and the scenery will only improve as chaparral begins to reemerge.

To begin, duck into a tunnel under one of Southern California's busiest freeways (**Interstate 15**), scoot under another overpass, then begin huffing upward. Drop down to cross an unpaved road, then pop through a corrugated metal tunnel under the **railroad tracks**. Head up a small embankment and look both ways to carefully cross at 1.2 miles, continuing uphill on the other side. As you curve around these slopes, the freeway (and its noise) recedes, and the **Rock Candy Mountains** (commonly referred to as the Mormon Rocks) come into view. These fascinating formations, named for the missionaries who passed

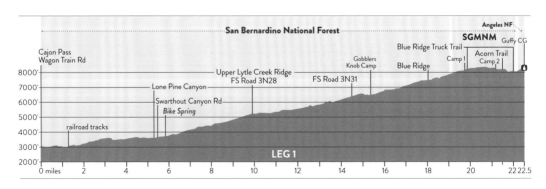

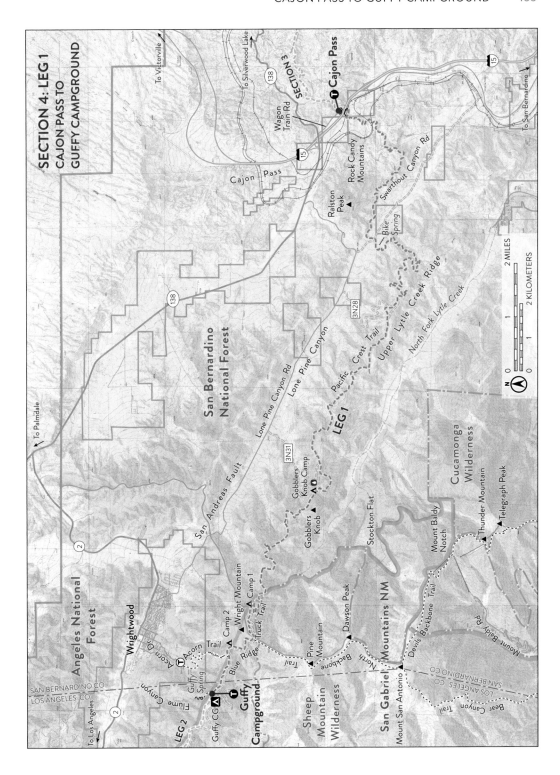

SECTION 4: LEG 1
CAJON PASS TO
GUFFY CAMPGROUND

To Victorville

To Silverwood Lake

SECTION 3

138

Cajon Pass

15

15

To San Bernardino

Wagon Train Rd

Rock Candy Mountains

Swarthout Canyon Rd

Ralston Peak

Bike Spring

To Palmdale

138

San Bernardino National Forest

Upper Lytle Creek Ridge

North Fork Lytle Creek

3N28

Lone Pine Canyon Rd

Lone Pine Canyon

Pacific Crest Trail

LEG 1

San Andreas Fault

3N31

Gobblers Knob Camp

Gobblers Knob

Stockton Flat

Cucamonga Wilderness

Thunder Mountain

Telegraph Peak

2

Angeles National Forest

Wrightwood

Wright Mountain

Camp 1

Camp 2

Truck Trail

Acorn Trail

Blue Ridge

Pine Mountain Trail

Dawson Peak

Mount Baldy Notch

Devils Backbone Trail

San Gabriel Mountains NM

North Backbone Trail

Mount Baldy Rd

Bear Canyon Trail

LOS ANGELES CO
SAN BERNARDINO CO

SAN BERNARDINO CO
LOS ANGELES CO

Wrightwood

Acorn Dr.

Guffy Spring

Flume Canyon

Guffy CG

Guffy Campground

LEG 2

To Los Angeles

2

Sheep Mountain Wilderness

Mount San Antonio

N

0   1   2 MILES

0   1   2 KILOMETERS

RUMBLE AND SHAKE

The San Gabriel Mountains owe their dramatic peaks and valleys to the seismic rumblings of the San Andreas Fault, which borders the range to the northeast. Formed over 28 million years ago, this "thrust" fault, caused by the powerful collision of two tectonic plates (the Pacific and North American), stretches over 800 miles from Southern California's Salton Sea to Northern California's Cape Mendocino. While its ability to cause catastrophic earthquakes keeps Californians shaking in their boots, its history of violent collisions also gives the state some of the best mountain geography in the country. You'll see three interesting examples of seismic upheaval along this section—the Mormon Rocks at Cajon Pass, the Devils Punchbowl as you enter the midsection of your journey, and Vasquez Rocks near the end in Agua Dulce.

through on the Mormon Trail in the mid-19th century, were created by seismic activity on the adjacent San Andreas Fault and angle out of the ground like giant sandstone fins; watch for trains chugging through them every few minutes.

Temporarily join and then cross several unpaved roads as you ascend—the trail is well marked in each instance. Around 2.6 miles, earn fantastic views back toward I-15, but also to the rugged slopes of **Ralston Peak** ahead and down to the wide chasm of **Lone Pine Canyon**, home of the San Andreas Fault. Eventually begin descending toward the latter, reaching the fault at 5.2 miles, a lumpy, unattractive area filled with yucca, rocks, and spent shotgun shells.

Reach unpaved **Swarthout Canyon Road** just 0.2 mile later, then head uphill for nearly the remainder of this leg, first toward Upper Lytle Creek Ridge. The grade is gentle and you're rewarded with expanding views the higher you go. At 5.8 miles, reach a trail register on your right and the concrete box marking perpetually dry **Bike Spring** on your left. The grade steepens a bit, but distract yourself with views to the rapidly receding canyon bottom and across to Ralston Peak. Once you're high enough you'll also gaze back down to Interstate 15 and the Mormon Rocks—a nice indicator of how far you've come.

Cross unpaved **Forest Service Road 3N28** at 9.9 miles, now on **Upper Lytle Creek Ridge** itself instead of traversing the slopes below. You're still headed uphill, but it's a bit gentler, offering a chance to shake out your wobbly legs. Now that you're above 5000 feet, snow and ice are real

possibilities—nearby Wrightwood is, after all, a ski town. The tread thins and becomes crumblier as you continue along north-facing slopes, so traction devices may be necessary if things get slippery. Ghost trees appear in the form of coniferous skeletons scattered around the slopes as you climb, but rest assured that you'll see real, live pines farther ahead.

At 14.3 miles, reach unpaved **Forest Service Road 3N31** (Sheep Creek Truck Trail), which leads back down to Lone Pine Canyon (and paved Lone Pine Canyon Road) below. Continue across on lightly forested south-facing slopes that offer views down to Stockton Flat and the North Fork Lytle Creek watershed. Reach a saddle at 15.3 miles just before **Gobblers Knob**, the large mound directly to the west. According to various local legends, the name is attributed to this being a perfect lunch stop for hungry hikers or to a flock of wild turkeys that used to roam the area. Should you decide to bed down with their ghosts for the evening, look right to spot a slanted clearing with several obvious tent platforms (**Gobblers Knob Camp**); you're quite close to Road 3N31, so don't be surprised to see weekend campers drive past. Also don't be surprised to see *bears* wander through camp—you've reached their, ahem, *bearritory* now. While bear-resistant containers aren't required, take proper precautions to ensure you're not awakened by the sound of a furry friend enjoying tomorrow's lunch.

You still have a bit of elevation gain from here, but feel free to celebrate a bit since you've accomplished the bulk of it already. Tree cover remains

Rest along Blue Ridge to take in a sweeping vista of the Antelope Valley.

thin until you head up **Blue Ridge** around 17.6 miles, where you'll enjoy the scent and feel of soft pine duff underfoot. Pop up to a flattish ridge at 19.8 miles, which offers not just epic views out to the Antelope Valley to the north but also shady camping (**Camp 1**) just before crossing unpaved **Blue Ridge Truck Trail**, your near constant companion for the remainder of this leg.

You're now in the **San Gabriel Mountains National Monument**; stay to the right to remain on trail, gazing down through the Jeffrey pines to spot houses on the fringes of Wrightwood below. Wind along the southern slopes of **Wright Mountain**, scoring great views toward Mount San Antonio and its barren top (hence its nickname, Mount Baldy) almost directly to the south. Trekking to the summit is widely regarded as a rite of passage for Southern California hikers. The **North Backbone Trail** departs from Blue Ridge Truck Trail just below the PCT about 20.7 miles into this leg, right along the ridgeline heading southwest from Wright Mountain, tagging Pine Mountain

155

The Mormon Rocks offer an intriguing geologic interlude near Cajon Pass.

WRIGHTWOOD

Wrightwood, a small but bustling ski hamlet, is one of the most hiker-friendly towns on the Southern California portion of the PCT—you just have to figure out how to get yourself down there from the trail. You have two options—the first is a steep 2.1-mile descent on the Acorn Trail, losing a knee-busting 1750 feet in elevation along the way. If you choose this route, remember: what goes down must come up! Your second option is to hike an additional 5 miles past Guffy Campground to meet Angeles Crest Highway (State Highway 2), where thru-hikers routinely catch rides into town; hitch at your own risk. Once in Wrightwood, you'll find a post office, hardware store, and grocery to help with resupply, a coffee shop and several restaurants to help with empty stomachs, and a number of motels, inns, and bed-and-breakfasts to help with weary bodies. There are a lot of trail angels in this area—information is usually available at the hardware store.

and Dawson Peak along the way; the side trip adds 7.8 roundtrip miles to your hike.

When you pop around to the west of Wright Mountain, look toward its north face—or what *remains* of it, I should say. These slopes have been scooped away over the years by repeated mudslides washing down into the canyon below. Continue on trail to your right along the cliff's edge to reach a lovely flat at 21.3 miles that offers several soft, pine-shaded spots to pitch a tent (**Camp 2**). Reach a junction with the **Acorn Trail** 0.2 mile ahead—it's possible to hike into Wrightwood from here if you dream of a cozy bed and meals that don't come served in foil pouches. From here, your path is pleasantly flat, making the first of several crossings of Blue Ridge Truck Trail at 22 miles, then reaching the boundary of the **San Gabriel National Forest** just ahead.

The last bit of trail to Guffy Campground is inexplicably steep; grunt through it, passing an obvious use trail on your right at 22.4 miles, which leads to seasonal **Guffy Spring 🌢**, located over 800 feet down in Flume Canyon. Ascend just past a guardrail to a big red tank marking your arrival at **Guffy Campground**. The campground is seasonally car accessible along **Blue Ridge Truck**

Trail (Adventure Pass required), so you're likely to see other people in the summer months—and almost nobody come fall. Your leg ends here, where you'll have the run of six duff-cushioned campsites, picnic tables, fire pits, and a pair of vault toilets that might smell better than you do after such a long day of hiking. You'll also have a nearly unobstructed view of the night sky, where you can wish upon a star for the pizza or adult beverage of your choice.

CAMP-TO-CAMP MILEAGE

Cajon Pass to Gobblers Knob Camp 15.3
Gobblers Knob Camp to Camp 1 . . . . 4.5
Camp 1 to Camp 2. . . . . 1.5
Camp 2 to Guffy Campground. 1.2

2 GUFFY CAMPGROUND TO VINCENT GAP

DISTANCE 9.6 miles

ELEVATION GAIN/LOSS
+1770/-3420 feet

HIGH POINT 8455 feet

CONNECTING TRAILS AND ROADS
Angeles Crest Highway, Blue Ridge Truck Trail, Jackson Lake Trail

ON THE TRAIL

Guffy Campground is surprisingly quiet considering how close it sits to the ski town of Wrightwood, probably because it's a little tricky to reach—and that's alright with me! While it's possible to drive here via rough, unpaved Blue Ridge Truck Trail, the average passenger car may not survive the trip with all parts and pieces intact, so it's best to hike this as a continuation of the last leg or come up via the Acorn Trail from Wrightwood to join the PCT 1 mile east.

This leg begins at the large metal water tank located at the west end of the campground. While you can't actually access any wet stuff here, it might be possible at Guffy Spring ⬤, located far below in Flume Canyon, described in the previous leg. This is a seasonal source, so it typically dries up by summertime. From here, begin a gentle ascent, immediately scoring impressive views to Wrightwood, the Antelope Valley, and on a clear day, well beyond. When wetted by spring snowmelt, this area glows with a vibrant mix of sage, ceanothus, manzanita, and grasses, with beautiful pops of color courtesy of wallflowers and paintbrush.

The trail quickly transitions from ascending a mellow plateau to descending along steep slopes populated with a sparse mixture of white fir and Jeffrey pine. A sweet fragrance hangs in the air, and the trees provide welcome shade as you hike along to the sound of birdsong and not much else. Quietude abounds! While this bit makes for easy walking, things begin to undulate as you continue along the spine of rollercoaster Blue Ridge. None of the climbs or descents is all that horrible, but the consistent elevation gain and loss does grow tiresome at points.

Around 2.2 miles, cross an unpaved road, landing at a fence that guards a reservoir holding future snow for skiers at popular Mountain High resort. Continue along the fence, around a metal gate, and briefly join Blue Ridge Truck Trail. Pause here to soak in the expansive vista south into the Sheep Mountain Wilderness, especially pretty when frothy cloud soup rolls through and fills the canyons. After gawking a bit, depart once more onto single-track trail to your right, ascending toward your first epic view of Mount Baden-Powell looming to the southwest.

Once you've snapped a few photos, continue through trees to pass right next to one of the

Glance over your shoulder from just above Guffy Campground to sneak one last look toward Cajon Pass.

Mountain High ski lifts. On a hot day, you'll be forgiven if your mind wanders to images of cool powder runs. Make a note to come back in the winter, then continue on, crossing Blue Ridge Truck Trail and curving around to a faint use trail on your right at 2.9 miles that leads to the **Blue Ridge Campground**. Though you won't find any water here, it does feature vault toilets, picnic tables, fire rings, and a handful of campsites.

Less than 0.5 mile ahead, re-cross your ol' pal Blue Ridge Truck Trail, then head uphill to spot another fenced-off ski resort reservoir. Quickly lose elevation after this, then just as quickly regain it. While the up-and-down nature of this leg might seem a little torturous, at least it feels like you're actually walking on the *crest*. On the uphill, you're rewarded

with even better views of Mount Baden-Powell while passing a second ski lift, this time servicing the west side of the resort. On the descent, a paved ribbon comes into view below—this is **Angeles Crest Highway** (State Highway 2), and you'll reach it at the 5-mile mark after intercepting Blue Ridge Truck Trail twice more. Be very cautious when crossing the highway lest you become a hiker pancake—the posted speed limit is 55 miles per hour, but many drivers cruise by faster than that.

When the coast is clear, zip across into the parking area for popular **Inspiration Point**, a scenic overlook located just west down the highway. If you need relief rather than inspiration, there are vault toilets in the parking area along with a picnic table, garbage receptacle, information kiosk,

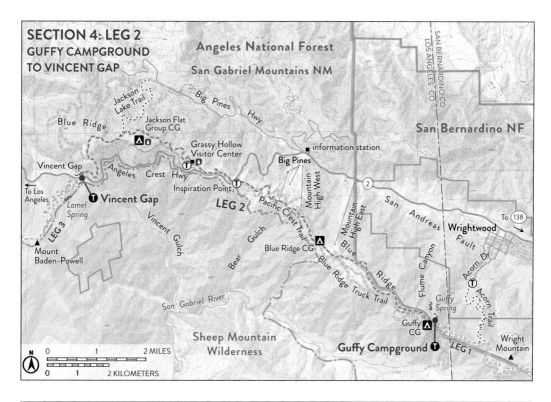

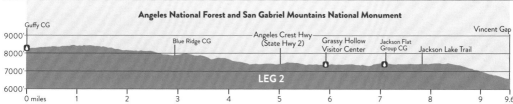

and horse corral. Instead of wandering down the road to catch a glimpse of the greatness, continue up the trail and look for a small use path to your left—this leads to a bench and a less crowded environment for you to soak in the stunning peaks and canyons carved into the San Gabriel River basin far below.

Reluctantly retreat from the sweeping views and continue along to reach a large mileage sign at 5.9 miles—only 2,277 miles to Canada (give or take)! There's also a bench here, along with a picnic area and the **Grassy Hollow Visitor Center** over to the left. Pop off trail here to fill your water bottles at a spigot **0** located near a garbage

receptacle and vault toilet. If you're feeling fancy, find flush toilets inside the center itself along with helpful staffers and interesting displays. The building is located right alongside Angeles Crest Highway, with ample parking, so this makes for an alternate access point.

Rejoin the trail to begin a short climb offering expansive views across the Antelope Valley to the north before dropping down to briefly join a paved road that leads to the **Jackson Flat Group Campground**. There's no need to leave the trail if you want to check out the accommodations—simply continue on, ascending a series of switchbacks. After topping out, keep your eyes peeled for a use

Mount Baden-Powell strikes an imposing silhouette.

trail on the left at 7.1 miles, opposite a small sign reading "To Jackson Lake." The short spur leads to the wooded campground, where you'll find typical amenities (picnic tables, fire pits, vault toilets), with an added bonus—a water spigot **◐** located near the toilets.

If you wondered about the mysterious sign mentioned above, there's an opportunity to satisfy your curiosity just ahead at 7.8 miles when you intersect with the **Jackson Lake Trail**, which descends to the right. If you choose to make the side trip, it's about 2.5 miles to the popular, if small, lake, where weekend picnickers and anglers abound. Otherwise continue on, staying to the right just ahead at a fork with an unpaved road, then begin a lengthy descent through a mixture of shady oak, manzanita, sage, and ceanothus. The trail is somewhat rocky and steepens as you descend, and you quickly reach a small parking area just shy of 9.6 miles. Walk

across it to reach Angeles Crest Highway, cross just as carefully as you did the first time around, and land at the absolutely massive parking area (Adventure Pass required) marking this leg's end at **Vincent Gap**. Here, you'll find vault toilets, garbage receptacles, picnic tables, and spectacular views down Vincent Gulch. You'll also find lots of people—Vincent Gap serves as trailhead for one of the most popular peakbagging objectives in the **Angeles National Forest**—Mount Baden-Powell, whose imposing flank you've been staring at for quite some time on this leg, and whose lofty peak you'll cruise near if you continue on the next leg.

CAMP-TO-CAMP MILEAGE

3 VINCENT GAP TO ISLIP SADDLE

DISTANCE 12 miles

ELEVATION GAIN/LOSS
+3610/-3530 feet

HIGH POINT 9226 feet

CONNECTING TRAILS AND ROADS
Angeles Crest Highway, Dawson Saddle
Trail, Windy Gap Trail, Little Jimmy Road

ON THE TRAIL

Perched alongside **Angeles Crest Highway,**
Vincent Gap offers a giant paved parking lot
(Adventure Pass required), a picnic table, two vault
toilets, garbage receptacles—and amazing views
into the Sheep Mountain Wilderness to the south.
Of course, these vistas will only get better as you
ascend, so look for the trailhead at the west end of
the parking lot and start heading uphill. Take heed
of the sign warning in both English and Spanish of
the hazards present in winter. Slipping down the
precipitous slopes is a real danger. Traction devices,
an ice axe, *and the knowledge to safely use them* are
crucial once the trail is coated in ice and snow.

You're likely to have a lot of company during
this first segment, since Vincent Gap also serves
as the primary trailhead for Mount Baden-Powell,
popular with peakbaggers not just for its unobstructed summit views, but also for the subsequent
access to a string of nearby peaks, all of which you'll
travel past on this leg. But you're not there yet, so
keep hustling uphill, via a set of steep, seemingly

interminable switchbacks through a dense forest of
Jeffrey pines, white fir, and lodgepole pines. You'll
likely break a sweat within minutes, unless you're
a serious endurance athlete or a cyborg. If you're
neither of those things and need a rest, there's a
small wooden bench located at a particularly scenic switchback just under 1 mile ahead.

Your first opportunity to tank up comes at
1.7 miles, when you reach a spur trail signed
for **Lamel Spring** ⬯. Hang a left to follow this
somewhat crumbly path about 400 feet south to
find water; be aware that this may dry up during
the warmer months and into fall. The next likely
source is Little Jimmy Spring, 8 miles ahead. As
you're moving upward, you'll notice that although
the air gets noticeably—*huff*—thinner—*puff*—the
views get better and better. You'll start scoring epic
panoramas of the Antelope Valley to the north,
spread far below like a beige patchwork quilt,
along with breathtaking (*literally*) scenes of the
undulating peaks of the San Gabriel Mountains to
your south. For locals, this is the next best thing to
being in the Sierra Nevada.

Just shy of the 3-mile mark, you'll spot a clearing
down the slope to your left and another smaller one
just ahead before making a switchback (**Camp 3**).
Each has room for a few tents, and each boasts
excellent views and good shade. Just after this,
you'll reach a set of short, tightly packed switchbacks that might cause you to explore the depths of
your curse word repertoire. Hang in there—these
switchbacks last for only a short bit—then level off
at a razor-thin ridge jutting ahead. From the north,
the trail looks as though it drapes precariously

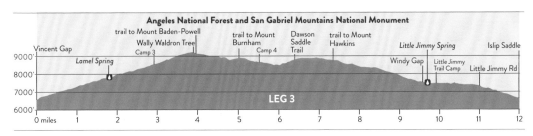

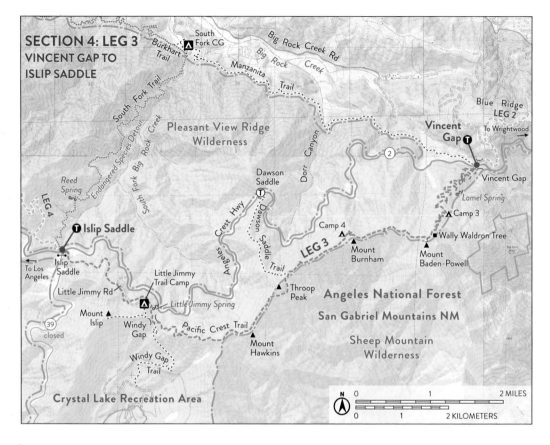

SECTION 4: LEG 3
VINCENT GAP TO ISLIP SADDLE

South Fork CG
Burkhart Trail
Big Rock Creek Rd
Manzanita Trail
Big Rock Creek
South Fork Trail
Blue Ridge
LEG 2
Pleasant View Ridge Wilderness
Dorr Canyon
Vincent Gap
To Wrightwood
Endangered Species Detour
South Fork Big Rock Creek
Reed Spring
Dawson Saddle
Vincent Gap
Lamel Spring
Camp 3
LEG 4
Islip Saddle
Crest Hwy
Dawson Saddle Trail
Camp 4
Wally Waldron Tree
To Los Angeles
Islip Saddle
Angeles
LEG 3
Mount Burnham
Mount Baden-Powell
Little Jimmy Rd
Little Jimmy Trail Camp
Throop Peak
Angeles National Forest
Mount Islip
Little Jimmy Spring
San Gabriel Mountains NM
39 closed
Windy Gap
Pacific Crest Trail
Mount Hawkins
Sheep Mountain Wilderness
Windy Gap Trail
Crystal Lake Recreation Area

N   0   1   2 MILES
0   1   2 KILOMETERS

across a steep bowl of scree (and it does), but as you approach, you'll see that although the path is slim, there's plenty of room to walk—just mind your feet. On that note, this is a great place to take photos that will horrify your more acrophobic friends.

Around the 3.9-mile mark, you'll reach the **Wally Waldron Tree**—a massive limber pine attached to the trail's eastern edge by some kind of nature voodoo. This knotted and gnarled giant, dedicated to longtime Los Angeles–area Boy

SCOUT'S HONOR

The Boy Scouts of America have a decorated history in the mountains surrounding Los Angeles. Their trail work has been most prolific in the San Gabriel Mountains, where in 1942, they established the 53-mile Silver Moccasin Trail, based on a path used long before by indigenous people and more recently by hunters. Beginning in Chantry Flat to the south and ending at Vincent Gap to the north, the route joins with the PCT for the 29 miles between Three Points Trailhead and Vincent Gap. Since backpacking the Silver Moccasin is a rite of passage for local Scouts, don't be surprised if you see packs of energetic boys (and their exhausted Scoutmasters) running past as you hike. The route reaches its high point at Mount Baden-Powell, named after Lord Robert Baden-Powell, who founded the Scouts after a lengthy stint with the British Army; there's a large monument to him located on the broad summit.

The thin north ridge of Mount Baden-Powell is much easier to navigate when it is not covered with snow and ice.

Scouts volunteer Michael H. "Wally" Waldron, is one of the most ancient in the San Gabriel range, estimated to be over 1500 years old.

Once you've taken your fair share of snaps with this arboreal celebrity, you'll have a choice—continue on the PCT to the right or head straight to take a short, less-than-0.1-mile detour to summit 9399-foot **Mount Baden-Powell**, whose slopes you've been trudging up these last few miles. Many hikers, including me, consider the summit a highlight of this entire section, so frankly, you'd be crazy not to head up there to score some of the best views in the San Gabriel Mountains. From this majestic height, your viewshed includes not just the full run of neighboring peaks and valleys, but also an aerial view of the famed Devils Punchbowl to the northwest, an alien landscape of tilted sandstone formations created by violent seismic

activity along the San Andreas Fault, which you'll skirt if you take the Endangered Species Detour detailed in the next leg.

Back down at the junction, begin traversing a ridgeline along north-facing slopes, whose crumbling facades will make you want to hug your trekking poles. As you move west, you'll pass near three prominent peaks, beginning with **Mount Burnham**, whose use trail you'll intercept on the mountain's east side at 5 miles. Considering the epic 360-degree views you scored at Mount Baden-Powell, it's up to you whether you feel it's worth dragging yourself up each of these peaks. If you want to hang out here for a while, keep your eyes peeled around 5.5 miles to spot a campsite tucked in a clearing down the slope to your right (**Camp 4**).

Continuing on the gentle trail on a thick bed of pine duff, you'll pass scampering squirrels and sunning western fence lizards to reach a junction with the **Dawson Saddle Trail** at 6.4 miles that's signed for Mount Baden-Powell behind you, Dawson Saddle down to your right, and Windy Gap up to the left—the latter is your route, unless you want to pick up a use trail and ascend **Throop Peak**, whose northeastern shoulder you're currently straddling. Walk the ridge, enjoying excellent views on both sides before approaching a use trail on your left at 7.4 miles that leads to the summit of **Mount Hawkins**. Unless you want to enjoy one last peakbagging experience on this leg, continue downhill on the PCT.

Squiggle along the ridgeline, then descend via several switchbacks to reach **Windy Gap** at 9.5 miles. This is a breezy little pass that often earns its name and then some. Stop for a breather on a downed log bench and consider your options—you can make a left on the **Windy Gap Trail** to descend toward the Crystal Lake Recreation Area, go straight for a lengthy detour to Mount Islip, or head right to reach Little Jimmy Trail Camp (hint: you want the latter).

Just ahead, spot a use trail descending to the right—this travels 0.1 mile to seasonally reliable **Little Jimmy Spring ◑**. The popular **Little Jimmy Trail Camp** is just ahead at 9.9 miles on the left; it's

not likely you'll have the place to yourself. Depart the PCT here on an obvious use trail to find vault toilets, picnic tables, wood-burning ovens, and ample room to pitch a tent for the night. You're in black bear territory, so although bear-resistant canisters aren't required, take care to prevent your food from being stolen overnight by our ursine friends.

Continue along the shady trail, crossing unpaved **Little Jimmy Road** at 11 miles. The road, camp, and spring are all named for a character created by cartoonist Jimmy Swinnerton, who spent time in the area. You're flying downhill now, undoing all of the hard work you did in the first 4 miles of this trip, scoring views of Mount Williamson ahead as you land at the edge of Angeles Crest Highway at **Islip Saddle** 1 mile later. Cars whiz by at breakneck speeds despite the curvy roadway; be very careful as you cross to find a paved parking lot (Adventure Pass required), picnic tables, vault toilets, garbage receptacles, and an information sign on the other side.

CAMP-TO-CAMP MILEAGE
Vincent Gap to Camp 3 . . . . 3.0
Camp 3 to Camp 4 . . . . 2.5
Camp 4 to Little Jimmy
    Trail Camp 4.4

4 ISLIP SADDLE TO BURKHART TRAIL

DISTANCE 8 miles; detour 20.7 miles

ELEVATION GAIN/LOSS
+2500 feet/-3460 feet;
detour +4764 feet/-5712 feet

HIGH POINT 7877 feet; detour 6936 feet

CONNECTING TRAILS AND ROADS
Angeles Crest Highway, South Fork Trail, Forest Service Road 4N11A, Burkhart Trail

ON THE TRAIL
Although the San Gabriel Mountains provide boundless recreation opportunities for outdoorsy humans, they also provide an important home for all kinds of wildlife, from black bears to much smaller creatures, including the mountain yellow-legged frog. Threatened by extinction from both disease and hungry trout introduced into its habitat, this riparian critter was listed as an endangered species in 2002. As a result, just under 4 miles of the PCT that run through its native habitat are currently a no-go zone to let our little friends prosper and enjoy amorous amphibious liaisons in peace.

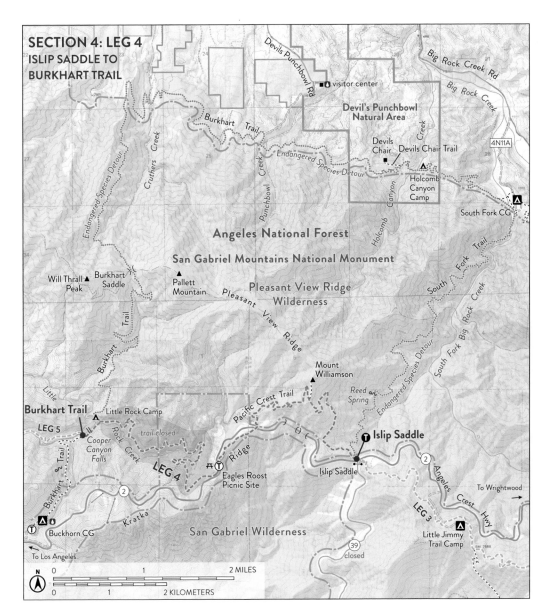

SECTION 4: LEG 4
ISLIP SADDLE TO
BURKHART TRAIL

Devils Punchbowl Rd

Big Rock Creek Rd

Big Rock Creek

visitor center

Devil's Punchbowl
Natural Area

Burkhart   Trail

Cuthers Creek

Endangered Species Detour

Punchbowl Creek

Endangered Species Detour

Devils
Chair

Devils Chair Trail

4N11A

Holcomb
Canyon
Camp

Holcomb Canyon

South Fork CG

Angeles National Forest

San Gabriel Mountains National Monument

South Fork Trail

Pleasant View Ridge
Wilderness

Will Thrall
Peak

Burkhart
Saddle

Pallett
Mountain

Pleasant View Ridge

South Fork Big Rock Creek

Burkhart   Trail

Mount
Williamson

Reed
Spring

Endangered Species Detour

Little

Burkhart Trail

Little Rock Camp

LEG 5

Cooper
Canyon
Falls

Rock Creek

trail closed

Pacific Crest Trail

Ridge

LEG 4

Eagles Roost
Picnic Site

Islip Saddle

Islip Saddle

2

Angeles

Burkhart Trail

2

Kratka

Crest Hwy

To Wrightwood

LEG 3

Buckhorn CG

San Gabriel Wilderness

Little Jimmy
Trail Camp

To Los Angeles

39
closed

BM 7686

N

0   1   2 MILES

0   1   2 KILOMETERS

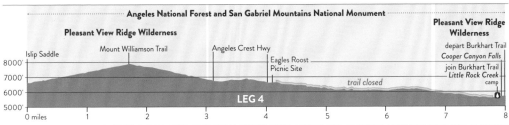

Angeles National Forest and San Gabriel Mountains National Monument

Pleasant View Ridge Wilderness

Pleasant View Ridge
Wilderness

Islip Saddle

Mount Williamson Trail

Angeles Crest Hwy

Eagles Roost
Picnic Site

depart Burkhart Trail
Cooper Canyon Falls

join Burkhart Trail
Little Rock Creek
camp

8000'

7000'

trail closed

6000'

5000'

LEG 4

0 miles   1   2   3   4   5   6   7   8

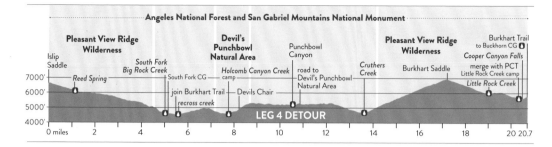

While the PCTA works with land managers to hatch a more permanent routing solution, hikers must choose between taking a popular shortcut that follows a segment of serpentine **Angeles Crest Highway**, or making a circuitous jaunt known as the "Endangered Species Detour." Since the former follows the official PCT track for more than half the route, I'll begin with that, followed by a detailed description of the latter. Mileage and elevation information is included for both the *actual* PCT and the Endangered Species Detour, although camp-to-camp mileages reflect only the latter since there are no campsites located along this leg of the PCT.

Begin at the **Islip Saddle** trailhead (Adventure Pass required), which features vault toilets, picnic tables, parking, and garbage receptacles. Head uphill through pine cover to top out on a ridge at 1.7 miles, intersecting with the **Mount Williamson Trail** on the right. Hop off trail here to bag the peak itself . . . or *one* of the peaks, since there's controversy over which of Pleasant View Ridge's high points should qualify as the true summit. Otherwise, stay left to switchback down to Angeles Crest Highway at 3.1 miles.

From here, ascend to more lovely views along **Kratka Ridge**, then descend a series of tight switchbacks to the shoulder of Angeles Crest Highway. Follow a faint trail to reach **Eagles Roost Picnic Site** just ahead at 4.1 miles, which offers parking (Adventure Pass required), vault toilets, and picnic tables. The PCT is closed north of here to protect the mountain yellow-legged frog, so you now walk *very* carefully alongside Angeles Crest Highway for the next 2.7 miles. Look for an unsigned paved driveway on your right 0.1 mile after spotting a sign for **Buckhorn Campground**. Turn here and exercise caution

while descending the narrow road. Upon reaching the campground, follow signs to the day use area, about 0.7 mile down from the highway; if you need water, stop by one of the campground's spigots ⬤ beforehand. Once at the day use parking area (Adventure Pass required, no overnight parking allowed), hop on the **Burkhart Trail**, passing a spring ⬤ 0.7 mile in. Land at the canyon bottom and this leg's end to rejoin the PCT 4.9 miles after you first left it at Eagles Roost for a grand total of 9 miles on foot.

If you don't fancy walking along a curvy mountain highway or are interested in a more scenic route, consider taking the **Endangered Species Detour** instead. As before, begin at Islip Saddle, but instead of heading uphill on the PCT, look for a path that descends to the right—this is the **South Fork Trail**, which constitutes the first part of this alternate. Due to a combination of decomposing granite and lack of maintenance, this segment of the route is in a sorry state with thin, uneven, and slippery tread that sometimes disappears altogether. Although the views down canyon are beautiful, I don't recommend this route for anyone with fear of heights or unsteady balance.

Channel your inner mountain goat (and perhaps, nerves of steel) to continue downhill. You'll pass **Reed Spring** ⬤ 1.1 miles in—in summer, this may be the only running water available until the end of this leg. If traveling in wetter months, however, it's likely that you'll find water when you reach the canyon bottom and a crossing of the **South Fork Big Rock Creek** ⬤ at 5 miles. The canyon widens just past this, and use trails on your right offer access to the **South Fork Campground**, accessible by car via unpaved **Forest Service Road 4N11A**. The location is beautiful, but the campground itself is in just as sorry shape as the trail that

The Endangered Species Detour is long, but brings you near the spectacular Devils Punchbowl formation.

leads to it, with an abundance of trash and graffiti. I recommend continuing on.

Reach a junction at 5.4 miles; ignore the right branch (the **Manzanita Trail**, which leads back up to Vincent Gap) and instead bank left to join the Burkhart Trail (also called High Desert National Recreation Trail and Punchbowl Trail here), your route for the rest of this leg. Quickly re-cross the South Fork Big Rock Creek **O** to head west. The trail in this area remains somewhat crumbly as you pop up to a saddle, then descend to beautiful Holcomb Canyon, where you'll find a large campsite (**Holcomb Canyon Camp**) at 7.7 miles, tucked in a shady glen next to **Holcomb Canyon Creek O**. Cross the creek a few moments later to ascend a scree slope that's doing its best to resist the trail—if you enjoy climbing sand dunes, you'll *love* this.

Reach the top at 8.2 miles, where a sign suggests a detour to the **Devils Chair**, a sandstone fin that overlooks the spectacular **Devils Punchbowl** formation. This adds about 0.5 mile roundtrip to your journey, but is worth it if you have the time. Otherwise, bear left to continue on much better trail, although it's still a bit of a sand slog to climb uphill. If you skipped the side trip, enjoy excellent views as you contour above Devils Punchbowl.

Continue on somewhat shady slopes dotted with manzanita, mountain mahogany, and pinyon pines to round **Punchbowl Canyon** and its

seasonal creek **O** at 10.5 miles. Angle slightly uphill to reach a junction with an unpaved road 0.3 mile later that leads to the parking area for **Devil's Punchbowl Natural Area**, just under 1 mile off-trail. Here, you'll find parking, vault toilets, and a nature center, with water available during business hours. Unless making a pit stop, veer left to stay on the single-track, marked with a sign for Buckhorn Campground. Continue meandering along through thick manzanita until making a noticeable drop to reach a mileage sign, fence, and unpaved road—make a left onto the latter, then cross seasonal **Cruthers Creek O** at 13.6 miles.

Just after the crossing, ignore an unpaved road along the creek and instead head uphill on the

DEVILISH GEOLOGY

Like the Mormon Rocks at the beginning of this section and the Vasquez Rocks at its end, the Devils Punchbowl formations are the fascinating result of seismic upheaval coupled with erosion and other geologic factors. Here, the San Andreas, Punchbowl, and Pinyon Faults all conspired to send layers of sedimentary rock skyward, a process set into motion an estimated 60 million years ago.

trail at the signed junction—it's time to regain all of the elevation lost on the descent to the South Fork Big Rock Creek. Enjoy a few remnants of shade in the canyon bottom, then slowly make your way up the sunny slopes. The trail is in much better shape than the South Fork segment, but you'll still encounter debris and slipped tread from time to time.

Pinyons dot the slope, eventually replaced with Coulter and Jeffrey pines as you ascend. Look over your shoulder for exceptional views across the desert before reaching **Burkhart Saddle** at 17.3 miles, perched between Will Thrall Peak and Pallett Mountain. From here, make a series of lazy downhill switchbacks to travel across ridges and gullies, landing at a branch of seasonal **Little Rock Creek 🄾** at 19 miles. Hop across to continue along, reaching a junction with the PCT 1.5 miles later. The southbound (read: closed) PCT heads steeply uphill to your left, marked as the Rattlesnake Trail,

but you turn right to stay on the PCT and Burkhart Trail combo. There's a small one-off campsite just to your right after this (**Little Rock Camp**), before you cross the main flow of **Little Rock Creek 🄾** at 20.5 miles. While finishing this last bit, look to your right to spot **Cooper Canyon Falls**, a popular destination for day hikers, just before reaching this leg's end at 20.7 miles. Here, the PCT and Burkhart trail split ways; the former continues straight, and the latter veers off to the left to climb 1.5 miles to Buckhorn Campground.

CAMP-TO-CAMP MILEAGE
Mileage is for camps along the Endangered Species Detour.

Islip Saddle to South Fork Campground....	5.2
South Fork Campground to Holcomb Canyon Camp........................	2.5
Holcomb Canyon Camp to Little Rock Camp.....................	12.8

5 BURKHART TRAIL TO THREE POINTS TRAILHEAD

DISTANCE 9.1 miles

ELEVATION GAIN/LOSS
+2400/-2180 feet

HIGH POINT 7037 feet

CONNECTING TRAILS AND ROADS
Burkhart Trail, Angeles Crest Highway

ON THE TRAIL
The PCT and the **Burkhart Trail** (also known as the High Desert National Recreational Trail) join for a short bit, and the trails' split offers a relatively easy starting point for this next leg since it's only 1.5 miles south from the PCT to reach a car accessible trailhead (Adventure Pass required) located at the far end of **Buckhorn Campground**. Unfortunately, this parking area is meant for day

use only, so backpackers are instructed to park in turnouts located along Angeles Crest Highway and walk down the campground's driveway instead. This section of the PCT is also part of the popular 53-mile Silver Moccasin Trail, so between that and proximity to the campground, you'll likely share the trek with at least a few day hikers and weekend backpackers.

WATER ALERT!
If you depart the PCT heading south on the Burkhart Trail toward **Buckhorn Campground**, you will cross a creek 🄾 less than 0.2 mile in, and if that's dry, you can try your luck at a spring 🄾 on your right side 0.6 mile farther. The campground itself is located 1.5 miles south of the PCT and features water spigots 🄾.

Enjoy forested views in part of the Angeles National Forest left unscathed by the Station Fire.

Your leg begins in shady **Cooper Canyon** at a sign that points toward its namesake camp ahead. In wet seasons, you'll almost immediately cross a small creek **◑**, but know that there's a chance this may run dry. The area is pretty and peaceful, dotted with boulders, Jeffrey pines, and incense cedars, so hopefully the natural beauty keeps you distracted from the fact that you almost immediately start angling uphill. Your path is a disused and annoyingly steep roadbed; continue on it for 1.2 miles. The now more obvious unpaved road continues straight, and you bank up on single-track to the right, just past a vault toilet. You also have the option of making a left here into signed **Cooper Canyon Trail Camp**, a popular backpacking destination for locals. Here you'll find tons of room to set down your tent, several wood-burning ovens, and an array of picnic tables. If the creek was running at the start of this leg, you'll likely find it flowing in the ravine down below **◑**, just south of the camping area.

After a bathroom break, snack stop, or shady slumber, continue up to ascend a ridgeline that offers nice northward views of the San Gabriel Mountains' many folds and a peek to the Antelope Valley beyond. The scenery is quite pretty here, so take your time undulating along these high points.

Continue along a smattering of scrub oak, chaparral, and conifers to cross the unpaved road you saw next to Cooper Canyon Trail Camp. Despite the relative proximity of Angeles Crest Highway, which you'll reach soon enough, it's quiet here, with only the sound of chirping birds and buzzing insects to break (or add to) the reverie.

Around 3.3 miles, you'll cross several channels at the head of Cooper Canyon that may contain water, though it's doubtful. Continue uphill, grunting your way to a small parking turnout on **Angeles Crest Highway** at 3.9 miles—this is the adorably named **Cloudburst Summit**, located almost directly between Winston Peak and Waterman Mountain, a popular ski area. When you arrive, you'll notice an unpaved road on your right—this is the one you crossed twice earlier. Look for a giant trail marker across the way, then very carefully cross the highway; you'll do this several more times on this trip, one of the less exciting aspects of traveling this section of trail. Once on the other side, ignore the dirt path headed straight, and instead make a quick switchback to stay along the north side of **Cloudburst Canyon**.

Cross Angeles Crest Highway for a second time at 4.8 miles and look for the trail to continue to the left of a yellow gate. The sound of traffic detracts

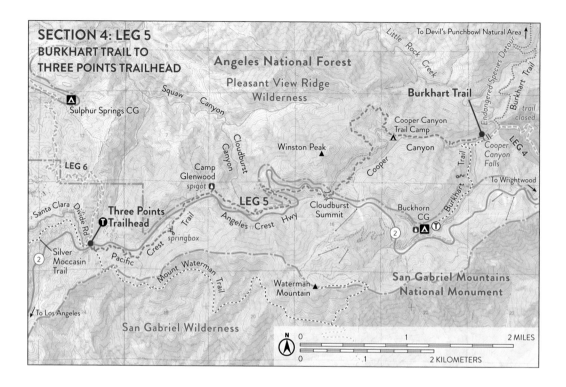

SECTION 4: LEG 5
BURKHART TRAIL TO
THREE POINTS TRAILHEAD

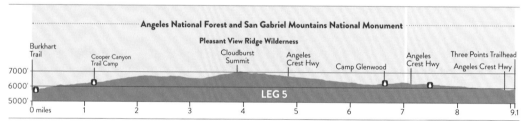

from the natural beauty in this area, but you can still appreciate the unique rock formations, pines, birds, and butterflies all around. Round a large gully to hit the 400-mile mark of the PCT—no doubt someone before you already spelled this out in rocks, twigs, or pinecones laid across the trail. Take the obligatory picture, then continue on to reach **Camp Glenwood** at 6.6 miles. While this is a private facility, you can still visit the vault toilets just to the right of the trail or walk straight ahead to find a seasonal water spigot **O** located near some picnic tables just below an informational sign.

From here, hang a left to join the camp's access road for a short bit. You'll see a sign jutting out of

the hillside on your left that mentions a "Curry Spring," but you will sadly find neither a spring nor any delicious curry at this juncture. Instead, depart the road on the right just ahead to return to the trail and descend to your third crossing of Angeles Crest Highway at 7.1 miles. Before you get to the road itself, you'll notice a large, paved parking area on its far side, complete with vault toilets, a picnic table, and a garbage receptacle—while the trail doesn't directly pass this area, it comes close enough. If catholes are more your thing, just continue on, joining an old roadbed soon thereafter.

You have one more chance for water on this leg—well, technically *four* more opportunities, the first at 7.5 miles when you pass a concrete spring box **O** on the left just before a gully. You'll pass two more in quick succession, but the fourth box is the most likely to contain the wet stuff, although it can be a little tricky to collect—patience, grasshopper. If you're continuing on beyond this leg, your next source is just under 5 miles ahead at Sulphur Springs Trail Camp.

Even though you're nearly to this leg's finish line, there's still a lot to enjoy as you hike through some beautiful Jeffrey pines. Don't be embarrassed—just push your nose right into the bark and inhale the sweet, torturous smell of butterscotch cookies. *Sigh.* Once you pry your face away, you'll probably realize that you're now within spitting distance of your last highway crossing, tucked between you and some interesting granite outcroppings across the way. You might be excited, but focus on the task at hand since you'll need to stay straight at 8.5 miles after the old roadbed peters off down to the right. You'll make your own right turn 0.3 mile ahead at a junction with the Mount Waterman Trail, where you might see some lingering poodle-dog bush, an irritating (literally) remnant of the heartbreaking, arson-caused Station Fire that burned for nearly two months in 2009, devastating over 160,000 acres and killing two firefighters.

Continue down to your last crossing of Angeles Crest Highway at 9 miles. It's just 0.1 mile more to reach a Y-intersection where the **Silver Moccasin Trail** continues to the left and you ascend to the right to reach the **Three Points Trailhead**. Here, you'll find a massive paved parking lot (Adventure Pass required), vault toilets, garbage receptacles, and a picnic table. Camping is available about 2 miles away at **Horse Flats Campground**. You can take partially paved **Santa Clara Divide Road** or the Silver Moccasin Trail to reach this seasonal, fee-based site. Don't come here looking for water, though, because you won't find any unless a kind fellow camper offers you a swig.

CAMP-TO-CAMP MILEAGE
Burkhart Trail to Cooper Canyon Trail Camp 1.2

AN ITCHY NEMESIS

Poodle-dog bush (*Eriodictyon parryi*)—or as I call it, The Notorious PDB—is a perennial shrub that typically sprouts up in certain Southern California mountain environments after wildfires, sticking around for upward of a decade until other plants stake their claim. It's been especially prolific in areas of the San Gabriel Mountains affected by the 2009 Station Fire. The pungent plant shoots out of the ground in huge clusters, its vivid green stalks sporting bright purple blossoms through summer, fading into withered droops as the seasons change. Trail workers have done a heroic job of pushing it back over the years, but if you come across the dreaded PDB, do everything you can to avoid touching it, as it releases a substance that is highly irritating to many people, producing blistered rashes similar to those caused by poison oak.

6 THREE POINTS TRAILHEAD TO MILL CREEK SUMMIT

DISTANCE 15.5 miles

ELEVATION GAIN/LOSS
+2510/-3520 feet

HIGH POINT 6781 feet

CONNECTING ROADS
Santa Clara Divide Road, Sulphur Springs Road, Pacifico Mountain Road, Angeles Forest Highway

ON THE TRAIL

Although bookended by major thoroughfares—Angeles Crest Highway and Angeles Forest Highway—this trip feels surprisingly remote, offering a fairly peaceful retreat from some of Angeles National Forest's busier attractions. Begin at the large paved parking area at the **Three Points Trailhead**, just off **Angeles Crest Highway** (Adventure Pass required). Visit the dank vault toilets if you must, then head west to find the trail marked by a brown post. Quickly cross **Santa Clara Divide Road** before rejoining on the other side, where you'll encounter a slightly alarming sign warning of any number of dangers: Flash floods! Falling trees! Loose rocks! For the majority of this leg—in fact, for the bulk of the rest of this section—you're walking through the extensive burn scars left by the 2009 Station Fire.

While the sign might prove intimidating, the Forest Service carefully assesses all burned lands before opening them to the public, so exercise caution around snags (dead trees) and loose ground, and you'll be good to go. It's also wise to keep an eye out for poodle-dog bush, a highly irritating plant that sprouts up after fire. It's probably a good idea to wear long pants through this leg and the remainder of the San Gabriels, since Notorious PDB tends to encroach on the trail no matter how often maintenance crews attempt to beat it back.

If you're feeling any hesitation, trust me when I say that there is a lot to love here, and that post-burn lands can hold pure magic as life blooms once again. With renewed optimism, hop along through abundant chaparral, with manzanita, mountain mahogany, and shrubby oaks flanking your path. In spring, scarlet bugler lends splashes of bright orange-red to the proceedings, and yucca blooms rise up in greeting. While you'll hear some traffic noise from the nearby highway, you hit the **Pleasant View Ridge Wilderness** boundary 0.3 mile in; quietude is on the way. Western fence lizards dart across the boulder-strewn slopes as the trail meanders along on a gentle contour. If you want to stay a bit, look to the right at just over 1 mile where the trail makes a hairpin turn to find a shadeless saddle with room for a few tents (**Camp 5**). There are better spots ahead, so continue walking on soft tread under thickening tree cover, which includes bigcone spruce and sugar pine. Briefly join an old roadbed at 1.6 miles, then depart back onto single-track to your right just ahead.

Besides the ever-present summertime hum of gnats, this is a peaceful area and the walking is extremely pleasant, especially as you make a gentle descent through an abundance of shade-giving oaks and conifers, including occasional appearances by scattered incense cedar and white fir. Dreamy! Skip along like this for a while until you come to a fork in the trail around 3.5 miles. The right prong is an equestrian alternate that ambles along on gentler ground, whereas the left side marks the main PCT, which heads uphill. Both options offer access to **Sulphur Springs Campground** just off trail—the horse route is more direct—but you'll find a use path just ahead on the regular route that descends to a large clearing below. There's ample room to throw down your shelter, along with possible water, from both a spring-fed trough and seasonal **South Fork Little Rock Creek** ⬤ that runs just beyond; however, the wet stuff may disappear by early summer. The

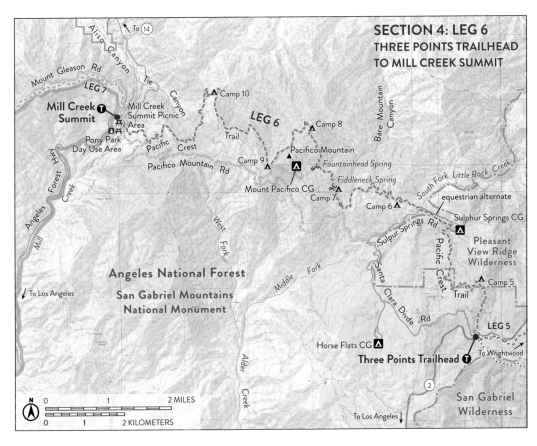

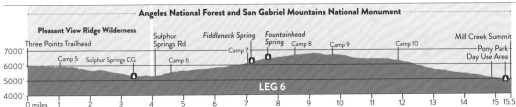

formal campground is located less than 0.25 mile to the east—follow any number of use trails or the obvious ribbon of nearby paved Sulphur Springs Road to access its picnic tables, fire rings, and vault toilets.

Continuing on, the reason for the equestrian alternate is clear as you curve onto crumblier slopes. After a short jaunt, descend to meet the alternate on your right, then hike a bit farther to reach **Sulphur Springs Road** at 4.2 miles. Before crossing, check to be sure you're properly slathered

in sunscreen—it's about to get sunny. While climbing, resist the urge to taunt yourself with wistful glances back toward the shade-giving pines below. If feeling droopy, look to the left to glimpse a one-tent spot perched on a ridgeline (**Camp 6**) just under 0.5 mile from the road.

Wiggle around for an eternity, crossing a saddle at the head of **Bare Mountain Canyon**, then head uphill onto the sunny eastern slopes of **Pacifico Mountain**. A well-worn campsite appears on your right at 7.2 miles (**Camp 7**); however, it's located

Your lofty forested perch offers expansive views of the desert terrain below.

right next to the trail, so consider moving on. Look for ferns decorating the left side of the trail just 0.1 mile later, obscuring piped **Fiddleneck Spring ⭕**, a seasonal source accessed via an opening in the foliage. Not to worry if it's dry—you'll find a second refill option ahead at 7.9 miles at the somewhat more reliable **Fountainhead Spring ⭕**. I will cop to arriving here on a hot day completely parched and low on water, then yelping with joy like a dust-covered lunatic once I saw the small pool and trickle.

There's more climbing to do, although your efforts are rewarded with expanded views down the giant maw of Bare Mountain Canyon and out to the Antelope Valley on a clear day. You also earn a bit of natural UV protection when pine and spruce reappear; keep quiet to spot mule deer snacking on scattered vegetation. There's an opportunity to continue your wildlife viewing once you reach a forested saddle at 8.6 miles—a use trail on the right leads to a camping area offering top notch vistas (**Camp 8**).

Continue curving around Pacifico Mountain, ducking in and out of tree cover—sometimes the starkness of the post-burn areas are just as beautiful as those that are more thickly forested. Finally round the peak's western side to hit a saddle at 9.9 miles, meeting a signed side trail to a dirt road that winds up to **Mount Pacifico Campground**, a waterless spot a full mile off-trail. Since it's a haul, I won't call it out in the camp-to-camp mileage at the end of this leg description, but peakbaggers may find it a worthy side trip as the mountain's boulder strewn summit is right next to the campground. If you're sleepy, but don't fancy an uphill slog, there are a few obvious campsites tucked away on the left side of the saddle (**Camp 9**).

There's a neat juxtaposition as you continue along through a mix of post-burn scenery, large boulders, and fragrant pines, while looking down into more desert-like environments far below. Eventually turn to head north on a prominent, sage-covered ridgeline offering stellar views from every angle. When you near the end around 11.9 miles, look to the left to spot a gravelly area ringed by silvery Fremont's bush mallow—this makes for a somewhat lumpy campsite boasting beautiful views (**Camp 10**).

WATER ALERT!

If you're continuing north, take enough water from the Pony Park Day Use Area to last the hot, dry 17.5 miles until North Fork Saddle. As a courtesy to hikers, water has been provided there for many years, but it's best to research online and check the information board at the Pony Park Day Use Area before counting on their kindness.

You're now staring down into nearby Tie Canyon and beyond to Aliso Canyon; the paved road squiggling far below is Angeles Forest Highway, which you'll meet soon enough. Until then, undertake what seems like an endless campaign to navigate the myriad gullies and ridges that make this final section seem much longer than it really is. Weave in and out and in and out for a shadeless eternity, the whole while spotting Mill Creek Summit at a gap in the mountains—so close, but so far away.

Yerba santa, chamise, and manzanita are your ever-present natural company as the rest of the scenery shifts toward man-made, with power lines, transformers, buildings, and speeding cars creeping closer. Your first option to depart comes at 15.3 miles

with a use trail skittering off to the left, leading to the **Pony Park Day Use Area**, a spot that doesn't quite live up to its cheery name but offers a vault toilet, water spigot **0**, picnic table, and garbage receptacle all the same. Continue downhill to reach an intersection with paved **Pacifico Mountain Road**; cross to reach the **Mill Creek Summit Picnic Area**, this leg's endpoint, at 15.5 miles. Located on busy **Angeles Forest Highway**, the neglected spot features a parking area (Adventure Pass required), vault toilets, garbage receptacles, and a smattering of picnic tables in various states of disrepair. While the area is fairly unsightly, it's worth walking up Pacifico Mountain Road a minute or two to soak in the pretty views down canyon, especially lovely at sunset. In the past, PCT hikers have been able to set up camp in the dilapidated day use site—signs at the Pony Park Day Use Area will announce whether this is still allowed.

CAMP-TO-CAMP MILEAGE

Three Points Trailhead to Camp 5 . . . . 1.1
Camp 5 to Sulphur Springs Campground. . . . 2.4
Sulphur Springs Campground to Camp 6. . . . . 1.1
Camp 6 to Camp 7 . . . . 2.6
Camp 7 to Camp 8 . . . . .1.4
Camp 8 to Camp 9 . . . . .1.3
Camp 9 to Camp 10 . . . . 2.0

7 MILL CREEK SUMMIT TO MESSENGER FLATS CAMPGROUND

DISTANCE 11.8 miles

ELEVATION GAIN/LOSS
+3250/-2280 feet

HIGH POINT 6421 feet

CONNECTING ROADS
Angeles Forest Highway, Mount Gleason Road, Forest Service Road 4N24, Santa Clara Divide Road

ON THE TRAIL
Whether you're starting from the front seat of a parked car or fresh off the last segment, you'll want to carry every drop of water you'll need on this leg (and into the next) since it's bone dry; the next likely source is provided by the kind caretaker at North Fork Saddle, about 17.4 miles ahead. If you need to top off on the wet stuff before setting out, backtrack to paved **Pacifico Mountain Road** and head uphill to pass a fire station and reach the **Pony Park Day**

Use Area, which features a parking area, vault toilet, picnic table, and water spigot ⬤.

Once you're loaded up, begin by carefully crossing **Angeles Forest Highway**, a busy thoroughfare that sees traffic at all hours. Your path on the other side isn't marked well, but logic leads you in the right direction as the indistinct, sandy trail runs between a smattering of wooden posts on the left and paved Mount Gleason Road down to the right. Waste no time climbing up through deep sand and shadeless chaparral containing a mixture of manzanita, chamise, and yerba santa, with intermittent bursts of bright scarlet bugler providing color in spring and early summer. It's best to knock this bit out before high noon unless you enjoy dabbling in heatstroke or lead a double life as a lizard.

As the trail climbs, the highway drops farther away and views open up back to the south and ahead to the north as you rise high above Aliso Canyon. The terrain changes after 1 mile or so as you curve around to north-facing slopes—here, the ground is pockmarked with boulders and interior live oaks. There used to be more of the latter, but the Station Fire ripped through in 2009, scorching nearly everything in its path and inviting repeated poodle-dog bush invasions. Still, a few hardy trees remain, and their presence is well appreciated, especially on a hot day. In a few spots you'll also find some resilient Coulter pines lending a hint of the alpine.

The trail mellows out as it contours around, and charred remnants aside, this area is actually quite pretty, especially when everything greens up in springtime; sweeping views down to the Antelope Valley below only add to the experience. If you want to stay for a bit, look for a sandy shelf located under some oaks to the right at 2.1 miles, offering room for about two tents (**Camp 11**). Just under 0.5 mile ahead, reach **Mount Gleason Road** and the remnants of what used to be a trailhead parking area, abandoned when the road closed to traffic after the Station Fire. Perhaps it will reopen someday, but until then, the coast is clear to walk across

The upside to the Station Fire's destruction is your ability to score views in nearly every direction.

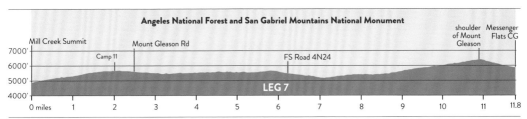

and rejoin the trail as it continues on north-facing slopes. The path can feel a bit overgrown as you continue along—long pants are a lifesaver when dodging the itchy reach of Notorious PDB and pushing through thick underbrush.

While the trail has remained mostly level, it now makes a noticeable drop along switchbacks that deposit you onto a rough road at 6.1 miles. Ignore that sinking realization that on the trail, what goes down must come up, and enjoy the break. Hang a right onto the dirt, quickly reaching the horseshoe curve of a much more well maintained road just ahead—this is **Forest Service Road 4N24** (Beartrap Truck Trail or Bear Trap Canyon Road on some maps). Curve right here, then immediately depart to the left to hop back

on single-track, meandering through a sage-filled canyon before making your way uphill once more. Drop into a gully at 7.1 miles, then round a much larger one at 8.2 miles where you'll notice a use trail jutting off to your left; this pops out at Mount Gleason Road, which follows the ridgeline you've been traveling beneath.

Once you finish traversing around this big gouge, it's time to head uphill. Luckily, a few trees survived to provide shade; you're luckier still if you catch a nice breeze while sweating it out. Huff up a short, but steep series of switchbacks to gain the eastern ridge of Mount Gleason, and admire the northward views while you ascend, often framed by charred branches. If all of this burned stuff makes you blue, rejoice when Jeffrey pines begin to

Charred branches frame endless waves of chaparral-clad slopes.

reappear during the ascent, the soft duff underfoot like a welcome mat.

Soar on that coniferous high to crest the northern shoulder of **Mount Gleason** around 10.8 miles. You can venture a short bit up an old roadbed to your left to tag the summit itself, otherwise crest a rise and let out a shout because it's all downhill from here! The upside to the lack of tree cover for the rest of this leg is that you suddenly earn views straight down gorgeous Pacoima Canyon and out to the ridgelines curving skyward to the southwest. Pull your gaze away long enough to notice an obvious pine-covered island almost directly to the west—this is **Messenger Flats**, and you're headed that way.

Soar down manzanita-lined switchbacks, eventually reaching a side trail at 11.8 miles that marks the end of this leg and your gateway to **Messenger Flats Campground**. Once accessible by car via **Santa Clara Divide Road**, the campground is now hike-in only, thanks to a longstanding post-fire road closure. The upside is that outside of the typical thru-hiking season in late spring, you'll find relative quiet here among a healthy stand of majestic ponderosa pines. To enjoy such wonderful surrounds, depart the PCT on the signed side trail, then make a quick left to follow the unpaved road into the campground. Here, you'll find a now useless parking area, horse corral, vault toilets, picnic tables, garbage receptacles, and plenty of clearings for tents—although there's no water available, so resist the temptation to use any of the fire pits. If there's anything you've learned throughout this leg and the one previous, it's that humans have the ability to irrevocably change the natural landscape—and it's our responsibility to ensure we don't leave things worse for the next generation.

CAMP-TO-CAMP MILEAGE

8 | MESSENGER FLATS CAMPGROUND TO ACTON

DISTANCE 13.8 miles

ELEVATION GAIN/LOSS
+1810/-5470 feet

HIGH POINT 5886 feet

CONNECTING ROADS
Santa Clara Divide Road, Forest Service
Road 4N33, Indian Canyon Road, Soledad
Canyon Road

ON THE TRAIL

When the Station Fire roared through a large swath of the San Gabriel Mountains in 2009, it rendered the burn zone unfit for public recreation for a very long time. Although foliage has reclaimed the ground, animals have returned to inhabit the lands, and hikers once more tromp along its myriad slopes, car access has been severely limited by long-term road closures in the area. The upside is that you have a shot at exceptional peace and solitude as you walk through these transformed lands, especially on this leg.

Begin just outside **Messenger Flats Campground**, a formerly bustling drive-up site that now sees only hiker traffic. If you choose to bunk here, you'll have the benefit of nestling under a stand of majestic ponderosa pines. The turnoff for the campground is well signed, and it's from that junction adjacent to **Santa Clara Divide Road** that you depart. From the get-go, spot Messenger Peak hovering over **Messenger Flats** to the west but also earn expansive views down to the desert environments of the Antelope Valley below, specifically the small community of Acton. You'll also notice the shocking green stripe of Soledad Canyon, created by the cottonwood-lined Santa Clara River—believe it or not, you'll end up down that way soon enough.

Contour along north-facing slopes as you curve around **Messenger Peak**, passing through a few scattered pines until chaparral dominates, with plenty of manzanita and chamise brightening the ground under charred tree skeletons. Drop down to reach a gully at 1.4 miles; pass a seasonal stream just beyond this (but don't get your hopes up unless coming through after rain or snowmelt) to cross rough, unpaved **Forest Service Road 4N33**.

Commence a short, but sweaty, climb to reach a saddle at 2.7 miles. Here, merge with unpaved **Santa Clara Divide Road**, following it briefly before rejoining the trail on the right. The views change as you're now looking southwest down the green folds of Iron Canyon. Up you go, eventually switching to vistas over the North Fork Pacoima Canyon, clothed in hazy silhouettes as the sun retreats. The trail here is lined with the pom-pom flowers of California buckwheat, and scattered yucca serve as reminder that the desert creeps ever closer.

Just over 0.5 mile past the saddle, the trail initiates a glorious downhill trend. Another low point becomes obvious in the distance—this is **North Fork Saddle**, your next checkpoint. To get there,

SAND FIRE

The Sand Fire began in July 2016 and quickly exploded to over 41,000 acres that affected the western San Gabriel Mountains, including nearly the entire Magic Mountain Wilderness. As with the Station Fire, the North Fork Saddle area was spared, but the rest of this leg (and part of the next) experienced intermittent damage. The trail was closed between Mill Creek Summit and Soledad Canyon Road directly after the fire and may be intermittently closed in the future to aid recovery efforts. Check with the Angeles National Forest and PCTA before planning any trips in this area.

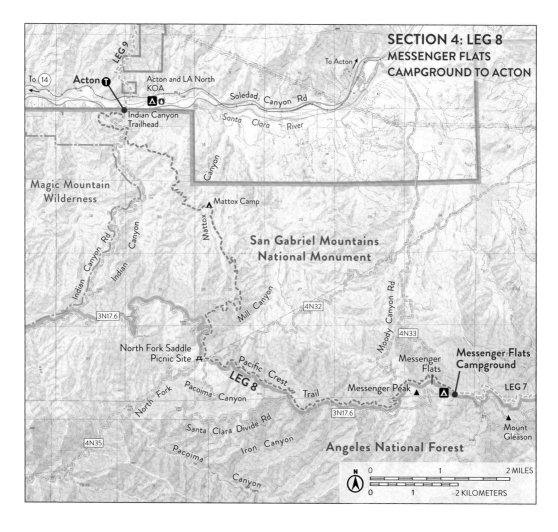

zigzag along a branch of **Mill Canyon**, enjoying the fluffy, Seussian seed heads of clematis punctuating the slopes if you come through in summer. Meet a rough dirt path at 5.6 miles and hang a left to reach your old pal Santa Clara Divide Road at the **North Fork Saddle Picnic Site**, a quiet shadow of its former self since car access was cut off after the Station Fire. Still, there are picnic tables and a vault toilet, and the caretaker here has provided water 🛢 as a courtesy to PCT hikers for many years—for your sake, hopefully that's still the case, since you're not likely to find it anywhere else along this leg. They've also allowed PCT hikers to camp in obvious spots near the picnic area and some horse corrals to the south—I can't guarantee this kindness will be extended into the future if the road reopens.

Once you're done poking around, depart Santa Clara Divide Road almost as quickly as you joined it, the single-track jutting off to the right just past an information sign. From here, you're entering an area that was affected by the 2016 Sand Fire. While it wasn't terribly destructive to the PCT, you'll still see the effects all the way to this segment's end at Soledad Canyon Road and for a few miles into the next leg. Be especially cautious as you navigate the steep slopes above Mill Canyon just past the saddle—while they begin innocuously enough with soft, sandy tread and sunlit foliage,

Early morning light filters through Mill Canyon.

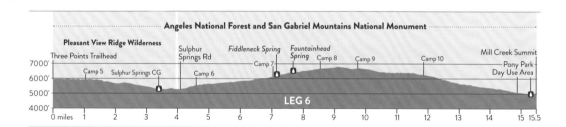

they rapidly transform to thin tread over friable rock that's historically been prone to slides and sloughing.

A slight uphill trend carries you above the vibrant folds of Mill Canyon, whose beauty is marred by the power lines running its length. Eventually the view changes back toward Soledad Canyon, much closer than the last time you caught a glimpse. Follow a series of rollercoaster, fin-like ridges and wiggle around past pockets of chia and yerba santa, marveling at the fact that earlier in this leg, you walked through pine trees, and now you're in a desert wonderland.

A series of switchbacks deposits you in a tree-filled gouge at 9.7 miles—this is **Mattox Canyon**,

and it's the only other spot that might contain water on this leg in wetter months. Sycamores offer a shady rest before you tackle your final section of uphill, regaining some of the elevation you just lost. If the task seems too daunting, you can call it a night here; there are plenty of sandy platforms scattered around the canyon that make excellent campsites (**Mattox Camp**).

Once you've mustered your (emotional) strength, it's time to grind out some uphill. The initial climb is the steepest, but the grade mellows as you make a series of long switchbacks to gain a ridgeline around 11 miles. The lush slash of **Soledad Canyon** is even closer now, and you might be able to make out the sounds of civilization—traffic,

Open slopes offer front-row views to Soledad Canyon below, here covered in a thick layer of fire-produced haze.

trains, and tigers. Okay, I'll explain that last bit—the canyon's Shambala Preserve serves as sanctuary for big cats rescued from improper care.

Head down with gusto, looking across the canyon to spot not only the trail ascending the opposite slope, but also a distinctive rock formation known as the Three Sisters, apparently named for three local women after a man petitioned the United States Geological Survey to honor his mother and aunts. Wiggle around to hit a saddle at 12.2 miles—unpaved **Indian Canyon Road** sits over to the left, but you'll continue straight to stay on trail and crank out one last short bit of uphill. Pop up to meet the road on a ridge less than 0.5 mile later, then cross and curve around to eventually reach the **Indian Canyon Trailhead**. Here, you'll find a shade structure, picnic table, garbage receptacle, vault

toilet, and parking (Adventure Pass required). While it's fine to end here if you arranged a car shuttle, the leg technically finishes at **Soledad Canyon Road** below at 13.8 miles. Walk across the parking lot, then make a left onto Indian Canyon Road, ending at the stop sign below. If looking for a place to spend the night, the **Acton and Los Angeles North KOA** ⬯ campground is just a few minutes east down Soledad Canyon Road; if you walk across the road to continue north, you quickly encounter a side path that leads directly there.

CAMP-TO-CAMP MILEAGE

Messenger Flats Campground to
    Mattox Camp 9.7
Mattox Camp to Acton and
    North Los Angeles KOA 4.1

9 ACTON TO AGUA DULCE

DISTANCE 10.3 miles

ELEVATION GAIN/LOSS
+2320 feet/-2020 feet

HIGH POINT 3163 feet

CONNECTING ROADS
Soledad Canyon Road, Escondido
Canyon Road, Agua Dulce Canyon Road,
Darling Road

ON THE TRAIL

While this leg begins at a busy road, it wastes no time heading up into quiet hills marking the last folds of the San Gabriel Mountains. The only potential unpleasantness (besides power lines above) is a burn scar from the 2016 Sand Fire crossing the first portion of this leg. Luckily, chaparral bounces back quickly after a fire, so things should get back to normal sooner rather than later.

Before embarking, consider your water supply—there are a few natural sources en route, but they tend to dry up by late spring or early summer. One option comes rather quickly, as you cross **Soledad Canyon Road** and pick up the trail on the north side. You almost immediately encounter a side path on the right, which leads to the **Acton and North Los Angeles KOA** campground, where you'll find a host of amenities, including a swimming pool, kitchen, and running water ⬤. Fun fact: this is where I received my trail name, Rustic—it's a long story.

It's just another 0.1 mile through assorted debris piles to cross the seasonal **Santa Clara River** ⬤,

The scenery grows more dramatic as you near Escondido Canyon.

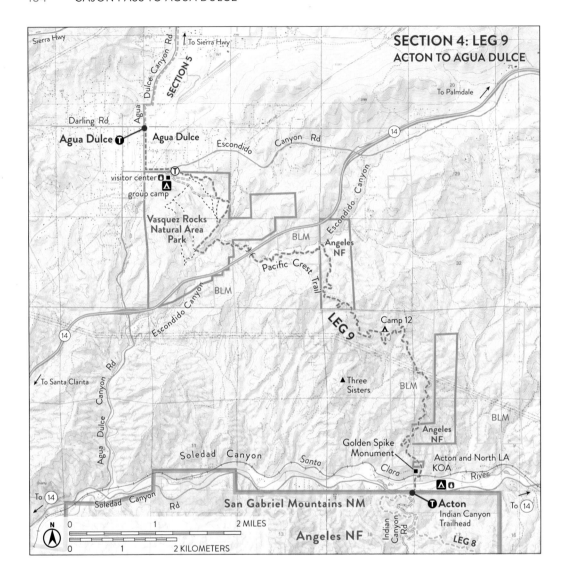

A MISLEADING MONUMENT

The phrase "golden spike" comes from railroad history, where it was common to celebrate a finished rail route by driving a spike into the ground; the original "golden spike" refers specifically to the completion of the First Transcontinental Railroad. While the PCT's Golden Spike Monument is located adjacent to a railroad, the name is merely symbolic—a way to signify the trail's "completion" in 1993 after a land easement was granted for one last bit of trail construction in the nearby Sierra Pelona.

often nothing more than a dank mud pit. Scan for trail markers to stay on track and avoid use trails, then rise up to meet a set of railroad tracks shortly thereafter. This is an active route, so cross carefully. Once safely across, a stone pedestal invites inspection—this is known as the **"Golden Spike Monument,"** a testament to the trail's technical completion in 1993.

After you spend some time soaking in the history, it's time to begin climbing out of the canyon. The sounds and sights of civilization quickly fade as you ascend through intriguing conglomerate rock formations, a warm-up for the main (geologic) event at Vasquez Rocks Natural Area Park. The gentle hillsides glow bright green in spring, dotted with a spectacular assortment of colorful wildflowers, including Indian paintbrush, baby blue eyes, and our state flower, the vibrant orange California poppy.

Cross a less poetic fire road around 2.1 miles, then join a firebreak for a moment about 0.8 mile ahead, quickly descending back to single-track on the left. In the absence of spring flora, this segment can feel a bit monotonous, but it does offer quietude (aside from the buzzing power lines). The only other humans you're likely to see are trail runners grinding out their regular route. You're not *totally* alone, however—mountain lions and coyotes frequent these hills, though you're not likely to see either one as you hike. If you want to bed down with the wildlife, there's a mediocre option around 3.3 miles via a few slightly sloped clearings atop a grassy ridge to your right (**Camp 12**).

Once **State Highway 14** appears in the near distance, quicken your pace to head downhill, wiggling toward **Escondido Canyon**, whose wide bottom you'll drop into just shy of 7 miles. While it's tempting to throw down a tent under the welcoming shade of sycamores, it's not the best

FROM BANDITS TO BIG SHOTS

The stunning Vasquez Rocks formations were carved over the last 25 million years from sandstone and fanglomerate beds along the Elkhorn Fault, a lesser cousin to the famed San Andreas Fault. The area was first inhabited by the Tataviam people, a hunter-gatherer tribe that left morteros and pictographs in the area; hop onto the park's Nature-Heritage Trail to see some of these artifacts. The Tataviam eventually disappeared (or assimilated) in the late 18th century after the Spanish came through and extinguished their way of life. The park's name comes from its next chapter in history, when the maze-like area served as hideout for a notorious outlaw named Tiburcio Vasquez in the mid-19th century. While some saw him as a Robin Hood type, others felt he was no more than a common crook. His eventual capture and execution came about not from his banditry, but by his lust—he was caught with the wife of one of his fellow baddies, who notified the authorities of his whereabouts. In modern times, Vasquez Rocks serves a more glamorous role as backdrop for countless film and TV productions, including *Blazing Saddles*, *Battlestar Galactica*, *Planet of the Apes*, and most famously, both the film and TV versions of *Star Trek*.

idea—not only is freeway traffic quite loud, but there's also a seasonal waterway that winds through the canyon in spring. Best to keep moving toward metal scaffolding guarding a slightly creepy, damp

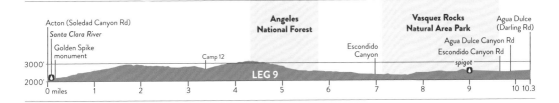

The enchanting Vasquez Rocks formations glow at dusk.

tunnel under Highway 14 that deposits you into a completely different world as you emerge into a lush riparian zone studded with giant conglomerate boulders.

You're heading into the truly spectacular **Vasquez Rocks Natural Area Park**, where you'll walk through some of the most interesting (and famous) rock formations in Southern California. Move away from the freeway, still in a branch of Escondido Canyon, possibly crossing several seasonal flows in late winter and early spring; wait until you reach the park's visitor center about 2 miles ahead for a better water source. The fascinating canyon walls steal your attention, so make sure you don't miss a crucial junction at 8.1 miles; turn right here and head uphill, lest you end up in the boondocks.

Black sage, California sagebrush, chamise, and juniper dot the slopes as you rise to greet a wide, grassy ridge offering absolutely spectacular views. Ignore the nearby houses and focus instead on the incredible formations just to the east—the famous

WHERE TO SNOOZE?

Agua Dulce is a tiny community that doesn't offer anything in the way of lodging. However, you might have two options to choose from, depending on time of year and availability. First, the kind folks at Vasquez Rocks Natural Area Park might let you camp there if you beg convincingly on a day when their group campground isn't already reserved. A second option exists if you're coming through during the late spring thru-hiking season, when perhaps the most famous trail angels of them all, the Saufleys, open their home to serve as the aptly named Hiker Heaven—a quick peek online will let you know if this is an option. If you strike out on both accounts, it's on to the next leg, where the nearest campsite is 4.1 miles in at the head of Mint Canyon.

Vasquez Rocks. These are the park's crown jewels, and a photographer's dream—time your visit to reach the ridge during the golden hour leading into sunset.

Reluctantly tear yourself away and finish walking along the ridge, staying right at a junction, then left to remain on track where the plateau peters out into a residential area. A picnic table 9 miles in offers a shady break spot adjacent to a large, grassy field prone to impromptu soccer matches and picnickers. Continue toward the rocks, crossing an area with horse troughs and a spigot **O**. Things get a bit jumbled from here, although just about any path headed west will deposit you at the park's visitor center. To stay on trail, look to the right when facing the troughs, scanning for trail markers outlining your path through more complex formations. Hit the park's entrance at **Escondido Canyon Road** around 9.6 miles—if you want to visit the visitor center, fill up your water bottles **O**, or use a flush toilet, follow the obvious gravel road away from the trail to land at the sleek building. Water is available only during business hours since it's located inside the building.

Cross Escondido Canyon Road to pick up the route on the other side—not so much a trail as it is a scraggly dirt path inches from asphalt and whizzing cars, but it'll do. You're now in the pastoral town of **Agua Dulce** and will hit its main drag, **Agua Dulce Canyon Road**, shortly; turn right when you reach it and pick up the trail on its left side. Before reaching this leg's end at 10.3 miles, where Agua Dulce Canyon Road intersects with **Darling Road**, stroll right past a grocery store, liquor store, restaurants, retail shops, a hardware store, offering possibly the easiest resupply stop on the entire PCT!

CAMP-TO-CAMP MILEAGE

Soledad Canyon Road to
  Acton and North Los Angeles KOA 0.1
Acton and North Los Angeles KOA
  to Camp 12 . . . . 3.2

AGUA DULCE TO TEHACHAPI PASS

HIKERS OFTEN FEAR The Desert, wondering if they will end up crawling across an infinite swath of blistering sand dunes, fending off small armies of scorpions, while generally dying a slow, thirst-induced death. Thus, no section of the PCT strikes as much dread in the hearts of hikers as this one, which cuts across the western-most Mojave Desert—but there's no need to get freaked out.

This is a beautiful area, and with a bit of careful planning, it's easy to enjoy not just the forested heights of the Sierra Pelona and Tehachapi Mountains but also the Joshua tree–filled expanse of the sandy Antelope Valley. The higher elevations, especially the Sawmill-Liebre sections, are absolutely stunning in spring, when neon green miner's lettuce explodes on the lush slopes beneath sun-drenched black oaks, mingling with stately Coulter pines. Your views out to the desert far below—and the distant Tehachapi and Piute Mountains—are simply spectacular.

Your start to The Desert itself is rather unexciting, through the far reaches of Lancaster alongside the almost entirely enclosed Los Angeles Aqueduct—it's a tease to walk along so much water, yet not be able to reach it. Give the Mojave a chance, though—the man-made structures in this area have a strange symmetry that works in tandem with the topography, and once you head farther north, the land is anything but a stereotypical, flat moonscape as it bends and folds into deep canyons and tall ridges south of Tehachapi. That said, this section of the PCT is in store for some radical changes in the future. The PCTA is currently working with the Tejon Ranch Conservancy to eventually relocate the trail from the hot, dry desert floor up into the cooler Tehachapi Mountains. This process will take quite some time, however, so make peace with the sand and the sun—and make plans to return for another hike once the trail moves to its new home on the crest.

Opposite: Hmmm . . . where to go, where to go?

DISTANCE 112 miles

STATE DISTANCE 454.5–566.5 miles

ELEVATION GAIN/LOSS +13,680/-12,370 feet

HIGH POINT 6302 feet

BEST TIME OF YEAR Oct–Apr

PCTA SECTION LETTER E

LAND MANAGERS Angeles National Forest (Santa Clara/Mojave Rivers Ranger District), Bureau of Land Management (Ridgecrest Field Office)

PASSES AND PERMITS Adventure Pass may be required to park at certain trailheads within the Angeles National Forest. California Campfire Permit.

MAPS AND APPS
- Halfmile's CA Section E
- USFS PCT Map #2 Transverse Ranges
- USGS Topo Quads: Agua Dulce, Sleepy Valley, Green Valley, Lake Hughes, Burnt Peak, Liebre Mountain, La Liebre Ranch, Neenach School, Fairmont Butte, Tylerhorse Canyon, Tehachapi South, Monolith
- Halfmile's PCT app
- Guthook's PCT app

LEGS

1. Agua Dulce to Bouquet
   Canyon Road
2. Bouquet Canyon Road to San
   Francisquito Canyon Road
3. San Francisquito Canyon Road
   to Upper Shake Trail
4. Upper Shake Trail to Horse
   Trail Camp
5. Horse Trail Camp to State
   Highway 138
6. State Highway 138 to Cottonwood
   Creek Bridge
7. Cottonwood Creek Bridge to
   Tylerhorse Canyon
8. Tylerhorse Canyon to Tehachapi
   Willow Springs Road
9. Tehachapi Willow Springs Road
   to Tehachapi Pass

Be prepared. Water is incredibly scarce throughout the area, so plan for strategic top-offs and heavy carries. If it's hot when you pass through, consider avoiding the midday bake with a siesta under a Joshua tree and continuing your hike at night under the canopy of a million twinkling stars—an unforgettable experience.

ACCESS
Agua Dulce
From Los Angeles, head north on Interstate 5 to State Highway 14 north (toward Palmdale and Lancaster). Continue on this road for 14.3 miles, exiting at Agua Dulce Canyon Road (exit 15). Head north for 1.8 miles, where you'll turn left to stay on the road (if you continue straight here, the road becomes Escondido Canyon Road, and you'll soon see Vasquez Rocks Natural Area on your right). This section formally ends at the intersection of Agua Dulce Canyon Road and Darling Road, but you'll have an easier time finding parking outside of Vasquez Rocks Natural Area Park on Escondido Canyon Road; overnight parking is not allowed inside the park.

Tehachapi Pass
From Los Angeles, head north on Interstate 5 to State Highway 14 north (toward Palmdale and Lancaster). Continue on this road for just under 69 miles until it becomes State Highway 58 Business as you pass through Mojave; 3.6 miles after this transition, merge onto State Highway 58 West. Drive 6 miles, then exit at Cameron Road (exit 159) and park in the large turnout on the north side of the road.

NOTES
Cities and Services
The southern trailhead is located on the main drag of Agua Dulce, a small town that boasts a grocery store, several restaurants, and a post office. The northern trailhead offers the choice to head 9 miles west to Tehachapi or 11 miles east to Mojave, both of which offer post offices and several grocery, dining, gas, and lodging options.

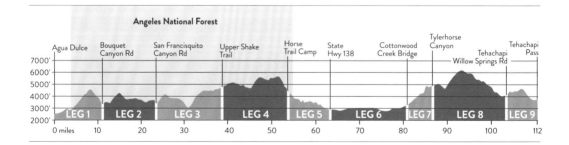

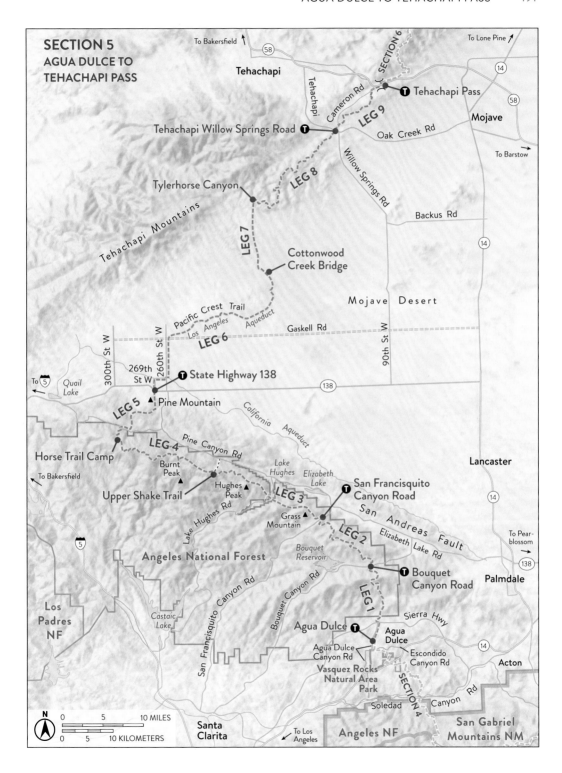

SECTION 5
AGUA DULCE TO
TEHACHAPI PASS

To Bakersfield
To Lone Pine
58
14
Tehachapi
SECTION 6
Tehachapi Pass
58
Mojave
Tehachapi Willow Springs Road
Cameron Rd
LEG 9
Oak Creek Rd
To Barstow
LEG 8
Willow Springs Rd
Tylerhorse Canyon
Backus Rd
Tehachapi Mountains
14
LEG 7
Cottonwood
Creek Bridge
Mojave Desert
Pacific Crest Trail
Los Angeles Aqueduct
Gaskell Rd
90th St W
300th St W
260th St W
LEG 6
269th
St W
State Highway 138
138
Quail
Lake
To 5
Pine Mountain
California Aqueduct
LEG 5
Pine Canyon Rd
LEG 4
Lancaster
Horse Trail Camp
Burnt
Peak
Lake
Hughes
Elizabeth
Lake
To Bakersfield
Upper Shake Trail
Hughes
Peak
San Francisquito
Canyon Road
LEG 3
San Andreas Fault
To Pear-
blossom
Grass
Mountain
LEG 2
Elizabeth Lake Rd
138
5
Lake Hughes Rd
Angeles National Forest
Bouquet
Reservoir
Bouquet
Canyon Road
Palmdale
San Francisquito Canyon Rd
Bouquet Canyon Rd
LEG 1
Los
Padres
NF
Castaic
Lake
Sierra Hwy
Agua Dulce
Agua
Dulce
14
Agua Dulce
Canyon Rd
Escondido
Canyon Rd
Acton
Vasquez Rocks
Natural Area
Park
SECTION 4
Canyon Rd
N
Soledad
0   5   10 MILES
Santa
Clarita
To Los
Angeles
Angeles NF
San Gabriel
Mountains NM
0   5   10 KILOMETERS

SUGGESTED ITINERARIES

Camps are either viewable from the trail or located within a few tenths of a mile from the noted location unless otherwise specified in leg descriptions.

8 DAYS

		Miles
Day 1	Agua Dulce to Camp 1	4.1
Day 2	Camp 1 to Camp 4	12.7
Day 3	Camp 4 to Fish Camp	18.6
Day 4	Fish Camp to Sawmill Campground	8.3
Day 5	Sawmill Campground to Horse Trail Camp	9.9
Day 6	Horse Trail Camp to Cottonwood Creek Bridge	26.8
Day 7	Cottonwood Creek Bridge to Tylerhorse Camp	6.7
Day 8	Tylerhorse Camp to Tehachapi Pass	24.9

7 DAYS

Day 1	Agua Dulce to Camp 4	16.8
Day 2	Camp 4 to Fish Camp	18.6
Day 3	Fish Camp to Sawmill Campground	8.3
Day 4	Sawmill Campground to Horse Trail Camp	9.9
Day 5	Horse Trail Camp to Cottonwood Creek Bridge	26.8
Day 6	Cottonwood Creek Bridge to Tylerhorse Camp	6.7
Day 7	Tylerhorse Camp to Tehachapi Pass	24.9

6 DAYS

Day 1	Agua Dulce to Camp 4	16.8
Day 2	Camp 4 to Fish Camp	18.6
Day 3	Fish Camp to Horse Trail Camp	18.2
Day 4	Horse Trail Camp to Cottonwood Creek Bridge	26.8
Day 5	Cottonwood Creek Bridge to Tylerhorse Camp	6.7
Day 6	Tylerhorse Camp to Tehachapi Pass	24.9

Camping and Fire Restrictions

Like many portions of Southern California's PCT, the trail in this section crosses a lot of private land; restrictive areas are mentioned in the text. Camping and campfires are prohibited while crossing the Tejon Ranch property from just south of Pine Canyon Road to State Highway 138. Fires are allowed only in designated fire rings. Check for seasonal fire restrictions in Angeles National Forest before heading out.

Water

There are few reliable water sources throughout this section, so plan carefully and prepare for heavy water carries. The longest likely waterless stretches are the 8.7 miles between Darling Road and Bear Spring, the 15 miles between Bear Spring and San Francisquito Canyon Road (at the Green Valley Fire Station spigot), the 10.4 miles between the spring at Horse Trail Camp and the California Aqueduct, the 20.7 miles between the Aqueduct faucet and Tylerhorse Canyon, and the 25.1 miles between Oak Creek and Golden Oaks Spring in the next section.

Hazards

The Mojave Desert portion of this section is notoriously hot and prone to high winds. Consider hiking the lower elevations during the cooler months or in evening hours; an umbrella or wide sun hat, plus layers of loose clothing and plenty of sunblock are also recommended. All of this isn't to say that the area is always broiling—the Sierra Pelona and Tehachapi Mountains can see snow, and cold, rainy conditions can hit the desert floor.

Other

Many thru-hikers rely on trail angels in this section to help with package resupply and lodging due to the lack of camping options in some areas.

1 AGUA DULCE TO BOUQUET CANYON ROAD

DISTANCE 11.1 miles

ELEVATION GAIN/LOSS
+3050/-2250 feet

HIGH POINT 4583 feet

CONNECTING ROADS
Darling Road, Agua Dulce Canyon Road, Sierra Highway, Mint Canyon Road, Peterson Road, Forest Service Road 6N07, Bouquet Canyon Road

ON THE TRAIL

This leg begins somewhat unconventionally, at the intersection of **Agua Dulce Canyon Road** and **Darling Road** in the small town of **Agua Dulce**. Before setting off, consider toting enough water for your entire trip—the only source is a spring 8.7 miles ahead that is usually dry by the warmer months. Luckily, the town has a great grocery store ⬤ (and liquor store, although that will only exacerbate dehydration) right on the trail just south of your start point, so it's easy to stock up here. Amble north along Agua Dulce Canyon Road, steering clear of

the pavement to avoid getting clipped by passing traffic. The people here are friendly—and very used to hikers coming through—so don't be surprised if you earn a few hoots, honks, and hellos.

Head north on Agua Dulce Canyon Road toward the distant foothills, following the road as it bends to the right past houses, horses, and a few small businesses. At 1.9 miles, cross **Sierra Highway** at an intersection, then quickly curve right up **Mint Canyon Road**, with another quick right to head north on **Peterson Road**. Keep your eyes peeled for a trail marker on the

SWEET WATER

Agua Dulce is a sweet little town in both name and character, and quite possibly the only place where you'll find a grocery store right on the trail since the PCT travels its main drag (Agua Dulce Canyon Road) for quite some time. Besides the market, you'll also find several restaurants and shops, along with the fantastic Vasquez Rocks Natural Area Park, which you'll travel through to arrive in town if you're hiking the trail.

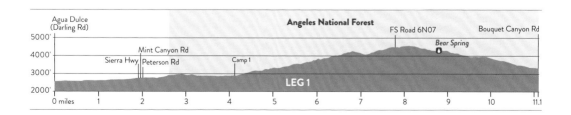

Bouquet Reservoir sparkles in the late afternoon light.

ALTERNATE START

If you'd like to skip the walk through town and shave off some mileage, an alternate start can be found 2.2 miles north underneath a transformer and power lines on a dirt road that marks where the PCT departs Petersen Road—there's a small dirt patch here with space for a few cars.

right side of the road at 2.2 miles—cross here and head up a wide dirt road underneath some power lines.

As you climb, it's hard not to notice the jet fuselage occupying sizeable real estate off of Peterson Road—this is actually one of the filming locations owned by the **Agua Dulce Movie Ranch**. Ignore a dirt road on your left and sweat upward to reach a trail marker at 2.6 miles guarding a blissful

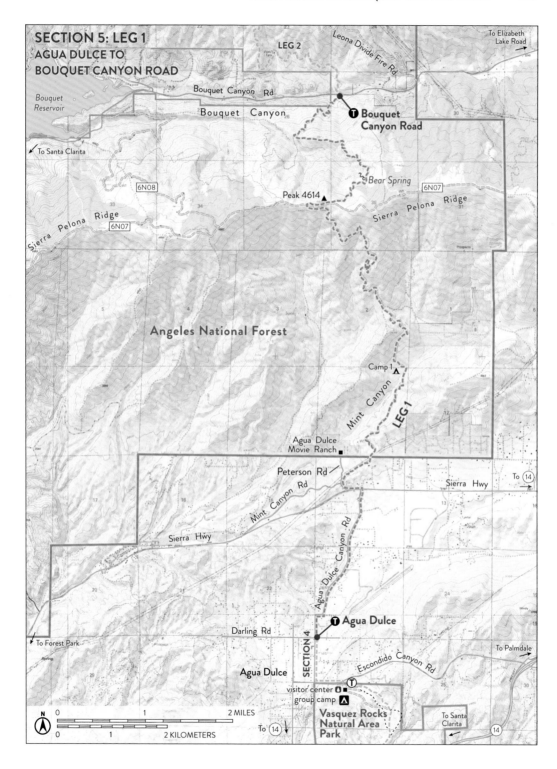

SECTION 5: LEG 1
AGUA DULCE TO
BOUQUET CANYON ROAD

LEG 2

Leona Divide Fire Rd

To Elizabeth
Lake Road

Bouquet Canyon Rd

Bouquet
Reservoir

Bouquet Canyon

T Bouquet
Canyon Road

To Santa Clarita

Bear Spring

6N08

Peak 4614 ▲

6N07

Sierra Pelona Ridge

Sierra Pelona Ridge

6N07

Angeles National Forest

Camp 1 ⚑

Mint Canyon

LEG 1

Agua Dulce
Movie Ranch ■

Peterson Rd
Rd

Sierra Hwy

To 14

Mint Canyon Rd

Agua Dulce Canyon Rd

Sierra Hwy

To Forest Park

Darling Rd

T Agua Dulce

SECTION 4

To Palmdale

Agua Dulce

Escondido Canyon Rd

visitor center ❶■
group camp ⚑

T

Vasquez Rocks
Natural Area
Park

To Santa
Clarita

14

N
0   1   2 MILES
0   1   2 KILOMETERS

To 14

single-track that wiggles around the gentle green slopes of gorgeous **Mint Canyon**. Wave goodbye to the jet plane and all other man-made stuff as you finally head back into nature, weaving through thick chaparral above the wide, braided canyon bottom.

Camping opportunities are sparse throughout this entire section, but there are a few mediocre spots scattered to your left after you wind around the canyon mouth to hit a rough dirt road at 4.1 miles (**Camp 1**). However, take heed: while the canyon is often dry, it does sometimes see a seasonal flow in wet years. Encounter a trail register shortly thereafter and make your mark. Before departing, consider taking a bathroom break deep in the plentiful chamise, because from here, the trail is going to wind around the kind of steep slopes that only a mountain goat could comfortably crouch upon.

Post-potty break, slather on sunblock and break out your wide-brimmed hat—it's time to head uphill along the shadeless slopes. Now on the far side of Mint Canyon, boulders dot the hillside and the climb offers views of bucolic ranchland filled with grassy pastures and grazing cows. Briefly join a firebreak at 5.4 miles and continue back on trail down to the left. Although the path winds along (and up) for what seems like an eternity, it does offer views to the sometimes snowcapped San Gabriel Mountains rising up in the distance. You can also see nearly all of the tread you just ascended—high five your hiking buddy (or yourself) for hoofing up all of that! You reach **Sierra Pelona Ridge** at 7.8 miles at **Forest Service Road 6N07**, which seems perpetually rutted out by any number of wheeled vehicles. Nevertheless, this is an awesome, shady spot to take a break under an array of welcoming oaks.

When you're ready to push on, make sure you stay on the road, heading down to the right to circle beneath, rather than over, **Peak 4614**—although if you do take the overland route, you'll still end up at the right place, a flat spot on the ridge at 8.1 miles, where the PCT makes an obvious departure to descend along the north slopes.

Stepping into a completely different world than the sunny southern side, you'll walk through a tunnel of scrub oak to pass through the first of

four pipe gates on this shady segment shortly after you begin the downhill. Watch for a horse trough down to the left at 8.7 miles after you round a large, rocky gully; while the water here is usually disgusting, you'll find less slimy refreshment at piped **Bear Spring** ⬤ in a clearing to the right. However, don't be surprised to find it dry if you come through in late summer.

Hit the next pipe gate at 9.4 miles and start walking along a wide, rocky ridge gazing west to Bouquet Reservoir, a man-made lake that packs a visual punch, especially in the hour or two before sunset when the surrounding mountains transform into hazy silhouettes. Your water views expand for a bit as you continue down; just be sure you also pay attention to your feet since the tread in this area isn't in the best shape and one tiny misstep might send you sailing into the dirt.

By the time you hit the third gate at 10.1 miles, you'll likely hear cars passing on nearby **Bouquet Canyon Road**. Continue down through manzanita to reach the final gate and finally the road itself at 11.1 miles, where you'll find a large dirt turnout for parking. If you're desperate for a place to throw down your tent, avoid the temptation to park yourself across the road in the canyon's depression—this area attracts partiers (and their accompanying noise and garbage). Instead, continue up the PCT another 0.3 mile to find several clearings scattered in the brush, described oh-so-eloquently in the next leg.

CAMP-TO-CAMP MILEAGE
Agua Dulce to Camp 1 . . . . .4.1

2 BOUQUET CANYON ROAD TO SAN FRANCISQUITO CANYON ROAD

DISTANCE 12.6 miles

ELEVATION GAIN/LOSS
+3130/-3060 feet

HIGH POINT 4327 feet

CONNECTING ROADS
Bouquet Canyon Road, Spunky Edison Road, San Francisquito Canyon Road

ON THE TRAIL

This leg begins at the trail's intersection with **Bouquet Canyon Road**, just east of a large parking turnout, with a slow, moderate climb out of **Bouquet Canyon**. You'll quickly trade the hum of occasional traffic for a surprising stillness as you weave through the tall chamise lining the trail. Be sure to carry all the water you need since there are no reliable sources along this leg. Around 0.3 mile in, notice a sloped grassy clearing to the left with room for one tent (**Camp 2**); there are a few more similar spots scattered throughout the gravelly brush along the next 0.1 mile. However, unless you've desperately worn yourself out in the first seven minutes of your hike, keep on hoofing since better sites await.

The gentle grade makes this a popular route for trail runners, who whiz by like so many Spandex-clad cheetahs, and it's no surprise that this area plays host to a popular trail race. As you amble along on the soft tread, listen for birdsong and sink into the peaceful vibes; considering you're within spitting distance of a fairly busy road, there's a real sense of serenity here.

At just under 2 miles, round a corner to earn a glimpse of Bouquet Reservoir and its surrounding peaks—as good as it seems now, this view improves the higher you go. And speaking of climbs, the gentle ascent is over—it's time to put in some grunt work. After a short burst of thigh-busting uphill along a ridge, you'll hit a set of power lines at 2.6 miles; just beyond this, crest the ridge to find a sandy area on your right through some scattered bushes—a perfect spot for a few small tents if you don't mind the slight buzz overhead (**Camp 3**).

The trail suddenly becomes a bit thinner, crumblier, and bushier as you continue, so mind your step and ensure you don't have anything dangling from your pack for the branches to grab. The slopes are eventually dominated by manzanita, the tread becomes a lot more pleasant, and the reservoir once again provides eye candy in the distance. Enjoy these last water views because when you hit the crest of the ridge, your views

A TRAGIC HISTORY

While the Bouquet Reservoir makes for a pretty sight down below, its history is actually quite sobering as it was built to replace the doomed St. Francis Dam, located several miles southwest in San Francisquito Canyon. In 1926, work was completed on the original dam, part of the complex aqueduct system designed to transfer water from the Owens Valley to the heavily populated Los Angeles area. Unfortunately, the dam was problematic from the start, with leaks occurring almost immediately. It failed completely just before midnight on March 12, 1968, sending a catastrophic flood rushing down the valley, carving a path of destruction all the way to the Pacific Ocean. It's estimated that nearly 500 people lost their lives as a result. All that remains today is a commemorative plaque and several massive concrete chunks that sit exactly where they fell, serving as haunting reminder of one of the worst disasters in California history.

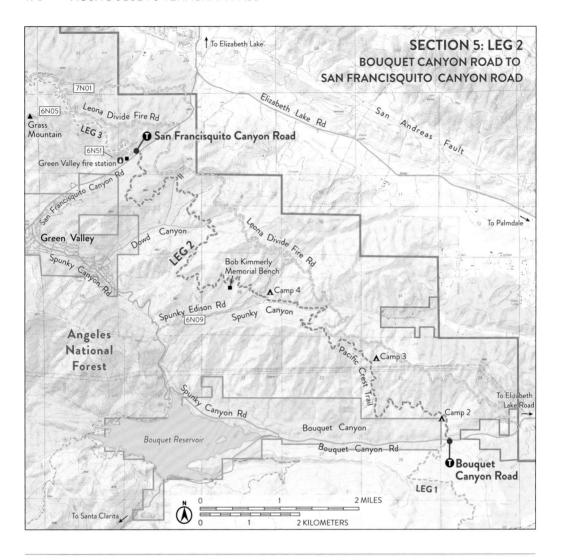

change dramatically as you peer down into **Spunky Canyon** and look north into the Mojave Desert.

Once you've marinated in the sights, head left along a firebreak to pick up the trail heading downhill into the canyon. Now that you're traveling along north-facing slopes, the foliage shifts from bushy chaparral to grasses and oaks, offering your first real respite from the sun. A shady nook offers a camping opportunity 5.6 miles in, with more spots located in the brush ahead (**Camp 4**).

A hiker enjoys the views into Dowd Canyon and beyond.

Cross unpaved **Spunky Edison Road** (Forest Service Road 6N09), heading uphill toward a marvelous sight—a shady bend in the trail at 6.7 miles that features a welcoming bench. Air out your dogs and sink into the wooden comfort of what's known as the **Bob Kimmerly Memorial Bench**, named for the originator of the Leona Divide trail races; a partial list of winners is carved into a sign next to the bench. Once you're finished admiring others' accomplishments, lift your weary bones and continue traversing the slopes above Spunky Canyon. As you make your way toward a prominent ridge, look for a rounded high point in the distance— this is Grass Mountain; the next leg of the PCT passes within spitting distance of its pine-dotted summit.

GREEN VALLEY

Green Valley is a small residential area with extremely limited services. If you're hungry or thirsty, head 1.5 miles south of the PCT where San Francisquito Canyon Road meets Spunky Canyon Road, and you'll find a café as well as a gas station that also serves as a small market. Green Valley is also home to a pair of beloved SoCal trail angels, the Andersons, who offer up their home (known in trail circles as Casa de Luna) as a Hawaiian shirt–filled, taco salad–stuffed oasis for thru-hikers. A quick search online will let you know if they're still hosting hikers when you roll through.

After you pop over the ridge you've been staring at, the trail becomes much rockier, and your views suddenly expand to include the small community of Green Valley, which sits in lush **Dowd Canyon** far beneath the trail. One glance at the massive chlorophyll explosion down below and you won't question how the town earned its name.

Once you look up again, you might notice a faint line running across the slopes ahead—this seemingly endless path is the trail, and despite the beautiful scenery, it can feel a bit monotonous as it winds steadily uphill around each little squiggle in the topography. Just when you think it's over, you turn a corner and . . . more squiggling. Distract yourself with the sweet smell of trailside sage and by taking in those valley views. If it's all getting a bit sweaty for your tastes, know that at 10.7 miles you'll turn a corner to enter a shady rock grotto that becomes a tiny seasonal waterfall in wetter years. The sign mentioning BSA Troop 415 is a relic from trail maintenance times past.

Hopefully revived, you're now in the home stretch! Reach a firebreak at 11.6 miles that marks the end of the uphill—go ahead and let out an excited squeal as you round a bend to begin coasting down. You might be shocked at just how close **San Francisquito Canyon Road** looks (if you set up a shuttle, you'll probably be able to spot your car parked along its edge) and even more shocked at how quickly you reach it—don't forget to pause and sign the trail register just before landing at the road itself at 12.6 miles. If thirsty, walk south on the road for a few minutes to reach the **Green Valley Fire Station** on the north side. They kindly allow passing hikers to avail themselves of their water spigot ◯ (located in a box attached to the main building), and you'll also find a small parking lot and picnic area here.

CAMP-TO-CAMP MILEAGE

Bouquet Canyon to Camp 2 . . . . 0.3
Camp 2 to Camp 3 . . . . 2.3
Camp 3 to Camp 4 . . . . 3.1

3   SAN FRANCISQUITO CANYON ROAD TO UPPER SHAKE TRAIL

DISTANCE 15.2 miles

ELEVATION GAIN/LOSS
+3920/-2580 feet

HIGH POINT 4787 feet

CONNECTING TRAILS AND ROADS
San Francisquito Canyon Road, Forest Service Road 6N51, Forest Service Road 7N01, Forest Service Road 7N02, Lake Hughes Road, Forest Service Road 7N08, Upper Shake Trail

ON THE TRAIL

As you've no doubt learned so far, wildfire is a constant threat to the trail and its surroundings. In Southern California, it's important to roll with the punches as Mother Nature and careless humans deal them. Nearly this entire leg was affected by the 2013 Powerhouse Fire, a power line–sparked blaze that knocked out more than 30,000 acres. Subsequent years of drought meant that new root systems weren't able to establish and bind together the weakened soil, and seasonal rains (including a particularly rough storm in October 2015) caused further deterioration of the already-wrecked slopes. However, trail crews finished repair work on this portion of trail as this book went to press, so now hikers are free to enjoy this excellent slice of the Sierra Pelona.

Consider hiking in springtime when the slopes glow bright green and on a clear day when you'll have great sightlines. Begin at the trail's

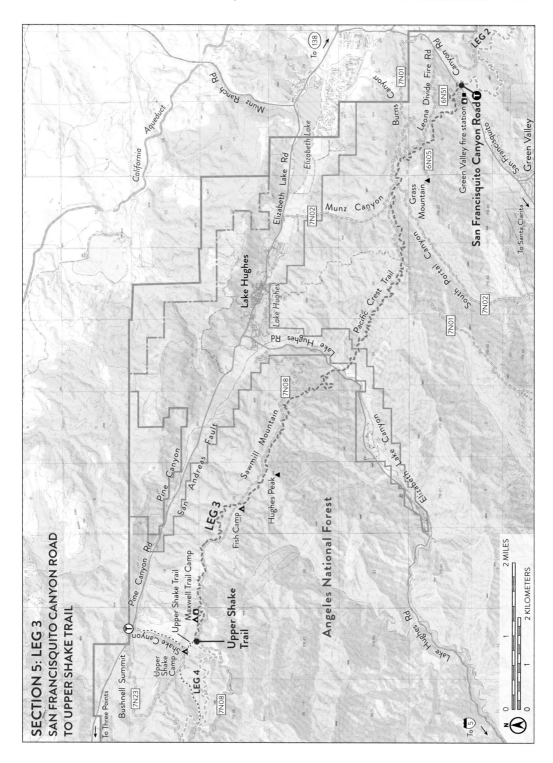

SECTION 5: LEG 3
SAN FRANCISQUITO CANYON ROAD
TO UPPER SHAKE TRAIL

To Three Points

Bushnell Summit

7N23

Pine Canyon Rd

LEG 4

7N08

Upper Shake Camp

Shake Canyon

Upper Shake Trail

Maxwell Trail Camp

Upper Shake
Trail

Fish Camp

LEG 3

San Andreas Fault

Pine Canyon

Hughes Peak

Sawmill Mountain

7N08

Angeles National Forest

Lake Hughes Rd

Lake Hughes

Lake Hughes

Lake Hughes Rd

Elizabeth Lake Canyon

Pacific Crest Trail

7N02

7N01

7N02

South Portal Canyon

Grass
Mountain

6N05

Munz Canyon

7N02

Elizabeth Lake Rd

Elizabeth Lake

Munz Ranch Rd

California Aqueduct

To 138

Canyon

7N01

Burns Canyon

Leona Divide Fire Rd

Canyon Rd

LEG 2

6N51

Green Valley fire station

San Francisquito Canyon Road

To Santa Clarita

Green Valley

San Francisquito

To I5

N

0   1   2 MILES

0   1   2 KILOMETERS

DIRTY WORK

The author takes a break from doing dirty work along the trail.

I was able to access part of the former Powerhouse Fire closure area when I joined the famous Trail Gorillas work crew to assist with some trail repair. These amazing people help maintain around 700 miles of the PCT between the southern terminus and Kennedy Meadows—no small task! On this trip, we dug out portions of the tread, which sat buried under large quantities of slide debris, and built rock walls to stabilize washouts. The crew planned to work hard throughout the year so that the closed trail could be reopened as soon as possible—in fact, I can promise that it will have happened by the time you're reading this book! I highly encourage you to consider volunteering for trail work—sweat equity is a wonderful way to give back to a trail that gives so much to all of us. Visit the PCTA website for a list of projects.

intersection with paved **San Francisquito Canyon Road**; if you want to leave a car in the area, find parking along the shoulder or in a lot located at the **Green Valley Fire Station** just a few minutes south. There's a shady picnic area; you'll also find a water spigot ⭕ attached to the building.

The trail teases you with a brief, shady interlude in pinyon pines, but as soon as you round a gully, the trees give way to sunny chaparral slopes abundant with manzanita, chamise, and fragrant yerba santa. You ascend from the road fairly quickly, although the sound of traffic below and crackling power lines above serve as reminder that civilization is not too far away. Reach unpaved **Forest Service Road 6N51** 0.3 mile in; from here, gaze down lush **San Francisquito Canyon** into the small town of Green Valley. Turn right on the road, then quickly depart to the

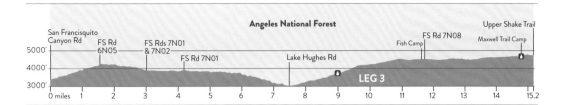

left to continue on trail. While climbing, it's easy to spot not only the previous leg's track running across the canyon but also **Grass Mountain** to the northwest.

If the lure of peakbagging is strong, the opportunity arises to tag Grass Mountain at 1.6 miles when you reach unpaved **Forest Service Road 6N05**. Head left on this gravelly route to climb about 0.75 mile to reach the summit, marked with communications equipment, a few hardy Coulter pines, and of course, grass. The views aren't too shabby, especially since you can see all the way to the Pacific Ocean on a clear day! However, great vistas abound even if you opt to skip this side trip—from a small clearing where the trail crosses the road, look down into **Burns Canyon**, out toward the small town of Elizabeth Lake (and possibly its rainfall-dependent namesake), and even farther north into the Antelope Valley, across the wind turbine–dotted sandy flats leading toward the Tehachapi Mountains.

Cross the road to leave San Francisquito Canyon (and traffic noise) behind, picking up the trail on the other side—the PCT is the right branch of the trail fork. Lose elevation at a gentle grade, contouring along slopes that offer bits of shade from clusters of scrub oak. Northward sightlines continue until obscured by surrounding hillsides; now, a sandy saddle comes into view along with massive **South Portal Canyon** to the southwest. Reach this area at 3 miles, at the intersection of unpaved **Forest Service Road 7N01** (Burns Fire Road) and **Forest Service Road 7N02**, with **Munz Canyon** cutting through just to the north.

The folded hills offer new views at every turn.

The ascent toward Grass Mountain offers expansive views over San Francisquito Canyon.

Continuing on, the trail traces the north side of South Portal Canyon for a bit before re-crossing Burns Fire Road at 4.2 miles. It then begins a northwestern arc, weaving out of a million gullies (rough estimate), before descending to **Elizabeth Lake Canyon** and paved **Lake Hughes Road** at 7.5 miles. This route offers another access point for the trail and will take you to the western edge of the small burg of Lake Hughes where you'll find a market, post office, the fantastic Rock Inn, and possibly even its ephemeral namesake if drought hasn't claimed the lake.

From its intersection with **Lake Hughes Road**, the trail climbs once more, continuing northwest to ascend the slopes of sprawling **Sawmill Mountain**, where you'll find a seasonal spring ○ sprouting from the hillside at 8.9 miles. Cross a few unpaved roads and continue along, eventually passing north of the summit of **Hughes Peak**. Just before crossing unpaved **Forest Service Road 7N08** (Maxwell Truck Trail) at 11.7 miles, look for a small wooden sign for "Fish Creek Canyon PCT Trail Camp" (**Fish Camp**); depart the PCT and walk downhill toward a rickety picnic table to find a grassy area suitable for camping, although digging gophers and overgrowth conspire to make it a little less so.

Continue winding along the ridgeline above numerous deep canyons to reach pine-shaded **Maxwell Trail Camp** on your left at 14.8 miles. Water is available nearby via a concrete wildlife guzzler ○. To find it, ignore the obvious grey concrete box south of the campsite and instead continue along the PCT for a moment to reach a wide dirt road; turn right here and walk less than 0.1 mile to spot the flat concrete guzzler to your right. It's just a short bit farther to reach the obvious, but unsigned junction with the **Upper Shake Trail** to **Upper Shake Campground** at 15.2 miles. From here, you can depart the PCT and descend to the right about 0.5 mile to reach the disused campground, now closed to car traffic. Here, you'll find a pair of terrifying pit toilets, some broken picnic tables, and plenty of space to plop down a tent. Seasonal water is available via a spring ○ that feeds into the canyon just below the northernmost picnic table; an obvious trail descends to it.

CAMP-TO-CAMP MILEAGE

4 UPPER SHAKE TRAIL TO HORSE TRAIL CAMP

DISTANCE 14.7 miles

ELEVATION GAIN/LOSS
+3690/-3610 feet

HIGH POINT 5751 feet

CONNECTING TRAILS AND ROADS
Upper Shake Trail, Maxwell Truck Trail,
Burnt Peak Road, Sawmill Mountain
Truck Trail, Liebre Road

ON THE TRAIL

There's a lot to feast your eyes upon while traveling across the backbones of both Sawmill and Liebre Mountains, from gentle slopes dotted with sun-dappled oak trees and heavily scented pine stands to the vast expanse of the flat Antelope Valley and the Tehachapi Mountains on its northern edge. Although the area has been ravaged by fire and windstorms over the years, this remains one of the most stunning segments of the Sierra Pelona.

Start where the PCT meets the unsigned **Upper Shake Trail**, which switchbacks down 0.5 mile to reach the abandoned **Upper Shake Campground**, described in the previous leg. As you begin to traverse the slopes of **Sawmill Mountain**, you'll almost immediately score fantastic views out to the sunny Antelope Valley below and the Tehachapi Mountains rising beyond. The views come and go as you weave in and out of gullies, sometimes obscured by a pleasantly shady mixture of oak and spruce. On a clear day, stop at one of the gaps to see if you can spot Telescope Peak towering over Death Valley over 150 miles away.

Skip along the grassy path to reach a PCT marker located across from a faint use trail on your right around the 2-mile mark; this is an alternate route that plunges steeply on sometimes crumbling slopes to meet Upper Shake Campground. Just ahead at 2.8 miles, emerge from the pristine beauty

and enter a large dirt clearing—this is **Burnt Peak Junction**, where **Maxwell Truck Trail** (Forest Service Road 7N08) comes in from the south, **Burnt Peak Road** (Forest Service Road 7N23A) proceeds straight ahead, and **Sawmill Mountain Truck Trail** (Forest Service Road 7N23) winds across to the north. Luckily, the PCT is well marked here, and you pick it up on the north side under a large, shady pine between the two spurs of Road 7N23. If you want to try topping off your reservoir before forging on, look uphill to the west to spot a tank ⬤ perched on the hillside—this deep basin usually holds some water after a rain.

ALTERNATE START

An alternate to this route's start point begins in **Shake Canyon**, just east of Bushnell Summit on Pine Canyon Road. Parking is available along the road here, with an unpaved lot farther up at Bushnell Summit itself. Depart the road on an unpaved path that quickly becomes an obvious trail (**Shake Canyon Trail**) as you enter the canyon. Pass the remnants of long-gone Lower Shake Campground in 0.3 mile, nothing more than a decrepit outhouse and an old spring pipe jutting out of the canyon wall to your left. From here, head up through the shaded canyon, scanning for possible water in the creek bed down to your right ⬤, fed by a spring located just below Upper Shake Campground, which you'll reach in just under a mile. Hop on a crumbling paved road, heading to the left through the remnants of the campground, to spot a PCT marker ahead. It marks the Upper Shake Trail, which switchbacks up to connect you with the PCT in about a half mile, where this leg starts.

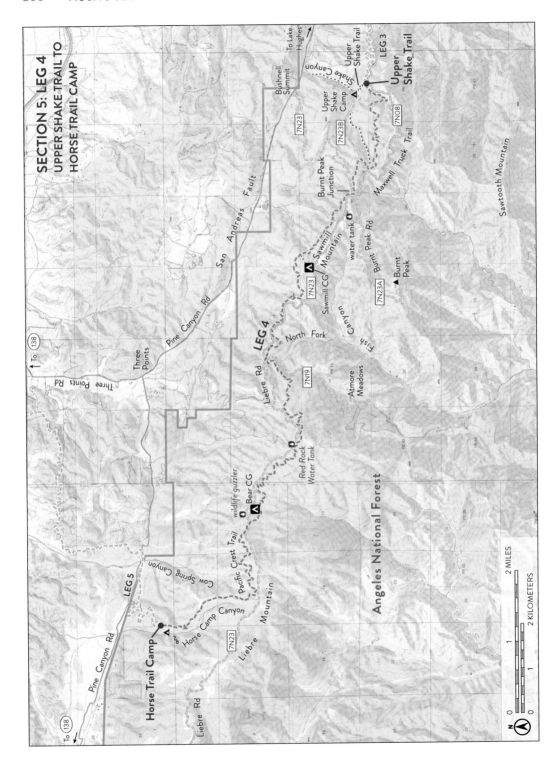

SECTION 5: LEG 4
UPPER SHAKE TRAIL TO
HORSE TRAIL CAMP

HUNTING SEASON

This area is popular with hunters, who come through in autumn in search of resident mule deer. The hunting season here usually lasts a month, between mid-October and mid-November, so unless you enjoy dodging lethal projectiles, wear bright colors or avoid the trail during this time.

As you descend, enjoy the shade of black oaks, inhale the sharp pine fragrance, and marvel at the blanket of miner's lettuce coating the hillsides with chlorophyll-induced enthusiasm in the spring—it's edible, with a slight spinachy taste, so feel free to dress up your lunch. Also scan for mistletoe clinging to the oaks—yes, it's a parasite, but it's also the same stuff you steal kisses under during the holidays, so have a go if your hiking partner's up for some romance.

At 4.8 miles, reach a signed junction with the **Sawmill Campground Trail**, which ascends to the left 0.25 mile to reach a waterless, but pretty area featuring a handful of campsites, picnic tables, fire rings, and a vault toilet (**Sawmill Campground**). Reach an intersection with Sawmill Mountain Truck Trail at the 6-mile mark—enjoy one last look out across the Antelope Valley (for now), then continue down into a small grove of tall Coulter pines and incense cedars, whose needles make for pleasantly soft duff underfoot. Take time to appreciate this fragrant shady patch because you're about to undertake a sweaty climb through sunny chaparral. Take this opportunity to reapply sunscreen and munch the high-energy food of your choice, then stroll on through thick clusters of manzanita and chamise dotted with the

occasional mountain mahogany. It's easy for the trail to become overgrown here, so consider long pants or resign yourself to being scratched by every wayward branch.

Even though the desert vistas disappear for a bit, you still have beautiful things to look at—now it's the lush folds of **Fish Canyon**'s north fork. This should provide motivation until you reach **Atmore Meadows Spur Road** (Forest Service Road 7N19) at 6.8 miles, hanging a left to follow it for a scant 200 feet until the PCT detours right into a brushy gully. Congratulations—you just transitioned from Sawmill Mountain to **Liebre Mountain**!

Around 8.6 miles, curl around to head along the spine of Liebre Mountain in earnest. Just to the north of the trail is Forest Service Road 7N23, now called **Liebre Road**, which ascends to the **Red Rock Water Tank ⬡**. You can reach this concrete cistern by diverting to the road whenever you have the chance; otherwise, a faint use trail cuts over from the PCT through a tunnel of scrub oak near the 9-mile mark. As with your previous water tank experience, there's no guarantee you'll find anything here, and if you do, it may be far beyond arm's reach.

From here, continue on blissfully level trail, admiring a parade of ridges and canyons that seem to go on forever. Scan for a break in the ubiquitous manzanita at 10.8 miles, guarding a spur to **Bear Campground**, a tiny outpost with a rustic outhouse, several campsites, and picnic tables. There's no water here, but when you hit Liebre Road just under 0.5 mile ahead, hang a right to not only access the camp, but also to locate a guzzler ⬡ hidden on a gentle slope to your left. Its corrugated metal "roof" peeks out as you head downhill; leave the road about 350 feet ahead to make your way down to the tank. Water collects here after rains, but so does algae, so bring a filter.

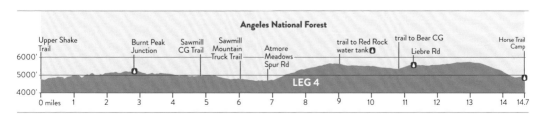

Bright miner's lettuce carpets trailside slopes in spring.

If you've enjoyed the trail so far, you'll be knocked out by it during these last few miles as you enter what I call the "fairy forest" portion, most magical in the spring when miner's lettuce completely clothes the gently rolling slopes, which are dotted with gnarly, sun dappled oaks, moss-covered boulders, and deer tracks. Be on the lookout for gnomes.

It's a bit sad to have to leave these magical surrounds when you hit an old jeep road at 13.1 miles, but the good news is that what you lose in greenery, you make up for in scenery. Hang right to head along the wide, gravelly track, which wastes no time losing elevation along a steep ridgeline that straddles **Cow Canyon** to the east and **Horse Camp Canyon** to the west. Prepare your camera for what will shortly become an unobstructed look down, across, and into what feels like The Entire Desert—there are no trees blocking the spectacular view, so soak it in.

Pull yourself away to continue the descent, dropping down past scattered pines, cedars, and oaks. The trail is quiet and shady as you skirt the eastern wall of Horse Camp Canyon, and you'll find its namesake camp is equally peaceful (**Horse Trail Camp**). Reach it on your left at 14.7 miles; it's marked by a sign and a solitary picnic table. The camp sits on a high bump overlooking the Antelope Valley—a perfect perch for settling in with your beverage of choice and watching the sunset (or sunrise). Speaking of liquids, there's a spring 🌢 here—look for a sign at the west side of the clearing, then zigzag your way down a very steep use trail to hit the canyon bottom—head upstream for the best flow, watching out for stinging nettle, and don't be surprised if it's bone dry in the warmer months.

CAMP-TO-CAMP MILEAGE
Upper Shake Trail to
    Sawmill Campground 4.8
Sawmill Campground to
    Bear Campground 6.0
Bear Campground to Horse Trail Camp 3.9

5 HORSE TRAIL CAMP TO STATE HIGHWAY 138

DISTANCE 9.5 miles

ELEVATION GAIN/LOSS
+1340/-3150 feet

HIGH POINT 4852 feet

CONNECTING ROADS
Pine Canyon Road, State Highway 138

ON THE TRAIL

Enjoy shade from a few last pine trees before hitting the hilly edge of the Mojave Desert in the Antelope Valley. While this route meanders up and down and every which way due to the jagged lines of a private property easement, your frustration at its nonsensical path will fade if you embrace the gorgeous views and wildflower display, especially if you come through in spring when fields of bright yellow-orange poppies erupt.

Before descending, fill up at the spring ⭘ in **Horse Camp Canyon**, described in the previous chapter—there's no reliable water on this leg or the next—in fact, it's quite possible that you won't hit water until the flow at Tylerhorse Canyon, 33.5 miles from here! When finished, head

straight down along a series of long, lazy switchbacks. Although they won't compare to watching sunrise or sunset from your lofty perch at **Horse Trail Camp**, the sweeping views are still pretty excellent as you gaze out toward the Tehachapi Mountains to the north. You can also spot Quail Lake to the northwest, a recreational watershed created from a branch of the California Aqueduct—its faraway waters a cruel tease as you drop toward the notoriously hot, dry Mojave Desert floor. Until then, there's plenty of flora to enjoy, from Coulter pines and black oak to chamise, wild cucumber, and mountain mahogany.

It doesn't take long for civilization to encroach, here in the form of an asphalt ribbon marking Pine Canyon Road below; you'll be near it at 1.9 miles when you cross a dirt parking area that serves as an alternate trailhead. You won't hit the road itself quite yet, although it will seem annoyingly close over the next mile. Hang a right from the parking area to stay on the trail and try to focus instead on the abundant wildlife you might spot in this area—western fence lizards, cottontail rabbits, and snakes all patrol these slopes.

Reach a possible opportunity for water on the shores of a small pond to your left at 2.5 miles, but don't count on it providing much beyond

TEJON RANCH

The large, privately held Tejon Ranch began with a land grant in 1843 and has long served as stomping grounds for cattle ranchers, farmers, and hunters. The PCT was originally supposed to stay high in the Tehachapi Mountains, but builders weren't able to secure an easement through the ranch's property in that area, so the trail was laid down far below—not exactly "crest" material. In 2014, after a lengthy process, the Tejon Ranch Company finalized paperwork with their own Tejon Ranch Conservancy to designate an easement that will allow for rerouting approximately 38 miles of trail up from the desert floor and across the spine of the Tehachapi Mountains, a process that will take many years, lots of work, and much more paperwork to complete. No doubt, future hikers will wonder why so many past trekkers dreaded this section of trail as they stroll along their cooler perch up high.

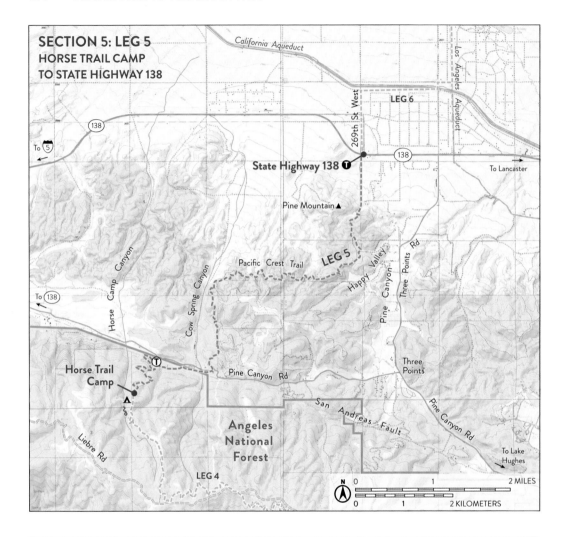

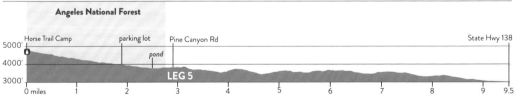

mud and desiccated vegetation except during the wettest times. Just past this, spot a sign warning that you're entering private land—you are now walking through a slice of the massive Tejon Ranch and will continue to do so for the next 7 miles. Stay on the trail in this area,

and know that camping and campfires are prohibited.

Just past the private land sign, cross a seasonal flow that shouldn't be counted on for refreshment. Continue on to reach **Pine Canyon Road**—and your old friend, the **San Andreas Fault**—at

In spring, wildflowers add a splash of color to the landscape.

2.9 miles. Weave through scarlet buglers, yerba santa, sage, and tall grasses (consider a tick check when through) and suppress the urge to turn and run back through all of it when you come across signage warning that you're hiking next to a hunting club. You may hear gunfire anytime between early September and the end of April; suffice it to say that you should definitely stay on the trail.

Head uphill, taking time to look back and admire the many folds of the pine-topped Sierra Pelona rising behind you. Uphill and downhill, left and right, squiggle and squaggle—this next bit of trail bounces all over the place, courtesy of the property boundary you skirt throughout the rest of this leg. Instead of feeling annoyed, remember that each time you come up a rise, you're likely to score some nice views across the Antelope Valley. Cold comfort for tired calves, I suppose.

Drop down into a small side canyon at 3.9 miles to cross a seasonal stream, not likely to have water unless you come through immediately after a rain. After another rise, look down to your left to spot Cow Spring Canyon; its namesake spring, the obvious green patch, teases from below. Continue along the rollercoaster sunny slopes and eventually

spot State Highway 138 in the distance. It will seem closer than it truly is since you have to duck around about a million gullies before arriving. *Sigh.*

While the meandering trail can become mentally exhausting, there's an extra incentive if you're traveling through in spring—fields of California

STAY OFF MY LAWN

You may have noticed that I haven't listed any campsites on this leg once you leave Horse Trail Camp—that's because you are traveling almost exclusively through private property and camping is not allowed. This is an issue in the next leg as well—while you might think that "desert" equals "wide open spaces upon which to pitch a tent," you also don't want to ruin your hike with a trespassing charge. Hikers have solved this issue over the years by staying the night with a local trail angel located near this leg's end; an online search for "Hiker Town" will let you know if this is an option as you plan your trip.

poppies (the state flower) come into view, bursting with vivid color against the desert floor. You might also spot goldfields, Indian paintbrush, lupine, and yerba santa, all swarming with butterflies.

Come to a small saddle around 6.9 miles, then duck back to traverse south facing slopes for a short bit. You're now looking down into optimistically named Happy Valley, and you see Three Points Road making its way through adjacent Pine Canyon. There's a startling difference between these slopes and the ones you just left—instead of being covered in chaparral, these are rockier, with only the occasional juniper hanging on for dear life.

In short time, make a turn to head mostly north for the remainder of this leg. Dense chaparral returns as you descend into a bit of a flat, then ascend to see a large, sparsely vegetated peak looming in front of you—this is **Pine Mountain**, and luckily, you don't have to climb it; the path you see winding up its slope is not for you.

Round a curve to begin the final descent, the desert heat suddenly swirling up to say hello on a warm day. Roosters crow as you drop down past farmland to make one last straightaway on a flat track next to a fence. Ignore any side trails flaring out to the left and make a beeline for **State Highway 138** ahead, which you reach at 9.5 miles after crossing through a gate. A few dirt turnouts here make fine day use parking spots, but don't leave your car overnight, lest you receive a present in the form of a warning slip for "abandoning" your vehicle, like a certain someone did. It's better to look for parking along the rural "side streets" to the north. If you want to reward yourself with a cold soda, ice cream, or even french fries, there's a small store and gas station located about 4 miles east on Highway 138.

CAMP-TO-CAMP MILEAGE
There are no viable campsites on this leg apart from its start point.

6 STATE HIGHWAY 138 TO COTTONWOOD CREEK BRIDGE

DISTANCE 17.3 miles

ELEVATION GAIN/LOSS +680/-630 feet

HIGH POINT 3159 feet

CONNECTING ROADS
State Highway 138, 269th Street West, Barnes Ranch Road, Neenach School Road, 260th Street West, Gaskell Road, Aqueduct Road

ON THE TRAIL
So begins The Leg That Shouldn't Have Been. The PCT was originally slated to route along the backbone of the Tehachapi Mountains, curling high above the Mojave Desert instead of crossing it, but builders weren't able to secure easement rights from Tejon Ranch back in the day, so here we are, about to traverse the flat, hot, nearly waterless (well—we'll get to that) desert floor instead. The good news is that the PCTA is working with the Tejon Ranch Conservancy to route the path up onto the crest, so look for this bit of the book to become deliciously obsolete years down the line once the trail is moved up high where it belongs.

Before making one step, get all of your sun protection in place—not just sunblock, but also a wide brimmed hat or umbrella, long sleeves, and possibly even sun gloves if you want to avoid crisping your paws since there aren't a lot of opportunities for true shade once you set out.

This leg travels through the outskirts of the city of **Lancaster**, so remain aware that you are

The California Aqueduct teases with a short segment of open water before the long, dry desert trek.

nearly always on—or very near—private property of some sort. For this reason, it's imperative that you stay on the trail and wait to set up camp until reaching the end—yes, 17.3 miles down the trail. Begin by carefully crossing **State Highway 138** (also known as West Avenue D and Lancaster Road) to walk along the left side of **269th Street West** for a moment before angling up to join actual trail. Goats bleat and roosters crow as you pass through a stock gate and head straight along a fence, tumbleweeds stereotypically blowing across your path. Behind you, the Sierra Pelona wave goodbye, making way for your eventual ascent into a small portion of the Tehachapi Mountains ahead. Pass through a gate to reach paved **Barnes Ranch Road** (West Avenue C-6); turn right, then quickly make a left onto **Neenach School Road** (270th Street West); some hikers park on this street as an alternate start point.

WATER ALERT!

Despite the fact that you will spend the bulk of this leg walking along the California and Los Angeles Aqueducts, water access is all but nonexistent. An official from the California Department of Water Resources told me that hikers are not allowed to pull water from the California Aqueduct, as tempting as it may be, and the Los Angeles Aqueduct is completely enclosed. While there might be water available at this leg's end, via a spigot ⦿ located above Cottonwood Creek, it's also quite common for the spigot to run dry. Your next likely option beyond that is in **Tylerhorse Canyon** ⦿ at the end of the next leg, 24 miles past this leg's start.

Wake up to unique sunrise views if you camp next to the Cottonwood Creek bridge.

A sign proclaims that you've reached The End at 0.9 mile, but really it's the beginning—pop up a short hill to stare down the tantalizing blue waters flowing through the **California Aqueduct**. Resist the urge to dive in or collect water—it's not allowed. (The aqueduct's managing entity, the California Department of Water Resources, cited the danger of hikers slipping down the slanted walls into the deceptively fast-moving flow.) Walk alongside the open canal for a short while before crossing through a pipe gate just shy of 2 miles to land at **260th Street West** (Three Points Road). Make a quick left, then a quick right to rejoin the trail, now on the north side of the aqueduct.

Turn left where a sign indicates the trail's continuation to leave behind the open waters of the California Aqueduct and transition to walking along an unpaved road adjoining the **Los Angeles Aqueduct**, an impenetrable metal tube that taunts you with every step. It does present some great photo opportunities, though, as it shoots across the desert floor. An endless cavalcade of barking dogs keep you moving past an outpost of scattered homes. While this area may feel remote, plenty of people live surprisingly close to the PCT here and you may also share the path with an assortment of vehicles along the way—unusual for the PCT, but it can't be avoided since the trail is located mostly on accessible roads rather than single-track.

If lack of access to all of that glorious water has you feeling blue, you may have reason to rejoice at 3.3 miles when you come across a funny looking contraption on the right side of the aqueduct—there's a spigot ⬤ here, and if you're lucky, one hard turn will grant access to the wet stuff. I've been

NIGHTWALKING

If you must travel through these next few legs when the desert is unbearably hot, you might choose to do so at night, using shady pockets for an extended siesta during the hottest part of the day. While many people dread this section of trail, it's actually quite beautiful (and sometimes much more tolerable) to walk in the moonlight, listening for coyote yips while strolling under an infinite blanket of stars.

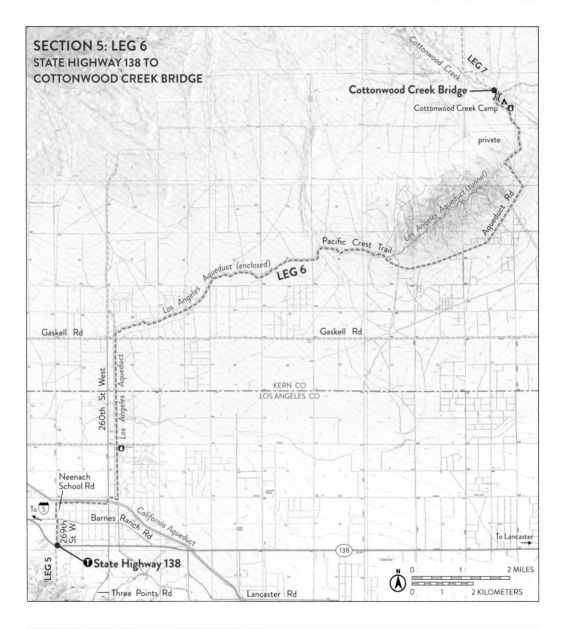

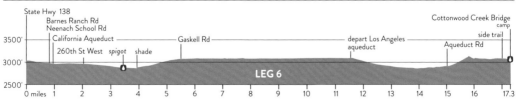

A CALIFORNIA CONTROVERSY

The Governor Edmund G. Brown California Aqueduct is so named for former California Governor "Pat" Brown, who oversaw the creation of the California State Water Project (SWP) via passage of the Burns-Porter Act, approved by voters in 1960. The SWP was (and is) one of the most ambitious public works projects of its kind, using a series of aqueducts, dams, reservoirs, and other mechanisms to redistribute (or *steal*, depending on with whom you're discussing the matter) water from the state's wetter, mountainous north to the dry, but heavily populated southlands. The SWP has been fraught with controversy from day one; properly detailing the lengthy fight over water rights would take longer than it would to hike the length of the California Aqueduct itself.

denied before, though, when it was frozen solid in winter. Reach a dip in the trail around 3.9 miles—here, the aqueduct rises above the depression and offers a chance for shade. The downside is that this is no oasis—garbage and spent shotgun shells litter the area and a general air of creepiness prevails.

There are a few more pleasant things to look at as you make this long, relatively flat trek across the open desert. Joshua trees begin to dot the landscape, their gnarled limbs adding a much-needed visual break to the somewhat monotonous scenery. Tumbleweeds pass by in the ever-present wind, lending a "Wild West" feel, and tufts of rabbitbrush often line the path, their yellowed blooms adding a splash of color.

Head straight at an intersection with unpaved, unsigned **Gaskell Road** at 5.4 miles. Afterward, make a right at another intersection to head east along the aqueduct, now marked by closed concrete boxes, remnants of a dreamy time in the past when small openings provided access to much-needed water. From here, there's not much

to break up the journey until you spot a small bridge on your left at 11.7 miles and bid adieu to the aqueduct (for now) to make a right and head downhill onto another unpaved, unnamed road.

Ignore any side paths and unmarked dirt roads to stay on the main track until you spot a marked intersection at 15.1 miles—hang a left here onto unmarked, unpaved **Aqueduct Road** to curve uphill and begin a generally northward progression. This is the first time you experience any noticeable gain in this section, and of *course* it has to come near the end! Make a right just over 0.5 mile ahead to rejoin the aqueduct, still frustratingly inaccessible beneath its concrete barricade. Let the sweeping views calm you—the Tehachapi Mountains draw nearer to the north, and what seems like the entire Antelope Valley spreads out beneath you. Draw your gaze up to see not just the Sierra Pelona but also the San Gabriel Mountains—and even the distant San Bernardino Mountains—rising to the southeast. If you've already hiked these sections of trail, it's a treat to look back at where you've been.

Spot a small building on your right just shy of 17.3 miles, followed by signage mentioning the availability of camping and water; your leg ends a moment ahead at the foot of a bridge spanning the wide, typically dry path of **Cottonwood Creek**. If you're looking to camp, you'll find ample space down below, near a small metal lean-to across the creek bed (**Cottonwood Creek Camp**).

Water—well, that's another story. The "creek" itself is typically bone dry. If you take the spur trail marked for "water," you will find a concrete box with a spigot **O** attached—and then you will cry meager, dehydrated tears if you turn and nothing comes out, which happens often. Console yourself with whatever you carted from the start of this leg and bed down for what turns out to be a fantastically unique camping experience underneath not just the glittering stars, but also the blinking lights of an endless field of wind turbines.

CAMP-TO-CAMP MILEAGE
State Highway 138 to Cottonwood Creek Camp 17.3

Walk on top of the enclosed aqueduct before departing into a sea of wind turbines.

7 COTTONWOOD CREEK BRIDGE TO TYLERHORSE CANYON

DISTANCE 6.7 miles

ELEVATION GAIN/LOSS
+2090/-340 feet

HIGH POINT 5003 feet

CONNECTING ROAD
Aqueduct Road

ON THE TRAIL
Here, we leave behind the water (at least, the tease of it) for wind (and lots of it), waving goodbye to the Los Angeles Aqueduct and welcoming miles of towering wind turbines that slice through the dry desert air to generate electricity for the good people of Southern California. If it's a hot day, try to avoid thinking about just how many air conditioners are running full blast thanks to the efforts of these giant towers rising out of the sand.

Cool thoughts, cool thoughts. Or warm thoughts if you're anything like me and decide to hike through in the dead of winter, when the wind slaps your face with an icy bite and snow powders the Tehachapi Mountains directly ahead. Most thru-hikers come through in late spring, so they'll never experience the true strangeness of waking up to a frozen water bottle in the Mojave Desert.

Cross a bridge spanning usually dry **Cottonwood Creek** and walk toward a forest of Joshua trees and wind turbines. This area is surprisingly beautiful both at night and in the early morning light, when the turbines—and Joshua trees—take on an otherworldly glow. Hit a Y-intersection just past the bridge crossing; turn left here to depart **Aqueduct Road**, then make another quick left to begin walking in earnest along an unpaved road through the wind farm. You'll notice a lot of short, gravel access roads leading directly to single wind turbines; these are

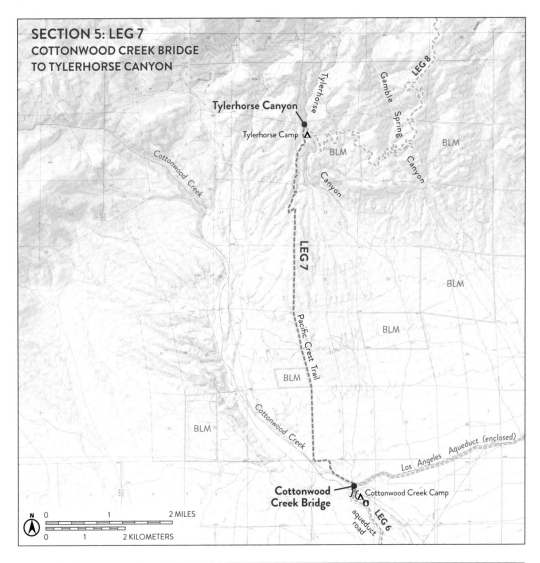

SECTION 5: LEG 7
COTTONWOOD CREEK BRIDGE TO TYLERHORSE CANYON

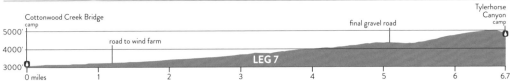

usually marked with a red post, as opposed to the trail's brown ones, so stick to the main path and keep your eyes peeled for PCT markers.

Depart the road at just over 0.5 mile and pick up the single-track heading up a small hill. You'll soon walk along a barbed wire fence bearing DANGER! signs that warn of possible electrocution due to high voltage. Considering the PCT passes through this fence, I suppose those signs are meant for everyone except hikers. Onward you go, with perhaps an extra jolt to your step. Just shy of 1.2 miles, reach one of the multitudes of gravel roads that radiate across the wind farm. In recent years, the kind folks here started offering hikers the opportunity to top off their water via a tank located near the main office, which you can spot to the east; if this is still the case when you come through, you'll know by signs posted at several of these intersections of trail and road. If you don't see any signs, please don't intrude on our energy-harnessing friends.

From here, head mostly north through the loud whir of whipped wind, first through relatively gentle flats, where the blades' shadows dance across the ground on a sunny day. Cross a few more gravel roads, then move into a series of increasingly undulating foothills, where you'll hop on a hamster wheel of elevation gain and loss. Take advantage of some of the uphill jaunts to look up toward the pine-tipped ridge far above you and back toward the Antelope Valley, Sierra Pelona, San Gabriel Mountains, and San Bernardino Mountains—if you've hiked through all of these already on the trail, give yourself a well-deserved high five.

The trail dips on and off unpaved roads in this area but is always signed, so keep an eye out for that familiar emblem and the typical brown marker posts. Cross one last gravel road around 5.1 miles and make a somewhat demoralizing descent into a small canyon only to climb right back out along a semi-steep, breezy ridgeline. Pass an unpaved road a few times, then leave it behind to begin the final descent into Tylerhorse Canyon. As you prepare for this last bit, you'll notice two things—first, the trees studding the hillsides far above the canyon and relative lushness of this area in comparison to the rest of this leg, and second, the start of the next leg angling uphill along the opposing canyon wall—cue the sad trombone.

Reach the bottom of **Tylerhorse Canyon** at 6.7 miles. Here, you may find a damp patch, a trickle of water, or a good flow **◑**, depending on the time of year. This is a somewhat reliable source since it's fed by a spring tucked deep in the canyon beyond the trail crossing, so if you come up empty at the crossing itself, walk upstream to look for pockets of water; a scoop comes in handy during times of extreme low flow. This leg ends on the far side of the canyon, where you'll find a sign proclaiming the next leg's destination (Tehachapi Willow Springs Road), and room for perhaps two tents (**Tylerhorse Camp**). You might also find some spots back across the canyon, although these were damaged by a flash flood in 2015—don't camp here if storm clouds are brewing unless you want to be flushed right back out to the wind farm.

CAMP-TO-CAMP MILEAGE

**Cottonwood Creek Bridge to
    Tylerhorse Camp** 6.7

---

8 TYLERHORSE CANYON TO TEHACHAPI WILLOW SPRINGS ROAD

DISTANCE 16.9 miles

ELEVATION GAIN/LOSS
+3010/-3710 feet

HIGH POINT 6302 feet

CONNECTING ROAD
Tehachapi Willow Springs Road

ON THE TRAIL

Before departing **Tylerhorse Canyon**, try to collect enough water from its seasonal flow **◑** to get you through this next leg and beyond. While there's a seasonal source at Oak Creek 16.6 miles ahead, it may be dry. Your next natural water source is a staggering 25.1 miles farther past that at Golden Oaks Spring, but you may choose to do as most hikers and hop off the trail

The climb offers expansive southward views across the Antelope Valley.

NO REST FOR THE TREKKER

As you may have noticed, there are very few campsites available before or after the Sierra Pelona since you're either traveling through private property or around steep slopes across the few pockets of BLM land that exist in this section. In fact, the next "legal" campsite after Tylerhorse Canyon is a staggering 27.7 miles ahead, a few miles north of Tehachapi Pass. Researching and coordinating with local trail angels is how most travelers—both thru-hikers and section hikers—navigate the situation, and many depart at Tehachapi Willow Springs Road to break up the long camp-less and waterless segment by detouring to nearby Mojave or Tehachapi for a night or two.

to tank up in one of the nearby towns of Mojave or Tehachapi.

Begin by heading uphill via a long traverse of the canyon's north side. In October 2015, an epic storm caused massive erosion in this area, and although the trail has been repaired, the effects will linger for quite some time. There's not a ton of vegetation here (partially due to flash flooding, partially due to the terrain), but you'll spot lonely trees in various finger canyons as you dip in and out of deep gullies and curve around protruding ridges in this stretch. The slopes mellow out a bit leading to a fat ridge that offers fantastic views back down to the wind farm you walked through on the last leg, and the Sierra Pelona, San Gabriel, and San Bernardino Mountains rising up in the distance.

Hit a confluence of dirt roads at 3 miles; walk straight across to make your mark in a trail register, lingering as long as possible before making a steep, demoralizing descent into the wide slash of

SECTION 5: LEG 8
TYLERHORSE CANYON TO
TEHACHAPI WILLOW SPRINGS ROAD

Gamble Spring Canyon below, made even worse by the fact that you can see the trail zigzagging right back up the other side. *Ugh.* Reach the dry canyon floor just over 0.5 mile ahead, the route across clearly marked by posts. Utter a few choice words, then begin plowing up a lengthy set of switchbacks to ascend a ridgeline on the other side.

Even though regaining all of that lost elevation can feel disheartening, you earn some nice views, including potentially snowcapped Mount

San Antonio and San Gorgonio Mountain far to the southeast. You'll also start to see a few pinyon pines dotting the trail, a welcome reprieve from the mostly barren slopes you've been traveling thus far. After far too many switchbacks, pop up on a ridge—this signals the end of the bulk of your uphill travel. You'll still need to work those calves, but it's a much gentler grade from here.

Cross a dirt road, then head northeast along a slight incline. Reach a saddle at 7.7 miles, where a larger clearing on the left might hold a few surprises courtesy of a longtime local trail angel. Although some hikers choose to bed down here, it is technically private property. Continue undulating along this gentle crest, now switching to north-facing slopes. If hiking in the winter months, don't be surprised to find snow underfoot—it gets pretty cold up here. The area you're traveling through is sparsely vegetated compared to the pine-filled slopes across the way and down below as a result of the 2007 White Fire, which destroyed over 12,000 acres and multiple homes. Farther along, you'll also see scars from the even more destructive 2011 Canyon Fire, ignited by a plane crash.

Still, all is not barren, and you'll find plenty of white sage and pockets of occasional pinyon pines, including a lovely shady pocket around 8.4 miles at a broad saddle—despite the obvious tent clearings under the trees, I'm sorry to say that this is also private land. Continue back into the burn area to a rise where you're suddenly confronted by the sight of wind turbines churning the air—if you continue on to the next leg, you'll walk directly under their towering blades.

Continue through the slightly apocalyptic landscape littered with the remnants of trees past—on a sunny day, you'll long for the shade they once offered. The terrain bumps up and down, but soon enough you're headed downhill, crossing a series of dirt paths. Around the 11-mile mark, look down upon wide **Oak Creek Canyon** below. Its relative lushness is the result of its namesake seasonal waterway, which you'll cross near the end of this leg. The canyon is home to a herd of beautiful wild horses. Some say they're descendants of animals left behind when Spanish explorers crossed the area long ago; some say they escaped from local breeders who ranched the area at the turn of the last century. No matter which history is correct, consider it your lucky day if you see these beautiful creatures as you pass through.

After a bit, reach a saddle and ignore the unpaved road banking straight up to **Peak 5580**. Instead, curve around to trace south-facing slopes before angling back to the north-facing views. The burn scars eventually fade and you'll notice scattered pines, scrub oak, juniper, and even some Joshua trees in the lower reaches.

Eventually descend to the shady canyon floor and hit a use trail to **Oak Creek** to your left at 16.6 miles. This is a seasonal source, so be prepared for the real possibility that it may run dry in summer and fall. In quick order, pass through a stock gate, sign the trail register, and cross a small footbridge. You'll find a horse corral and picnic table on the other side, a nice spot for a shady lunch break. One last uphill deposits you at a large unpaved parking lot and trailhead, where a brief continuation of trail deposits you at the edge of paved **Tehachapi Willow Springs Road**, where this leg ends. Many hikers choose to catch a ride here into nearby Mojave or Tehachapi for resupply and rest; local trail angel names are usually listed in the register 0.3 mile back.

CHOICES, CHOICES

Although this section ends 8 miles ahead at Tehachapi Pass, many hikers choose to depart from Tehachapi Willow Springs to resupply before tackling the hot, dry section ahead as it's a bit easier to hitch a ride here than at State Highway 58—look in the trail register to find contact info for local trail angels. The towns of Tehachapi (north on Tehachapi Willow Springs Road) and Mojave (east on Oak Creek Road) are nearly equidistant from the trail here; both offer an assortment of grocery and lodging options.

CAMP-TO-CAMP MILEAGE

There are no viable campsites other than the one located at the start of this leg.

9   TEHACHAPI WILLOW SPRINGS ROAD TO TEHACHAPI PASS

DISTANCE 8 miles

ELEVATION GAIN/LOSS
+1420/-1710 feet

HIGH POINT 4767 feet

CONNECTING ROADS
Tehachapi Willow Springs Road, Cameron
Road, State Highway 58

ON THE TRAIL

This leg of the Pacific Crest Trail is named the Cameron Ridge Segment for good reason—you follow a ridge above Cameron Canyon nearly the entire way! Before embarking on your somewhat brief journey, ensure you have enough water (there is none available along the way) and a windbreaker—this area is extremely breezy and can turn downright cold in winter. Many an unsecured hat has been sacrificed to this ridge. If it's a bit chilly as you hike, be grateful—this area can also see excessive heat that makes the lack of water and shade even more apparent.

Begin on the southwest side of **Tehachapi Willow Springs Road**, just to the right of **Cameron Road**, below a large, gravelly parking area. Carefully cross the road and pick up a trail on the other side that quickly leads to a dirt turnout, where you'll find interpretive signs offering a brief history of the area. Spoiler alert: it involves the wind turbines you're about to hike beneath, since the area is widely considered the birthplace of American wind power. One brisk gust will lead you to believe these claims.

Walk through low, rolling hills studded with sagebrush and wind turbines. The giant blades spin overhead for nearly your entire route, so learn to make peace with these alien towers, and you'll start to appreciate the unique landscape you're traveling through. There are a lot of access roads in this area (along with animal trails), but the

PCT is well marked, so it shouldn't be hard to follow. Head through a metal stock gate around 1.2 miles, then begin ascending the ridge, a somewhat sweaty prospect on a hot day. There's no shade here except for the occasional gnarled juniper, and there's not even much in the way of vegetation, but the upside is that you have nearly limitless views from whence you came (if you hiked the last leg) and beyond, including the distant San Gabriel Mountains to the south.

As you come over a noticeable rise, immediately dip back down the other side, likely casting wistful glances toward the pines dotting the ridge that you are *not* walking on; you'll get there if you continue into the next section. Until then, it's sagebrush and spinning blades! Continue through a series of gates, then right back to the uphill grind, finishing with the worst of it at the 2-mile mark. From here, it's mostly a gentle meander through the wind farm, accompanied by the strange whirs and whistles of the spinning giants towering above. Around 3.4 miles, pop down to a rough paved

NO SLEEP 'TIL TEHACHAPI?

This segment of trail passes through a wind farm (and private property) via an easement, which means you can't just throw your tent down any ol' place you like. Truthfully, most trekkers (including thru-hikers) day hike or "slackpack" this leg, either by setting up a relatively easy car shuttle or by enlisting willing locals to help with rides; a list of trail angels is usually found at the register just south of Tehachapi Willow Springs Road near Oak Creek on the previous leg. Sleep-time options include walking 2.8 miles into the next leg to find the first of several camping options in that area or heading into nearby Tehachapi or Mojave to grab a hotel room.

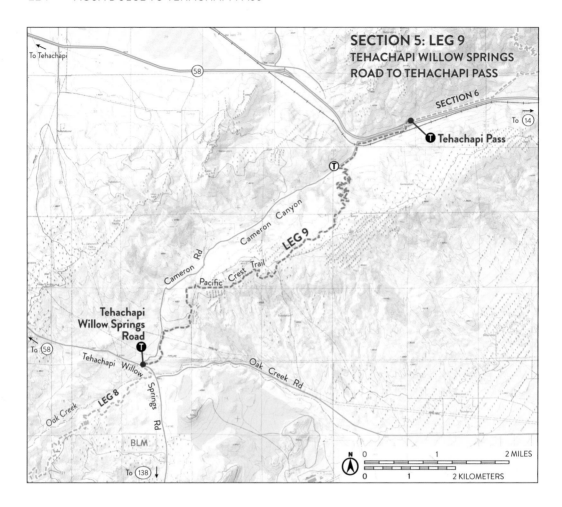

SECTION 5: LEG 9
TEHACHAPI WILLOW SPRINGS
ROAD TO TEHACHAPI PASS

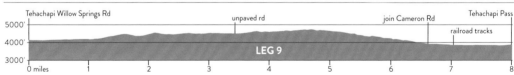

access road—if the vegetation on the other side is overgrown, it might be hard to see the trail, but trust that it's over there. Traverse a footbridge, pass through a gate, and cross yet another access road to continue on your way.

Around the halfway point, the views turn back to the north and west, while closer to the trail you'll spot beavertail cactus, California poppies, and lupine. Pass through a ninth stock gate at 4.7 miles, after which the ground turns from soft sand to hard-packed dirt studded with rocks. A few more juniper and even some scrub oak appear along your path, with an awesome handmade mileage sign tacked to a barbed wire fence. Shortly after this sign, look down to spot bustling **State Highway 58** running through **Tehachapi Pass**. It seems closer than your remaining 3 miles would indicate, but your path is not a straight shot.

Wind farms offer a unique hiking experience.

Reaching the endpoint requires some serious downhill action, which you'll accomplish via a lengthy series of switchbacks. Crows squawk above and horned lizards scurry below as you make your way down a pair of ridgelines studded with wildflowers in the spring, including the beautiful white blooms of desert evening primrose, which fade to light pink as they wilt. Traipse through the beauty until you reach the harsh reality of asphalt at 6.6 miles when you drop down to pass through yet another pipe gate and meet **Cameron Road** once more. Turn right to walk along the shoulder of the road, crunching along to the sound of squirrel chatter and train clatter. Reach the tracks at just over 7 miles and be very careful while crossing—this is an active route. Once on the other side, stay on the right side of the road as it curves upward to become a freeway overpass. While this isn't the busiest interchange, cars *do* exit and enter from Cameron Road—stay aware as you walk. Once you've cruised above the bustling traffic below, walk straight ahead to a dirt parking area, ending at its eastern end near a PCT marker. While it's possible to leave your car here overnight, don't be surprised to see a big rig taking up most of the space—this is a popular snooze spot for weary drivers.

CAMP-TO-CAMP MILEAGE
There are no viable campsites on this leg.

TEHACHAPI PASS TO WALKER PASS

THIS SECTION IS widely regarded as one of the hottest, driest portions of the entire PCT (because it is), but it also plays host to an incredible ecological transition zone offering a fascinating journey through an ever-changing assortment of landscapes. Yes, you will need to prepare for long, heavy water carries (and for plenty of shadeless uphill jaunts that increase your thirst), but if you plan to hike in early spring when natural sources are more likely to flow and temperatures haven't yet reached apocalyptic levels, you'll find a lot more here to enjoy than to complain about.

Begin by traversing across, then quickly rising above the Mojave Desert floor, sweating through sunny mixed chaparral en route to the welcoming shade of pinyon pines gracing the upper reaches of the Piute Mountains. The landscape constantly undulates, flipping between lofty ridgelines that host wind turbines (and stiff breezes) and low, moist valleys that play host to grasslands and gorgeous stands of oak. Vibrant wildflowers color the ground in springtime, when the surrounds are surprisingly verdant.

As you continue your ascent, the trail rises up to meet a variety of conifers, including butterscotch-scented Jeffrey pine, before angling east and dropping back down to the impressive desert landscape surrounding Mayan Peak. You're now heading into the much drier Scodie Mountains, where the trail wiggles up, down, and all around, dipping in and out of chaparral, Joshua trees, and pines, eventually making a sharp drop down to relatively quiet Walker Pass Campground and the pass itself just beyond. After such a long stretch of solitude (and lack of pavement), the constant flow of traffic on Highway 178 might prove a bit startling—all the more reason to continue your northward journey into the heart of the Sierra.

DISTANCE 85.5 miles

STATE DISTANCE 566.5–652 miles

ELEVATION GAIN/LOSS
+12,570/-11,150 feet

HIGH POINT 6975 feet

BEST TIME OF YEAR Mar–Apr and Sep–Nov

PCTA SECTION LETTER F

LAND MANAGERS Bureau of Land Management (Ridgecrest Field Office, Kiavah Wilderness), Sequoia National Forest (Kern River Ranger District, Kiavah Wilderness)

PASSES AND PERMITS California Campfire Permit

MAPS AND APPS
- Halfmile's CA Section F
- USFS PCT Map #3 Southern Sierra
- USGS Topo Quads: Monolith, Tehachapi NE, Cache Peak, Cross Mountain, Emerald Mountain, Claraville, Pinyon Mountain, Cane Canyon, Horse Canyon, Walker Pass
- Halfmile's PCT app
- Guthook's PCT app

LEGS
1. Tehachapi Pass to Golden Oaks Spring
2. Golden Oaks Spring to Jawbone Canyon Road
3. Jawbone Canyon Road to Kelso Valley Road
4. Kelso Valley Road to Bird Spring Pass
5. Bird Spring Pass to Walker Pass

Opposite: *Spring blooms decorate the Piute Mountains.*

Wind turbines glow at dusk on Sweet Ridge.

ACCESS
Tehachapi Pass

From Los Angeles, head north on Interstate 5 to State Highway 14 North (toward Palmdale and Lancaster). Continue on this road for just under 69 miles until it becomes State Highway 58 Business as you pass through Mojave; 3.6 miles after this transition, merge onto State Highway 58 West. Drive 6 miles, then exit at Cameron Road (exit 159) and park in the large turnout on the north side of the road.

Walker Pass

From Los Angeles, head north on Interstate 5 (toward Sacramento), then take exit 162 for State Highway 14 northbound (Antelope Valley Freeway) toward Palmdale and Lancaster. Drive 110.8 miles, then make a left onto CA Highway 178 westbound. You will reach Walker Pass in 8.3 miles—there are small parking pullouts located on either side of the road, but it's best to park 1 mile farther west on CA 178 at Walker Pass Campground if leaving your car overnight. You then depart the campground from a well-signed connector trail to hit the PCT and head 0.7 mile northeast on the PCT to reach Walker Pass.

NOTES
Cities and Services

The southern trailhead offers the choice to head 9 miles west to Tehachapi or 11 miles east to Mojave, both of which offer post offices and several grocery, dining, gas, and lodging options. The northern trailhead is a bit more remote, with access to services in the resort town of Lake Isabella about 36 miles to the west, or in the community of Ridgecrest, approximately 25 miles to the east.

Fire Restrictions

Camp 100 feet from water and trails. Check for seasonal fire restrictions in Sequoia National Forest before heading out.

Water

This section is widely considered one of, if not *the* driest portion of the PCT. The first source is Golden Oaks Spring, 16.8 miles into the hike. The next source, Robin Bird Spring, is 18.8 miles farther. The next source from here is the spring at Landers Camp, just off the PCT, only 6.8 miles ahead—but the sources become less reliable after this spring, and the bulk of the remaining 43.1 miles of this section may be completely dry by late spring or early summer save for the generosity of locals who occasionally cache water at road crossings. Remember: carry what you need between sources and *never* rely on caches! Luckily, there's a fairly reliable spring located near the Walker Pass Campground toward the end of this section that may provide respite.

Hazards

Excessive heat is possible between late spring and early fall, while extreme cold, ice, and snow may exist through the winter months, especially at higher altitudes.

Other

Unpaved access roads throughout this section may be rough, rutted, and occasionally washed out. Off-road vehicle use is heavy throughout the bulk of this section.

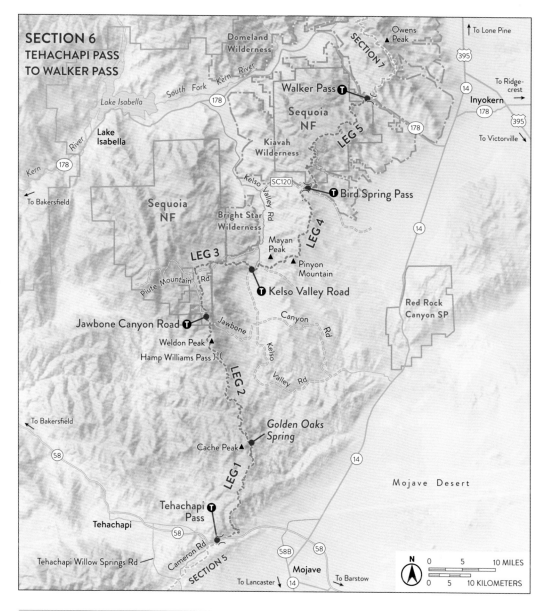

SECTION 6
TEHACHAPI PASS TO WALKER PASS

Domeland Wilderness

Owens Peak

To Lone Pine

SECTION 7

395

Kern River

South Fork

Lake Isabella

178

Walker Pass

Sequoia NF

To Ridge-crest

14

Inyokern

178

395

To Victorville

River

Kern

Lake Isabella

178

Kiavah Wilderness

LEG 5

Kern

178

To Bakersfield

Sequoia NF

Bright Star Wilderness

Kelso Valley Rd

SC120

Bird Spring Pass

LEG 4

Mayan Peak

Pinyon Mountain

14

LEG 3

Piute Mountain Rd

Kelso Valley Road

Red Rock Canyon SP

Jawbone Canyon Road

Jawbone

Canyon

Rd

Weldon Peak

Hamp Williams Pass

Kelso

LEG 2

Valley Rd

Golden Oaks Spring

Cache Peak

14

Mojave Desert

LEG 1

To Bakersfield

58

Tehachapi Pass

Tehachapi

58

Tehachapi Willow Springs Rd

Cameron Rd

SECTION 5

58B

58

Mojave

To Barstow

To Lancaster

14

N

0   5   10 MILES

0   5   10 KILOMETERS

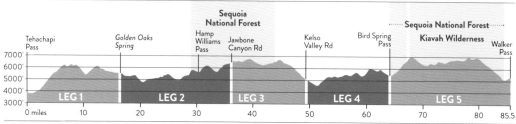

Tehachapi Pass

Golden Oaks Spring

Sequoia National Forest

Hamp Williams Pass

Jawbone Canyon Rd

Kelso Valley Rd

Bird Spring Pass

Sequoia National Forest

Kiavah Wilderness

Walker Pass

7000'
6000'
5000'
4000'
3000'

LEG 1

LEG 2

LEG 3

LEG 4

LEG 5

0 miles   10   20   30   40   50   60   70   80   85.5

Baby blue eyes burst from the ground in spring.

SUGGESTED ITINERARIES

Camps are either viewable from the trail or located within a few tenths of a mile from the noted location unless otherwise specified in leg descriptions.

7 DAYS

		Miles
Day 1	Tehachapi Pass to Camp 8	12.2
Day 2	Camp 8 to Camp 10	14.4
Day 3	Camp 10 to Robin Bird Camp	9.0
Day 4	Robin Bird Camp to Landers Camp	6.8
Day 5	Landers Camp to Camp 12	15.4
Day 6	Camp 12 to Camp 14	11.1
Day 7	Camp 14 to Walker Pass	16.6

6 DAYS

Day 1	Tehachapi Pass to Camp 9	12.8
Day 2	Camp 9 to Camp 10	13.8
Day 3	Camp 10 to Landers Camp	15.8
Day 4	Landers Camp to Camp 12	15.4
Day 5	Camp 12 to Camp 14	11.1
Day 6	Camp 14 to Walker Pass	16.6

5 DAYS

Day 1	Tehachapi Pass to Camp 9	12.8
Day 2	Camp 9 to Robin Bird Camp	22.2
Day 3	Robin Bird Camp to Camp 12	22.8
Day 4	Camp 12 to McIvers Camp	19.5
Day 5	McIvers Camp to Walker Pass	8.2

1 TEHACHAPI PASS TO GOLDEN OAKS SPRING

DISTANCE 16.8 miles

ELEVATION GAIN/LOSS
+4090/-2460 feet

HIGH POINT 6211 feet

CONNECTING ROADS
State Highway 58, Cameron Road

ON THE TRAIL

Much like San Gorgonio Pass and Cajon Pass farther south on the PCT, **Tehachapi Pass** serves less as scenic stopover and more as major thoroughfare. However, this makes the trailhead, along bustling **State Highway 58**, very easy to reach, both by car and by public transportation (a Kern Transit bus stops near the trailhead upon request). As a result, you'll fight sleepy semi-truck drivers (and plenty of wind-whipped trash) for parking space in the small, unpaved lot located at the northern terminus of **Cameron Road**.

Before setting off, ensure you have enough water to last the very dry, usually warm, and generally uphill 16.8 miles to Golden Oaks Spring—you won't find a single drop until you arrive there. When you've made peace with your heavy pack, depart from the east end of the unpaved parking area, which bears a sign marking the start of the trail's Cache Peak Segment, then begin hiking parallel to the drivers speeding past down to your right. Just a moment ahead, take a quick break to sign the trail register, then continue your pleasantly (and deceptively) flat meander. Be especially

careful to stay on the trail here as it passes through a private property easement—if it's not clearly marked when you come through, know that your route stays far right, just above Highway 58.

About 1.2 miles in, scoot around a gated fence, then dip into a flood channel popping right back up on the other side. The terrain here remains gentle, covered in a layer of chia, sage, and yucca, with scattered Joshua trees and a few junipers offering shady nooks. Eventually start gaining ground as you briefly join a rough unpaved road, then depart to join the single-track angling up to the left around 2.3 miles. This is where the fun begins—and by "fun," I mean "uphill."

You'll yearn for the flat valley below as you trudge up a series of lengthy switchbacks. The upside to all of

MOTHER NATURE'S FURY

In October 2015, a large storm system rumbled across segments of Southern California, causing destructive flooding in several areas, including Tehachapi Pass. Under heavy rains, a massive mudslide formed and raced down toward Highway 58, trapping almost 200 vehicles in its wake. The first mile of the trail heading north from the Tehachapi Pass trailhead was also mostly obliterated in the flow and was somewhat indiscernible when I hiked through, although it's easy enough to trace its intended path as the route parallels the highway in this segment.

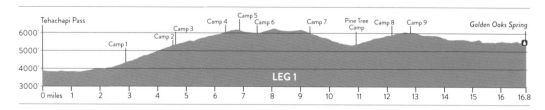

A springtime climb is rewarded when you reach a scenic plateau carpeted in wildflowers.

this hard work is that you'll not only lose some of the highway noise but also gain ever-expanding views—first to a wind turbine-topped ridgeline across the way then eventually past it toward the greater Antelope Valley. If you need a break, look to the left at around 2.8 miles to spot a small use trail leading toward a tiny patch of Joshua trees that make a sweet little camp with room for one tent (**Camp 1**).

Continue uphill to find a few more camping opportunities ahead. Spot another use trail jutting off to the left at 4.4 miles that offers a shady nook with room for one tent (**Camp 2**) or walk another 0.1 mile to find a few mediocre sites scattered on either side of the trail (**Camp 3**). Otherwise, keep trucking to easier ground ahead. If you're heading through in spring, especially in April, you're in for a treat—right as the terrain mellows out, you'll notice a veritable rainbow of wildflowers carpeting the ground.

This gentler landscape also offers a smattering of craggy pinyon pines, a welcome sight after so many miles of sun-beaten trail. If you want to stay for a while and commune with the conifers, there's room for perhaps two tents in a small clearing under some trees to your left around the 6.4 mile mark (**Camp 4**). Just 0.5 mile up, find another clearing on the left with room for another two (**Camp 5**). Now walking along west-facing slopes, your views change as you gaze upon the lovely green slash of **Waterfall Canyon** and the colorful hills beyond.

Another small campsite appears 7.5 miles in, tucked a bit deeper into the pinyons over to the left (**Camp 6**). Just after this, encounter a sign warning that you're entering an area popular with off-road vehicle enthusiasts, then step over a wooden barrier—the first of many to come—crossing a rough unpaved road. You'll repeat this pattern several more times over the next mile,

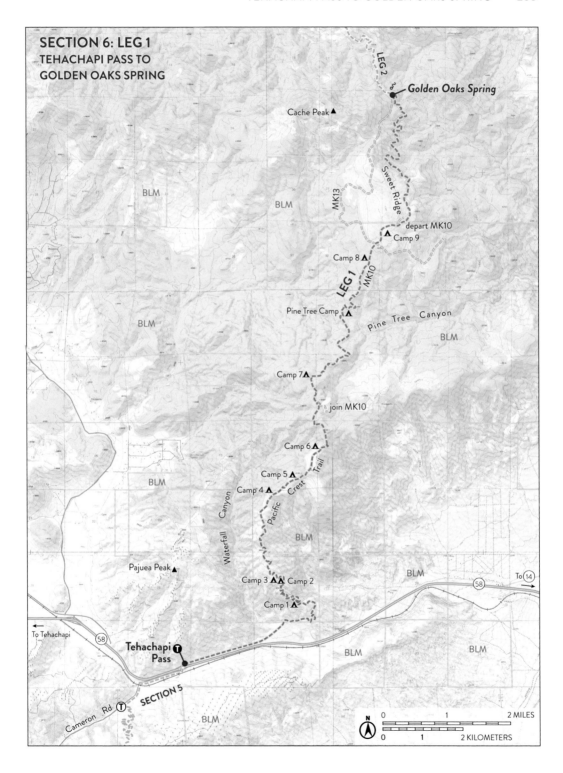

SECTION 6: LEG 1
TEHACHAPI PASS TO
GOLDEN OAKS SPRING

LEG 2

Golden Oaks Spring

Cache Peak ▲

BLM

BLM

MK13

Sweet Ridge

depart MK10

Camp 9 ▲

LEG 1

MK10

Camp 8 ▲

BLM

Pine Tree Camp ▲

Pine Tree Canyon

BLM

Camp 7 ▲

join MK10

BLM

Camp 6 ▲

Camp 5 ▲

Crest Trail

Camp 4 ▲

Waterfall Canyon

Pacific

BLM

Pajuea Peak ▲

BLM

To (14)

Camp 3 ▲▲ Camp 2

58

Camp 1 ▲

← To Tehachapi

58

BLM

BLM

Tehachapi Pass (T)

BLM

BLM

Cameron Rd (T)

SECTION 5

BLM

N

0   1   2 MILES

0   1   2 KILOMETERS

YOU ARE NOT ALONE

The Piute and Scodie Mountains (i.e., Section 6 of the PCT) are flush with BLM and private land that is incredibly popular with off-road vehicle (OHV) users, and the trail is hashed with OHV trail crossings; only the main ones are included on the maps. It's not uncommon to hear the sound of revved motors and to see many types of wheeled wonders whizzing past, and it's best to stay alert as you're hiking and avoid camping or stopping in the middle of any OHV paths. While it's unfortunately not uncommon to see tire ruts damaging portions of the PCT in this area, most riders I've encountered are friendly toward hikers and steer clear of the trail.

eventually throwing in the trail towel and actually joining jeep road **MK10** for quite some distance. Keep your ears open and your eyes peeled for motorized users sharing your path.

Sharp eyes will spot another potential campsite on the left at 9.1 miles—not the obvious clearing literally next to the trail, but rather the somewhat hidden spots tucked in the trees behind it, accessed via a faint use trail (**Camp 7**). As you continue past, still hiking along MK10, views open up a bit more to the north and upon consultation with your map, you'll face the daunting realization that you're about to lose a significant amount of elevation, only to pick it right back up as you head toward the wind turbines guarding Sweet Ridge. Stifle your sobs and try to enjoy the downhill while it lasts.

If the emotion of it all becomes too much to bear, find a huge clearing on the right with room for a small city of tents, just as you bottom out near the head of **Pine Tree Canyon** at 10.8 miles (**Pine Tree Camp**). Even if you're moving on, take a moment to enjoy the surrounding greenery and plentiful shade, then stretch your legs and prep your lungs for the climb up **Sweet Ridge**. While ascending, glance over your shoulder from time to time and try to appreciate the views back toward whence you came.

Another tenting opportunity presents itself in a clearing around 12.2 miles, tucked back on your left, with room for multiple occupants (**Camp 8**). Just after this, encounter the deafening whir of wind turbines erected like sentinels along the ridge. If you enjoy sleeping with a white noise machine at home, you'll *love* camping almost directly under this racket on a moonscape-like flat on the right at about 12.8 miles (**Camp 9**), just after passing **MK13**—be sure your tent is not pitched on any vegetation, no matter how small it seems.

Finally bid adieu to your old pal MK10 in 0.2 mile ahead, making a right to rejoin single-track and start heading downhill. There's not a lot in the way of shade from here, but the lack of trees offers unrestricted views to an endless sea of valleys and peaks, the latter often topped with wind turbines, whose stark white towers add a sort of alien beauty to the surroundings. This segment's namesake promontory, Cache Peak, sits to the west. If you come through in spring (which I strongly suggest), prepare to traipse through an endless accompaniment of Bigelow's coreopsis, whose bright yellow blooms seem to illuminate your path.

Continue weaving in and out of the earth's folds until you reach an unpaved road at 16.8 miles; drop down on the other side and avail yourself of trailside refreshment at **Golden Oaks Spring 🅞** as you bask in the shade. The spring itself is within a private land easement; while you're allowed to grab water here, you're not supposed to make a home of it, so keep on trucking into the next leg if you're looking for a place to spend the night.

CAMP-TO-CAMP MILEAGE

Tehachapi Pass to Camp 1	2.8
Camp 1 to Camp 2	1.6
Camp 2 to Camp 3	0.1
Camp 3 to Camp 4	1.9
Camp 4 to Camp 5	0.5
Camp 5 to Camp 6	0.6
Camp 6 to Camp 7	1.6
Camp 7 to Pine Tree Camp	1.7
Pine Tree Camp to Camp 8	1.4
Camp 8 to Camp 9	0.6

2 GOLDEN OAKS SPRING TO JAWBONE CANYON ROAD

DISTANCE 19.2 miles

ELEVATION GAIN/LOSS
+4220/-3060 feet

HIGH POINT 6611 feet

CONNECTING ROADS
Back Canyon Road, Jawbone Canyon Road

ON THE TRAIL

While lingering at **Golden Oaks Spring O**, make sure to filter enough wet stuff to last all the way to Robin Bird Spring, 18.8 miles away. Once you've tanked up, walk along pinyon pine–dotted slopes that offer some of the only shade you'll see for a bit. Wind turbines also make an appearance, although considering the abundance you've already encountered in this section and the last, you should not be too surprised—they are as much a part of the Southern California landscape as chaparral, Joshua trees, and extremely tanned beachgoers.

Cross a wind farm access road at 0.8 mile, then leave human encroachment behind (for a few miles, at least) to continue winding along somewhat exposed slopes lined with wildflowers in spring—paintbrush, goldfields, and baby blue eyes are some of the showiest. The open space also offers views of Cache Peak, whose summit rises to the south. Just over 3 miles past your start point, the landscape shifts toward a spooky post-burn

zone, the result of the 2012 Jawbone Complex Fire, a lightning-sparked blaze that scorched over 12,000 acres, taking out a smattering of Coulter pines in its wake. Slather on the sunblock and lament the lack of trees to once more contour below towering wind turbines, losing a significant amount of elevation before reaching a small, shady flat around 4.1 miles.

Vegetation remains sparse as you move back uphill through the burnscape, although you'll find pockets of chia, fiddleneck, and miner's lettuce in springtime. You might also notice some residual poodle-dog bush popping up in a few spots—prepare to dance around it if you encounter it. As with any post-burn area, there's also the possibility that you'll need to hop over any number of downed trees ("blowdowns"). While trail crews work hard to keep the path clear for hikers and equestrians, the same stiff breezes that fan the wind farms can also dislodge trees with fire-weakened root systems.

At 6.7 miles, pass through a gate and barbed wire fence to continue the somewhat hilly path—the trail is anything but level through here. The routing might test your patience, but a reward arrives around 9.1 miles when you not only emerge from the burn area, but also bank east to land on a picturesque ridge pointing the way toward pastoral rolling hills complete with green grasses, mountain mahogany, sage, and even some lovely pinyon pines. Enjoy a blissful skip down to an obvious grassy flat at 9.8 miles to find scattered campsites

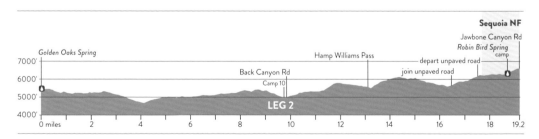

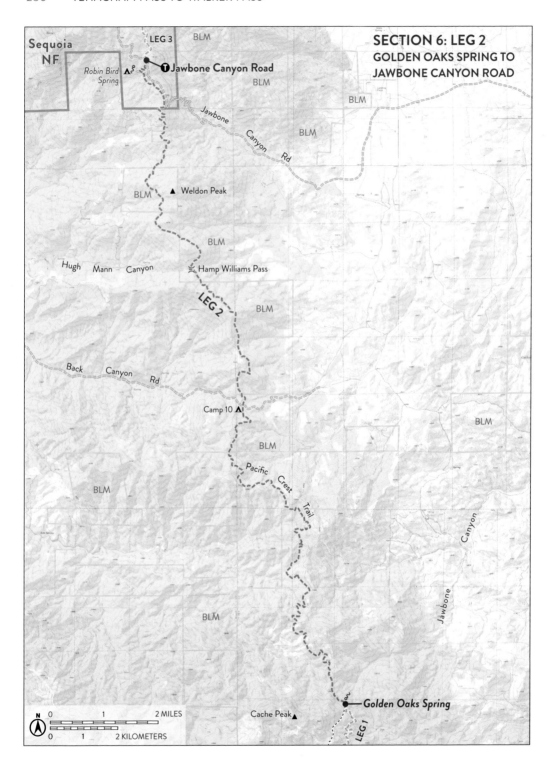

Sequoia NF

LEG 3

BLM

Robin Bird Spring

Jawbone Canyon Road

SECTION 6: LEG 2
GOLDEN OAKS SPRING TO
JAWBONE CANYON ROAD

BLM

BLM

Jawbone Canyon Rd

BLM

BLM

▲ Weldon Peak

BLM

Hugh Mann Canyon

Hamp Williams Pass

LEG 2

BLM

Back Canyon Rd

Camp 10 ▲

BLM

BLM

BLM

Pacific Crest Trail

BLM

Jawbone Canyon

BLM

N

0   1   2 MILES

0   1   2 KILOMETERS

Cache Peak ▲

Golden Oaks Spring

LEG 1

Emerge from a burn zone to land on this grassy ridge, offering a sneak peek of the distant Owens Valley.

tucked under beautiful oaks (**Camp 10**). Rabbits and squirrels scamper around here, but it's also prime breeding ground for ticks—do a thorough check if you decide to twirl around the grass, Von Trapp–style.

Head on with renewed energy, crossing unpaved **Back Canyon Road** 0.1 mile past the camp. A sign explains that you're now passing through private property and that livestock may be present—no surprise since there's plenty of green grass for the four-legged types to munch on in spring. Head uphill now, with intermittent oak cover quickly giving way to thick Jeffrey pine forest—the change is abrupt and magical. Coast through the fragrant stands to land near **Hamp Williams Pass** at 13.2 miles. The pass is simply a forested notch, and you'll likely only notice it because of the steep ascent waiting just on the other side; however, the views provide some solace for the uphill grunt. The path meanders up and down through a mixture of pine and oak, with occasional views westward into the gaping maw of **Hugh Mann Canyon**. Skirt around below

the western ridge of **Weldon Peak**, eventually descending to an unpaved road at 16.4 miles. Hang a right to follow this gravelly path uphill for just over 1 mile until departing back onto single-track trail to the left. Even though private residences sit tucked into the pines here and there, it's really quite peaceful, with little more than occasional birdsong interrupting the silence.

Meander along until you intersect an unpaved road at 18.8 miles, where you can depart to the left to reach **Robin Bird Spring** ⬤ about 300 feet downhill. Here, find the fenced-off spring, which offers two points of collection—via a pipe poking out through the barbed wire or by passing through the awkward wooden gate and walking uphill to find a natural flow coursing down the hillside. There's also nearby camping in an obvious flat just west of the spring (**Robin Bird Camp**).

To finish, continue sharply uphill past the Robin Bird Spring turnoff to end at unpaved **Jawbone Canyon Road** at 19.2 miles, where it intersects the PCT at a saddle. There's no formal parking area here, although there are a few places where you might wedge a vehicle into the sand. While this is a moderately traveled road, don't expect to find a hitch—you're more likely to see off-road vehicles than passenger cars.

3 JAWBONE CANYON ROAD TO KELSO VALLEY ROAD

DISTANCE 13.4 miles

ELEVATION GAIN/LOSS +1430/-3090 feet

HIGH POINT 6795 feet

CONNECTING ROADS
Jawbone Canyon Road, Forest Service Road 29S19, Piute Mountain Road, Forest Service Road 29S05, Kelso Valley Road

ON THE TRAIL

If I had to choose only one leg of the trail to hike in this section, this is it! While I dig the ridgeline views near Tehachapi Pass and love the expansive high desert views waiting as you near Walker Pass, I can't resist the siren call of wandering through sun-dappled pine forest. It kicks in right at the beginning, from the trail's dusty intersection with unpaved **Jawbone Canyon Road** as you head downhill on soft duff straight into a beautiful stand of deliciously fragrant Jeffrey pines. *Swoon.*

While many people mistakenly think that everything south of Kennedy Meadows is a beige swipe of hot sand, the Piute Mountains prove them wrong as manzanita, white fir, and live oaks join the party, the latter offering bright pops of color in fall. Boulders stud the hillsides, and it's easy to remember that you're actually walking through the **Sequoia National Forest** here. If you want to linger awhile, there is a campsite just shy of 1.5 miles at an obvious clearing on your right (**Camp 11**). In spring, you may find water just 0.1 mile ahead at a branch of **Cottonwood Creek** ◐, but it's more likely that you'll encounter nothing more than desiccated willows as summer rolls around.

Cross the stream (or its muddy remnants) once more, then continue along a series of gentle ups and downs. Pass a few dirt paths in this area, first a narrow bike trail at 2.7 miles, then unpaved **Forest Service Road 29S19** not quite 0.1 mile past that. If you're thirsty, another possible hydration option appears at 3.2 miles on your right via a dammed spring ◐ wedged into the hillside. Continue scampering along through gorgeous, sun-dappled pines, passing yet another bike trail, descending toward lovely Landers Creek. History enthusiasts

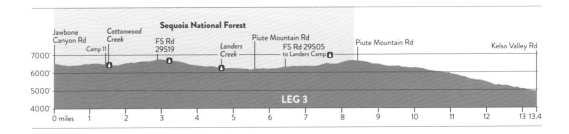

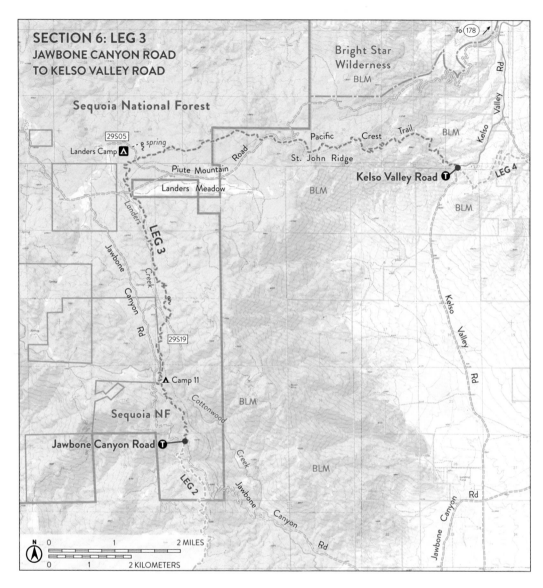

SECTION 6: LEG 3
JAWBONE CANYON ROAD
TO KELSO VALLEY ROAD

To 178

Bright Star
Wilderness
– BLM

Sequoia National Forest

Kelso Valley Rd

29S05

spring

Landers Camp

Pacific   Crest   Trail   BLM

St. John Ridge

Piute Mountain

Kelso Valley Road

LEG 4

Landers Meadow

BLM

BLM

Landers

LEG 3

Jawbone

Creek

Canyon Rd

Kelso

Valley

29S19

Camp 11

Rd

Cottonwood

BLM

Sequoia NF

Jawbone Canyon Road

Creek

BLM

LEG 2

Jawbone

Rd

Canyon

Jawbone Canyon

Rd

N   0   1   2 MILES

0   1   2 KILOMETERS

will appreciate a weathered sluice box sunk into the mud, a remnant of the Piute Mountains' rich mining past.

After walking alongside it for a short bit, you'll actually cross **Landers Creek** at 4.6 miles, then once more just ahead. As with Cottonwood Creek, this waterway may evaporate by late spring, depending on snowpack levels. The walking is easy here, and before no time you reach the western edge of **Landers Meadow**, a lush, grassy area fed by the ephemeral creek waters. Resist the urge to roll around like a puppy and instead move uphill to reach the first crossing of unpaved **Piute Mountain Road**. Unattractive metal barricades guard each side of the road to keep off-road vehicle enthusiasts at bay but allow you to pass back into a beautiful mixture of large boulders, vibrant sage, and heavenly pines. Before continuing on, pause a moment to relax on some cozy benches and scrawl your name in the trail register located here.

Pine trees abound in the Sierra National Forest.

WATER ALERT!

The spring ⬤ at **Landers Camp** is the most reliable source for the duration of this section. The next option, **Willow Spring ⬤**, is 11.1 miles ahead, **McIvers Spring ⬤** is 17 miles past that, and the spring ⬤ near **Walker Pass Campground** is 14.3 miles farther. The latter is typically fairly dependable, but the two previous sources can dry up by summer, especially during drought conditions. Trail angels sometimes leave water caches scattered around, but these tend to be small, seasonal, and depleted after large numbers of hikers pass through the area. Plan your hike through this section *very* carefully to assure you have adequate *agua*.

Continue through more forested loveliness to reach a junction with yet another unpaved road at 6.4 miles—this time, **Forest Service Road 29S05**. If you're tired or thirsty, hang a left here to reach **Landers Camp** less than 0.25 mile down the way, which is really just a large, pine-ringed clearing available for camping that's frequented mostly by hikers and off-road vehicle enthusiasts; don't expect to find picnic tables or toilets here. Directly across from the camp entrance is a dirt path that leads to a metal trough filled by a piped spring ⬤, typically the most reliable water in the area.

From the junction to Landers Camp, hop over another unsightly metal barricade and head uphill on a fairly gentle grade. Great Basin sagebrush sprouts from the ground in thick tufts, surrounded by Jeffrey pines and birdsong—until it all just stops about 0.5 mile from the camp junction. Here, cross an unpaved road that serves as a sort of depressing boundary between the forest and the scar left by the 2008 Piute Fire, a month-long blaze that devegetated almost 37,000 acres. The tree cover is all but gone, save for a few hardy pinyon pines holding fort among the spooky, wind-whipped skeletal remnants.

Luckily, the somewhat apocalyptic scene doesn't last too long—after making the second crossing of Piute Mountain Road (called the "Harris Grade" here) at 8.7 miles, things become a lot more attractive as you wiggle around below **St. John Ridge**. You're now in an obvious transition zone, moving from conifer forest down toward more desert climes, where pinyons and oaks dot the slopes before becoming sparser. The scattered coverage offers one especially great advantage, though—views straight north toward loftier Sierra environments, including Mount Langley and Olancha Peak rising on the horizon.

Sagebrush begins to dominate the descent, and eventually yucca, Mormon tea, juniper, and bitterbrush pop up along the increasingly barren slopes, the latter hosting pretty blooms in spring. The low chaparral offers unrestricted views of the sandy desert suddenly surrounding you, the most prominent feature being the soaring pyramid of Mayan Peak just to the northeast. The mountain stays in sight as you squiggle all the way down to a trailhead parking area adjacent to **Kelso Valley Road**, which you reach at 13.4 miles after passing over a wooden barrier. If tackling this section in chunks, this is a good location for one end of a car shuttle since the road is paved from this point all the way north to State Highway 178. You can also access this spot from the south, but it requires driving a long distance on unpaved roads; choose your own adventure.

CAMP-TO-CAMP MILEAGE
Jawbone Canyon Road to Camp 11 . . . . 1.5
Camp 11 to Landers Camp 4.9

Towering Mayan Peak can't help but dominate its surroundings as you near this leg's end.

4 KELSO VALLEY ROAD TO BIRD SPRING PASS

DISTANCE 14.9 miles

ELEVATION GAIN/LOSS
+2990/-2580 feet

HIGH POINT 5978 feet

CONNECTING ROADS
Kelso Valley Road, Butterbredt Canyon
Road, Dove Spring Canyon Road, Bird
Spring Canyon Road

ON THE TRAIL

If you hiked the previous pine-filled segment through the Piute Mountains, it might seem a bit startling to find yourself out of the woods (literally), surrounded by sandy beige, but you'll quickly adjust and begin to appreciate the expansive beauty of the high desert. This leg is accessible year-round, and if you choose to make the journey in winter to avoid the heat, you might end up prancing along snow-covered slopes that offer an otherworldly contrast to the normally dry surroundings.

It's best to carry all of the water you'll need; the only natural source on this leg is Willow Spring, considerably off-trail and prone to disappearing by late spring. Begin at the trailhead parking area on the west side of **Kelso Valley Road**, cross the pavement, and walk over a wooden barrier on your left, passing a trail register shortly thereafter. From the outset, Mayan Peak dominates the landscape, its pointy summit towering to the northeast. Closer to your feet, jackrabbits and lizards scurry around sparse patches of Great Basin sagebrush, Mormon tea, bitterbrush, and gnarled Joshua trees.

In just over 0.25 mile you'll hit one of many unpaved "roads" in this area—don't expect any street signs out this way, since most of these are OHV tracks. Nearly all (including this one) will feature some sort of wooden barrier to prevent less

responsible riders from encroaching on the PCT; step over and continue on the other side. The shadeless trail meanders gently through this area, dipping to cross a gully, then arriving at unpaved **Butterbredt Canyon Road** (SC 123) at 1.9 miles before swinging back uphill. While Mayan Peak is an attention stealer, definitely glance back from whence you came toward the slowly receding Piute Mountains. Joshua trees become more dominant the farther you hike, and taller ones provide small pockets of shade on a hot day while also serving as decent windbreaks on a breezy one.

The terrain changes slightly, eventually blocking westward views as you wind toward the northern slopes of **Pinyon Mountain** and into steeper territory. Just before this, a short bit of downhill deposits you at the edge of a prominent gully at 4.1 miles, where wooden posts guard a rough use trail leading about 1.5 miles north to **Willow Spring ⬡**, adjacent to Dove Spring Canyon Road (SC 103). A bit of boulder hopping and sand walking is required to navigate to the spring trough and pond; the upside

DESERT SNOW?!

While it broils in summer, the high desert is no stranger to chilly weather—in colder months, snow covers sand, ice slicks the trail, and frosty winds whip all around. I came through in January one year, breaking trail in calf-deep powder while wearing running shoes; waterproof boots would have been a better choice. On that same trip, one companion sat on a rock after a sweaty ascent only to realize upon standing up that he now had a frozen wedgie. Check the weather before heading out anywhere in the Piute or Scodie Mountains in winter or during the shoulder seasons—this area is remote, and if a storm descends, frozen undies will be the least of your worries.

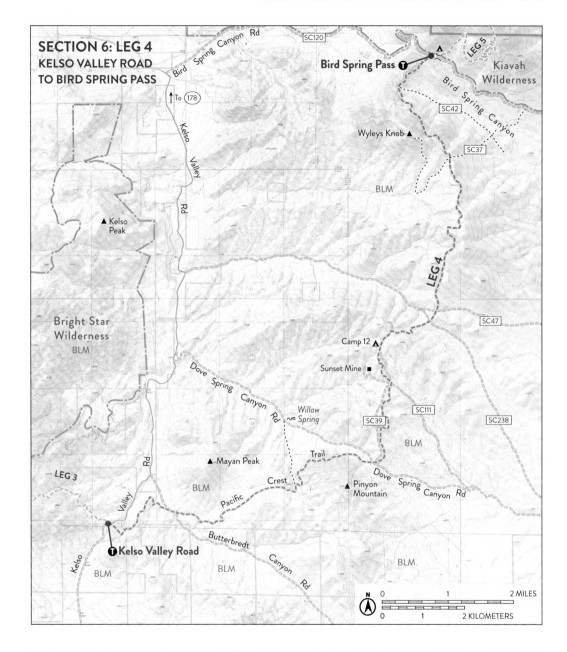

SECTION 6: LEG 4
KELSO VALLEY ROAD
TO BIRD SPRING PASS

Bird Spring Canyon Rd

SC120

Bird Spring Pass

LEG 5

Kiavah
Wilderness

Bird Spring Canyon

To 178

Kelso Valley Rd

SC42

Wyleys Knob

SC37

BLM

LEG 4

Kelso
Peak

SC47

Camp 12

Bright Star
Wilderness
BLM

Sunset Mine

Dove Spring Canyon Rd

Willow
Spring

SC39   SC111   SC238

BLM

LEG 3

Mayan Peak

Trail

BLM

Crest

Dove Spring Canyon Rd

Pacific

Pinyon
Mountain

Kelso Valley Rd

Butterbredt

Kelso Valley Road

BLM

BLM

Canyon Rd

BLM

N   0   1   2 MILES

0   1   2 KILOMETERS

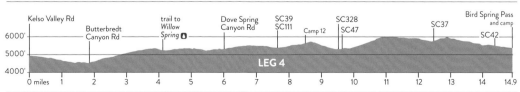

Kelso Valley Rd

Butterbredt
Canyon Rd

trail to
Willow
Spring

Dove Spring
Canyon Rd

SC39
SC111

Camp 12

SC328
SC47

SC37

Bird Spring Pass
and camp

SC42

6000'

5000'

4000'

LEG 4

0 miles 1   2   3   4   5   6   7   8   9   10   11   12   13   14   14.9

Yes, that's snow in the desert! Always check the weather before heading out to ensure you're prepared for a range of conditions.

is that you don't have to backtrack—just pop onto Dove Spring Canyon Road and head southeast to rejoin the trail where it intersects. Otherwise, stay on the trail as it rounds one more gully, then traverses the slopes north of Pinyon Mountain, covered in—*wait for it*—a welcome assortment of pinyon pines and boulders.

Spot the dirt ribbon of **Dove Spring Canyon Road** snaking below and eventually reach it at the 6-mile mark. The area might seem a little confusing—unpaved **SC 39** shoots uphill to the left, but the PCT continues straight to the east across a dirt clearing. It's worth taking a short break here at a seemingly random picnic table; the spot also features an area map and an interpretive display about the desert tortoise, called the Mojave Desert's "living symbol." You'd be very lucky to see this reptilian superstar out and about, although I wouldn't count on snagging an autograph if you do.

Once rested and adequately informed, continue along the trail, now heading north. The sparse sage scrub offers unlimited views across the impressive Indian Wells Valley to the east. Climb gently uphill, traversing around Joshua tree–dotted hillsides to cross two rugged unpaved roads, eventually reaching a four-way junction at 7.6 miles. This is the intersection of your old pal SC 39 and **SC 111**, marked by a giant dirt flat in the middle. While the level sand might beckon for tents, remember that this area is popular with OHV riders—several whipped by as I stood near the junction. Continue on to the northwest over a wooden barrier as the trail curves around a ridgeline, once more opening up to westward views.

Just over 8 miles in, a faint use trail departs in a gully toward the remnants of the Sunset Mine. Your eyes do not deceive—that *is* an old school bus rusting away on the desert floor. Less than 0.5 mile up, find a campsite tucked into a small Joshua tree–ringed flat to your left (**Camp 12**); the views from here are pretty excellent. Just ahead, cross **SC 39** and ascend a slope across from another old mining claim that now seems to serve as a makeshift target range, judging from the shots ringing out as I passed.

Cross another unpaved path then crest a ridge to spot a tower-topped high point to the north—this is **Wyleys Knob**, and you'll pass to its east while approaching the end of this leg. Until then, cruise down to reach wooden barriers guarding **SC 328** at 9.5 miles, then pass **SC 47** just 0.1 mile ahead. Work up a knobby ridgeline that presents ever-expanding views to the southwest, skipping past yet another unpaved track. The scenery improves as you move along—large boulder piles create intriguing formations, and massive **Bird Spring Canyon** suddenly jumps into view—you're getting close.

At 12.5 miles, cross unpaved **SC 37** and look to the right for a wooden barrier guarding the continuation of the PCT. Head uphill to curve below a fence line on the eastern side of Wyleys Knob. Pinyon pines reappear as you angle northwest, moving downhill. Bird Spring Canyon opens up in a sandy slash just below, an impressive sight at any time of day, but particularly beautiful around dusk—especially so if dusted with snow. Pass **SC 42** to reach the canyon's head and this leg's end, **Bird Spring Pass**, at 14.9 miles. Here, find unpaved **Bird Spring Canyon Road** (SC 120) as well as a small dirt parking area. I made it up here in my Honda Civic, but you may want to consider a higher clearance vehicle since the road experiences washouts from time to time. Sleepyheads will find flattish clearings on the north side of the road (**Bird Spring Camp**); just be prepared for a windy snooze.

CAMP-TO-CAMP MILEAGE

Kelso Valley Road to Camp 12. . . . . 8.4
Camp 12 to Bird Spring Camp 6.5

5 BIRD SPRING PASS TO WALKER PASS

DISTANCE 21.2 miles

ELEVATION GAIN/LOSS
+3410/-3500 feet

HIGH POINT 6975 feet

CONNECTING TRAILS AND ROADS
Bird Spring Canyon Road, Forest Service Road 27S11, Walker Pass Campground Trail, State Highway 178

ON THE TRAIL

After a brief foray into the world of Joshua trees and sandy vistas, it's time to head back into pines, courtesy of this scenic journey through the Scodie Mountains. From **Bird Spring Pass** (specifically, unpaved **Bird Spring Canyon Road**), head north to hop over a wooden barrier and enter what's signed as the Scodie Segment of the PCT. Almost immediately, you'll notice some flat spots carved out to the left of the trail—these make for decent, if sloped (and breezy) campsites (**Bird Spring Camp**).

Begin with gentle contouring, moving into a deep gully lined with sagebrush and yucca. In 0.5 mile, a trail register appears on the left—scrawl something impressive, then pop back out onto south-facing slopes, where pinyon pines and boulders begin to appear. The first part of this leg features the biggest gain of the trip, but expansive views east along massive **Bird Spring Canyon**, south to Wyleys Knob, and beyond absolutely make up for the well-graded grind. After a slew of switchbacks beginning around 1.5 miles in, ascend into not only the **Sequoia National Forest** but also the **Kiavah Wilderness**, where you'll remain until just before State Highway 178 at the end of this section.

Pop up to a saddle to begin traversing below a rock-studded ridgeline that serves as the southeast spur of nearby **Skinner Peak**, whose slopes you'll reach shortly. Before then, enjoy a few more steep switchbacks dotted with pinyons and fascinating rock formations. Grunt along to reach another

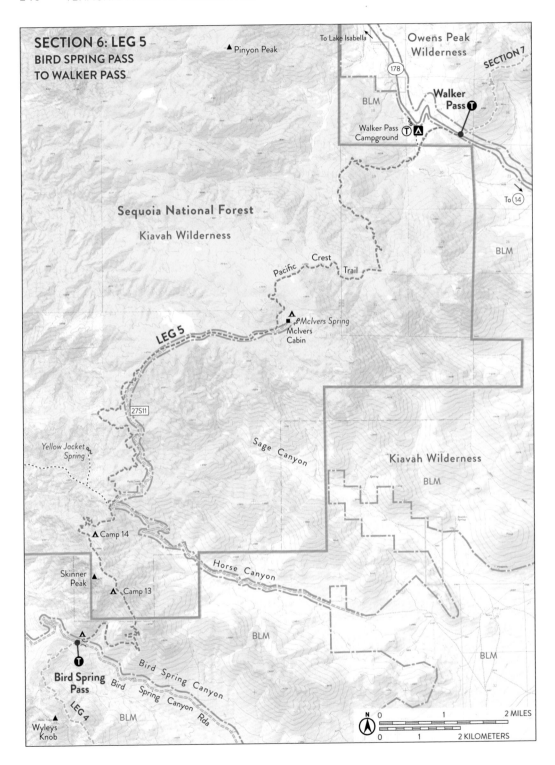

SECTION 6: LEG 5
BIRD SPRING PASS
TO WALKER PASS

saddle at 3.4 miles, this one offering a few scattered campsites (**Camp 13**) just south of the peak.

The going is easy as you move downhill, with scattered pinyons offering shade. As you wind below the summit, eastward views open into vast **Horse Canyon** and then quickly switch to westward ones above **Cane Canyon**. Look to the right at 4.6 miles on a saddle to find a small campsite with room for at least one tent (**Camp 14**). Long, lazy switchbacks then descend from the ridgeline, transitioning back to eastward vistas.

Although this area feels wonderfully secluded, you might encounter off-road vehicle enthusiasts traveling nearby—if so, you'll hear them before you see them. Cross an unpaved road, pass a "No Motorbikes" sign, and arrive at the signed turnoff to **Yellow Jacket Spring** ⬤ at 6.2 miles. The path is just under 1 mile long, delivering you to a small pool seep in the grass, where you'll likely either need a pump filter or scoop to gather the wet stuff, if it's there at all. If you arrive to find just a mud patch, hope that piped McIvers Spring is running about 6.8 miles ahead.

Round a gully, then continue along mellowing slopes under pine cover. If the mechanical sound of wheeled recreation grinds your gears, now is the time to make peace with it—you're in mixed-use territory, with popular OHV routes scattered around the area. The terrain makes gentle waves as you walk through thick forest cover, now with bonus oak trees. Eventually emerge into sunnier terrain, hiking up to meet unpaved **Forest Service Road 27S11** at 10.7 miles; make a left to join it for the next 2.3 miles. While the landscape has flattened out considerably, the road doesn't make for easy going, especially after a rain or snowmelt—you now share the "trail" with OHV riders, and the path is incredibly rutted out. Take your earbuds out and move to the side as vehicles

approach, especially since some are nearly as wide as the road itself.

Although it's annoying to dodge wheeled machines, expansive views to the southeast promise to balance the equation, especially as tree cover thins and sagebrush becomes the dominant foliage. Traipse along the sunny plateau, passing the rusted skeleton of some form of dearly departed wheeled recreation, and reach a fork in the road at 13 miles. The PCT continues as single-track up to the left, but the road heads downhill to the right toward a cluster of Jeffrey pines, reaching **McIvers Cabin** less than 0.25 mile ahead. This area is popular with OHV enthusiasts, but it also offers dusty (or muddy) campsites (**McIvers Camp**) and water via seasonal **McIvers Spring** ⬤, dripping from a pipe located in a gully next to the cabin. While some might want to bed down in the dilapidated structure, my companions and I nicknamed it the "Hantavirus Cabin" since we were convinced a night there meant snuggling with rodents and their droppings. One last note—if the rustic outhouse is still around, it's best not to make a deposit here since there's no floor—just a rancid pile of poop and toilet paper heaped up on the ground below.

Ascending past the McIvers junction, manzanita, sagebrush, and even beavertail cactus join the pinyon pines and boulders. The terrain remains flattish until traversing the steep cliffs above **Boulder Canyon**, then another deep, unnamed canyon to its northeast. Move along the pine-dotted hillsides, contouring to reach the beginning of the final descent toward Walker Pass around 18.6 miles; from here, the trees all but disappear, replaced with sand and chaparral. Switchback alongside a gully while enjoying views to the north that offer a glimpse of not only State Highway 178, but also what's to come if you continue into the next section. Before then, cross the

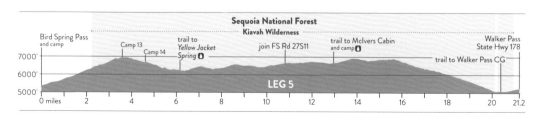

Even when it's cold and gloomy, the descent to Walker Pass still offers exceptional beauty.

WATER ALERT!

If you are thirsty, exit **Walker Pass Campground** and walk a few minutes west along the shoulder of Highway 178 to reach an obvious use trail descending on the south side of the road. Here, find three concrete spring boxes **0**; the largest one (usually with an assortment of cattails sprouting from its interior) has a metal pipe that feeds into a metal basin; this is the easiest place to access the good stuff.

gully, grind out a short bit of uphill, and arrive at a trail junction on the left at 20.5 miles, signed for **Walker Pass Campground**. Depart here for vault toilets, picnic tables, and parking—leave your car here instead of at Walker Pass itself if setting up a shuttle. There's no water at the campground itself, but there is a fairly reliable spring **0** located just west of the entrance.

Before continuing to finish this leg, you may want to take note of the Kern Transit sign posted here—if you have cell service, it's possible to request a pickup on the bus route that runs along State Highway 178. Otherwise, continue through

EAST OR WEST?

Walker Pass is a natural launchpad for resupply. Kern Transit operates a bus through the area (although you must call ahead of time to request a pickup), and brave types can try for a hitch going either direction on busy Highway 178. Most hikers choose to visit either Lake Isabella, 34 miles to the west, or Ridgecrest, 25 miles to the east, for food and rest. I've eaten delicious Mexican food in both towns (availability of mole enchiladas being my personal barometer of a good trail town), so I can't play favorites here—although the latter has more "big box" stores if that's your thing.

sagebrush, pinyon pines, and yucca, now walking parallel to the highway itself. Pass through a somewhat tricky cattle gate and continue on the faint tread to reach **State Highway 178** and **Walker Pass** at 21.2 miles. Cars whip by at breakneck speeds, so mind your step while visiting a large stone monument commemorating Joseph R. Walker, the first Euro-American to traverse the pass—of course, there's also a lengthy history of indigenous people inhabiting and navigating the area long before he came through.

CAMP-TO-CAMP MILEAGE

Bird Spring Pass to Camp 13 . . . . 3.4
Camp 13 to Camp 14 . . . . 1.2
Camp 14 to McIvers Camp 8.4
McIvers Camp to Walker Pass
    Campground 7.5

WALKER PASS TO KENNEDY MEADOWS

ENJOY ONE LAST TRIP through the wind-swept sand and rocky spires of the high desert as the scenery slowly transforms into alpine with plentiful pines and your first views out to the High Sierra. This section begins with a bit of history at Walker Pass on State Highway 178, part of a route originally pioneered by indigenous people and later followed by Euro-American explorers and purveyors of gold fever, but you'll quickly step away from human history to wind through the natural kind on myriad sandy slopes pockmarked by pinyon pines and boulders.

Traverse high above the wide, flat Owens Valley before entering a magical world filled with the twisted wonder of Joshua trees (actually a form of yucca!) and occasional flows of life-sustaining water. After climbing back into the pines, pass the ruins of a once-bustling mining operation and trudge through many shadeless miles of bleak, fire-scorched hillsides before descending into the relatively green expanse of Rockhouse Basin—also somewhat burn-scarred, but leagues better in the scenery department.

Rejoice when you reach the South Fork Kern River—while you're not yet totally out of the waterless woods, this flow will prove a trusted companion into the beginning of the next section. Finally, drop down into quiet, residential Kennedy Meadows, where a short walk will carry you to food, sundries, and all manner of libations. Congratulations—you've made it to what's commonly (if somewhat erroneously) considered the "Gateway to the Sierra!"

DISTANCE 50.2 miles

STATE DISTANCE 652–702.2 miles

ELEVATION GAIN/LOSS
+8480/-7750 feet

HIGH POINT 8012 feet

BEST TIME OF YEAR Apr–Oct

PCTA SECTION LETTER G

LAND MANAGERS Bureau of Land Management (Bakersfield Field Office, Owens Peak Wilderness, Chimney Peak Wilderness, Domeland Wilderness), Sequoia National Forest (Kern River Ranger District, Domeland Wilderness)

PASSES AND PERMITS California Campfire Permit

MAPS AND APPS
- Halfmile's CA Section G
- USGS PCT Map #3 Southern Sierra
- USGS Topo Quads: Walker Pass, Owens Peak, Lamont Peak, Sacatar Canyon, Rockhouse Basin, Crag Peak
- Halfmile's PCT app
- Guthook's PCT app

LEGS
1. Walker Pass to Joshua Tree Spring
2. Joshua Tree Spring to Canebrake Road
3. Canebrake Road to Manter Creek
4. Manter Creek to Kennedy Meadows

Opposite: By late summer (earlier in drought years), the South Fork Kern River dwindles to a lazy flow.

ACCESS
Walker Pass
From Los Angeles, head north on Interstate 5 (toward Sacramento), then take exit 162 for State Highway 14 northbound (Antelope Valley Freeway) toward Palmdale and Lancaster. Drive 110.8 miles, then make a left onto State Highway 178 westbound. You will reach Walker Pass in 8.3 miles—there are small parking pullouts located on either side of the road, but it's best to park 1 mile farther west on CA 178 at Walker Pass Campground if leaving your car overnight. You then depart the campground from a well-signed connector trail to hit the PCT; head 0.7 mile northeast on the PCT to reach Walker Pass.

Kennedy Meadows
From Los Angeles, head north on Interstate 5 (toward Sacramento), then take exit 162 for State Highway 14 northbound (Antelope Valley Freeway) toward Palmdale and Lancaster. Drive 117.7 miles, then merge onto US 395 northbound. In 9.9 miles, turn left onto 9 Mile Canyon Road, continuing onto Kennedy Meadow Road (Sherman Pass Road) after 9.8 miles. In 14.1 miles, make a left to stay on Sherman Pass Road. The PCT crosses the road 0.8 miles ahead. There is no parking at this intersection—either make arrangements to park at the Kennedy Meadows General Store 0.7 mile east on Sherman Pass Road, or head north on Kennedy Meadow Road for another 2.7 miles to reach Kennedy Meadows Campground and a large parking lot; the PCT passes through the campground.

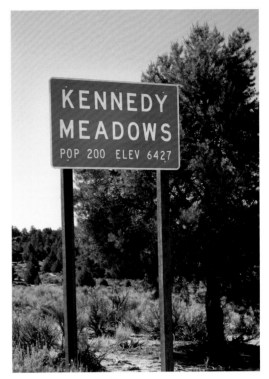

Welcome to paradise!

NOTES
Cities and Services
From the southern trailhead, head to the resort town of Lake Isabella about 36 miles to the west or the community of Ridgecrest, approximately 25 miles to the east, for an array of services. Kennedy Meadows is a small community near the northern trailhead, where you'll find a general store, a restaurant, and not much else.

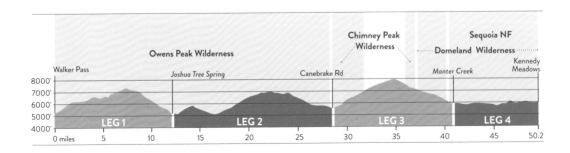

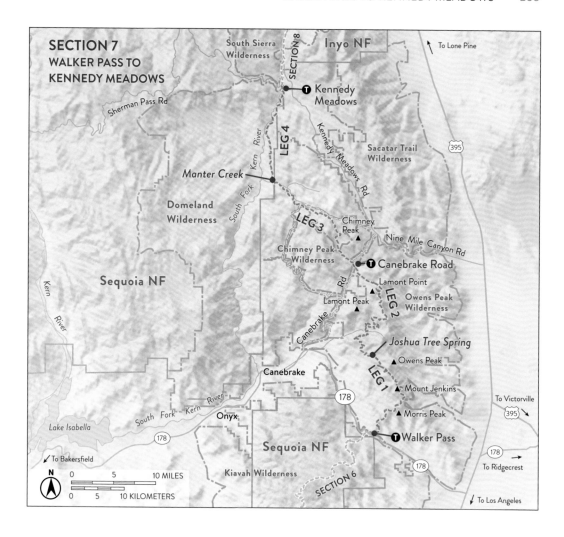

Camping and Fire Restrictions

Camp 100 feet from water and trails. Campfires must be at least 100 feet from the South Fork Kern River. Check for seasonal fire restrictions in Sequoia National Forest before heading out.

Water

Natural water sources are few and far between, and they begin to dry up by late summer (if not earlier)—check water reports before venturing out. The longest waterless stretches are the 11.7 miles between Walker Pass and Joshua Tree Spring, the 10.6 miles between Spanish Needle Creek and Chimney Creek, and the 10.4 miles between Fox Mill Spring and Manter Creek. The water from Joshua Tree Spring is reported to contain high levels of uranium.

Hazards

This section can see extreme heat in the summer months and extreme cold, ice, and snow in the winter months.

Other

The general store in Kennedy Meadows has reduced hours outside of the summer hiking season—call ahead if you plan to visit.

SUGGESTED ITINERARIES

Camps are either viewable from the trail or located within a few tenths of a mile from the noted location unless otherwise specified in leg descriptions.

5 DAYS

		Miles
Day 1	Walker Pass to Joshua Tree Camp	11.8
Day 2	Joshua Tree Camp to Camp 6	9.0
Day 3	Camp 6 to Chimney Creek Campground	8.1
Day 4	Chimney Creek Campground to Camp 9	11.0
Day 5	Camp 9 to Kennedy Meadows	10.3

4 DAYS

Day 1	Walker Pass to Joshua Tree Camp	11.8
Day 2	Joshua Tree Camp to Chimney Creek Campground	17.1
Day 3	Chimney Creek Campground to Camp 10	16.0
Day 4	Camp 10 to Kennedy Meadows	5.3

3 DAYS

Day 1	Walker Pass to Joshua Tree Camp	11.8
Day 2	Joshua Tree Camp to Chimney Creek Campground	17.1
Day 3	Chimney Creek Campground to Kennedy Meadows	21.3

1 WALKER PASS TO JOSHUA TREE SPRING

DISTANCE 11.8 miles

ELEVATION GAIN/LOSS
+2970/-2760 feet

HIGH POINT 7346 feet

CONNECTING ROAD
State Highway 178

ON THE TRAIL

Before you embark on this leg of your journey, take a moment to read the plaque embedded in the historic marker on the south side of **Walker Pass**, commemorating Joseph R. Walker, "American trailblazer." When you've had your fill of brief historic information, carefully cross busy **State Highway 178**, lest you become part of the roadway, continue along the short access road, and venture up toward a trail marker and glorious single-track tread leading to a register. Welcome to the Owens Peak Segment of the PCT! Before getting too far along, make sure you have as much water as you need for this leg since you won't encounter any until the very end. If you're traveling during the shoulder season, especially closer to the summer months, this will be a sweaty trip—bring adequate sun protection as well.

Take solace in the fact that this leg's beginning is its steepest part. The hills here are sparsely populated, with soft sand dominating

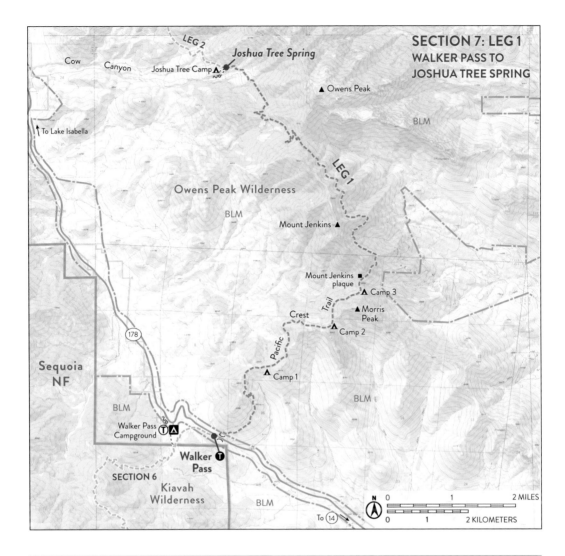

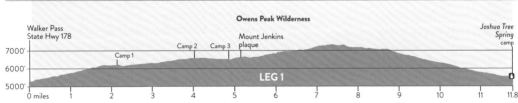

the landscape. Enjoy the expanding views back down toward Walker Pass as you rise higher into the dry slopes. Knock out a few switchbacks and begin to encounter scattered pinyon pines among the sagebrush. Pockets of granite appear on the hillsides around you, a sure sign that you're beginning the gradual shift from high desert to High Sierra.

Pinyon pines dot the slopes as you ascend the ridgeline toward Morris Peak.

Around 1.8 miles, round a curve, earning views out to the northwest. If you're already tuckered out, spot an assortment of small campsites beginning just under 0.3 mile ahead and continuing along the ridge, mostly on the right side (**Camp 1**). Oak and pinyons provide a bit of shade, and sage provides a nice scent to the surroundings. If you can wait, however, better sites appear around the 4-mile mark—here, a pair of well-trodden use trails lead to an obvious clearing with room for several tents (**Camp 2**). If *that* camp's occupied, skirt around the western slopes of **Morris Peak** to find a similar spot ahead another 0.8 mile up on the right (**Camp 3**).

Venture back to east-facing slopes to begin a long traverse with sweeping views out to the southern end of the Owens Valley. At 5.1 miles, encounter your second plaque of the trip, this time commemorating Sierra enthusiast and guidebook author James Charles Jenkins for whom **Mount Jenkins**—the peak you're currently traveling underneath—is named. Enjoy intermittent pinyon shade as you navigate the steep slopes, and mind your feet as you dance around darting western fence lizards and tiptoe over broken talus—if it makes you feel any better, imagine you're getting a free foot massage along the way.

Eventually the twisted pinyons yield to an expansive burn area (courtesy the 2010 Indian Fire), where the trees' striking white and black bark stands in spooky relief against the slopes. The upside is that you earn clear views out to Owens Peak, a promontory named for Richard Owens, who explored the area with John C. Fremont in the mid-1840s. Owens must have been one helluva guy because Fremont not only named a few more natural features after him but also named him Secretary of State during his very brief, self-appointed gubernatorial tenure. By the way, if you look at certain maps, you'll see that the PCT track appears to continue along the Sierra Crest (in the southern Sierra, this is the prominent ridgeline dividing Inyo and Tulare counties) heading north past Owens Peak. This old routing was abandoned in favor of dropping lower on the slopes to give trekkers opportunities to access water.

The hardest work is done—from here, begin a series of long downhill switchbacks, snagging dramatic westward views. The slopes here mellow out, dotted with an array of sage, grasses, pinyons, scrub oak, and manzanita that creates a vibrant green glow in spring. Skip around an assortment of boulders and enjoy the rapid descent.

SUPERHERO SPRING

Joshua Tree Spring 🅾 has been found to contain "unacceptable" levels of uranium; because of this, some folks avoid this water source. However, most hikers accept that brief exposure to this radioactive element isn't going to turn them into a three-armed mutant, so they take the risk and filter carefully. To this day, I haven't developed a green glow or any noticeable superpowers, so I'd say a one-time fill-up is safe enough.

Your final approach involves a few false side trails leading down toward an assortment of gullies. Ignore all of these—the path to **Joshua Tree Spring** 🅾 is marked with a very obvious sign at 11.8 miles, which denotes the end of this leg. If you're ready to rest your weary head or soothe your dry throat, head left here, passing some exposed campsites (**Joshua Tree Camp**) to reach the spring (piped into a trough) 0.25 mile downhill—this source tends to dry up by late summer or early fall. Obvious camping is available near the spring but isn't recommended due to its proximity to the water source—and nothing will turn you off

more quickly than the dried turds and used toilet paper dug up all over the place. One more word of warning: this spring is frequented by not just bloodthirsty mosquitos but also by water-thirsty resident black bears—be mindful of your food storage. I met a hiker up the trail whose dog earned the trail name "Bear Chaser" due to an encounter here.

CAMP-TO-CAMP MILEAGE
Walker Pass to Camp 1 . . . . 2.1
Camp 1 to Camp 2 . . . . 1.9
Camp 2 to Camp 3 . . . . 0.8
Camp 3 to Joshua Tree Camp 7.0

2 JOSHUA TREE SPRING TO CANEBRAKE ROAD

DISTANCE 17.1 miles

ELEVATION GAIN/LOSS
+3840/-3760 feet

HIGH POINT 6995 feet

CONNECTING ROAD
Canebrake Road

ON THE TRAIL
You will go up, then down, then up, then down, all while playing a game of water roulette—will the next stream have a better flow? Or will it be bone dry? Speaking of, tank up on tasty uranium-enhanced water at **Joshua Tree Spring** 🅾 (see directions in the previous leg) and get a move on as early as you can—as the temperature rises, so will your annoyance at the shadeless uphill.

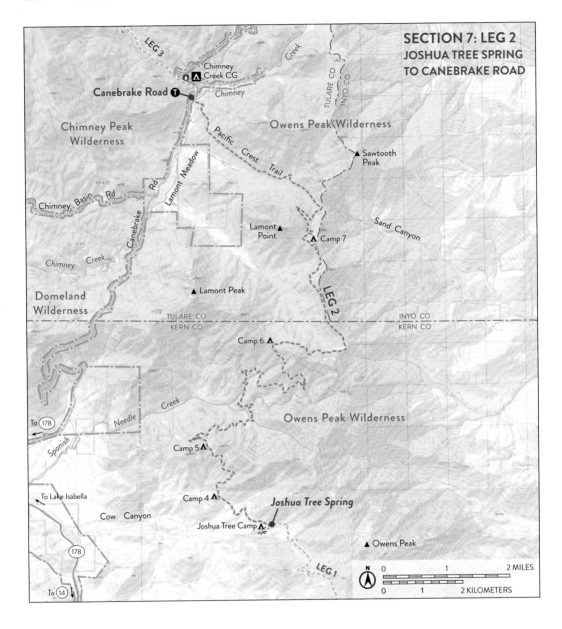

SECTION 7: LEG 2
JOSHUA TREE SPRING
TO CANEBRAKE ROAD

LEG 3

Chimney
Creek CG

Canebrake Road

Chimney

Chimney Peak
Wilderness

Owens Peak Wilderness

TULARE CO
INYO CO

Pacific Crest Trail

Sawtooth
Peak

Lamont Meadow

Chimney Basin Rd

Canebrake Rd

Sand Canyon

Lamont
Point

Camp 7

LEG 2

Chimney Creek

Lamont Peak

Domeland
Wilderness

TULARE CO
KERN CO

INYO CO
KERN CO

Camp 6

To 178

Needle Creek

Owens Peak Wilderness

Spanish

Camp 5

Camp 4

To Lake Isabella

Cow Canyon

Joshua Tree Spring

Joshua Tree Camp

Owens Peak

178

LEG 1

To 14

N

0   1   2 MILES

0   1   2 KILOMETERS

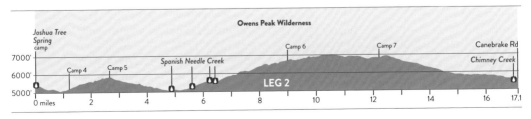

Joshua Tree Spring camp

Owens Peak Wilderness

7000'

6000'

5000'

Camp 4

Camp 5

Spanish Needle Creek

Camp 6

Camp 7

Canebrake Rd

Chimney Creek

LEG 2

0 miles   2   4   6   8   10   12   14   16   17.1

Looking back to Lamont Peak from Canebrake Road

The consolation prize, however, is that as you rise above the flats of **Cow Canyon**, you'll enjoy some nice views to the west in the company of any number of desert denizens—yucca, junipers, Joshua trees, and a plethora of lizards. Find your first option to call it quits around 1.2 miles, via a well-defined use trail on the left of a saddle that leads to a small dirt patch with room for a few tents (**Camp 4**). Not exactly a scenic wonderland, but it'll do—and it's better than the next saddle's campsite at 2.7 miles—here, there's just enough room for one tent in the scraggly brush (**Camp 5**).

From this perch, settle in for the first significant downhill of the leg, switchbacking down along moderate slopes, weaving in and out of numerous gullies, with intermittent pinyon shade offering some respite. The scent of sage and the sight of beavertail cactus serve as a reminder that you're still in the high desert; the occasional sunbathing snake will reinforce the point.

Your mounting thirst may also serve as a sharp reminder of your desiccated surrounds, but you'll hopefully find refreshment at any one of the upcoming branches of **Spanish Needle Creek 0**, the first in a gully at 4.9 miles. You'll know you've hit a waterway when you spot bright green willows, sometimes accented by winged creatures (including an assortment of colorful butterflies) flitting about. If this branch is dry (and it may be in late season or in a drought year), continue to the 5.6-mile mark, where you'll find the second crossing **0**.

This course sits in another gully—this time filled with leafy oaks—and even if you come up empty, it provides an enjoyable shady rest before you emerge back onto sunnier slopes.

The third crossing of **Spanish Needle Creek** ⭕ at 6.2 miles is the most reliable due to a spring source located uphill. Even if the crossing is dry, follow a use trail up the gully to hopefully find a small trickle. Reach the final crossing ⭕ 0.2 mile ahead—this one provides a bit less shade than its predecessors, so you may want to time your break for one of the other three spots. From here, it's a sunny, steep slog, especially if you're now toting a full water bladder. Try to let the decent views mitigate the sweaty ascent.

Continue ahead to a saddle 9 miles in where you'll find limited camping on either side (**Camp 6**). If it's a hot day, take a rest on this breezy perch and enjoy views across the way to prominent Lamont Point—the rest of this trip is a bit more forgiving. Once your legs are ready, pop around the other side of the ridge to begin a traverse around the canyon. In contrast to the mostly shadeless slopes you just climbed, these provide a lot more cover in the form of beautiful Jeffrey and sugar pines. The grade is mellow, the wildflowers pop in spring, and the views are beautiful, especially when you reach the canyon's apex, rejoining the Sierra Crest to catch a brief glimpse down into the Owens Valley.

Eventually end up across the way from the two-camp saddle, earning views back to the pinnacles of Lamont Peak and below to grassy Lamont Meadow. The latter is fed by Chimney Creek, whose waters you'll encounter in just a few miles. If you have enough of the wet stuff and want to bed down for the night, look for campsites beginning around 12.2 miles on a breezy ridge, where you'll find some small, scattered spots under tree cover (**Camp 7**). Better sites are located a short bit ahead once the ridge widens out near the slopes of **Lamont Point**. If running low on energy, you'll appreciate that the route is mostly downhill from here, dipping down along the back side and winding through sage, scrub oak, pinyons, and an array of seasonal wildflowers, including Indian paintbrush.

WATER ALERT!

If both access points for **Chimney Creek** ⭕ are dry, you might try **Chimney Creek Campground**, which provides seasonal water from a spigot ⭕ near site #36. The only issue is that the site is about 1 mile past the camp entrance—although that's nothing compared to the distance you've already hiked! Parts of the campground were scorched when the Chimney Fire swept through in June 2016, but luckily the bulk of the sites—and the water spigot—remain unscathed.

Descend to a mellow saddle just to the west of **Sand Canyon**; this area may look inviting, but it's not quite flat enough for camping, so carry on. Lamont Meadow feels a lot closer now, and you earn a different view of its namesake peak. Here, leave the Sierra Crest to angle northwest and start making tracks on this final stretch. Granite boulders pop up along the trail, a mere hint of what you'll encounter upon reaching the High Sierra, if headed that far. For now, they seem pretty impressive.

Dip into a line of willows around 17 miles to cross **Chimney Creek** ⭕. If it's run dry (which can happen in drought years and by mid-summer), continue just a short bit to spot an array of obvious use trails headed through the high grasses to your right—these provide additional creek access, where you'll likely find at least a small pool, if not a small flow. This leg ends 0.1 mile ahead at unpaved **Canebreak Road**—you'll find free camping (plus picnic tables, fire rings, and a set of vault toilets) 0.2 mile farther north up the road at **Chimney Creek Campground**.

CAMP-TO-CAMP MILEAGE

Joshua Tree Spring to Camp 4 . . . . 1.2
Camp 4 to Camp 5 . . . . 1.5
Camp 5 to Camp 6 . . . . 6.3
Camp 6 to Camp 7 . . . . 3.2
Camp 7 to Chimney Creek Campground 4.9

Views into the Domeland Wilderness offer hope after a shadeless, burn-scarred climb.

3 CANEBRAKE ROAD TO MANTER CREEK

DISTANCE 12.6 miles

ELEVATION GAIN/LOSS
+3100/-2820 feet

HIGH POINT 8012 feet

CONNECTING ROADS
Canebrake Road, Chimney Basin Road

ON THE TRAIL

Begin where the PCT crosses unpaved **Canebrake Road**, leaving your mark in the trail register before entering the **Chimney Peak Wilderness**. You waste no time climbing uphill, but there's plenty to distract, from colorful lichen to blocky granite to heavenly sage. Plentiful oaks provide some shade as you meander up and down (okay—mostly up). Your reward for this minor workout is the impressive view back toward a parade of summits,

including that of Lamont Peak, whose lofty spires dominated the second half of the previous leg.

Farther up, history buffs might enjoy the scattered remnants of the old Fox Mill on the trail's uphill side at 2.2 miles. Even if you're not into piles of rusted-out stuff, you might enjoy what is down a short, but somewhat steep, signed use trail to the right of the ruins—**Fox Mill Spring ⓪**, seasonal source of liquid refreshment. If the pipe

WATER ALERT!

If you need water at the start of this leg, hike 0.1 mile south on the trail to a crossing of **Chimney Creek ⓪** or head 0.2 mile north on the road to **Chimney Creek Campground ⓪**, which offers seasonal water via a spigot located at site #36—it's an additional 1-mile walk through the campground to access it, though, so mentally prepare yourself.

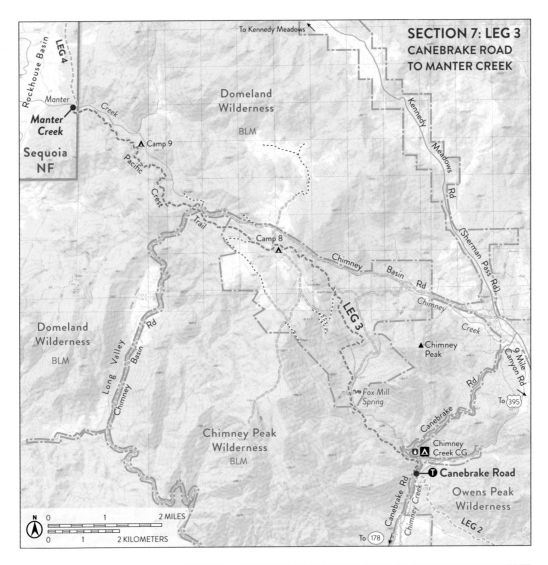

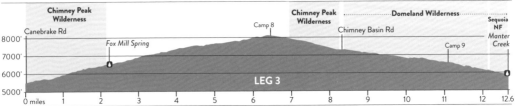

isn't flowing or if the water looks stagnant, walk around the trough to find a creek hidden just behind. Tank up here, because you won't hit the wet stuff again until the end of this leg at Manter Creek (and if that's dry, it's another 4.4 sweaty miles beyond that to reach the more reliable South Fork Kern River), and this can be a tough hike on a hot, cloudless day.

Cross an unpaved road 0.1 mile ahead and continue a mellow stroll through pleasant pinyon forest. As you meander uphill through aromatic sage, decent views occasionally open up to the east, across green meadows and up to Chimney Peak, whose namesake wilderness area you're traversing. Try to appreciate this bit as much as possible while you're in it because these are the last trees you're going to see for quite some time—right before you cross an unnamed dirt road at 4.8 miles, the tree cover disappears, victim to the Manter Fire, which ravaged a large swath of the Sequoia National Forest and Domeland Wilderness in 2000.

I'm not going to sugarcoat it—this portion is miserable on a hot, sunny day. There's a sense of desolation here—all of the surrounding hillsides lay bare, dotted with only the gnarled remnants of burnt trees and bushes. Traverse endlessly along these slopes, your only companion the continual beige ribbon of Chimney Basin Road down below. You will wonder if the burn will end around the next curve—I'm sorry to say that no, it will not. In fact, it feels like it will *never* end. To that point, if you see a spot of shade, grab it—it may be the only one for miles. While massively overheating, with sunblock-infused sweat burning my eyes and the

hot ground scorching through my shoes, I crawled under a low bush here like a desperate animal, wedging as much of my body as possible under the minimal cover. It was not my best moment.

It'll be a while before you earn a reprieve from the endless burn area, so try to find some small joys along the way—the first major one coming at 6.4 miles, when you top out on a plateau of sorts. There are a few exposed campsites to the right (**Camp 8**), along with epic views north to the beautiful white granite slabs of the Domeland Wilderness—and to the iconic slopes of distant Mounts Langley and Whitney beyond! If that consolation prize doesn't put a little wind in your sails, you have my sympathy.

Use that extra pep in your step to coast downhill for a bit, reaching an unpaved road at 6.6 miles, then meeting up with your old buddy **Chimney Basin Road** farther along at 8.2 miles. Head up this for a moment, scanning for a PCT marker lurking behind a bush to your left, marking your departure back onto the trail. In case you're wondering: yes, everything is still scorched. When you reach the 11-mile mark, rejoice, for there will appear a small pinyon-dotted ridge on your right—the first real shade in 6.2 miles! Crawl over

Fox Mill Spring isn't the most attractive source, but it does the trick.

for a brief rest, a lunch break, or even an overnight stay—there's room for at least one tent, although you might be in for a windy evening (**Camp 9**).

Hopefully you feel a renewed spirit from here as you close in on the goal. A green squiggle in the canyon floor below hints at the water that (hopefully) lies ahead. Quicken your step while barreling downhill, finally landing at the edge of massive **Rockhouse Basin** around 12.4 miles. You may not be out of the burn area quite yet, but something about the towering peaks in the Domeland Wilderness across the way and the pines on the horizon offer hope. Walk just 0.2 mile more on flat territory to reach the willow-flanked crossing of **Manter Creek ⊘**, marking this leg's end. If the creek bed is dry (which happens earlier than you'd like some summers), cross and walk down along the creek just a bit to the right, where you might find a small seep in the creek bed; bring a scoop and prepare to deploy every filtering mechanism you own. If the waterway is completely dry and you need to fill up, continue 4.4 miles north on the PCT into the next leg to reach a narrow canyon and your first visit with the **South Fork Kern River ⊘**; use trails offer water access on your left. There are obvious sandy clearings next to Manter Creek that seem like perfect campsites, but this isn't an appropriate location considering it's right next to the creek itself—there's a much better spot a couple miles ahead into the next leg.

CAMP-TO-CAMP MILEAGE

Canebrake Road to Camp 8 . . . . 6.4
Camp 8 to Camp 9 . . . . 4.6

4 MANTER CREEK TO KENNEDY MEADOWS

DISTANCE 8.7 miles

ELEVATION GAIN/LOSS
+1090/-920 feet

HIGH POINT 6089 feet

CONNECTING ROAD
Sherman Pass Road

ON THE TRAIL

Even though you begin this leg surrounded by the somewhat barren remnants of the Manter Fire, it's not long before you duck into shady trees, sidle up to a refreshing river, and make your way to what's widely regarded as the "Gateway of the Sierra!" If you need water, tank up at willow-lined **Manter Creek ⊘** before venturing out. Be aware that this source can dry up in early summer—if that's the case, cross and head right for a moment, looking for an opening in the brush, where you might find a muddy seep to pull from. Filter, filter, filter . . . and filter again—I saw tons of tiny creatures wiggling around when I pulled from the seep (but hey, maybe you need the protein).

Begin your traverse of eastern **Rockhouse Basin** with a short climb, affording a view of the sparkling South Fork Kern River snaking along in the distance—you'll get there soon enough! This area looks downright lovely during the pre-sunset golden hour—the views back toward the basin's south end are worth the price of admission, and it's a special treat to spot jackrabbits darting around in the waning light.

Ambling along the moderately graded path, you begin to encounter stands of pinyon pines mixed in with the sand and sagebrush. Large boulders also start to pop up—maybe I was a bit nutrient deprived and slightly dehydrated when I passed through, but I swear that I saw one that looked like a narwhal and one that looked like a T-rex. Your mileage may vary.

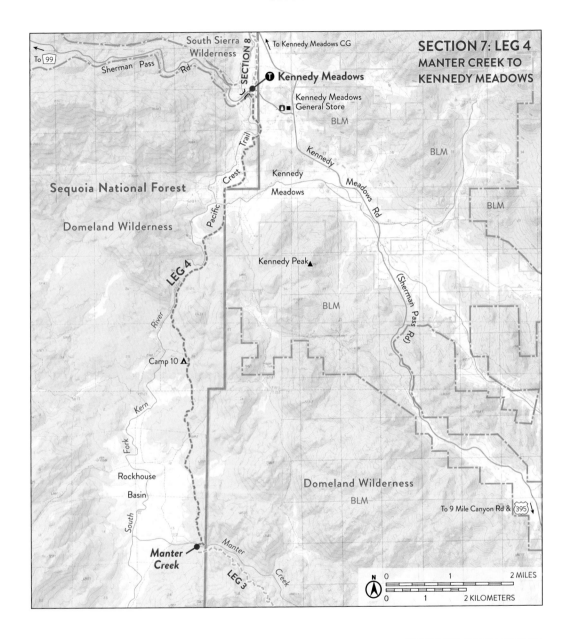

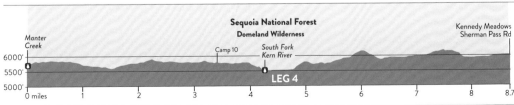

Sunlight gives Rockhouse Basin an ethereal glow.

A RIVER BY ANY OTHER NAME

The South Fork is a major tributary of the Kern River, a popular recreation corridor that carves a path beginning just west of Mount Whitney all the way down to the northern reaches of Bakersfield. The waterway earned many appellations before its present one—Po-sun-co-la, La Porciuncula, Rio Bravo—but explorer John C. Fremont named it in honor of his expedition-mate and topographer Edward M. Kern, and the designation stuck.

If you're feeling sleepy, keep your eyes peeled around 3.4 miles after rounding a prominent gully to find a good-sized sandy area on the left with room for quite a few tents (**Camp 10**)—walk back into the trees a bit to find the best spots. From here, you're within spitting distance of the South Fork Kern River **0**, which weaves a green path into a narrow canyon guarded by willows and alders, which you'll enter at 4.3 miles. Several use trails lead to the good stuff, the most obvious located 0.1 mile ahead, across from a useful rock shelf. You'll have other opportunities to tank up ahead, but this spot provides the easiest access.

Once your reservoirs are full, head out of the canyon and uphill through scattered Jeffrey pines, then across a fragrant carpet of sagebrush. The upside to the minor workout is that the higher you get, the better views you earn of the river wiggling around below. If you didn't follow my advice earlier and need to top off, find another access point downhill at 5.4 miles.

From here, it's up through hot, shadeless scrub—a reminder that you're not out of the high desert quite yet. Eventually begin descending toward **Kennedy Meadows**, more of a sagebrush flat than a grassy expanse, but still pretty enough.

SIERRA GATEWAY

Kennedy Meadows is a small community located 0.7 mile east of the PCT crossing at Sherman Pass Road. The general store offers food, beverages, and some gear for sale, plus laundry, showers, mail services, water **O**, toilets, a pay phone, a hiker box, and camping out back. It also sports a large deck that serves as home base to any number of stinky backpackers enjoying adult beverages and increasing their caloric intake during the summer months—you'll often receive a deafening round of applause if you walk up to join their ranks. I also had my dirt-encrusted toenails painted by a fellow hiker within an hour of arrival the first time I came through, although I can't guarantee that will happen to you. Many backpackers choose to send a resupply package here, often including a bear canister, traction devices, and an ice axe for the High Sierra; you must pay a fee when you retrieve your goods. Farther into "town," you'll find a hiker-friendly bar and restaurant—and not much else. If you choose to begin your hike at Kennedy Meadows, park in the large lot at the **Kennedy Meadows Campground** up the road instead of at the store.

Human encroachment appears in the form of barbed wire fences and scattered, dilapidated structures—resist the temptation to explore because private property abounds. If you'd rather not focus on the man-made intrusions, it's easy enough to be distracted by the distant tree-covered peaks looming ahead.

The surrounds are peaceful enough that the residential portion of Kennedy Meadows kind of sneaks up on you—from a high point around 7.5 miles, you're suddenly looking down on not just the shimmering South Fork, but also (relative) civilization! If you've been on the trail for a while, you might be forgiven for running the rest of the way toward cold drinks and hot food. I was hungry enough at this point in my journey that when I finally sat down to breakfast, I nearly salted my hash browns with tears of joy.

As you barrel downhill with visions of candy bars dancing in your head, let the ever-present mosquito hum propel you along. You'll hit several metal gates in this area—make sure to latch them all after passing through. Down through a short willow tunnel, up through some soft sand, and you'll finally spot a small bridge in the distance that marks **Sherman Pass Road**. Hit this paved wonder at 8.7 miles, just after passing through another metal gate. Sign the trail register, and if you're hungry or need a place to pitch your tent, hang a right to walk 0.7 mile east along the road to reach the **Kennedy Meadows General Store O**, where you'll likely find an array of fellow hikers and where all of your calorie-laden dreams may come true.

CAMP-TO-CAMP MILEAGE
Manter Creek to Camp 10 . . . . 3.4

KENNEDY MEADOWS TO COTTONWOOD PASS

FEEL THE EXCITEMENT BUILD as you begin in sage-scented flats and climb up toward the soaring Sierra peaks. Water is still a concern as you make your way to higher, wetter ground, but the cooler air and spectacular scenery should make the heavier carries less of a burden.

Start with a deceptively flat walk through the outer reaches of Kennedy Meadows as you meander toward its namesake campground, then into the South Sierra Wilderness to cross the refreshing South Fork Kern River. A scorched section mars the otherwise lovely Clover Meadow area, where you'll begin an ascent to the large, green expanse of Beck Meadow. Meet up with the South Fork again at a large steel bridge, tanking up next to grazing cattle and swooping swallows before making the long ascent to the trail's first climb above the 10,000-foot mark, near Olancha Peak.

Get used to huffing and puffing your way through the thinner air because it's here to stay as you begin the typical Sierra pattern of long descents and steep ascents—down to Death Canyon Creek, up to Sharknose Ridge, down to Diaz Creek, and then up to the triple guardians of Horseshoe Meadow: Mulkey Pass, Trail Pass, and finally, Cottonwood Pass. Dip off trail at any of these passes to reach several campgrounds and trailheads—along with a long, winding, precipitous paved road that drops over 5000 feet to the rustic Owens Valley town of Lone Pine, where you'll find places to load up on gear, scarf down some food, drink celebratory beverages, and rest your weary head.

DISTANCE 48 miles

STATE DISTANCE 702.2–750.2 miles

ELEVATION GAIN/LOSS
+9120/-3990 feet

HIGH POINT 11,135 feet

BEST TIME OF YEAR May–Oct

PCTA SECTION LETTER G

LAND MANAGERS Sequoia National Forest (Kern River Ranger District, South Sierra Wilderness), Inyo National Forest (Mt. Whitney Ranger District, South Sierra Wilderness, Golden Trout Wilderness)

PASSES AND PERMITS Wilderness permits are required for all overnight trips in the Golden Trout Wilderness; they are only required for the South Sierra Wilderness if you are entering via Inyo National Forest rather than from Kennedy Meadows. California Campfire Permit.

MAPS AND APPS
- Halfmile's CA Section G
- USGS PCT Map #3 Southern Sierra
- USGS Topo Quads: Crag Peak, Long Canyon, Monache Mountain, Haiwee Pass, Olancha, Templeton Mountain, Cirque Peak
- Halfmile's PCT app
- Guthook's PCT app

Opposite: *Looking out toward Clover Meadow*

LEGS

1. Kennedy Meadows to South Fork Kern River
2. South Fork Kern River to Death Canyon Creek
3. Death Canyon Creek to Diaz Creek Trail
4. Diaz Creek Trail to Cottonwood Pass

ACCESS

Kennedy Meadows

From Los Angeles, head north on Interstate 5 (toward Sacramento), then take exit 162 for State Highway 14 northbound (Antelope Valley Freeway) toward Palmdale and Lancaster. Drive 117.7 miles, then merge onto US Highway 395 northbound. In 9.9 miles, turn left onto 9 Mile Canyon Road, continuing onto Kennedy Meadows Road (Sherman Pass Road) after 9.8 miles. In 14.1 miles, make a left to stay on Sherman Pass Road. The PCT crosses the road 0.8 mile ahead. There is no parking at this intersection—either make arrangements to park at the Kennedy Meadows General Store 0.7 mile east on Sherman Pass Road or head north on Kennedy Meadows Road for another 2.7 miles to reach Kennedy Meadows Campground and a large parking lot; the PCT passes through the campground.

Cottonwood Pass

Cottonwood Pass is accessed via a 3.7-mile hike from Horseshoe Meadow, which has trailhead parking. From Los Angeles, head north on Interstate 5 (toward Sacramento), then take exit 162 for State Highway 14 northbound (Antelope Valley Freeway) toward Palmdale and Lancaster. Drive 117.7 miles, then merge onto US Highway 395 northbound. In 60.2 miles, turn left onto Lubken Canyon Road. Continue for 3.4 miles, then make a left onto Horseshoe Meadows Road. Continue up this road until you reach the Cottonwood Pass trailhead. Horseshoe Meadows Road is typically closed from mid-November to late May.

NOTES

Cities and Services

Kennedy Meadows is a small community near the southern trailhead, where you'll find a general store, a restaurant, and not much else. At Horseshoe Meadows near the northern trailhead, you'll find several campgrounds; for anything more, take paved Horseshoe Meadows Road down to the small town of Lone Pine.

Camping and Fire Restrictions

Camp at least 100 feet from water and trails. Fires are allowed only in existing fire rings. Check for seasonal fire restrictions in Sequoia and Inyo National Forests before heading out.

Water

Water is still somewhat scarce in this section—while the South Fork Kern River will never run completely dry, segments of it can vanish and many of the smaller creeks and springs will become unusable by late summer—earlier in a dry year. The longest waterless stretch is the 10.9 miles between Death Canyon Creek and the Diaz Creek Trail.

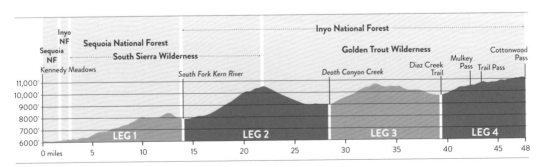

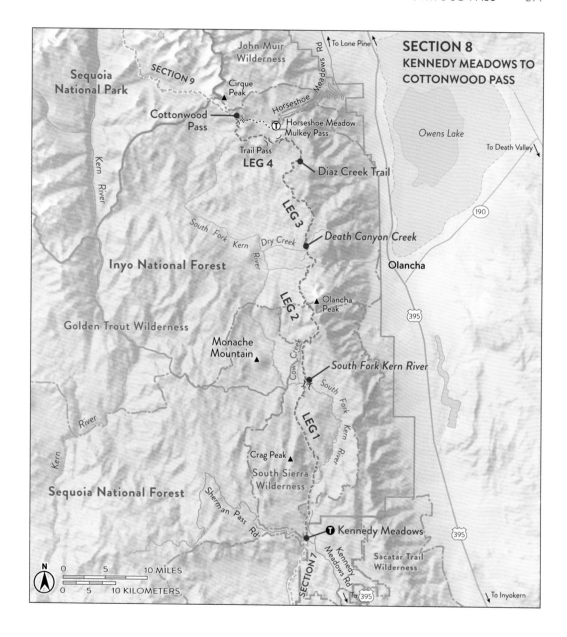

Hazards

Snow and ice may linger in the high-altitude portions of this section well into early summer. Use of traction devices and an ice axe may be required to safely navigate these areas.

Other

The general store in Kennedy Meadows has reduced hours outside of the summer hiking season—call ahead if planning a visit. Horseshoe Meadows Road is steep and narrow in sections. Bear-proof containers are required in the Cottonwood Pass area.

SUGGESTED ITINERARIES

Camps are either viewable from the trail or located within a few tenths of a mile from the noted location unless otherwise specified in leg descriptions.

5 DAYS

		Miles
Day 1	Kennedy Meadows to Clover Camp	7.3
Day 2	Clover Camp to Camp 2	12.3
Day 3	Camp 2 to Camp 3	10.9
Day 4	Camp 3 to Dutch Meadow Camp	10.4
Day 5	Dutch Meadow Camp to Cottonwood Pass	7.1

4 DAYS

Day 1	Kennedy Meadows to South Fork Camp	14.3
Day 2	South Fork Camp to Death Canyon Camp	14.3
Day 3	Death Canyon Camp to Diaz Creek Camp	10.9
Day 4	Diaz Creek Camp to Cottonwood Pass	8.5

3 DAYS

Day 1	Kennedy Meadows to South Fork Camp	14.3
Day 2	South Fork Camp to Death Canyon Camp	14.3
Day 3	Death Canyon Camp to Cottonwood Pass	19.4

1 KENNEDY MEADOWS TO SOUTH FORK KERN RIVER

DISTANCE 14.3 miles

ELEVATION GAIN/LOSS
+3050/-1230 feet

HIGH POINT 8379 feet

CONNECTING TRAILS AND ROADS
Sherman Pass Road, Kennedy Meadows Road, Haiwee Trail

ON THE TRAIL

Whether or not you ducked into **Kennedy Meadows** for a sleep or snack as part of a longer journey, or are just beginning your hike, rejoice, for you are now entering what most people (erroneously) call the "Gateway to the Sierra." Fact check: the Sierra Nevada range actually begins quite a bit south of where you're currently standing on **Sherman Pass Road**.

The trail begins in the mellow, but shadeless, meadow, filled with sand, sagebrush, and only the occasional patch of grass. You'll encounter several unpaved roads and cattle gates in this area; continue straight at each to stay the course. The only time you may want to deviate is 1.2 miles in, when an outhouse beckons down a dirt road to your left. Unless it's urgent, wait it out, since there's another opportunity to avoid cathole digging at Kennedy Meadows Campground just ahead.

Cliff swallows make their home under the metal bridge spanning the South Fork Kern River.

Cross **Kennedy Meadows Road** at 1.8 miles, then re-cross it a short bit later, arriving at a parking lot at 2.4 miles. Head straight toward a trail register and information sign—welcome to **Kennedy Meadows Campground**! This is a great camping alternate for those who don't wish to walk into town to camp behind the store—or for those who find that environment a little too party hardy. Note that while there are water spigots at the campground, they were cut off after a management change between Sequoia and Inyo National Forests. I can't say whether they'll be turned on again, but if not, know that you'll cross the South Fork Kern River soon enough.

Continue downhill, reaching a large sign at 2.6 miles marking the boundary of the **Sequoia National Forest's South Sierra Wilderness**. As if spurred on by such a grand proclamation, the scenery evolves to include glimpses of bright granite and an assortment of large trees, including Jeffrey pines, accented by the sound of the South Fork Kern River burbling down below.

Wind quietly uphill in soft sand, admiring the intoxicating mix of willows, pines, sagebrush, and cacti. Shade here is only intermittent, so find relief on a warm day when you arrive at a small, scenic bridge at 4.4 miles that spans the **South Fork Kern River ❶**. This is a beautiful spot to tank up, take a rest, and cool your feet (literally). The next few

TIMING IS EVERYTHING

Kennedy Meadows offers a multitude of services, outlined at the end of the last leg in this section. If you want to travel with thru-hikers or intend to continue into the High Sierra, aim to depart Kennedy Meadows no earlier than mid-June. By that time, the higher elevations are usually less snowy, although you will likely have to deal with snowmelt-fed water crossings. Folks at the Kennedy Meadows General Store may be able to share weather intel to help you decide whether to continue north or hang back a bit (with a beer or three) as you wait for conditions to improve.

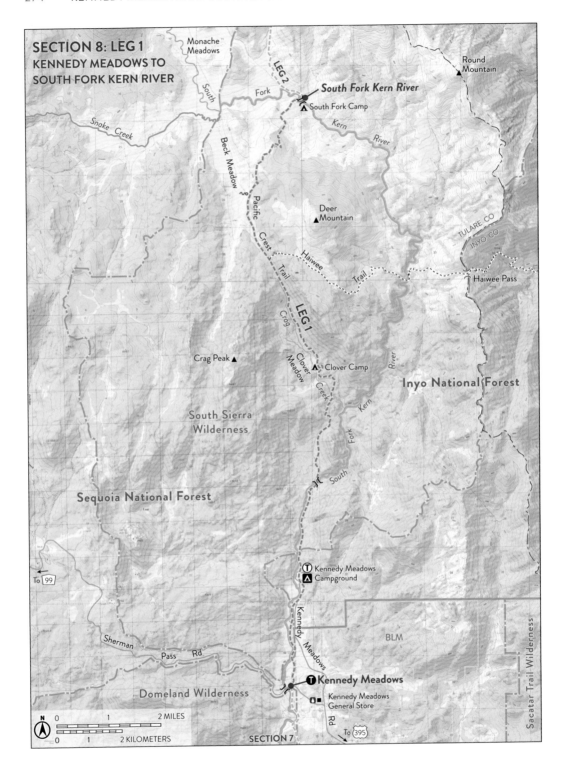

SECTION 8: LEG 1
KENNEDY MEADOWS TO
SOUTH FORK KERN RIVER

Monache Meadows

LEG 2

South Fork

Round Mountain

South Fork Kern River

South Fork Camp

Snake Creek

Kern River

Beck Meadow

Deer Mountain

TULARE CO
INYO CO

Pacific

Haiwee

Crest

Trail

Haiwee Pass

Trail

LEG 1

Crag

Crag Peak

Clover Meadow

Clover Camp

Kern River

Inyo National Forest

South Sierra Wilderness

Creek

South Fork

Sequoia National Forest

South

To 99

Kennedy Meadows
Campground

BLM

Sherman   Pass   Rd

Kennedy   Meadows

Kennedy Meadows

Sacatar Trail Wilderness

Domeland Wilderness

Kennedy Meadows
General Store

N
0   1   2 MILES
0   1   2 KILOMETERS

SECTION 7

Rd

To 395

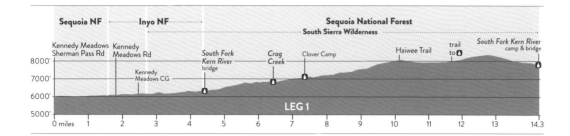

DON'T TIPTOE THROUGH THE MEADOWS

The deeper you climb into the Sierra, the more meadows you encounter, and the wetter they'll be. These moist environments teem with plant life, and are some of the most fragile montane ecosystems along the PCT. Take care to stay on trail when you pass through or next to them—human intrusion leaves a lasting impact that takes quite a long time to reverse.

water sources are seasonal, so it's best to take what you need to reach the end of this leg.

Cross the bridge, then bank uphill to the right through scattered boulders, trees, and sagebrush. It's pretty in here, but that ends soon enough when you spot a large burn area in the distance, left by the 2008 Clover Fire; reach its perimeter at 6.2 miles. The saving grace in this somewhat bleak patch of charred destruction is the bright green swath of seasonal **Crag Creek O**, which you cross at 6.4 miles; but this may be no more than a puddle or patch of sticky mud by early summer.

As you wind through slopes littered with the remnants of once-stately trees, try not to feel discouraged—soon enough you'll spot bright **Clover Meadow** down below. Several use trails appear on your left around 7.3 miles, descending to a huge camping area under a cluster of pines (**Clover Camp**), with nearby access to **Crag Creek O**. The incline sharpens from here, but the effort rewards with fantastic views back down to Clover Meadow and across to Crag Peak.

The trail mellows out after climbing through a constriction in the canyon, and the scenery opens up to include meadowy flats dotted with wildflowers in early summer. Reach a junction with the **Haiwee Trail** at 10.2 miles, an overgrown and nearly indiscernible route that leads east toward Dutch John Flat and merges with the Haiwee Pass Trail, eventually exiting down to the Owens Valley. More exciting is the view down to **Beck Meadow** 0.5 mile ahead. Upon reaching its fringes, veer off to the right through scrub and grasses, angling up above the meadow. If you're desperate for water, keep your eyes peeled for a spring-fed trough **O** situated down a gully to the left around 11.6 miles; a rough and unmarked but obvious use trail deposits you there.

Continue the ascent along the edge of Beck Meadow, rising through rockier trail to reach a set of switchbacks at 12.8 miles that signals the start of your drop toward the end of this leg. The green

THE MONO

The name "Monache" refers to the Monache, Monachi, or more commonly, Mono people, whose tribes are indigenous to portions of the central Sierra. These hunter-gatherers moved seasonally to various elevations to procure sustenance: acorns, pigeons, deer, and even bear. Although they remained fairly insulated from the Spanish, the Mono were eventually pushed from their land, forced to work for prospectors, and required to assimilate as a result of the Gold Rush influx and subsequent policies.

patch far below is part of **Monache Meadows,** a popular grazing spot for neighborhood cattle. Soon, you'll also see the slim ribbon of the **South Fork Kern River O** and will likely start to hear a somewhat deafening trill, courtesy the hordes of cliff swallows taking up residence under a steel bridge that spans the flow. Follow their calls through scented sagebrush and swirling dust, eventually descending back into blissful tree cover to finally reach the bridge—which you won't see until you're nearly on top of it—and the end of this leg at 14.3 miles. Peek underneath to spot a veritable village of mud nests tucked under the span.

Camping is available on dirt platforms carved into a shady slope on the near side of the bridge (**South Fork Camp**). You can access the potentially cow-fouled water **O** on either side of the bridge, but if you have a sensitive palette, make sure you filter adequately and have some type of flavoring to add to your haul. Hikers I met variously described the water as tasting like dirt, cigarette butts, and a less euphemistic term for excrement, and after a sampling, I understood why.

CAMP-TO CAMP MILEAGE

Kennedy Meadows to Kennedy Meadows
    Campground 2.4
Kennedy Meadows Campground to
    Clover Camp. 4.9
Clover Camp to South Fork Camp 7.0

2 SOUTH FORK KERN RIVER TO DEATH CANYON CREEK

DISTANCE 14.3 miles

ELEVATION GAIN/LOSS
+3030/-1920 feet

HIGH POINT 10,564 feet

CONNECTING TRAIL
Olancha Pass Trail

ON THE TRAIL

Scoop up some cow-flavored water from the **South Fork Kern River O**, cross the large steel bridge that spans the flow, and head off to the sound of deafening sparrow song into the green expanse of **Monache Meadows**, now walking in the **Inyo National Forest**. Get an early start here to avoid walking this first bit in the heat of the day—the only available shade is whatever you have sitting on top of your head.

The sagebrush flats eventually give way to a mellow, pine-dotted slope that allows you to gaze across the meadow without actually having to broil your way through it. If you can't stomach the taste of the South Fork water sloshing around your reservoir, you might have an opportunity to switch it out upon reaching the first crossing of

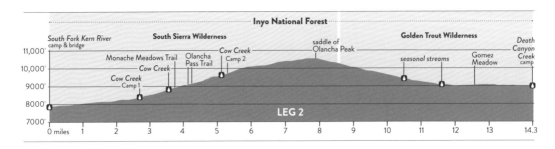

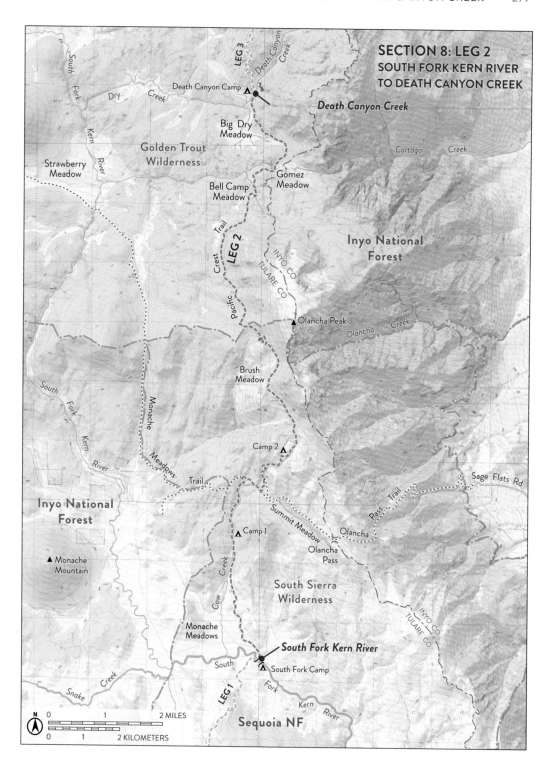

SECTION 8: LEG 2
SOUTH FORK KERN RIVER
TO DEATH CANYON CREEK

LEG 3

Death Canyon Creek

Death Canyon Camp

Big Dry
Meadow

Death Canyon Creek

Golden Trout
Wilderness

Gomez
Meadow

Strawberry
Meadow

Cartago Creek

Bell Camp
Meadow

Inyo National
Forest

South Fork Dry Creek

Kern River

Crest Trail

LEG 2

Pacific

INYO CO.

TULARE CO.

Olancha Peak

Olancha Creek

Brush
Meadow

South Fork Kern River

Monache Meadows Trail

Camp 2

Sage Flats Rd

Pass Trail

Inyo National
Forest

Summit Meadow

Olancha

Camp 1

Olancha Pass

Monache Mountain

Cow Creek

South Sierra
Wilderness

INYO CO.

TULARE CO.

Monache
Meadows

South Fork Kern River

South Fork Camp

South

LEG 1

Snake Creek

Fork

Kern River

Sequoia NF

N

0   1   2 MILES

0   1   2 KILOMETERS

Alpine vibes begin as you climb above 10,000 feet for the first time.

the surprisingly less bovine tasting **Cow Creek ⬤** at 2.6 miles. You'll also find a few scattered camp-sites here—one on the right side under some pines before crossing the creek, another just ahead after-ward (**Camp 1**). If the creek is dry here, you'll have several opportunities over the next mile as you weave back and forth across the slender waterway and hike alongside it. Chipmunks skitter across the forest floor and mule deer sneak around in the trees, but all will disappear if an equestrian passes through—not an uncommon occurrence in this area.

Try not to become too distracted as you weave through the trees, since there are a few key junc-tions coming up. At 3.5 miles, a second trail sud-denly appears on the right—ignore this and head downhill to cross your old friend **Cow Creek ⬤**. Not too long after, intersect the **Monache Meadows Trail** at 3.7 miles and continue right on the PCT toward Olancha Pass. Travel uphill through thick forest and large granite boulders to your next crossroads at 4.1 miles—this is the first

junction with the **Olancha Pass Trail**, which descends to the right; continue straight at this and the next junction 0.1 mile ahead.

The higher you climb, the more stunning the scenery. Large lodgepole and occasional foxtail pines blanket the slopes, their bright green needles a welcome sight after so much gray-green sage-brush. Large, blocky granite formations rise from the earth like Cubist sculptures, and surprisingly far below, the green meadow shows just how far you've come.

A branch of **Cow Creek ⬤** appears one last time at 5.1 miles—if the other crossings were dry, this one might still produce water since it's spring-fed. Tank up among the bright, leafy corn lilies and continue up another 0.2 mile toward a small, sandy outcropping on the right with space for two or three tents (**Camp 2**) and plenty of room to look up and enjoy the night sky.

Continuing up, heavy mouth breathing might serve as a reminder that you've crested the

10,000-foot mark—the first time the PCT rises above that magical elevation! If you're planning to stay in the Sierra for a while, you'll spend a lot of time in this thin air—enjoy a slower pace here as your lungs work to catch up. Weave along the slopes above **Brush Meadow** to reach a saddle at around 6.8 miles that makes a shady rest spot. However, know that there's an even *better* forested saddle just ahead at 7.8 miles on the shoulder of **Olancha Peak**, which towers over to your right— it's better not just because it's slightly bigger but also because it marks the last of the uphill trudge for this leg!

Switchback downhill into the **Golden Trout Wilderness**, enjoying fragrant pines and epic alpine views out to Mount Langley—it seems a world away, but you're creeping ever closer to the High Sierra. Views widen once the slopes transition to manzanita cover instead of trees, including sightlines to Bell Camp Meadow below and Gomez Meadow just beyond.

Continue the pleasant descent through intermittent pines and manzanita, traipsing past vivid snow plant, Indian paintbrush, and scattered wildflowers in early summer. You'll also encounter willows and other riparian greenery at two seasonal streams **◑**, the first at 10.5 miles, the second at 11.6. You're moving closer to **Gomez Meadow**, which you finally cross on a wooden boardwalk at 12.6 miles. Scan for mule deer nibbling away at the grasses, especially during dusk and dawn. Rock formations loom all around—as do marmots, the adorable, yet curious critters you'll find darting around boulders and eyeing your candy bars throughout the Sierra.

Once you're done being taunted by marmots, continue through soft sand, with *just* enough uphill to annoy your calves. Nearing this leg's end, pass **Big Dry Meadow** on the left—big, yes, but at times surprisingly vibrant given the name. Finally, hit tiny **Death Canyon Creek ◑** at 14.3 miles, named after the canyon it flows through. Ample camping is available on sandy flats just across the creek on both sides of the trail (**Death Canyon Camp**). The ominous name belies the fact that this pine- and boulder-filled area is actually quite scenic. If the creek is dry, you might have better luck upstream at a spring **◑**—hang a right after the crossing and follow a use trail for 0.2 mile to find a small pool tucked under a dripping rock on the right.

CAMP-TO-CAMP MILEAGE

South Fork Kern River to Camp 1. . . . . 2.6
Camp 1 to Camp 2. . . . . 2.7
Camp 2 to Death Canyon Camp. 9.0

THE CUTEST JERKS OF THE PCT

Yellow-bellied marmots are absolutely adorable giant rodents (related to squirrels and prairie dogs) who make their homes at elevations above 6500 feet in the Sierra. However, they are also The Cutest Jerks of the PCT because they want your food and they will stop at nothing to steal it with their clever little paws. They are like furry ninjas, darting behind rocks until suddenly appearing within arm's reach of your backpack. While I've never had any serious marmot encounters, I know people who've had edibles snatched from their side and holes chewed through their packs when they weren't paying attention. Never leave your food (or backpack) unattended!

3 DEATH CANYON CREEK TO DIAZ CREEK TRAIL

DISTANCE 10.9 miles

ELEVATION GAIN/LOSS
+2360/-1640 feet

HIGH POINT 10,699 feet

CONNECTING TRAILS
None

ON THE TRAIL

This leg begins by crossing **Death Canyon Creek ⓞ**, where you'll find a sprawling array of boulder-strewn campsites (**Death Canyon Camp**), mostly on the left side of the trail. You can't judge a canyon by its name, because if that were the case, I'd vote to rename this particular one Pretty Pinkish Boulder–filled Canyon.

After tanking up at the creek (or if it's dry, 0.2 mile upstream at a spring ⓞ), stretch and mentally prepare for the burly climb out—if there's a chill in the air, this massive undertaking will definitely warm you up. Zigzag through western junipers, foxtail pines, and manzanita as you switchback up past numerous false summits for what seems like an eternity. Your consolation prize is a lofty perch that offers expanding views down to Big Dry Meadow far below, back south toward Olancha Peak, and across to prominent Kern Peak in the

west. Continue up the ridgeline past soaring spires of geometric granite that occasionally frame Mount Langley and friends, all closer than they were on the prior leg.

The terrain flattens out a bit around 1.9 miles, and you'll find a few suitable one-off campsites over the next 0.5 mile (**Camp 3**)—none of these see heavy use, so they may not appear terribly obvious to the casual observer. Continue on, with just enough gain to make you appreciate a breather at 3.9 miles, when you reach a flat area and scenic overlook. To the west, Kern Peak continues to dominate its surroundings, and to the east, you look down upon the Owens Valley far below, including the typically dry flats of Owens Lake. Depending on your service provider, you might actually have cell phone coverage here—but depending on your desire to disconnect, you may not want to find out.

Although you're still ascending, know that the lion's share of the quad work is over for now. Catch another glimpse down to Owens Valley around 4.6 miles, where you might have another opportunity to phone home (or not), then begin a small descent to a flat, forested area. You'll hit a faint side trail on the right at 5.6 miles that leads north to a seasonal spring ⓞ about 0.3 mile down a gully. From here, it's back to the uphill grind, sometimes trudging through deep, sandy gravel that might inspire you to deploy a few choice words. Luckily,

MOUNT LANGLEY

Perched high atop the Sierra Crest, Mount Langley is the ninth tallest peak in California. It's named after Samuel Pierpont Langley, astronomer, professor, inventor, aeronautics guru, and former secretary of the Smithsonian Institution who helmed a scientific trip to the peak's nearest fourteener neighbor, Mount Whitney, in 1881. Most people make the summit via a non-technical route ascending from either "old" Army Pass or New Army Pass, accessible via the Cottonwood Lakes area or by taking a detour farther down the PCT, shortly after crossing into Sequoia National Park. While it's a bit out of the way for PCT hikers, it's a worthy bucket list item if you're planning to spend some time in the area.

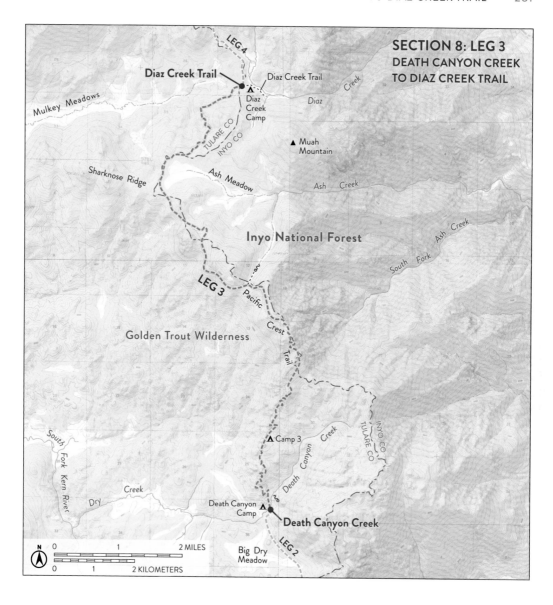

**SECTION 8: LEG 3
DEATH CANYON CREEK
TO DIAZ CREEK TRAIL**

LEG 4

Diaz Creek Trail

Diaz Creek Trail

Mulkey Meadows

Diaz Creek Camp

Diaz Creek

▲ Muah Mountain

Sharknose Ridge

Ash Meadow

Ash Creek

TULARE CO.

INYO CO.

Inyo National Forest

South Fork Ash Creek

LEG 3

Pacific Crest Trail

Golden Trout Wilderness

▲ Camp 3

Death Canyon Creek

INYO CO.

TULARE CO.

South Fork Kern River

Creek

Dry

Death Canyon Camp

Death Canyon Creek

LEG 2

Big Dry Meadow

N

0   1   2 MILES

0   1   2 KILOMETERS

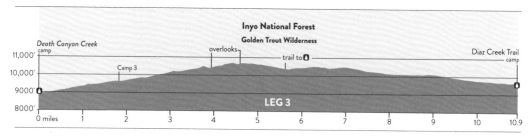

Inyo National Forest
Golden Trout Wilderness

Death Canyon Creek
camp

overlooks

trail to ⛺

Diaz Creek Trail
camp

11,000'

10,000'

9000'

8000'

LEG 3

0 miles   1   2   3   4   5   6   7   8   9   10 10.9

The windblown ridge above Death Canyon is studded with gnarled western junipers.

there are plenty of shady nooks offering break spots, and inspiring views out to the High Sierra will help keep you sufficiently motivated.

Just after 8 miles, reach a small saddle and then, glory be: downhill! **Sharknose Ridge** continues off to the left, while you instead move northeast to pass

WATER ALERT!

Diaz Creek ⓞ shrivels to a trickle by late summer, earlier in drought years—you may need to carefully navigate the steep banks to drop down into the creek bed itself to gather water; bring a scoop. If you come up empty, your next possible source is 1.4 miles ahead at **Dutch Meadow Spring** ⓞ—cross your fingers and hike on.

above **Ash Meadow** below to your right; Mount Langley beckons through the tree cover. As you descend, the foliage skews back to sagebrush, a reminder that the desert is never too far away on this section of the PCT. The end of this leg isn't as well marked as you'd hope, so pay attention once the trail flattens out—unless you're looking at a GPS, the only thing denoting the oddly unsigned, but obvious, side trail to **Diaz Creek** ⓞ at 10.9 miles is a small cairn on your right and perhaps the word "WATER" spelled out in rocks and twigs next to it on the ground. Here, it's possible to head right for 0.1 mile to find a use trail leading to the grass-lined creek on the left and a few clearings for tents on the right (**Diaz Creek Camp**). Tank up, huddle down, or breeze right past—the choice is yours.

CAMP-TO-CAMP MILEAGE

Death Canyon Creek to Camp 3 . . . . 1.9
Camp 3 to Diaz Creek Camp 9.0

4 DIAZ CREEK TRAIL TO COTTONWOOD PASS

DISTANCE 8.5 miles

ELEVATION GAIN/LOSS
+2060/-600 feet

HIGH POINT 11,135 feet

CONNECTING TRAILS
Mulkey Pass Trail, Trail Pass Trail,
Cottonwood Pass Trail

ON THE TRAIL

Although this leg involves a lot of uphill movement, it also offers up some gorgeous high alpine scenery as a worthy reward for all of that huffing and puffing through the ever-thinning air. Begin at the unsigned junction with the **Diaz Creek Trail** described in the previous leg; if you want to grab water before departing, walk 0.1 mile down this path and look for obvious use trails branching off to your left toward **Diaz Creek ◐**.

Enjoy the relatively relaxed gradient through scattered foxtail pines and fascinating granite formations—this easy grade isn't going to last long, so relish it while you can. **Dutch Meadow** soon comes into view, and you'll find an unsigned access path on your right at 1.4 miles, just before a noticeable bend and uphill turn in the trail. Depart the PCT here to find a somewhat creepy looking horse corral and several possible campsites (**Dutch Meadow Camp**). To access seasonal **Dutch Meadow Spring ◐**, continue downhill to the left of the corral toward an obvious line of grasses and corn lilies that guard the flow. The climb back up to the trail will feel a bit annoying, especially if you just made your pack heavier with water weight.

You won't complain for very long about the water dragging your pack down, though, since you'll likely start swigging it with a vengeance as the climb steepens through giant boulders and plentiful pines. The upside is that once back up on the Sierra Crest, you earn views down to verdant Mulkey Meadows and the peaks beyond. Express gratitude when things finally mellow out as you near **Mulkey Pass** at 2.8 miles. The spot is unmarked, but you'll know you're there once you spot a wooden sign tacked to a tree that points back to Olancha Pass and toward Trail Pass. You also have the option of departing the PCT here on the right to drop down a rough trail to **Horseshoe Meadow** and its myriad facilities far below.

Continue through the trees to **Trail Pass**, which you reach at 3.6 miles. **Trail Pass Trail** offers another departure point for Horseshoe Meadow (and to Mulkey Meadows to the south), but it is more frequently traveled and gently graded

MULKEY PASS

Mulkey Pass is the first northbound jump-off point for Horseshoe Meadow, a popular camping, trailhead, and equestrian area with paved road access, reached via 1.7 miles of knee-pounding descent and a traverse of the meadows. Depart the PCT on the right (north) side of the pass, heading down the path marked "Horseshoe Meadow," descending a steep gully on a somewhat loose, unmaintained trail that once served as a passage for stock to graze in Mulkey Meadows on the south side of the pass. The meadows and pass are named for Cyrus Mulkey, who served as sheriff for Inyo County in the latter part of the 19th century. When you reach the bottom at Round Valley, stay to the right to cross the eastern portion of Horseshoe Meadow, pass the Golden Trout Wilderness boundary, and ease left past a horse corral to pop out on paved Horseshoe Meadows Road—from here, you can head left to walk toward the campground facilities, or try your luck at snagging a ride.

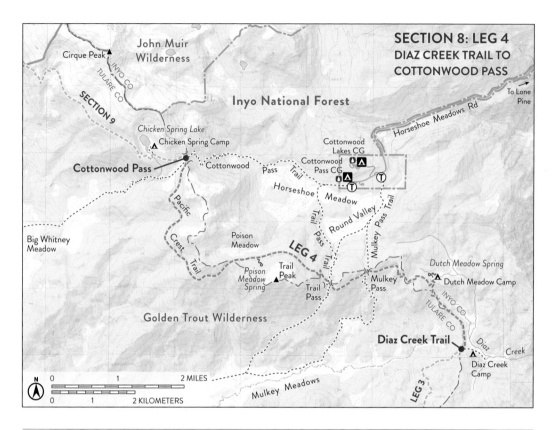

than the path from Mulkey Pass; you'll reach the bottom in 2.1 miles. However, as the sign indicates, Cottonwood Pass is next in line, so if you don't need a break, continue ahead, now walking along north-facing slopes underneath **Trail Peak**.

Ground squirrels scamper around as you wander through thick forest, whose branches occasionally give way to views of Poison Meadow far below. Perfectly framed openings also offer the best look at Mount Langley you've had yet—its decisive summit ridge rises up like a ship's prow, extra photogenic when frosted in a layer of gleaming white snow.

If all of this lovely scenery sparks a thirst, stay on the lookout for **Poison Meadow Spring** spilling over a small rockfall to your left at 5.1 miles. Don't let the name dissuade you—as long as you filter, it'll be fine to drink. In late summer, this source can reduce to a trickle, so look deeper in the rocks to see if you can find an accessible drip. Continue uphill to reach a gravelly plateau just over 0.5 mile ahead. Dipping back onto south-facing slopes, you're headed toward the highest elevation on the PCT thus far; make sure you take it slow, sip lots of water, enjoy some snacks, and

Mount Langley says "Hello" from across the way.

keep tabs on any developing headaches. When you're about 1 mile away from your final pass (and this leg's end), walk along a beautiful marmot-filled meadow with views of the hulking granite mass of Cirque Peak. If you look to the west, you'll also see the unmistakably saw-toothed ridge of the impressive Great Western Divide.

After one last uphill sprint, reach the signed trail junction and gap in the ridge that marks **Cottonwood Pass** at 8.5 miles. If you went left from here, you'd land at Big Whitney Meadow; a right zigzags east to Horseshoe Meadow via the **Cottonwood Pass Trail**, which descends a series of endless switchbacks, plunging you into a deep sand traverse that ends at the Cottonwood Pass Trailhead and campground in 3.7 miles. It's the longest of the three side trails you've encountered, and is a total knee-buster on the descent, but it's also the most popular access point for backpackers jumping on trail since it's the only one of the three paths to offer northbound wilderness permits.

If you don't want to check out Horseshoe Meadow, but seek rest and relaxation, continue straight for 0.6 mile along the next leg to find a wet, green strip that marks the outlet for **Chicken Spring Lake** ⬤. Hang right on the faint use trail

HORSESHOE MEADOW

Horseshoe Meadow is the colloquial term for not just the meadows itself, but also the general area where you'll find the **Cottonwood Pass Campground, Cottonwood Lakes Campground**, vault toilets, seasonal water spigots ⬤, equestrian facilities, parking, and paved road access. Many hikers choose to try their luck at hitching into Lone Pine, a small town about 22 miles—and more than 6200 feet of elevation—down dizzying Horseshoe Meadows Road into the hot, arid Owens Valley below.

running along the outlet to find a series of sandy campsites scattered above the lake itself (remember to practice Leave No Trace ethics when selecting a site). Have a brisk swim if you're feeling brave, then sit back and watch the granite cliffs shift from orange to pink to purple in the setting sun.

CAMP-TO-CAMP MILEAGE

Diaz Creek Trail to Dutch Meadow Camp.... 1.4

COTTONWOOD PASS TO FLORENCE LAKE TRAIL

HIKE THROUGH SOME of the most iconic scenery in the United States on this epic adventure through an endless parade of lush valleys and soaring peaks. You'll likely share the path with a host of other travelers, including John Muir Trail (JMT) hikers, but it's easy to find peace and solitude if you step off trail from time to time.

Leave water worries behind as you pass the Chicken Spring Lake outlet—from here on out, the wet stuff is plentiful. Stroll through thick forests of foxtail pine, past whitewashed granite outcroppings, lush meadows, and burbling waterways as you head into Sequoia National Park toward Crabtree Meadow, launch pad for an attempt on Mount Whitney, the highest peak in the Lower 48. From here, enjoy a quick word in passing with scores of JMT pilgrims making their typical southbound treks—you'll cross paths throughout this entire section.

Steel your nerves as you ascend toward somewhat imposing Forester Pass—the PCT's high point and your entry to Kings Canyon National Park. Dance on top, then barrel down toward the Bubbs Creek drainage, continuing through a magnificent assortment of peaks and passes, lakes and streams, meadows and glaciers. Each pass brings a new literal and metaphoric high, leading to a different valley, canyon, or watershed to explore.

Once you tag the last pass of this section, pausing for some quiet reflection or joyous celebration at the famous Muir Hut, descend into stunning Evolution Basin, brave the notorious waters of Evolution Creek, and stroll through humbler surrounds to reach the somewhat unceremonious endpoint at the Florence Lake Trail junction. From here, it's possible to visit Muir Trail Ranch for a resupply (or R & R, if you've made reservations),

Opposite: *The South Fork San Joaquin River carves a picturesque path.*

DISTANCE 107.5 miles

STATE DISTANCE 750.2–857.7 miles

ELEVATION GAIN/LOSS +18,180/-21,420 feet

HIGH POINT 13,123 feet

BEST TIME OF YEAR July–Oct

PCTA SECTION LETTERS G, H

LAND MANAGERS Inyo National Forest (Mt. Whitney Ranger District, Golden Trout Wilderness), Sequoia National Park (Sequoia–Kings Canyon Wilderness), Kings Canyon National Park (Sequoia–Kings Canyon Wilderness), Sierra National Forest (High Sierra Ranger District, John Muir Wilderness)

PASSES AND PERMITS Wilderness permits are required for all overnight trips in the Golden Trout, John Muir, and Sequoia–Kings Canyon wildernesses. A separate permit is required to exit via the Mt. Whitney Trail; none is required to simply summit from the west. California Campfire Permit.

MAPS AND APPS
- Halfmile's CA Section G and H
- USFS PCT Map #3 Southern Sierra and #4 Central Sierra
- USGS Topo Quads: Cirque Peak, Johnson Peak, Mount Whitney, Mount Kaweah, Mount Brewer, Mount Williamson, Mount Clarence King, Mount Pinchot, Split Mountain, North Palisade, Mount Goddard, Mount Darwin, Mount Henry
- Halfmile's PCT app
- Guthook's PCT app

LEGS

1. Cottonwood Pass to Crabtree Meadow
2. Crabtree Meadow to Forester Pass
3. Forester Pass to Glen Pass
4. Glen Pass to Pinchot Pass
5. Pinchot Pass to Mather Pass
6. Mather Pass to Muir Pass
7. Muir Pass to McClure Meadow
8. McClure Meadow to Florence Lake Trail

or soak in nearby Blayney Hot Springs as a reward for all of your hard work.

ACCESS

Cottonwood Pass

Cottonwood Pass is accessed via a 3.7-mile hike from Horseshoe Meadow, which has trailhead parking. From Los Angeles, head north on Interstate 5 (toward Sacramento), then take exit 162 for State Highway 14 northbound (Antelope Valley Freeway) toward Palmdale and Lancaster. Drive 117.7 miles, then merge onto US Highway 395 northbound. In 60.2 miles, turn left onto Lubken Canyon Road. Continue for 3.4 miles, then make a left onto Horseshoe Meadows Road. Continue up this road until you reach the Cottonwood Pass trailhead. Horseshoe Meadows Road is typically closed from mid-November to late May.

Florence Lake Trail

The Florence Lake Trail is reached via a lengthy and convoluted route that involves driving on winding mountain roads, possibly taking a boat, and hiking. If you're up for it, head north from Fresno on CA Highway 41, taking exit 128A for CA Highway 180 eastbound (toward Kings Canyon National Park). Drive about 1.4 miles, then keep left to take Route 168 eastbound (toward Clovis and Huntington Lake). Continue following this road for 67.4 miles and make a right onto Kaiser Pass Road, which will shortly dwindle to one hair-raising lane as you wind up the twisted mountain track. The end of the line is Florence Lake, which offers seasonal camping, groceries, recreation opportunities, and ferry service. Park here in the larger paved lot and either check in with the general store to arrange for boat transportation across the lake or hop on the trail, which skirts the southwestern side of the lake to deposit you at Muir Trail Ranch in approximately 8 miles. From here, you have two options for reaching the PCT—continue on the Florence Lake Trail for 1.6 miles or bypass 1.8 miles of PCT by hopping on a steep "cutoff" trail on the left.

NOTES

Cities and Services

At Horseshoe Meadow, near the southern trailhead, you'll find several campgrounds; for anything more, take paved Horseshoe Meadows Road down to the small town of Lone Pine. Muir Trail Ranch is a private guest ranch located near the northern trailhead; services are limited to resupply

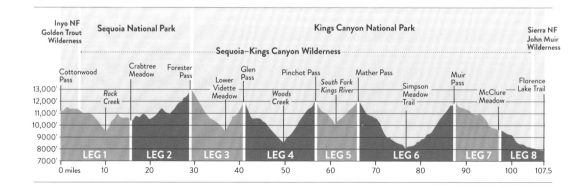

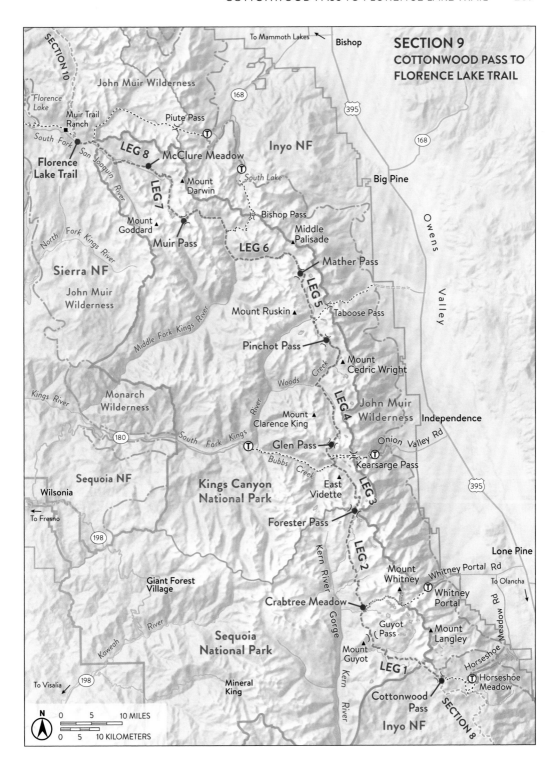

SECTION 9
COTTONWOOD PASS TO
FLORENCE LAKE TRAIL

SECTION 10

To Mammoth Lakes

Bishop

John Muir Wilderness

Florence Lake

Muir Trail Ranch

Piute Pass

168

LEG 8

McClure Meadow

Inyo NF

South Fork

San Joaquin River

Florence Lake Trail

LEG 7

Mount Darwin

South Lake

Big Pine

Mount Goddard

Muir Pass

Bishop Pass

Middle Palisade

395

168

North Fork Kings River

Sierra NF

John Muir Wilderness

LEG 6

Mather Pass

Owens Valley

LEG 5

Taboose Pass

Mount Ruskin

Middle Fork Kings River

Pinchot Pass

Mount Cedric Wright

Woods Creek

Kings River

Monarch Wilderness

River

Mount Clarence King

LEG 4

John Muir Wilderness

Independence

180

South Fork Kings River

Glen Pass

Onion Valley Rd

Kearsarge Pass

Bubbs Creek

Sequoia NF

Wilsonia

Kings Canyon National Park

East Vidette

LEG 3

395

To Fresno

198

Forester Pass

Giant Forest Village

Kern River

LEG 2

Lone Pine

Mount Whitney

Whitney Portal Rd

To Olancha

Whitney Portal

Crabtree Meadow

Guyot Pass

Mount Langley

River

Sequoia National Park

Mount Guyot

LEG 1

Horseshoe Meadow Rd

To Visalia

198

Mineral King

Kaweah

Horseshoe Meadow

Cottonwood Pass

SECTION 8

Kern River

Inyo NF

N

0   5   10 MILES

0   5   10 KILOMETERS

A hiker takes in the view on Bighorn Plateau.

(fee required; see Appendix 3 for more information), water, and electrical outlets for non-guests.

Camping and Fire Restrictions
In Sequoia–Kings Canyon Wilderness, camp only in well-established sites, preferably 100 feet (but at least 25 feet) from water. No camping within 0.25 mile of Bullfrog Lake. Camping limits: one night at each lake between Upper Rae Lake and Dollar Lake; two nights at any one site along the trail between Upper Vidette Meadow and the Woods Creek bridge. Fires are allowed only in existing fire rings, and are not allowed at Chicken Spring Lake, above 10,000 feet in Sequoia–Kings Canyon National Park, or above 10,400 feet in the John Muir Wilderness. Check for seasonal fire restrictions in the Inyo and Sierra National Forests, and in Sequoia–Kings Canyon National Park before heading out.

Water
The Chicken Spring Lake outlet and Guyot Creek can both run dry by late summer.

Hazards
River and creek crossings can be dangerous at times of high water, particularly during early summer snowmelt—Evolution Creek is typically the trickiest crossing in this section. Snow and ice may linger, especially on north-facing slopes and passes well into the summer months—use of traction devices and an ice axe may be required to safely navigate these areas. It is advisable to plan your trips over the high passes for morning—if there's snow present, it will be firmer and easier to navigate, and you'll face less danger of being caught in one of the afternoon thunderstorms frequent in the High Sierra.

Other

Use of an approved bear-resistant food storage container is required for overnight travel in these areas: Cottonwood Pass to just north of Guyot Creek and Forester Pass to Pinchot Pass. Food storage lockers ("bear boxes") are to be used only by hikers camping in their vicinity; caching of food or equipment is not allowed. Pets, with the exception of certified service animals, are not allowed on any trails in Sequoia–Kings Canyon National Parks, including the PCT. Ranger stations are only staffed during the summer months; rangers may be away from their stations for several days when on duty.

SUGGESTED ITINERARIES

Camps are either viewable from the trail or located within a few tenths of a mile from the noted location unless otherwise specified in leg descriptions. Realistically, you will need to resupply during this section. Most people exit over Kearsarge Pass to accomplish this, so plan your trip accordingly.

10 DAYS

		Miles
Day 1	Cottonwood Pass to Rock Creek Camp	10.3
Day 2	Rock Creek Camp to Tyndall Ponds Camp	13.6
Day 3	Tyndall Ponds Camp to Middle Vidette Camp	12.9
Day 4	Middle Vidette Camp to Middle Rae Camp	6.5
Day 5	Middle Rae Camp to Camp 13	9.1
Day 6	Camp 13 to Camp 16	10.4
Day 7	Camp 16 to Deer Camp	11.0
Day 8	Deer Camp to Camp 26	10.8
Day 9	Camp 26 to McClure Camp	13.3
Day 10	McClure Camp to Florence Lake Trail	9.6

9 DAYS

Day 1	Cottonwood Pass to Rock Creek Camp	10.3
Day 2	Rock Creek Camp to Tyndall Creek Camp	14.2
Day 3	Tyndall Creek Camp to Lower Vidette Camp	12.6
Day 4	Lower Vidette Camp to Woods Camp	12.5
Day 5	Woods Camp to South Fork Camp	11.5
Day 6	South Fork Camp to Deer Camp	12.7
Day 7	Deer Camp to Monster Camp	9.6
Day 8	Monster Camp to McClure Camp	14.5
Day 9	McClure Camp to Florence Lake Trail	9.6

8 DAYS

Day 1	Cottonwood Pass to Crabtree Meadow Camp	16.0
Day 2	Crabtree Meadow Camp to Camp 5	12.5
Day 3	Camp 5 to Camp 12	11.3
Day 4	Camp 12 to Camp 13	12.6
Day 5	Camp 13 to Camp 16	10.4
Day 6	Camp 16 to Big Pete Camp	19.6
Day 7	Big Pete Camp to McClure Camp	15.5
Day 8	McClure Camp to Florence Lake Trail	9.6

1 COTTONWOOD PASS TO CRABTREE MEADOW

DISTANCE 16.1 miles

ELEVATION GAIN/LOSS
+2580/-3370 feet

HIGH POINT 11,519 feet

CONNECTING TRAILS
Cottonwood Pass Trail, Rock Creek Trail, New Army Pass Trail, Crabtree Ranger Station Trail

ON THE TRAIL

Standing at **Cottonwood Pass**, you quickly forget about cars and pavement far below at Horseshoe Meadow—you're in rarified air up here, surrounded by sparkling granite and chattering ground squirrels. Okay, you might also hear the chattering of *humans* with cell reception right at the pass, but it disappears soon enough once you begin your ascent.

You'll likely hike in the company of at least a few non-PCT backpackers (or even day hikers) during this first bit since popular **Chicken Spring Lake ✪** is only a hop-skip from the pass. Reach its outlet in 0.6 mile—you'll know it from the ribbon of green crossing the trail, even if you don't see any water—and hang a right on a use trail to find not just the lake itself, but also an array of beautiful, sandy campsites perched above the water (**Chicken Spring Camp**). Make sure you're at least

200 feet from the lake and resist the temptation to build a fire—they're not allowed.

Whether or not you spend the night at this magical place, your route continues up a set of steep granite steps along a ridge. Contour along slopes beneath **Cirque Peak**, scoring amazing views south to Big Whitney Meadow and out to the sharp ridgelines of the Great Western Divide. While I love those views, my favorite part of this segment is the thick foxtail pine forest you're wandering through—it's particularly magical during early morning and the golden hour before sunset, when the trees take on an otherworldly glow.

Arrive at a metal sign marking the boundary of **Sequoia National Park** at 3.7 miles, then shuffle

PROTECTIVE MEASURES

Bear-resistant food containers are required from Cottonwood Pass to just north of Guyot Creek. Check the Sequoia–Kings Canyon National Parks website to see which canisters are currently approved. While it may seem like a pain to haul extra weight and bulk up your pack, these will not only keep your food from disappearing, but they've also been proven to help keep resident black bears safe and healthy by dissuading them from attempting to eat human food. Plus, they make great stools, washtubs, kitchen sinks, and drums.

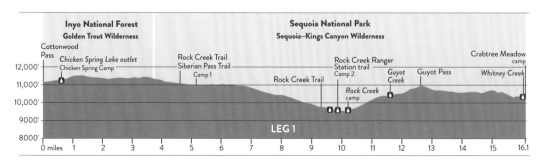

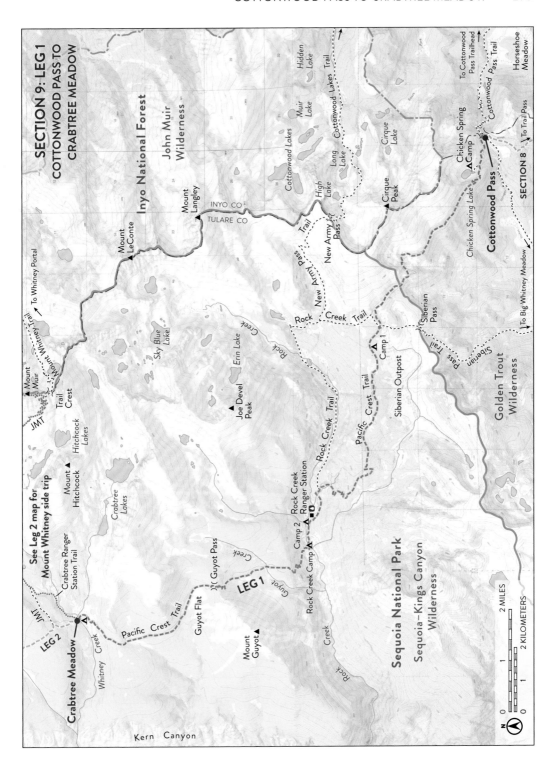

SECTION 9: LEG 1
COTTONWOOD PASS TO
CRABTREE MEADOW

Inyo National Forest

John Muir Wilderness

Hidden Lake

Muir Lake

Cottonwood Lakes

Cirque Lake

Cottonwood Lakes Trail

Long Lake

High Lake

Cirque Peak

New Army Pass

New Army Pass Trail

Mount Langley

INYO CO
TULARE CO

Mount LeConte

Chicken Spring

Chicken Spring Lake

Camp

Cottonwood Pass

To Cottonwood Pass Trailhead

Horseshoe Meadow

Cottonwood Pass Trail

SECTION 8

To Trail Pass

Rock   Creek   Trail

Siberian Pass

Siberian Pass Trail

Golden Trout Wilderness

To Big Whitney Meadow

Rock Creek Trail

Pacific   Crest   Trail

Camp 1

Siberian Outpost

Sky Blue Lake

Erin Lake

Joe Devel Peak

Rock   Creek

To Whitney Portal

Mount Whitney Trail

Mount Muir

Trail Crest

JMT

Hitchcock Lakes

Mount Hitchcock

Crabtree Lakes

Crabtree Ranger Station Trail

See Leg 2 map for Mount Whitney side trip

Pacific   Crest   Trail

Guyot Flat

Guyot Pass

Guyot Creek

Mount Guyot

Rock Creek Ranger Station

Camp 2

Rock Creek Camp

LEG 1

Rock   Creek

Sequoia National Park

Sequoia–Kings Canyon Wilderness

Whitney Creek

JMT

LEG 2

Crabtree Meadow

Kern   Canyon

N

0   1   2 MILES

0   1   2 KILOMETERS

ROVING RANGERS

There are several seasonally staffed ranger stations along the PCT in Sequoia and Kings Canyon National Parks, all serving as residence for "summer rangers" (and winter snow surveyors). You won't find any interpretive dioramas or gift shops here, just a private place for these hard-working folks to lay their heads. You can certainly stop by if you have a question—or an emergency—but do know that they often go out on patrol, sometimes for multiple days, so your knock may go unanswered.

mostly downhill through sand, dirt, and more gorgeous trees. Barren Siberian Outpost looms below, and you reach a junction at 4.6 miles that offers the opportunity to exile yourself there (via the **Siberian Pass Trail** on the left) or visit the **Rock Creek Trail** on the right. Instead, stay straight.

The terrain flattens out a bit, and the views disappear, although the forest is still plenty pretty enough. If feeling sleepy, scan both sides of the trail around 5.1 miles to find a few scattered sites (**Camp 1**)—this isn't a popular camping area, so you'll likely find some solitude here. If you still have some pep in your step, continue along the relaxed terrain, where you'll notice Joe Devel Peak rising steeply to the north.

Around 7.4 miles, the trail switchbacks downhill with gusto, gliding through scattered boulders and pines, with views to beautiful meadows and toward the Great Western Divide beyond. Reach a T-junction at 9.3 miles that marks the **Rock Creek Trail**, which veers off to the right, eventually meeting up with the New Army Pass Trail

Views of Mount Whitney and the Sierra Crest stop traffic en route to Crabtree Meadow.

to New Army Pass. Stay left to continue that glorious elevation loss—of course, not so glorious when you realize that the High Sierra is one giant roller coaster and you'll be cranking uphill soon enough.

Cross a small creek 🅞 about 0.2 mile ahead and continue through a gorgeous meadow that's an absolute vision in early summer when tiny wild-flowers speckle the grasses. After skipping through that dreamy wonderland, stroll through fragrant lodgepole pines to reach a use trail at 9.8 miles signed "Ranger Station"—this path leads back to the **Rock Creek Ranger Station**, a rustic cabin built in 1948.

Just after the path to the ranger station, find a few campsites (**Camp 2**) tucked off to the right under a stand of pines next to rushing **Rock Creek** 🅞. A larger, more established camp is just ahead at 10.3 miles (**Rock Creek Camp**) along the near side of your first significant water cross-ing of the Sierra, which is—you guessed it—**Rock Creek** 🅞. If you're feeling tired, set up camp here and use the metal food storage locker (bear box) to store any odorous items that don't fit in your canister. Be especially cautious when taking bath-room breaks since you're partially hemmed in by a meadow and the creek; head back up trail if you can't find a suitable spot away from water.

When you're ready to move on, carefully ford the creek, then dry off quickly as you regain a noticeable chunk of the elevation you spent so much time losing. Switchback up a steady grade,

perhaps passing a few seasonal flows as you go, until reaching **Guyot Creek** 🅞 at 11.6 miles, named (as is the nearby peak) after Swiss geologist Arnold Henry Guyot. This source can disappear by late summer, so you may want to carry what you need from Rock Creek instead.

Curve around the base of **Mount Guyot**, the prominent point to your left as you continue uphill to meet a saddle (sometimes called **Guyot Pass**) around 12.8 miles. Your hard work is rewarded with a downhill coast, depositing you at dusty, tree-ringed **Guyot Flat**. After a short ascent, reach a vantage point that begs you to stop: while Mount Young demands attention straight ahead, train your eyes eastward to set them upon the Sierra Crest and Mount Whitney, the tallest mountain in the continental United States at a lofty 14,505 feet!

Zigzag down an assortment of blocky granite, pass through a wooden stock gate, then let a phalanx of bright blue Steller's jays escort you to the spacious surrounds of **Crabtree Meadow**. Reach the meadow's edge at 16 miles, where you'll find a bear box and scattered campsites to the left (**Crabtree Meadow Camp**). Just ahead, ford **Whitney Creek** 🅞 (or cross on exposed rocks during low water), reaching a Y-intersection at 16.1 miles that marks the end of this leg. Head left to continue toward Wallace Creek on the PCT or right along the **Crabtree Ranger Station Trail** to locate a few more campsites scattered above the meadow and up near the station itself.

PEAKBAGGING

Mount Whitney (the tallest peak in the continental United States) is a worthy side trip, and no spe-cial permit is required for PCT trekkers who day hike to its summit; a Whitney Zone permit (and fee) is required, however, to continue over Trail Crest to Whitney Portal via the Mount Whitney Trail. From here, it's possible to catch a ride into the town of Lone Pine. To make the approxi-mately 17-mile roundtrip from the PCT, hang right at the Crabtree Ranger Station Trail, then make a right on the John Muir Trail, passing both Timberline Lake and Guitar Lake (no camping allowed) before ascending to Trail Crest and joining hikers on the main Mount Whitney Trail to make the final summit push. If you're comfortable hiking on exposed, talus-filled slopes in the dark, con-sider coordinating a sunrise arrival to make for an unforgettable summit experience. See the Leg 2 map for more detail.

Crabtree Meadow is an idyllic staging ground for an ascent of Mount Whitney.

Be cautious if you venture near the meadow's edge to enjoy a stunning sunset—despite the marmots and mule deer running around like they own the joint (and they do), this is a very fragile environment, and human encroachment has a lasting negative impact. Tread lightly—meaning: not at all.

CAMP-TO-CAMP MILEAGE

Cottonwood Pass to Chicken Spring Camp . . 0.6
Chicken Spring Camp to Camp 1 . . . . 4.5
Camp 1 to Camp 2. . . . . 4.7
Camp 2 to Rock Creek Camp 0.5
**Rock Creek Camp to Crabtree
    Meadow Camp**. 5.7

2 CRABTREE MEADOW TO FORESTER PASS

DISTANCE 13.2 miles

ELEVATION GAIN/LOSS
+4250/-1470 feet

HIGH POINT 13,123 feet

CONNECTING TRAILS
Crabtree Ranger Station Trail, John Muir Trail, High Sierra Trail, Shepherd Pass Trail

ON THE TRAIL
The magic of the High Sierra fully unveils itself on this leg as you hike in a world of endless granite spires and plentiful water sources, moving against a seasonal tide of southbound **John Muir Trail** (JMT) trekkers. From the junction with the **Crabtree Ranger Station Trail**, bid good day to the marmots scampering around **Crabtree Meadow** and head toward Wallace Creek. From here, you're in full-on rollercoaster

mode, good preparation for the final push to Forester Pass.

Reach a junction at 0.6 mile that marks the point where the PCT and JMT join. Continue straight toward Wallace Creek and, of course, Forester Pass. After some foxtail-enhanced uphill, flatten out a bit to stroll past lovely **Sandy Meadow**, with views to the stunning Kaweah Peaks beyond. Switchbacks lead down to **Wallace Creek ◖**, which you'll reach at 4.1 miles. Camping is possible underneath fragrant lodgepole pines before the crossing (**Wallace Camp**); a bear box is also located on the near side. You're likely to encounter a wade here unless the water is low.

Shake off on the other side, then proceed 0.1 mile to find a well-marked junction with the **High Sierra Trail**; head uphill toward Forester Pass and Tyndall Creek. Stroll through shady pine forest to reach burbling **Wright Creek ◖** at 4.7 miles; wade across or spend the night on the near side (**Wright Camp**).

Because it is The Way Of The Sierra, head uphill again after this crossing. Find a mediocre site about 0.2 mile afterward in a sandy clearing (**Camp 3**). For something better, look around the 5.2-mile mark to spot a jumble of trees down to your right at the edge of a pretty meadow, with room for a few tents (**Camp 4**). Top out around 6.5 miles at **Bighorn Plateau**, where you're greeted with 360-degree views of High Sierra magic, including the Great Western Divide, which dominates the skyline to the west, and a glittering tarn set in the middle of a meadow. It might be brisk and windy, but that doesn't diminish the wonder most hikers feel when they arrive.

Now full of alpine awe, begin a lengthy descent through scattered pines as you curve around **Tawny Point**. Once down low, reach a bear box

SHEPHERD PASS TRAIL

The Shepherd Pass Trail runs just about 14 miles from the Owens Valley up to Shepherd Pass, ultimately meeting with the PCT and JMT. You can use the trail as a bailout or entry point, but consider yourself warned—the trailhead is seldom visited, so you'll likely exhaust your thumb before getting a ride, and the price for entering this way is a hefty 6000 feet of gain from the desert floor.

on the right at 7.8 miles, just after a seasonal flow—this denotes the unmarked junction to the colloquially named **Tyndall Frog Ponds ◖**. Hang a right here to find a few sandy clearings for tents (**Tyndall Ponds Camp**). Otherwise, continue downhill to reach the **Tyndall Creek Ranger Station** junction at 8.2 miles. Hang a left to make a visit, find a bear box, or snag any number of campsites scattered in the dirt (**Tyndall Ranger Camp**); **Tyndall Creek ◖** is nearby.

Reach a junction with the **Shepherd Pass Trail** 0.1 mile ahead and stay straight to find a major crossing of **Tyndall Creek ◖** at 8.4 miles. The water runs fast and furious, so take extra care, especially if hitting this at the end of the day with tired legs (and brain)—this may be a somewhat tough wade when the water is high. If the crossing proves exhausting, you'll be grateful to find a large campsite on the other side (**Tyndall Creek Camp**), complete with bear box and plentiful clearings under the trees.

Tree cover thins, ending right around a junction with the **Lake South America Trail** at 8.6 miles.

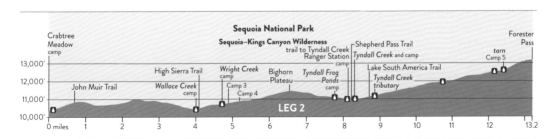

Sky pilot bursts from the granite as you near Forester Pass.

While this makes for a sunny final approach to the pass ahead, it also means that an incredible tundra-like landscape begins to unfold in front of you, full of grassy tufts, scattered wildflowers, and cunning marmots. The disappearing trees also offer a straight view of what you're in for—the ridgeline ahead sports a squared notch that marks somewhat intimidating Forester Pass. The pointed peak directly to its right is Junction Peak, and in front of that is the large formation known as Diamond Mesa.

You'll have a few more opportunities to fill your reservoir before the final ascent, first at 8.9 miles when crossing a small tributary of **Tyndall Creek** ⭕. Pass through a brief interlude of hardy trees, then again into the open—turn around here for a view back to the Great Western Divide and one last glimpse of Mount Whitney poking out to the southeast.

A few gorgeous tarns come into view at the base of **Diamond Mesa**. If these provoke thirst,

find refreshment as you cross a small stream ⭕ at 10.7 miles; another lies ahead at 12.2 miles. Look up to spot the trail snaking toward Forester Pass; know that while it's not a piece of cake, it's also not quite as bad as it looks from this angle. Unless everything is covered in snow (possible into early summer), reach a final tank-up point at 12.4 miles at a large tarn ⭕. To the right, spot several single-tent clearings; camp here instead of on the foliage ringing the tarn (**Camp 5**), but remember—you are completely above tree line here, fully exposed to the elements.

Even when acclimated, you'll still feel the thin air forcing your lungs into overdrive on the final ascent. After a few switchbacks, take a break at a memorial to Donald Downs, a young trail worker who died during the construction of this segment. Continue up with a new appreciation for how difficult it must have been to carve this path into such an imposing granite cliff.

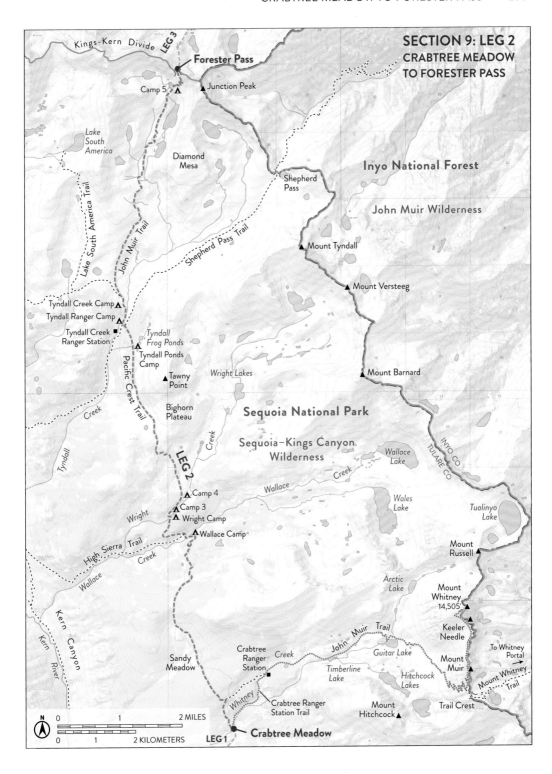

SECTION 9: LEG 2
CRABTREE MEADOW
TO FORESTER PASS

Kings-Kern Divide   LEG 3

Forester Pass

Camp 5   Junction Peak

Lake
South
America

Diamond
Mesa

Shepherd
Pass

Inyo National Forest

John Muir Wilderness

Lake South America Trail

John Muir Trail

Shepherd Pass Trail

Mount Tyndall

Mount Versteeg

Tyndall Creek Camp

Tyndall Ranger Camp

Tyndall Creek
Ranger Station

Tyndall
Frog Ponds

Tyndall Ponds
Camp

Tawny
Point

Wright Lakes

Mount Barnard

Bighorn
Plateau

Pacific Crest Trail

Creek

Tyndall

Creek

Sequoia National Park

Sequoia–Kings Canyon
Wilderness

Wallace
Lake

Wallace   Creek

Wales
Lake

Tualinyo
Lake

INYO CO
TULARE CO

LEG 2

Wright

Camp 4

Camp 3

Wright Camp

Wallace Camp

Wallace   Creek

High Sierra Trail

Creek

Wallace

Arctic
Lake

Mount
Russell

Kern Canyon

Kern
River

Sandy
Meadow

Crabtree
Ranger
Station

Creek

John Muir   Trail

Guitar Lake

Timberline
Lake

Hitchcock
Lakes

Mount
Whitney
14,505'

Keeler
Needle

Mount
Muir

To Whitney
Portal

Mount Whitney
Trail

Whitney

Crabtree Ranger
Station Trail

Mount
Hitchcock

Trail Crest

N
0   1   2 MILES
0   1   2 KILOMETERS

LEG 1   Crabtree Meadow

WINTRY WONDERLAND

Snow lingers well into summer on High Sierra passes and north-facing slopes. Many backpackers choose to carry an ice axe and traction devices while hiking this part of the trail in early summer. There are many tools available online to keep tabs on the Sierra snowpack, and you'll also glean intel from the folks at the Kennedy Meadows general store and from both the outfitter and the Eastern Sierra Interagency Visitor Center in Lone Pine. If you choose to bring an ice axe and traction devices with you on your trip, you need to *know how to use them*, otherwise they'll serve no purpose. Many outfitters and guide services offer day-long classes on using these tools; consider taking one before you find yourself careening down an icy slope.

Walk carefully over slippery talus chunks (or icy snow), stopping occasionally to appreciate the tenacity of sky pilot, a purple perennial in the phlox family that bursts with life through cracks in the granite. A final straightaway leads to perhaps the most-feared point on the PCT, where the trail curves around a gully known as "The Chute." Except for late season and in severe drought years, a giant snow bank usually builds across the trail here, creating a slippery, nearly vertical runout that makes for dangerous passage. Most hikers negotiate this section with traction devices on their shoes and white knuckles wrapped around an ice axe, prepared to self-arrest should they slip.

Once you've regained your composure, it's a quick, steep jaunt to reach **Forester Pass** on the **Kings-Kern Divide** at 13.2 miles, named by Sequoia National Forest supervisor Frank Cunningham to commemorate his fellow foresters. Here, you'll find company in snack-stealing marmots while straddling the dividing line between **Sequoia National Park** to the south and **Kings Canyon National Park** to the north. This small notch offers limited seating but unlimited views, including one last hurrah from the Great Western Divide and an introduction to the beautiful Bubbs Creek drainage to the north. Congratulations—you made it to the **highest point** on the entire PCT!

CAMP-TO-CAMP MILEAGE

Crabtree Meadow to Wallace Camp	4.1
Wallace Camp to Wright Camp	0.6
Wright Camp to Camp 3	0.2
Camp 3 to Camp 4	0.3
Camp 4 to Tyndall Ponds Camp	2.6
Tyndall Ponds Camp to Tyndall Ranger Camp	0.4
Tyndall Ranger Camp to Tyndall Creek Camp	0.2
Tyndall Creek Camp to Camp 5	4.0

3 FORESTER PASS TO GLEN PASS

DISTANCE 11.6 miles

ELEVATION GAIN/LOSS +2710/-3900 feet

HIGH POINT 13,123 feet

CONNECTING TRAILS Bubbs Creek Trail, Bullfrog Lake Trail, Kearsarge Pass Trail

ON THE TRAIL

The moment you head north from **Forester Pass**, you leave behind **Sequoia National Park** to enter **Kings Canyon National Park**. Even from this lofty vantage point, you get a sense of the beauty contained in nearby Center Basin and the Bubbs Creek drainage ahead—aquamarine alpine tarns dot the foreground, while high peaks (including dominant Center Peak) and a verdant canyon lie beyond.

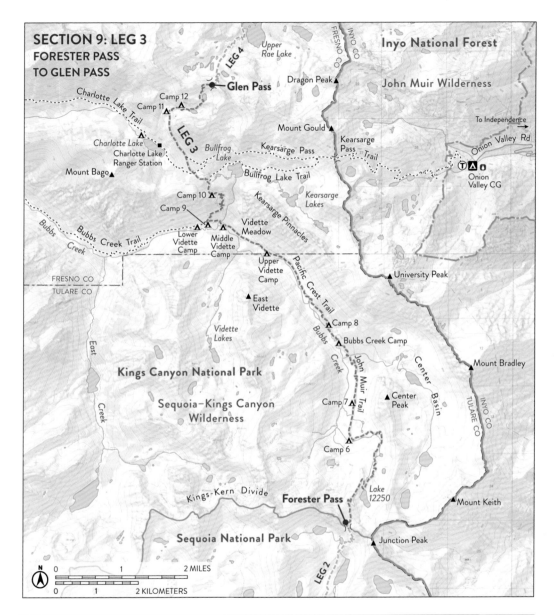

SECTION 9: LEG 3
FORESTER PASS
TO GLEN PASS

Inyo National Forest

John Muir Wilderness

Glen Pass

LEG 4

Upper Rae Lake

Dragon Peak

FRESNO CO

INYO CO

Camp 12

Camp 11

Charlotte Lake Trail

LEG 3

Charlotte Lake

Charlotte Lake Ranger Station

Mount Bago

Bullfrog Lake

Mount Gould

Kearsarge Pass

Kearsarge Pass Trail

To Independence

Onion Valley Rd

Onion Valley CG

Bullfrog Lake Trail

Kearsarge Lakes

Kearsarge Pinnacles

Camp 10

Camp 9

Bubbs Creek Trail

Bubbs Creek

Lower Vidette Camp

Middle Vidette Camp

Vidette Meadow

Upper Vidette Camp

East Vidette

FRESNO CO
TULARE CO

Pacific Crest Trail

University Peak

Vidette Lakes

Bubbs Creek

Camp 8

Bubbs Creek Camp

John Muir Trail

Center Basin

Mount Bradley

Kings Canyon National Park

Sequoia–Kings Canyon Wilderness

East Creek

Camp 7

Center Peak

Camp 6

TULARE CO
INYO CO

Kings-Kern Divide

Forester Pass

Lake 12250

Mount Keith

Sequoia National Park

Junction Peak

LEG 2

N

0   1   2 MILES

0   1   2 KILOMETERS

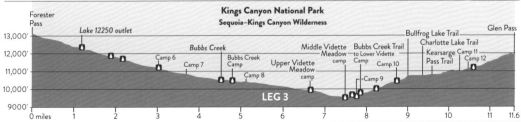

Kings Canyon National Park
Sequoia–Kings Canyon Wilderness

Forester Pass

Glen Pass

13,000'

Lake 12250 outlet

Bubbs Creek

Bullfrog Lake Trail

Charlotte Lake Trail

12,000'

Camp 6

Bubbs Creek Camp

Middle Vidette Meadow camp

Bubbs Creek Trail to Lower Vidette Camp

Kearsarge Pass Trail

Camp 11

Camp 12

11,000'

Camp 7

Camp 8

Upper Vidette Meadow camp

Camp 9

Camp 10

10,000'

LEG 3

9000'

0 miles   1   2   3   4   5   6   7   8   9   10   11   11.6

Descend a tight series of switchbacks (or make a lengthy glissade if the north side is coated with snow and you possess the skills to do so safely), then make your way down a ridgeline with stunning views of the Kearsarge Pinnacles in the distance. Drop down to cross the outlet of **Lake 12250 ⚪** at 1.2 miles, located at the foot of **Junction Peak** and Forester Pass. The descent continues on ankle-rolling chunks of talus that test your agility and patience. Totter down to cross a small stream ⚪ at 1.9 miles, meeting it again at 2.2 miles. Skip past an array of dainty bog orchids, red mountain heather, and wild buckwheat, eventually descending into light tree cover, courtesy of a smattering of whitebark pines. Look to the left at the 3-mile mark to spot shady platforms under the trees (**Camp 6**); a short trail on the north side of camp offers access to the creek ⚪.

Despite that pleasing pine interlude, pop back into the sun and onto annoying talus chunks as you continue the descent. Postcard views to the north should take your mind off your aching ankles. Find another camp at 3.6 miles (**Camp 7**), to the left under tree cover, although it's not nearly as nice (or large) as the previous one. Snap a few more photos before dropping into thick lodgepole forest. Hear a feeder branch of **Bubbs Creek ⚪** (also called Center Basin Creek here) before reaching it at 4.5 miles—this is often a ford. A scant 0.3 mile ahead, spot a large clearing below the trail (**Bubbs Creek Camp**)—an obvious path leads to ample campsites and a bear box next to the creek itself.

Spot another campsite to the left (**Camp 8**) just ahead at 5.1 miles in a small clearing under trees. This is fairly subpar, considering how many amazing options you have in this area, so skip along unless you need to grab some water from the creek. A bit farther up, glance through a break in the trees to spot a line of rocky spires towering above—these are the **Kearsarge Pinnacles**, so named for the nearby pass. The dominant feature on the other side of the canyon is impressive **East Vidette**.

An obvious clearing at 6.6 miles marks a campsite at the southern end of **Vidette Meadow**, colloquially known as Upper Vidette Meadow (**Upper Vidette Camp**). There's plenty of room for tents plus a bear box and access to **Bubbs Creek ⚪**. Continue on to reach Middle Vidette Meadow at 7.5 miles, with campsites scattered on both sides of the trail (**Middle Vidette Camp**) along with a bear box and access to water ⚪. Cross several seasonal streams ahead, the widest around 7.7 miles, featuring water that once flowed through Bullfrog Lake.

Just before reaching a junction with the **Bubbs Creek Trail** (marked for Cedar Grove) 0.1 mile ahead, spot a huge camping area below—there are plenty of places to pitch a tent here (**Camp 9**), but water access can be tricky. Instead, you might consider making a swing to the left to follow the Bubbs Creek Trail for a few minutes to a much better camp (**Lower Vidette Camp**), with a bear box, fire rings, and easier access to water ⚪ via a use trail on the west end. You might also find weekend backpackers who will happily unload some of their overstuffed bear canister delights. Enjoy your spoils while swatting away ever-present mosquitos as you watch a series of sublime sunset colors paint the granite all around.

It's now time to start gaining ground as you head toward Glen Pass. The path (signed as John Muir Trail North) swings sharply to the right and your legs crank like pistons as you

SHORTY'S CABIN

Beginning in 1912, a trapper with the fantastic name of Shorty Lovelace built a system of cabins sprinkled around what is now Kings Canyon National Park. He lived year-round in the mountains here and made a living selling pelts from the animals he hunted. Although he ranged farther abroad after the park was created, many of his cabins still stand and are collectively listed on the National Register of Historic Places as the Shorty Lovelace Historic District. Perhaps the most intact of his structures is located in Vidette Meadow, a surprisingly short jaunt from the trail . . . if you can find it. Ask a friendly ranger for directions.

KEARSARGE PASS

There are several ways to exit the trail over Kearsarge Pass. The Bullfrog Lake Trail offers a southerly route with waterside walking, and camping at gorgeous **Kearsarge Lakes**  just before the final ascent to the pass. The Kearsarge Pass Trail heads across slightly upslope, offering a dry campsite just under 1 mile in and a stunning view over Bullfrog Lake far below. If you head over Kearsarge Pass, you'll end up at Onion Valley, where you'll find a popular (read: always full in summer) campground, vault toilets, bear boxes, water spigots , and a giant parking lot. If hoping to catch a ride down the road to the small Owens Valley town of Independence (with limited lodging, a few restaurants, a gas station, and small market) or to larger Bishop to the north, switch to your least smelly shirt and try your hand at a hitch. I've never had a problem snagging a ride during summertime, and was especially thrilled when a benevolent trail angel offered up cold juice, frozen candy bars, and some refreshing oranges.

wind up the steep trail. Views down canyon, including East Vidette and Kearsarge Pinnacles, are breathtaking—literally and metaphorically. While you're still in scattered pines, you'll also spot ferns, corn lilies, mountaineer shooting stars, and great red paintbrush—all telltale signs of nearby water, which makes sense as you're ascending the Bullfrog Lake drainage. Access the wet stuff while crossing a small stream at 8.4 miles, then again at 8.8 miles. Find a beautiful little campsite (**Camp 10**) to the left

after the second crossing, with room for perhaps two tents.

Reach a junction with the **Bullfrog Lake Trail** just ahead at the 9-mile mark, which leads to not just Bullfrog Lake, but also to Kearsarge Lakes, Kearsarge Pass, and Onion Valley beyond. Tackle a steep uphill to reach the **Charlotte Lake Trail** on your left at 9.4 miles. If you choose this detour, drop down just shy of 1 mile to beautiful **Charlotte Lake** , where you'll find the **Charlotte Lake Ranger Station**, a bear box, and plentiful camping along the northeast shore. You can also turn right at the junction to join a spur trail that links with the **Kearsarge Pass Trail**, whose main path you'll cross at 9.6 miles on your right.

Continue uphill, spotting deep blue Charlotte Lake far below along with the obvious cirque of Mount Bago nearby. You pass a few less-than-stellar camping options, with small spots to the left of the trail at 10.3 (**Camp 11**) and 10.5 miles (**Camp 12**). Just after the second, cross a small stream **◐** and veer toward an amphitheater where short, but steep, granite switchbacks steal your breath. Huff above a small aquamarine tarn, then look across the way to spot your final zigzagging route. The path is narrow and the granite becomes slick when wet, so take caution as you finish the ascent.

Top out at 11.6 miles on the dizzying knife-edge ridge of **Glen Pass**, once known as Blue Flower Pass, but later named for a Forest Service ranger and former United States Geological Survey worker named Glen H. Crow. Steady your legs because the view threatens to sweep them from under you—down below sit the magnificent Rae Lakes, a backpacker's paradise surrounded by towering peaks all around. Luckily, you'll end up next to those stunning waters soon enough.

CAMP-TO-CAMP MILEAGE

Forester Pass to Camp 6 . . . . 3.0
Camp 6 to Camp 7 . . . . 0.6
Camp 7 to Bubbs Creek Camp 1.2
Bubbs Creek Camp to Camp 8 . . . . 0.3
Camp 8 to Upper Vidette Camp 1.5
Upper Vidette Camp to Middle
    Vidette Camp. 0.9
Middle Vidette Camp to Camp 9. . . . . 0.2
Camp 9 to Lower Vidette Camp. 0.1
Lower Vidette Camp to Camp 10. . . . . 1.0
Camp 10 to Camp 11 . . . . 1.5
Camp 11 to Camp 12 . . . . 0.2

4 GLEN PASS TO PINCHOT PASS

DISTANCE 16 miles

ELEVATION GAIN/LOSS
+3950/-3800 feet

HIGH POINT 12,133 feet

CONNECTING TRAILS
Baxter Pass Trail, Woods Creek Trail, Sawmill Pass Trail

ON THE TRAIL

If you arrive on the narrow ridge of **Glen Pass** in early summer, you might gaze upon a steep snowfield covering the north-facing slope below; at other times of year, you'll find a series of switchbacks over softball-sized talus—watch your step either way. Aquamarine Rae Lakes sparkle below, and you'll get there soon enough via a lush route through scattered pines and seasonal flows; the most reliable is a lovely stream **◐** you'll cross 1 mile in.

Another 0.8 mile down the way, encounter the **Sixty Lakes Basin Trail** veering to the left. Fantastic campsites are scattered around the gentle terrain northwest of this junction (**Sixty Lakes Camp**)—I actually prefer to camp here instead of at the crowded campsites on the other side of Rae Lakes. Continue straight to reach an isthmus, crossing the outlet for **Upper Rae Lake ◐** at 1.9 miles. Once across, turn your gaze south toward a prominent formation—this striated mass is the **Painted Lady**, and unsurprisingly, she dominates many a photo of the Rae Lakes area.

Reach a metal sign reading "Food Storage Box" at a fork in the trail at 2.4 miles—depart here to find some of the most deservedly popular campsites in the Sierra at **Middle Rae Lake ◐** (**Middle Rae Camp**); there's a one-night maximum at each lake

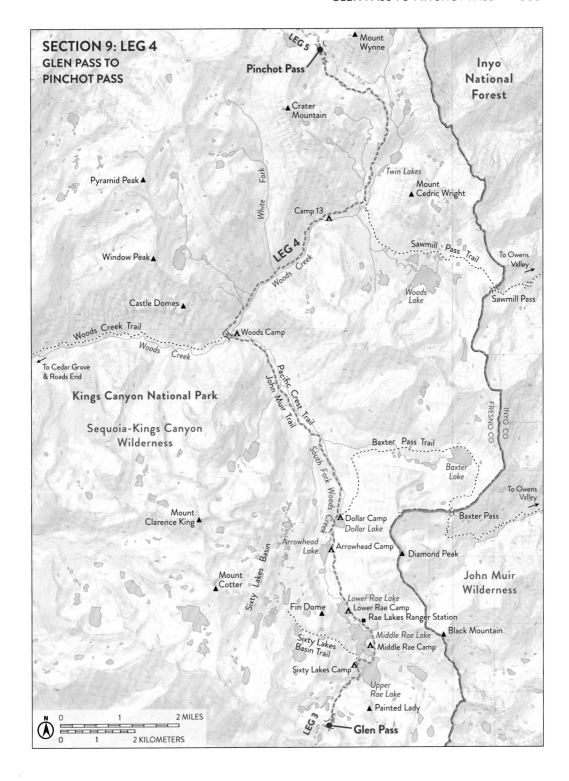

SECTION 9: LEG 4
GLEN PASS TO
PINCHOT PASS

LEG 5

Mount Wynne ▲

Pinchot Pass

Inyo National Forest

Crater Mountain ▲

Pyramid Peak ▲

White Fork

Twin Lakes

Mount Cedric Wright ▲

Camp 13 ⛺

LEG 4

Sawmill   Pass   Trail

To Owens Valley

Window Peak ▲

Woods Creek

Woods Lake

Sawmill Pass

Castle Domes ▲

Woods Creek Trail

⛺ Woods Camp

Woods   Creek

To Cedar Grove & Roads End

Kings Canyon National Park

Pacific Crest Trail

John Muir Trail

Sequoia-Kings Canyon Wilderness

Baxter   Pass   Trail

South Fork Woods Creek

Baxter Lake

FRESNO CO.

INYO CO.

Mount Clarence King ▲

⛺ Dollar Camp
Dollar Lake

To Owens Valley

Baxter Pass

Arrowhead Lake

⛺ Arrowhead Camp

Diamond Peak ◆

John Muir Wilderness

Mount Cotter ▲

Sixty   Lakes   Basin

Fin Dome ▲

Lower Rae Lake
⛺ Lower Rae Camp
■ Rae Lakes Ranger Station

Black Mountain ◆

Middle Rae Lake
⛺ Middle Rae Camp

Sixty Lakes Basin Trail

⛺ Sixty Lakes Camp

Upper Rae Lake

Painted Lady ▲

LEG 3

Glen Pass

N

0   1   2 MILES
0   1   2 KILOMETERS

The Rae Lakes area is one of the most popular places in the Sierra for good reason.

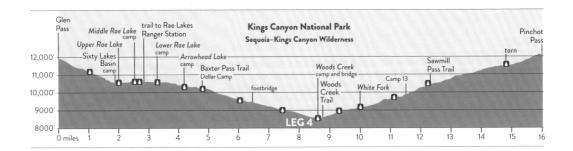

between here and Dollar Lake farther up. Various sites fan out across a hilly area under scattered tree cover; toward the bottom, find the noted bear box and use trails to the lake, where you can tank up, go for a dip, catch trout for dinner, or play tag with a small army of mosquitos.

Head gently uphill from here, under Black Mountain and Diamond Peak on the right, with Fin Dome, Mount Cotter, and Mount Clarence King looming to the west. Cross a small stream ⬤ at 2.6 miles as you spot the attractive **Rae Lakes**

Ranger Station straight ahead; reach its spur trail 0.2 mile farther. The ground becomes a bit more saturated, swampy even, but the upside is that you'll walk past an array of flowers if in season, including great red paintbrush, delicate bog orchids, and purple-flowered swamp onion.

Reach another large camping area on the left at 3.2 miles, adjacent to **Lower Rae Lake** ⬤ (**Lower Rae Camp**), featuring a bear box and water access. This site plays second fiddle to Middle Rae Lake, but it's plenty beautiful, regardless. Next, land near the shores of **Arrowhead Lake** ◐ at 4.1 miles; a bear box, water access, and good campsites abound (**Arrowhead Camp**). If you want to snap epic photos of this area, continue to the lake's outlet just ahead, offering a stunning view of Fin Dome and its watery reflection.

Drag yourself across the outlet on an assortment of logs, then contour around to spot **Dollar Lake** ◐ shimmering below. Traverse its shoreline and pop around to a junction with the **Baxter Pass Trail** at 4.7 miles; find camping here on granite slabs, with easy water access (**Dollar Camp**). The Baxter Pass Trail is an unmaintained path that leads up and over its namesake pass, then makes a dizzying drop to the Owens Valley far below. A map, compass, and navigation skills are recommended if you attempt to exit (or enter) this way.

Steal one last glance back to Fin Dome, then head down through chunky talus and foxtail pines, listening to the **South Fork Woods Creek**, born out of Dollar Lake and the chain above it. Despite its seeming proximity, you can't actually access water here, but you can at 6 miles, when crossing a stream ◐ created in faraway Sixty Lakes Basin. This can be tricky—you may find a (slippery) log bridge or perhaps some rocks, but might just want to wade.

Leave crunchy granite behind for a while as the ground moistens up ahead, the surrounding grass and mud dotted with more bog orchids, Sierra primrose, corn lilies, and even a few mushrooms. Cross the mushiest part on a small wooden footbridge at 6.4 miles, where you might be able to fill your bottles. There's better water up ahead at 7.4 miles at a seasonal flow and then a deeper stream ◐ that can prove a tricky wade in early season.

Before dropping into thick tree cover, enjoy the stunning views ahead, including Castle Domes, Window Peak, and Pyramid Peak. Soon enough, stroll up to the somewhat imposing (or fun, depending on your perspective) **Woods Creek** suspension bridge at 8.7 miles. The near side hosts a popular camping area (**Woods Camp**), with a bear box, fire rings, and water access ◐. The rushing creek, lodgepole pines, and red firs make this a wonderful place to bed down for the night.

Summon the spirit of adventure as you cross the bridge—one person at a time, lest you inadvertently bounce someone off the side. Once across,

CLOSE ENCOUNTERS OF THE FURRED KIND

I experienced a solo bear encounter just short of the Woods Creek bridge when I turned a corner to find I was within arm's reach of a bruin high five. Luckily, all turned out well and we both went on our merry way. While they tend to avoid human contact, black bears frequent the larger, more well-loved campsites in the Sierra (like this one), so remain extra vigilant with your smelly stuff and use the bear boxes if all of your goods don't fit into your bear canister.

hit a junction with the **Woods Creek Trail**; stay right. Weave through thick patches of manzanita as you sweat uphill, watching Woods Creek cascade below. The surrounds become lush, with seasonal flows running down the slopes above, providing nourishment for pockets of wildflowers and ferns. Hit a reliable stream crossing ◐ at 9.3 miles, the first of several. Pound up a series of granite steps to find your next source just after a cattle gate 10 miles in—this is the **White Fork** ◐, which can prove somewhat difficult in high water. Find a third source at 11.1 miles, where you cross a minor stream ◐.

Backpackers come in all shapes and sizes.

A scant 0.4 mile (and some uphill) ahead, find a Jeffrey pine–shaded clearing on the right that makes for a wonderful camp (**Camp 13**). If you're thinking about staying here, tank up at the last water source since there's not another chance until you cross a stream ⬡ at 12.2 miles; this one is much wider than the previous few, but you'll have rocks to cross over if the water is low enough.

Hoof up granite steps to reach the **Sawmill Pass Trail** junction 0.1 mile ahead; this unmaintained path veers right to offer rough passage up and over Sawmill Pass, down to the Owens Valley. A whole host of new peaks now come into view, notably the reddish ridgeline of Crater Mountain to the northwest, Mount Wynne to the north, and **Mount Cedric Wright** (with **Twin Lakes** beneath it) almost directly to the east. Continue up past granite slabs through scattered pines, accompanied by the ever-present squawks of Clark's nutcrackers overhead.

As you walk upward, pass through lovely alpine meadows and stare at the jagged ridgeline ahead, playing a game of "Is *That* The Pass?" I'll save you the trouble—no, it's not. While you wait to find out which notch *is* the pass, meander past a tiny tarn ⬡, then summon your quads to ascend a rocky ridgeline, stealing glances back toward the rusted hulk of Crater Mountain standing in stark contrast to the green below.

Continue huffing upward and your destination will soon reveal itself. Reach broad **Pinchot Pass** at 16 miles, named for former Forest Service Chief Gifford Pinchot. As you struggle to catch your breath (or do a little happy dance), enjoy views back down to the lush wonderland you traversed and out to the South Fork Kings River drainage, Upper Basin, and more beauty beyond.

CAMP-TO-CAMP MILEAGE

Glen Pass to Sixty Lakes Camp 1.8
Sixty Lakes Camp to Middle Rae Camp 0.6
Middle Rae Camp to Lower Rae Camp 0.8
Lower Rae Camp to Arrowhead Camp 0.9
Arrowhead Camp to Dollar Camp 0.6
Dollar Camp to Woods Camp 4.0
Woods Camp to Camp 13 . . . . 2.8

5 PINCHOT PASS TO MATHER PASS

DISTANCE 9.8 miles

ELEVATION GAIN/LOSS
+2230/-2220 feet

HIGH POINT 12,106 feet

CONNECTING TRAIL
Taboose Pass Trail

ON THE TRAIL

From your breathless perch atop **Pinchot Pass**, enjoy one last glance back to the beautiful meadows spread across the southern approach, take a moment to appreciate bright purple sky pilot shooting out of granite crevices, and then sail down lazy switchbacks toward a series of gemstone tarns. A slow pace offers ample time to pause and take in the sights of conical, grey **Mount Wynne** directly to your right and Mount Pinchot hovering directly north of it. While you might pass a seasonal flow or two and come somewhat close to the tarns you spotted from high above, your first reliable water option is a small stream ⬡ at 1.3 miles. This will likely serve as a reminder that unless you want to act as an unlimited buffet for hungry mosquitos, some form of chemical or clothing protection is warranted throughout this very wet section of trail.

From here, look down upon **Lake Marjorie** ⬡, whose outlet you'll skirt 0.5 mile later—this is an easy place to tank up, and the area offers a few sandy campsites (**Lake Marjorie Camp**) scattered

Throughout the Sierra, hikers must cross waterways multiple times a day—good balance and trekking poles will help with the rock-hopping.

around granite slabs. Be extra cautious to avoid trampling the delicate ground cover in this area. Beginning at 2.1 miles, pass another beautiful tarn, then the first of several stream **O** crossings; the next two occur at 2.2 and 2.8 miles. Head uphill from the latter to find several sites hidden in the trees upslope to the left, planting you across from yet another scenic tarn (**Camp 14**).

As you look northward, you'll notice two things: the obvious curve in the earth that marks Upper Basin and the distant ridgeline that hosts your objective for this leg, Mather Pass. Even if you're worried about the latter (which you shouldn't be), the meadow-filled, pine-scented splendor should take your mind off any brewing anxiety. Enjoy more downhill, depositing you at a junction with the **Bench Lake Trail** at 3 miles, which leads 2 miles to—you guessed it—lovely Bench Lake, offering good trout fishing and secluded camping.

Unless you want to step off the beaten path, continue right to ford a stream **O** and pass a spur

to the **Bench Lake Ranger Station**. Unlike the others you've passed so far, this is not a building, but a seasonal tent. Hit another junction a mere 0.1 mile ahead, this time with the **Taboose Pass Trail**. From here, dip into a pleasant lodgepole forest, making steady downhill progress toward the sound of South Fork Kings River rushing below. Before reaching it, hit a beefy stream **O** crossing at 4 miles that serves as teaser for the main event. Another 0.2 mile ahead, peer through the

TABOOSE PASS

The somewhat gnarly Taboose Pass Trail climbs over its namesake pass to descend a dizzying 6000 feet to the Owens Valley below. Although it provides a PCT exit or entry point, it's not commonly used due to the remote nature of the trailhead below, the lack of suitable campsites and shade and the huge elevation gain on the way up.

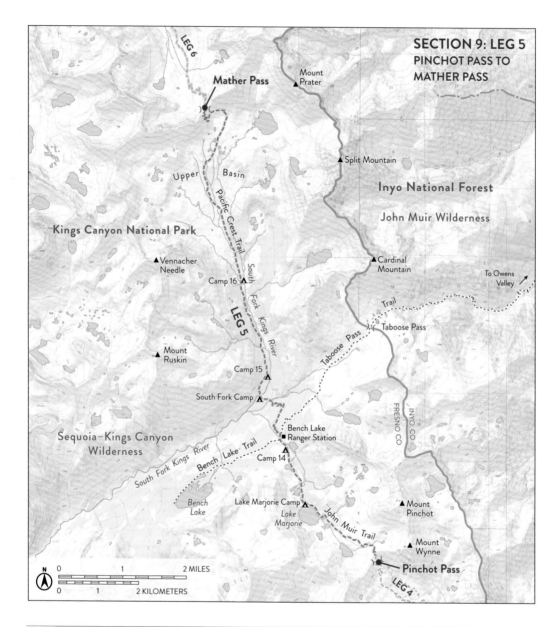

SECTION 9: LEG 5
PINCHOT PASS TO
MATHER PASS

LEG 6

Mount Prater

Mather Pass

Split Mountain

Inyo National Forest

John Muir Wilderness

Upper Basin

Pacific Crest Trail

Kings Canyon National Park

Vennacher Needle

Cardinal Mountain

To Owens Valley

South Fork Kings River

Camp 16

LEG 5

Taboose Pass Trail

Taboose Pass

Mount Ruskin

Camp 15

South Fork Camp

FRESNO CO

INYO CO

Sequoia–Kings Canyon Wilderness

Bench Lake Ranger Station

Camp 14

South Fork Kings River

Bench Lake Trail

Bench Lake

Lake Marjorie Camp
Lake Marjorie

John Muir Trail

Mount Pinchot

Mount Wynne

Pinchot Pass

LEG 4

N

0   1   2 MILES
0   1   2 KILOMETERS

Kings Canyon National Park
Sequoia–Kings Canyon Wilderness

Pinchot Pass

Lake Marjorie camp

Bench Lake Trail

trail to Bench Lake Ranger Station

Camp 14

Taboose Pass Trail

South Fork Kings River
South Fork Camp

Camp 15

Camp 16

Mather Pass

12,000'

11,000'

10,000'

9000'

LEG 5

0 miles   1   2   3   4   5   6   7   8   9   9.8

woods to find clearings to the left that make for pleasant camping (**South Fork Camp**); more sites are located ahead on the right as you approach the near side of the South Fork Kings crossing, although this area is sometimes closed for restoration.

At 4.3 miles, find yourself standing at the edge of the raging slash of water that marks your arrival at the frothing, imposing **South Fork Kings River 🌢**. If it's late in the day and the river seems particularly beastly, set up camp on the near side and wait for morning, when flow will be lowest. Most folks find that it's easiest to make the daunting crossing on logjams just downstream of the trail, where a small island splits the river into two channels, or across jumbled boulders upstream during times of lower flow. You *will* get wet, no doubt about that.

Once your shoes are back on and your nerves have calmed, continue on past an array of granite slabs to pick up the trail, now headed uphill. The pine forest is mixed with wetland, which means you're likely to spot a smattering of pretty purple mountaineer shooting stars along the way. If you're ready to bed down, look to your right at 4.7 miles for a few spots (**Camp 15**) carved under a smattering of pines between the trail and the **South Fork Kings River 🌢**.

Eventually leave the dense tree cover to score views of Mount Ruskin to the west and the pointy fin of Vennacher Needle to the northwest. Another two-pronged stream 🌢 crossing awaits at 5.1 miles; scout upstream to find an easier route. This area flattens out and becomes quite marshy, so expect to find water flowing over the trail in

Towering peaks, burbling streams, and lush meadows make Upper Basin a delight to traverse.

spots, especially in early summer. Cross another stream **O** at 5.9 miles and look to your right for a small campsite (**Camp 16**) tucked in the sandy slabs; be cautious to avoid trampling nearby foliage. Continue sloshing through the moist environs, tiptoeing through what seems like more water than dirt at times. Even though your instinct might suggest avoiding what might become a channel of mud and water, stay on the trail itself to avoid creating social trails and eroding the route.

Well within **Upper Basin**, continue a rather gentle ascent toward Mather Pass, the deep notch becoming more obvious in the distance the higher you climb. Before then, you have more water to contend with, including a rather wide stream **O** crossing at 6.6 miles then another **O** at 7.4 miles—this second will most certainly be a wade, even if the first is navigable on rocks. All of this wetness means you'll likely find an abundance of wildflowers in early summer, including purple tundra aster, magenta penstemon, tufts of yellow Muir's ivesia, and mats of wild buckwheat, among so many others.

The beauty continues as you cross a lovely stream **O** through the tundra-like meadows at 8.1 miles, passing above blue tarns dotting the alpine landscape. To the east, spot the darkened granite of Mount Prater, and up ahead, the final ascent to the pass becomes visible. Swing around to the east, then begin a long traverse through blocky talus. Continue on well-graded switchbacks—a marvel of engineering on this imposing granite wall—to reach **Mather Pass** at 9.8 miles, named for inaugural National Park Service Director Stephen Mather. No surprise, you'll find great views once you arrive—back across the verdant path you just ascended and north to more tarns and the Palisade Crest, whose lofty spires you'll travel under in the next leg.

CAMP-TO-CAMP MILEAGE

Pinchot Pass to Lake Marjorie Camp 1.8
Lake Marjorie Camp to Camp 14 . . . . 1.0
Camp 14 to South Fork Camp 1.4
South Fork Camp to Camp 15 . . . . 0.5
Camp 15 to Camp 16 . . . . 1.2

6 MATHER PASS TO MUIR PASS

DISTANCE 21.7 miles

ELEVATION GAIN/LOSS
+4360/-4480 feet

HIGH POINT 12,106 feet

CONNECTING TRAIL
Bishop Pass Trail

ON THE TRAIL

From high atop **Mather Pass**, glimpse just a hint of the immense beauty you'll walk through on this leg as the Palisade Lakes come into view, topped off by the soaring Palisade Crest. Descend switchbacks

comprised of ankle-turning chunks of talus, then ponder whether it should be called the Pacific *Creek* Trail due to an abundance of water flowing underfoot. Even in drier times, find a stream **O** at 1.2 miles, then continue down past bursts of bright penstemon, buckwheat, and both red and white heather, the latter appearing as droopy, but pretty white bells sporting reddish caps.

Nearing the 2-mile mark, rock-filled meadows begin morphing into tree-filled slopes. The trail ventures high above **Upper Palisade Lake**, with a few dry campsites tucked down to the left at 2.3 miles (**Camp 17**). Continue along toward another creek **O** crossing at 2.5 miles, with room for a small group to camp under a stand of pines just past it (**Camp 18**). A few more spots appear

Dear readers: Was eaten by LeConte Canyon rock monster. Please send help.

on the left just before another stream 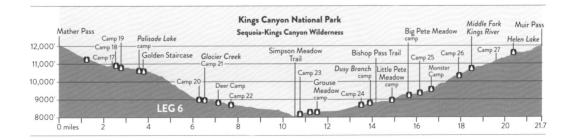 crossing 0.3 mile ahead (**Camp 19**).

Water drenches the trail in this area, and it might look like the entire Palisade Crest is one giant waterfall at this point. Follow the cascades down while zigzagging toward **Lower Palisade Lake** ⬤. Follow the lakeside path to eventually find campsites scattered around slabs north of the trail, just before the lake's outlet ⬤ at 3.6 miles (**Palisade Camp**).

Just ahead sits one of the most impressive segments of trail in the Sierra—the (in)famous **Golden Staircase**, which begins after yet another

stream crossing ⬤ at 3.8 miles. The tightly carved path winds through a narrow gap in the granite alongside roaring **Palisade Creek**, the outflow from Palisade Lakes. While wiggling down the dizzying trail, it's obvious why this was the final segment of the John Muir Trail to be completed— the route seems impossible until each turn reveals a path through myriad slabs, cliffs, and gullies. As you descend, the valley below opens up to offer views of toothy Devils Crags along the Black Divide.

The descent softens in an abundance of ferns, kept lush by multiple flows draining from Palisade

313

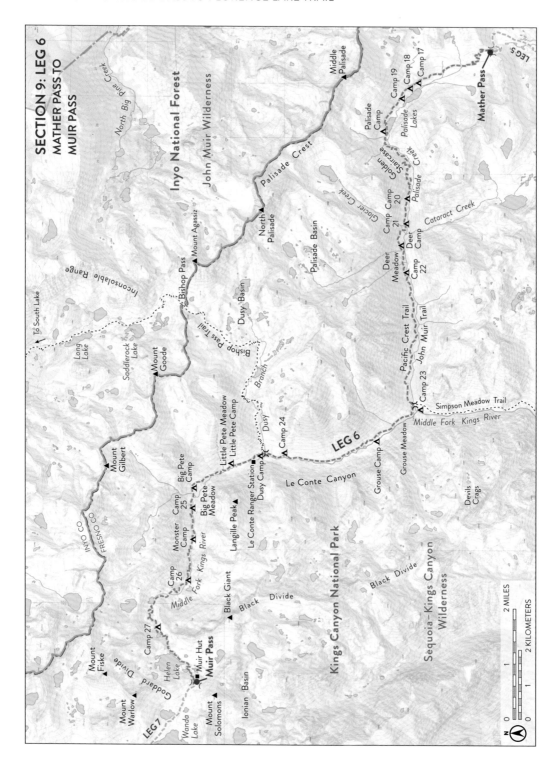

SECTION 9: LEG 6
MATHER PASS TO
MUIR PASS

Inyo National Forest

John Muir Wilderness

North Big Pine Creek

Inconsolable Range

Palisade Crest

Middle Palisade

Camp 19
Camp 18
Camp 17

LEG 5

Mather Pass

Palisade Camp

Palisade Lakes

Golden Staircase

Glacier Creek

Palisade Creek

Cataract Creek

North Palisade

Mount Agassiz

Bishop Pass

Palisade Basin

Camp 20
Camp 21

Deer Meadow

Deer Camp

Camp 22

To South Lake

Long Lake

Saddlerock Lake

Mount Goode

Dusy Basin

Bishop Pass Trail

Pacific Crest Trail

John Muir Trail

Camp 23

Branch

Dusy

Little Pete Meadow
Little Pete Camp

Simpson Meadow Trail

Middle Fork Kings River

Mount Gilbert

Camp 24

LEG 6

Grouse Camp

Grouse Meadow

Le Conte Canyon

Devils Crags

Big Pete Camp

Camp 25

Big Pete Meadow

Langille Peak

Le Conte Ranger Station
Dusy Camp

INYO CO
FRESNO CO

Monster Camp

Camp 26

Middle Fork Kings River

Black Giant

Black Divide

Kings Canyon National Park

Black Divide

Sequoia–Kings Canyon Wilderness

Camp 27

Mount Fiske

Goddard Divide

Helen Lake

Muir Hut
Muir Pass

Ionian Basin

Mount Warlow

Mount Solomons

LEG 7

Wanda Lake

N

0   1   2 MILES

0   1   2 KILOMETERS

The ascent to Muir Pass is a lot more enjoyable when it is not covered in deep snow.

Basin to the north and now-raging Palisade Creek to your left. Continue down a boulder-strewn slope toward the thick stand of pines marking the edge of **Deer Meadow** ahead. Find the first of several campsites at 6.3 miles, with several spots tucked between the trail and creek (**Camp 20**) **O**. Mosquitos nip at every inch of exposed skin in the moist forest; if you want to escape their incessant probing, another site appears 1 mile past the last (**Camp 21**) **O**. Otherwise, continue to multi-pronged **Glacier Creek O** 0.1 mile up—if your feet weren't wet before, they might be now.

Find one of the biggest camps in the area at 7.1 miles, in a massive clearing reached via a use trail to the left. One summer evening, I watched a mama deer birth two fawns here, so in honor of that magic, I deem this spot **Deer Camp O**. I always appreciate it when natural features live up to their names.

Cross another drainage **O** just afterward and enter a small burn area filled with spooky snags. Look for paintbrush, alpine buttercups, and bright pink wild roses to brighten the mood in early summer. More flows abound, then a small camp appears on your left at 7.6 miles (**Camp 22**), and another less than 0.25 mile beyond that, both with creek **O** access. Pass through a stock gate, earning more incredible views toward the Black Divide. These, too, will soon disappear as the trail bends to the north after a junction with the **Simpson Meadow Trail** on your left at 10.5 miles; stay straight toward Grouse Meadow.

Shortly after the junction, a use trail banks downhill to a shady campsite (**Camp 23**) near the powerful **Middle Fork Kings River O**. Vibrant **Grouse Meadow** comes into view after a stream crossing **O** at 11.2 miles. The area is gorgeous in early summer, flush with grasses, ferns, corn lilies, pines, and blueberry bushes. Find a few campsites scattered around, with the largest on your left at 11.5 miles (**Grouse Camp**). Access paths cut through to water; avoid trampling fragile meadow foliage.

Paintbrush, mariposa lilies, penstemon, and aster sprinkle color along the way as you move gently uphill, passing through a wooden stock gate. Campsites abound along the corridor, all near the **Middle Fork Kings River 🌢**. The first is on the left at 13.6 miles (**Camp 24**); two more are located within the next 0.3 mile. Just past the last spot, cross a small stream, then much larger **Dusy Branch 🌢** via a footbridge. Another campsite is found not much farther past this via an obvious use trail descending to the left (**Dusy Camp**) 🌢.

Encounter the **Bishop Pass Trail** on the right at 14.1 miles, a popular access point for **LeConte Canyon**, whose myriad wonders you're traveling through. A trail to the left leads to the rustic **LeConte Ranger Station**. Your path heads straight, angling up canyon a bit more steeply now. **Langille Peak** rises sharply to the west as the trail begins to turn in that direction, landing at **Little Pete Meadow** 0.5 mile past the junction. The

White heather glows in sunlight.

BISHOP PASS

The Bishop Pass Trail ascends from the South Lake trailhead past a beautiful array of lakes en route to the pass, tucked between Mount Goode and Mount Agassiz. The route then drops into gorgeous Dusy Basin and descends steeply to reach the PCT in LeConte Canyon. It's possible to resupply via the Bishop Pass Trail if you send a resupply (fee required) to Parchers Resort, located 1 mile south of the South Lake trailhead. The resort also offers pay showers, lodging, and a small seasonal café.

Middle Fork weaves lazily through the meadow, with two obvious camping spots nearby—a massive site on your left at 14.8 miles (**Little Pete Camp**) and then a smaller one tucked just ahead, both with water access 🌢.

Cross two small streams 🌢, pass another stock gate, then ascend to larger **Big Pete Meadow**, with a large campsite on your left at 15.7 miles (**Big Pete Camp**) 🌢. Cross a trickier multibranched flow 🌢 to find more sites on the other side. Find three more spots beginning at 16.1 miles (**Camp 25**); the last at 16.7 miles boasts an incredibly photogenic boulder, and once you see it, you'll understand why I've dubbed it **Monster Camp**.

The trail steepens as you begin the final ascent toward Muir Pass. To your left, the Black Divide, including the massive Black Giant, dominates the surroundings. Ascend past a raging waterfall created by the Middle Fork, zigzagging up to reach a few more camps—one at 17.9 miles (**Camp 26**), then another 0.1 mile ahead past a small stream crossing. You finally breach the **Middle Fork Kings River 🌢** via a series of flat rocks at 18.6 miles.

If hiking in early summer when snow is still present, the ascent to Muir Pass can present challenges—snow bridges form over the Middle Fork, and the route to the pass can become obscured. Come prepared with the right equipment and know-how to safely navigate this

The iconic Muir Hut sits atop breezy, beautiful Muir Pass.

terrain. The route still offers difficulties without snow, including your traverse of a small lake's fairly wide inlet ◐.

Climb several rocky, wildflower-dotted benches, crossing multiple flows along the way. A final campsite appears on the left at 19.8 miles, where a use trail leads to a secluded site tucked into a stand of whitebark pine (**Camp 27**). From here, continue on to cross the outlet and inlet of another small lake ◐, taking care over waterlogged, loose talus on the far side. Beautiful **Helen Lake ◐** (one of two named for John Muir's daughters) appears on your right; cross its boulder-strewn outlet then an inlet.

The **Goddard Divide** now rises up to greet you; **Mount Solomons** (named for John Muir Trail idea man and Sierra explorer Theodore Solomons) flanks Muir Pass to the south, and Mount Warlow takes northern duty. The final switchbacks are well graded (though you'll have to make your own if slogging through snow), and soon the John Muir Memorial Shelter (known as the **Muir Hut**) comes into view. Reach it, **Muir Pass**, and the end of this leg, at 21.7 miles. Enjoy spectacular views all around and lounge in the historic stone building,

erected by the Sierra Club in 1930 as a dedication to noted environmentalist and Sierra raconteur John Muir. The shelter was added to the National Register of Historic Places in 2016, a deserving designation for an iconic location.

CAMP-TO-CAMP MILEAGE

7 MUIR PASS TO McCLURE MEADOW

DISTANCE 9.5 miles

ELEVATION GAIN/LOSS
+540/-2840 feet

HIGH POINT 11,969 feet

CONNECTING TRAILS
None

ON THE TRAIL

Oh, an entire leg of glorious downhill! In one of the most beautiful places on earth, nonetheless! This segment might just be the best 9.5 miles on the entire PCT. At least, that's what I thought once I crested **Muir Pass** and looked down upon spectacular **Evolution Basin**, where sky-blue lakes sit cradled beneath a cavalcade of towering, glacier-carved peaks. Of course, the whole thing might be covered in a thick layer

Evolution Basin offers one of the most stunning alpine landscapes on Earth.

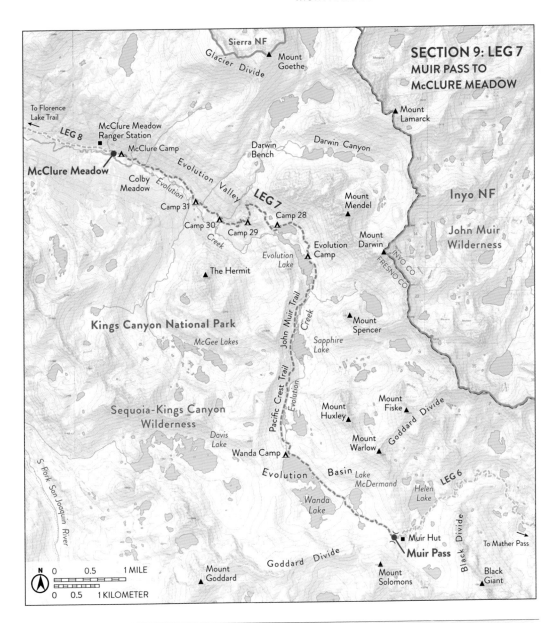

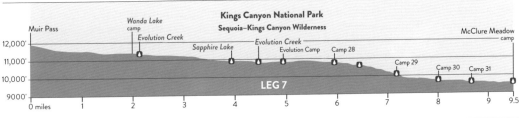

Bed down near McClure Meadow for spectacular sunset views back toward Evolution Valley.

of snow, but that just adds to the magic (even as you curse along with every single posthole on the way down).

Resist the urge to spend the rest of your life at the stone **Muir Hut** and head down the rocky trail toward the breathtaking (literally) surroundings, maneuvering across a few small flows in the first mile as you scoot around the south side of **Lake McDermand 0**. After a short bit of uphill, drop down to walk alongside massive **Wanda Lake 0**, the second of two area lakes named for John Muir's daughters. While it appears inviting, the prevailing semi-Arctic breeze might dissuade you from taking a swim. As the terrain flattens out toward the northern tip of the lake at the 2-mile mark, look for a few exposed campsites scattered around the granite (**Wanda Camp**). A night here offers starlit views around the massive basin,

whose surrounding summits were all named by explorer Theodore Solomons to honor various evolutionary philosophers, including Thomas Henry Huxley, John Fiske, and of course, Charles Darwin.

Make your way toward a two-branch crossing of Wanda Lake's outlet, which serves as headwaters for **Evolution Creek 0**. In early summer, wildflowers offer contrast against the granite— white heather, red heather, and alpine daisies are common sights in the area. You might not notice the tiny flowers, though, because the landscape is so massive—more peaks come into view as you descend, as does **Sapphire Lake 0**, whose waters you can access once you near its midpoint around 3.9 miles.

Another lake awaits, but first, head over to the east side of the valley via a wide crossing of **Evolution Creek ⏺** at 4.4 miles, possible on stepping stones. Once across, walk along beautiful **Evolution Lake**, another jewel in the sparkling chain of lakes dotting your path. If you want to stay a while and meditate on the magic, scan for a use trail descending less than 0.5 mile past the crossing toward a series of granite shelves with a few sandy tent spots (**Evolution Camp**); be cautious to avoid trampling nearby vegetation in your quest for the perfect perch. Farther along, find another few sites at the lake's northern tip at 5.9 miles, again on sandy slabs (**Camp 28**). Here, you're also near a small tarn ⏺ that offers easy water access along with spectacular views back toward Evolution Basin. Sweet dreams, indeed.

From here, the scenery changes as you transition into U-shaped **Evolution Valley**, a green, glacier-carved gorge teeming with fragrant lodgepole pines and gorgeous meadows. While The Hermit rises impressively to the south, the majority of the high peaks begin to disappear as you descend through thicker tree cover, but trust me—they'll show up again in a magical way. Wiggle steeply downhill on a mixture of dirt, granite steps, tree roots, and pine needles, crossing a pair of meadow-fringed streams ⏺ beginning at 6.4 miles. Although they lack the majestic views found in Evolution Basin, a few campsites appear as you descend. The first occurs at 7.2 miles, with spots first to the right, then shortly after, to the left of the trail (**Camp 29**). Less than 0.25 mile ahead, cross a multibranch stream ⏺, then continue to the 8-mile mark to find some sandy clearings tucked off the trail along with nearby water from **Evolution Creek ⏺** (**Camp 30**).

Continue toward **Colby Meadow**, its green expanse visible through the forest. Enjoy this fragrant stroll through the pines, passing a great campsite tucked under some trees on your left at 8.7 miles (**Camp 31**); find water via a stream ⏺ crossing less than 0.25 mile ahead. From here, the greenery on your left becomes **McClure Meadow**, and you reach this leg's end at a use trail that descends to a massive (and massively popular) campsite (**McClure Camp**) at 9.5 miles. **Evolution Creek ⏺** runs through the meadow, and use trails deposit you at its waters. From here, look back to the high peaks of Evolution Basin towering far above, and if you're lucky, watch the most spectacular sunset you've ever seen in your life. At least, I did.

CAMP-TO-CAMP MILEAGE

Muir Pass to Wanda Camp 2.0
Wanda Camp to Evolution Camp 2.8
Evolution Camp to Camp 28 . . . . 1.1
Camp 28 to Camp 29 . . . . 1.3
Camp 29 to Camp 30 . . . . 0.8
Camp 30 to Camp 31 . . . . 0.7
Camp 31 to McClure Camp 0.8

8 McCLURE MEADOW TO FLORENCE LAKE TRAIL

DISTANCE 9.6 miles

ELEVATION GAIN/LOSS
+640/-2410 feet

HIGH POINT 9662 feet

CONNECTING TRAILS
Piute Pass Trail, Florence Lake Trail

ON THE TRAIL

After the awe-inducing beauty of Evolution Basin and Evolution Valley throughout the last leg, I'll admit that this segment might feel a little less exciting—there are no big peaks, and you spend a lot of time walking through forest cover with little in the way of views. However, the landscape has a few excellent surprises in store, so keep the faith!

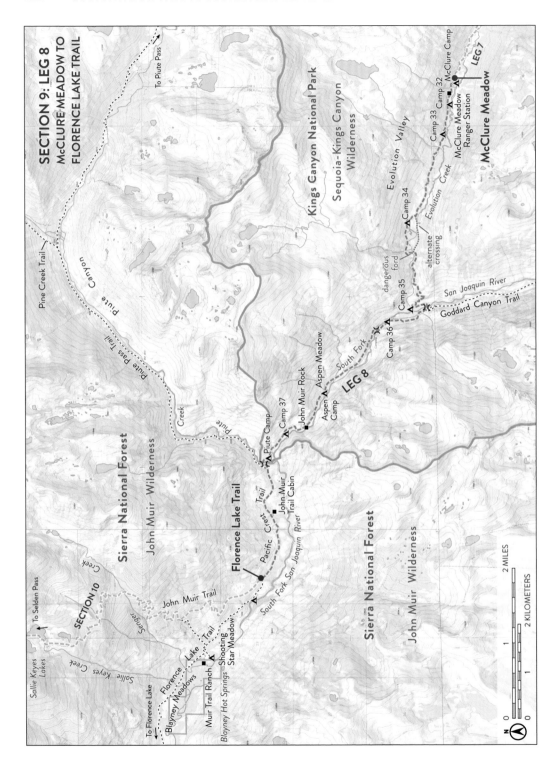

SECTION 9: LEG 8
McCLURE MEADOW TO
FLORENCE LAKE TRAIL

To Piute Pass

Pine Creek Trail

Piute Canyon

Piute Pass Trail

Creek

Piute

Piute Camp

Camp 37

John Muir Rock

Aspen Meadow

Aspen Meadow Camp

LEG 8

South Fork

Camp 36

Camp 35

dangerous ford

Camp 34

Evolution Valley

Evolution Creek

alternate crossing

San Joaquin River

Goddard Canyon Trail

Kings Canyon National Park

Sequoia–Kings Canyon Wilderness

McClure Camp

Camp 32

Camp 33

McClure Meadow Ranger Station

McClure Meadow

LEG 7

Florence Lake Trail

Pacific Crest Trail

John Muir Trail Cabin

John Muir Wilderness

Sierra National Forest

SECTION 10

To Selden Pass

Sallie Keyes Lakes

Sallie Keyes Creek

Senger Creek

John Muir Trail

Shooting Star Meadow

Florence Lake Trail

Muir Trail Ranch

Blayney Hot Springs

Blayney Meadows

To Florence Lake

South Fork San Joaquin River

Sierra National Forest

John Muir Wilderness

2 MILES

2 KILOMETERS

N

0   1   2

0   1   2

HIGH WATERS

The ford of **Evolution Creek**  in Evolution Meadow is perhaps the most feared water crossing in the Sierra due to its high, wide, swift-moving waters and the fact that it turns into a bit of a roaring deathtrap just downstream. If traveling through in early summer, during peak snowmelt, consider taking the alternate route offered 2 miles into this leg for a slightly mellower crossing. The alternate rejoins the PCT on the far side of the usual crossing.

Begin near **McClure Meadow**, where a use trail descends to a massive camp (**McClure Camp**), which makes for a fantastic place to spend the night. From here, quickly cross a small stream ⬦, then pass the **McClure Meadow Ranger Station**, where you can gain intel about the much feared Evolution Creek crossing ahead. Another camping option arrives 0.3 mile past the first, tucked under the trees to your left (**Camp 32**), with a slightly larger area appearing at 0.6 mile (**Camp 33**); both offer access to **Evolution Creek** ⬦.

Pass through a slightly complicated stock gate to cross another stream ⬦ at 1 mile. Another mile ahead, begin to walk alongside **Evolution Meadow**, where a sign indicates an alternate crossing of Evolution Creek. Afterward, more forested campsites appear, with water ⬦ access nearby (**Camp 34**). A stream ⬦ drains over the trail at 2.7 miles, nothing compared to **Evolution Creek** ⬦ 0.1 mile ahead. It's possible to shuffle against the current when the water is low, but if the "creek" appears too beastly for mere mortals to navigate, backtrack to take the alternate route.

Dry your feet for a short bit of uphill before descending along now-foaming Evolution Creek, whose waters can't wait to cascade into the South Fork San Joaquin River below. Zigzag through fragrant pines until the rocky trail deposits you near a large camp to the right at 4.1 miles (**Camp 35**); another site appears less than 0.25 mile ahead, just before a scenic wooden bridge over the **South Fork San Joaquin River** ⬦. On the other side, meet a trail junction marked for Goddard Canyon (**Goddard Canyon Trail**) on your left or Florence Lake on the right—choose the latter.

Cross a small footbridge at 4.4 miles to walk along a small feeder stream ⬦, then find a small campsite on the right (**Camp 36**) about 0.25 mile before reaching a third (but not final) bridge, a large steel-and-wood construction. As you move out of the tree cover, you are now walking along a mix of sage and manzanita dotted with occasional pines. The upside to the sunnier surrounds is a clear view down to the South Fork San Joaquin River, which is quite beautiful in its own right. Trees reappear in **Aspen Meadow**, which makes up for its lack of meadow with a small stand of aspens, whose leaves quake with the slightest breeze. It's a tight squeeze, but you might be able to fit two tents into a small spot on the left, just past a seasonal stream ⬦ at 6.5 miles (**Aspen Camp**).

Look to the left at 7.1 miles to search for a large stone engraved with "1917 Muir Trail." The "**John Muir Rock**" is nearly impossible to spot, but makes for a nice photo op once located. Past this, a few more campsites appear down to your left, situated between the rising trail and rushing river under a canopy of Jeffrey pines—the first at 7.4 miles (**Camp 37**), the second less than 0.25 mile ahead. Find a few more spots tucked between manzanita bushes to your left (**Piute Camp**) at 7.8 miles, just

A few key bridges help ease the way across the roiling South Fork San Joaquin River.

before crossing the final bridge on this leg, which spans **Piute Creek ⓞ**. Unless descending to Muir Trail Ranch, the next sure water source is 5.6 miles ahead at Senger Creek—tank up here, especially since the next leg begins with a sun-baked uphill grind.

Wave goodbye to **Kings Canyon National Park** as you enter the **Sierra National Forest** and **John Muir Wilderness**. Stay straight toward Florence Lake and Selden Pass at a trail junction with the **Piute Pass Trail**, which travels about 17 miles through Humphreys Basin and over Piute Pass, landing at the North Lake trailhead. After a brief foray across sunny manzanita slopes, the remainder

of this leg ducks into a thick forest of Jeffrey pines. About 0.25 mile past the bridge, see if you can find a rustic cabin hidden near the trail; a faint use path guides the way. Known as the "**John Muir Trail Cabin**," it's named for the man who dedicated much of himself to these mountains.

After a dry, forested descent, reach this leg's end at 9.6 miles at a junction with the **Florence Lake Trail**. It's possible to depart the PCT here, hiking 1.5 miles to **Muir Trail Ranch**, a popular resupply location. The **South Fork San Joaquin River ⓞ** continues to the left of this side route, easily accessible near a campsite on your left about 0.4 mile down the trail. You can also find

MAGIC BUCKETS

Muir Trail Ranch is a small mountain resort located 5.5 miles from Florence Lake via the Florence Lake Trail. Cabins are rarely available for walk-ups, so make reservations in advance. If you are not staying at the Ranch, services are limited to water refills **O**, power access, a small (foodless) gear shop, and resupply (fee required). For the latter, follow the very detailed instructions on the ranch's website to ship your package. When you arrive, follow more instructions to retrieve it, then head over to a tented area to dig through your spoils with gleeful abandon. The resort also runs a "hiker bucket" system where people dump unwanted food and supplies into a mesmerizing array of five-gallon buckets, divvied up by contents like a free, outdoor grocery store. In addition to grabbing powdered drink mixes, candy bars, and soup, I was able to apply deodorant for the first time in weeks, my friend fixed another's hiking pole, and we sat down to a delicious scavenged meal of canned chicken, melted processed cheese slices, and tortillas.

camping near (but not at) Muir Trail Ranch by taking a spur toward Blayney Hot Springs just before descending to the ranch itself. Reach those relaxing waters by crossing the feisty **South Fork San Joaquin River O**; luckily, the campsites are located on the near side. Overuse has been a problem in recent years, although the Forest Service is working to restore the area—camp high instead of next to the trail or water.

CAMP-TO-CAMP MILEAGE

McClure Meadow to Camp 32 . . . . 0.3
Camp 32 to Camp 33 . . . . 0.3
Camp 33 to Camp 34 . . . . .1.4
Camp 34 to Camp 35 . . . . .2.1
Camp 35 to Camp 36 . . . . 0.9
Camp 36 to Aspen Camp 1.5
Aspen Camp to Camp 37 . . . . 0.9
Camp 37 to Piute Camp 0.4

FLORENCE LAKE TRAIL TO TUOLUMNE MEADOWS

WHILE IT DOESN'T BOAST quite the same amount of showstopper terrain you saw in the heart of the High Sierra, this final jaunt has more than its fair share of towering peaks, sparkling lakes, and trout-filled creeks.

Begin with a grueling ascent toward Selden Pass, stopping to enjoy the wildflower-strewn shores of Sallie Keyes Lakes along the way. Equally impressive is sprawling, island-filled Marie Lake, a perfect spot to seek tranquility before plunging down toward the raging waters of Bear Creek. After crossing the wily waterway, traverse its idyllic drainage and grunt out an ascent of equally notorious Bear Ridge. From here, you'll find a number of ways to reach the hiker haven of Vermilion Valley Resort across Lake Thomas Edison.

Once recharged, motivate yourself up to Silver Pass and plunge down toward burbling Fish Creek and grassy Tully Hole. As you near exit points for the resort town of Mammoth Lakes, decide whether you want to detour to historic Red's Meadow Resort for a resupply, lunch, laundry—or even a night in one of their real, live beds. Pass the geologic wonder of Devils Postpile and wave goodbye to your John Muir Trail buddies as they diverge from the PCT for a bit, then ascend toward iconic Thousand Island Lake before a short (but steep) hop down to Rush Creek.

There's one last uphill slog to Donohue Pass, your gateway to Yosemite National Park, then it's smooth sailing down through lush Lyell Canyon, where you'll spot a rare breed known as "day hikers." Cast one last longing glance back at the glacier-draped high peaks before joining the tourist throngs in Tuolumne Meadows, then march straight over to the seasonal grill near the store and stuff your face with as much food as you can muster. You earned it!

DISTANCE 84.8 miles

STATE DISTANCE 857.7–942.5 miles

ELEVATION GAIN/LOSS +14,280/-13,570 feet

HIGH POINT 11,076 feet

BEST TIME OF YEAR July–Oct

PCTA SECTION LETTER H

LAND MANAGERS Sierra National Forest (High Sierra Ranger District, John Muir Wilderness), Inyo National Forest (Mammoth Ranger District, Ansel Adams Wilderness), Devils Postpile National Monument, Yosemite National Park (Yosemite Wilderness)

PASSES AND PERMITS Wilderness permits are required for all overnight trips in the Ansel Adams, John Muir, and Yosemite wilderness areas. Use fee or Interagency Annual Pass required if beginning in Yosemite National Park. California Campfire Permit.

MAPS AND APPS
- Halfmile's CA Section H
- USFS PCT Map #4 Central Sierra
- USGS Topo Quads: Mount Henry, Mount Hilgard, Florence Lake, Graveyard Peak, Bloody Mountain, Crystal Crag, Mammoth Mountain, Mount Ritter, Koip Peak, Vogelsang Peak, Tioga Pass
- Halfmile's PCT app
- Guthook's PCT app

Opposite: *Sunrise at Thousand Island Lake is nothing short of majestic.*

LEGS

1. Florence Lake Trail to Selden Pass
2. Selden Pass to Silver Pass
3. Silver Pass to Duck Pass Trail
4. Duck Pass Trail to Reds Meadow
5. Reds Meadow to Agnew Meadows
6. Agnew Meadows to Donohue Pass
7. Donohue Pass to Tuolumne Meadows

ACCESS
Florence Lake Trail
The Florence Lake Trail is reached via a lengthy and convoluted route that involves driving on winding mountain roads, possibly taking a boat, and hiking. If you're up for it, head north from Fresno on Highway 41, taking exit 128A for Highway 180 eastbound (toward Kings Canyon National Park). Drive about 1.4 miles, then keep left to take Route 168 eastbound (toward Clovis and Huntington Lake). Continue following this road for 67.4 miles and make a right onto Kaiser Pass Road, which will shortly dwindle to one hair-raising lane as you wind up the twisted mountain track. The end of the line is Florence Lake, which offers seasonal camping, groceries, recreation opportunities, and ferry service. Park here in the larger paved lot and either check in with the general store to arrange for boat transportation across the lake or hop on the trail, which skirts the southwest side of the lake to deposit you at Muir Trail Ranch in approximately 8 miles. From here, you have two options for reaching the

PCT—continue on the Florence Lake Trail for 1.6 miles, or bypass 1.8 miles of PCT by hopping on a steep "cutoff" trail on the left.

Tuolumne Meadows
From Mammoth Lakes, head north on US Highway 395 (toward Lee Vining). Travel for 25 miles, then make a left onto Highway 120 westbound (Tioga Road), which is usually closed by late fall after the first significant snowfall of the year (typically reopening sometime between mid-May and late June). This road leads directly into Yosemite, and you will have to pay an entrance fee (or show your Interagency Annual Pass) to complete your journey. Travel 19 miles to reach the trailhead on the south side of the intersection of Highway 120 and Yosemite National Park Road. Overnight parking can be confusing in this area. Directly across Highway 120 from this section's end is the Lembert Dome Picnic Area parking lot, but this is not an approved location for overnight parking while backpacking on the PCT. You will likely need to park at the Dog Lake or Wilderness Center parking areas; the friendly rangers at the Wilderness Center will review options when you pick up your permit.

NOTES
Cities and Services
Muir Trail Ranch is a private guest ranch located near the southern trailhead; services are limited to resupply, water, and electrical outlets for non-guests. At the northern trailhead, Tuolumne Meadows has a seasonal array of services, including a post office, groceries, grill, camping, and other lodging.

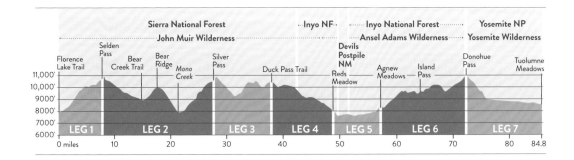

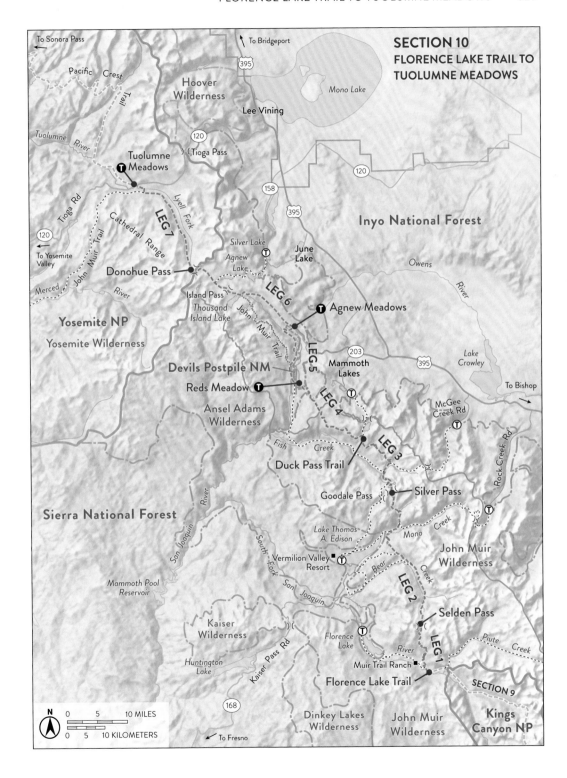

SECTION 10
FLORENCE LAKE TRAIL TO
TUOLUMNE MEADOWS

To Sonora Pass
To Bridgeport
395
Pacific   Crest
Hoover
Wilderness
Mono Lake
Trail
Tuolumne   River
Lee Vining
120
Tioga Pass
Tuolumne
Meadows
158
395
Inyo National Forest
LEG 7
Lyell Fork
120
Tioga Rd
Cathedral Range
To Yosemite
Valley
John Muir Trail
Silver Lake
Agnew
Lake
June
Lake
Owens
Donohue Pass
LEG 6
Merced
River
Island Pass
Thousand
Island Lake
River
Agnew Meadows
Yosemite NP
John   Muir   Trail
Yosemite Wilderness
LEG 5
Lake
Crowley
To Bishop
Devils Postpile NM
203
Mammoth
Lakes
395
Reds Meadow
LEG 4
McGee
Creek Rd
Ansel Adams
Wilderness
Rock Creek Rd
Fish   Creek
LEG 3
Duck Pass Trail
Goodale Pass
Silver Pass
Sierra National Forest
River
Lake Thomas
A. Edison
Mono   Creek
John Muir
Wilderness
Mammoth Pool
Reservoir
Vermilion Valley
Resort
Bear   Creek
LEG 2
San Joaquin
South Fork
San   Joaquin
Selden Pass
Kaiser
Wilderness
Florence
Lake
LEG 1
River
Piute   Creek
Huntington
Lake
Kaiser Pass Rd
Muir Trail Ranch
SECTION 9
168
Florence Lake Trail
To Fresno
Dinkey Lakes
Wilderness
John Muir
Wilderness
Kings
Canyon NP

N
0   5   10 MILES
0   5   10 KILOMETERS

The ascent from Agnew Meadows is dotted with wildflowers in early summer.

Camping and Fire Restrictions

Camp only in well-established sites, at least 100 feet from water. Camping is not allowed within 0.25 mile of the Thousand Island Lake outlet, within 300 feet of the Purple Lake outlet, or along the northbound PCT outside of established camp-grounds beginning 5.5 miles south of Tuolumne Meadows in Yosemite National Park. Fires are allowed only in existing fire rings, and are not allowed within 0.25 mile of the Thousand Island Lake outlet, in the Purple Lake drainage, above 9600 feet in the Yosemite Wilderness, and above 10,000 feet in the Ansel Adams and John Muir

wilderness areas. Check for seasonal fire restrictions in Sierra and Inyo National Forests, Devils Postpile National Monument, and Yosemite National Park before heading out.

Hazards

River and creek crossings can be dangerous at times of high water, particularly during early summer snowmelt—Bear Creek is typically the trickiest crossing in this section. Snow and ice may linger, especially on north-facing slopes and passes well into the summer months—use of traction devices and an ice axe may be required to safely navigate these areas. It is advisable to plan your trips over the high passes for morning—if there's snow present, it will be firmer and easier to navigate, and you'll face less danger of being caught in one of the afternoon thunder storms frequent in the High Sierra.

Other

Use of an approved bear-resistant food storage container is required for overnight travel in these areas: just south of Lake Virginia to just north of Duck Pass Trail; just north of Deer Creek to just south of Reds Meadow, and north of Devils Postpile National Monument to Tuolumne Meadows. Food storage lockers ("bear boxes") are to be used only by hikers camping in their vicinity; caching of food or equipment is not allowed. Pets, with the exception of certified service animals, are not allowed on any trails in Yosemite National Park, including the PCT.

SUGGESTED ITINERARIES

Camps are either viewable from the trail or located within a few tenths of a mile from the noted location unless otherwise specified in leg descriptions. You may want to resupply during this section, especially if continuing your hike from the previous section. Most people choose to visit Muir Trail Ranch, Vermilion Valley Resort, or Red's Meadow Resort to accomplish this, so plan your trip accordingly.

7 DAYS

		Miles
Day 1	Florence Lake Trail to Camp 2	13.2
Day 2	Camp 2 to Pocket Camp	10.2
Day 3	Pocket Camp to Purple Camp	12.5
Day 4	Purple Camp to Reds Meadow Campground	13.1
Day 5	Reds Meadow Campground to Thousand Island Camp	16.2
Day 6	Thousand Island Camp to Lyell Bridge Camp	9.2
Day 7	Lyell Bridge Camp to Tuolumne Meadows	10.4

6 DAYS

Day 1	Florence Lake Trail to Bear Camp	14.6
Day 2	Bear Camp to Squaw Camp	14.2
Day 3	Squaw Camp to Deer Camp	14.5
Day 4	Deer Camp to Upper Soda Springs Campground	10.0
Day 5	Upper Soda Springs Campground to Camp 12	15.9
Day 6	Camp 12 to Tuolumne Meadows	15.6

5 DAYS

Day 1	Florence Lake Trail to Camp 3	15.4
Day 2	Camp 3 to Camp 9	16.1
Day 3	Camp 9 to Reds Meadow Campground	17.5
Day 4	Reds Meadow Campground to Thousand Island Camp	16.2
Day 5	Thousand Island Camp to Tuolumne Meadows	19.6

1 FLORENCE LAKE TRAIL TO SELDEN PASS

DISTANCE 7.9 miles

ELEVATION GAIN/LOSS
+3530/-500 feet

HIGH POINT 10,915 feet

CONNECTING TRAIL
Florence Lake Trail

ON THE TRAIL

Begin at the PCT's junction with the **Florence Lake Trail**, which offers a departure point for **Muir Trail Ranch ◑**, a popular resupply stop located in idyllic Blayney Meadows. If you're returning to the trail with a full stash of food, you'll notice the extra weight as the day's theme is Uphill, Then More Uphill . . . With a Side of Uphill. The climb starts off innocently enough with a stroll through fragrant pine forest interspersed with bright green hillsides of manzanita. At 1.8 miles, reach an unnamed "cutoff" trail on the left that descends sharply to meet the Florence Lake Trail, offering a shortcut back to the PCT from Muir Trail Ranch for northbound travelers who don't mind skipping a little bit of mileage.

The trail toughens up a bit from here—a quick glance at your topo map offers the grim news that you're ascending progressively steepening slopes for the next 2 miles. I got through this with sheer grit, determination, and a *lot* of saltwater taffy. The scenery also helps things along—after hiking past some gorgeous western junipers, zigzag up open slopes clothed in manzanita, with views back down to Blayney Meadows, Shooting Star Meadow, and beyond. It's smart to knock this segment out in the early hours (or late in the day) to avoid overheating.

If things feel a bit hot under the collar, rejoice when you're spit back into the forest on more level ground, reaching the refreshing waters of **Senger Creek ◑** at 3.8 miles. Secure in the knowledge that you've accomplished the steepest gain of this leg, continue along a more gradual ascent, where mountaineer shooting stars and asters sprinkle color around the lush understory. Less than 1 mile up from the creek crossing, pass through a relatively large meadow, where it's possible to find seasonal water in early summer. Camping is available just a short bit afterward to your left in a large, tree-lined clearing (**Camp 1**) right before crossing a small stream ◑.

If you think the surrounds are pretty now, just wait until you reach **Sallie Keyes Creek ◑**, outlet for **Sallie Keyes Lakes ◑**, at the 6-mile mark—both Sallie Keyes Creek and Senger Creek flow downslope to keep Blayney Meadows well watered.

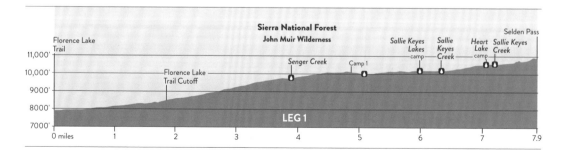

Opposite: *The climb up from the Florence Lake Trail is sweaty, but beautiful.*

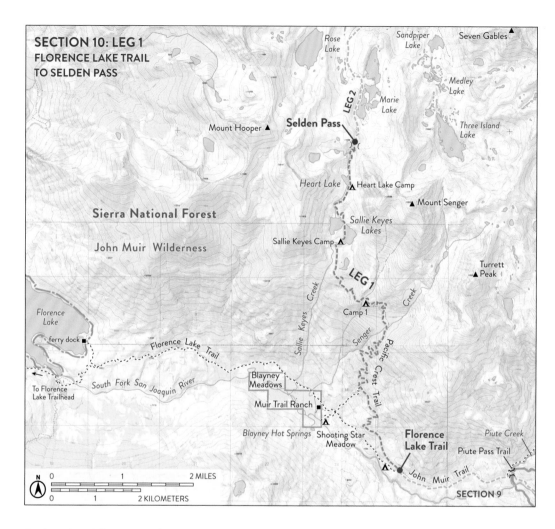

Soak in the idyllic surroundings, where the bright blue waters sit tucked just west of Mount Senger. Some trivia: the lakes are named for Sallie Keyes Shipp, daughter of some of Muir Trail Ranch's early owners. If you want to relax a while, look for a faint use trail jutting off to the right before crossing the outlet, leading to spots near the south shore of the first lake; more appear in the forest on the far side (**Sallie Keyes Camp**).

As you walk along the lakeshore, trout beckon—and don't be surprised to see any number of anglers, some of them day hikers from Muir Trail Ranch. Cross **Sallie Keyes Creek** ⬤ a second

time, here acting as connector between the upper and lower lakes. Sadly, your shoreline stroll is over as you meander uphill along rocky bluffs. Views back to the southeast offer some comfort, as do the wildflowers sprouting out of nearly every crack in the granite during early summer. After crossing more water at 6.6 miles, begin to follow the path of Sallie Keyes Creek more closely; the wet stuff is nearby for much of the rest of this leg.

The creek cascades down the narrowing canyon, and it's sometimes hard to know which is prettier—the views ahead, or the ones behind. Use your imagination to see the namesake shape of **Heart Lake** ahead as you rise past it at 7.1 miles; a use trail departs to the right, where you'll find a few campsites tucked into the rocks (**Heart Lake Camp**). Cross **Sallie Keyes Creek** ⬤ again just ahead, squiggling along a vibrant green path to reach **Selden Pass** at 7.9 miles. This perch, named for Selden S. Hooper, a member of the United States Geological Survey (this is the same guy nearby Mount Hooper is named for), offers a stunning vista over island-dotted Marie Lake, whose waters you'll skirt on the next leg.

CAMP-TO-CAMP MILEAGE

Florence Lake Trail to Camp 1 . . . . 4.8
Camp 1 to Sallie Keyes Camp 1.2
Sallie Keyes Camp to Heart Lake Camp 1.1

2 SELDEN PASS TO SILVER PASS

DISTANCE 19.3 miles

ELEVATION GAIN/LOSS
+4120/-4270 feet

HIGH POINT 10,915 feet

CONNECTING TRAILS
Lake Italy Trail, Bear Creek Trail, Bear Ridge Trail, Edison Lake Trail, Mono Pass Trail

ON THE TRAIL

Selden Pass offers stunning views of **Marie Lake** ⬤, whose island-speckled waters you'll reach shortly. Wave goodbye to the marmots no doubt eyeing your pack and head down a series of gentle switchbacks dotted with penstemon, heather, and aster. When you reach the lake, wander over and sit for a while, enjoying views of the impressive pyramid formation of Seven Gables across the way.

Cross the lake's outlet ⬤ just under 1 mile into this leg and let birdsong guide you down a slabby path through lodgepole pines and mountain hemlock to meet the **Rose Lake Trail** running through vibrant green **Rosemarie Meadow** on the left at 2.3 miles. Reach another junction just ahead, this time with the **Lou Beverly Lake Trail** on the right. At 0.3 mile past the first junction, reach a large clearing with room for several tents (**West Fork Camp**), just before crossing the **West Fork Bear Creek** ⬤. A more difficult ford appears when you reach the main **Bear Creek** ⬤ below at 3.5 miles. You'll wet your feet no matter which way you cross, and it's better to wade rather than try to balance on slippery rocks—I watched several people tumble into the cold water. Look downstream for an easier crossing when the water is high with snowmelt runoff.

Dry off your toes (and possibly your gear), then continue straight past the **Seven Gables Lakes Trail**

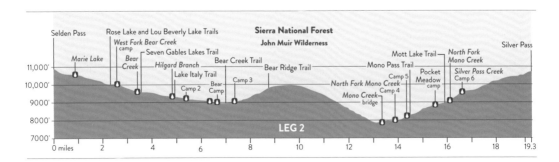

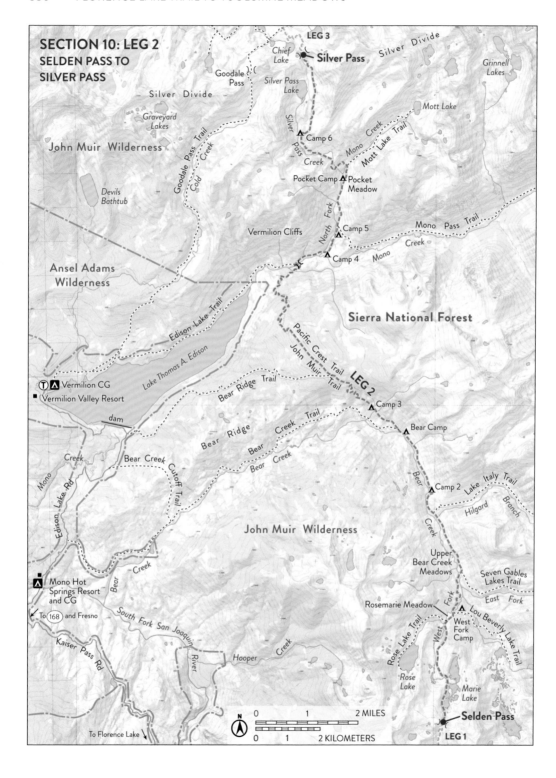

SECTION 10: LEG 2
SELDEN PASS TO
SILVER PASS

LEG 3

Chief Lake
Silver Pass
Silver Divide
Grinnell Lakes

Goodale Pass
Silver Pass Lake

Silver Divide

Graveyard Lakes

Mott Lake

Mono Creek

John Muir Wilderness

Goodale Pass Trail

Cold Creek

Silver Pass

Camp 6
Silver Pass Creek

Mott Lake Trail

Devils Bathtub

Pocket Camp
Pocket Meadow

Mono Pass Trail

Ansel Adams Wilderness

Vermilion Cliffs
North Fork
Camp 5
Mono Creek

Camp 4

Edison-Lake-Trail

Sierra National Forest

Pacific Crest Trail
John Muir Trail
LEG 2

Lake Thomas A. Edison

Bear Ridge Trail

Camp 3

Vermilion CG
Vermilion Valley Resort

Bear Camp

dam

Bear Ridge

Bear Creek Trail

Bear Creek

Lake Italy Trail

Mono Creek

Bear Creek Cutoff Trail

Bear Creek

Camp 2

Hilgard Branch

Bear Creek

Edison Lake Rd

John Muir Wilderness

Upper Bear Creek Meadows

Seven Gables Lakes Trail

Mono Hot Springs Resort and CG

Bear Creek

East Fork

Rosemarie Meadow

West Fork

Lou Beverly Lake Trail

To 168 and Fresno

Rose Lake Trail

West Fork Camp

Kaiser Pass Rd

South Fork San Joaquin River

Hooper Creek

Rose Lake

Marie Lake

Selden Pass

N
0   1   2 MILES
0   1   2 KILOMETERS

LEG 1

To Florence Lake

Marie Lake is a gorgeous sight even on a stormy day.

to begin a peaceful stroll through the fringes of **Upper Bear Creek Meadows**, falling back into the pines along Bear Creek. The water is mellower here, and as long as you don't mind fending off hordes of mosquitos, there are a few opportunities to take a dip or stay the night. Cross multipronged **Hilgard Branch** ⭘ at 4.8 miles, where a variety of logs and rocks offer a (mostly) dry route. Afterward, pass another junction, this time with the **Lake Italy Trail**. Each of these paths tempts discovery of even more remote lakes and stunning views—come back and explore when you have the opportunity.

The first campsite arrives at 5.3 miles, with several spots tucked under a stand of lodgepole pines (**Camp 2**). Continue strolling through the thick mosquitos—I mean, *forest*—crossing a sizeable stream ⭘ about 1 mile past the camp. There's a larger snooze spot 0.3 mile ahead (**Bear Camp**); a use trail leads to creek access on the

left ⭘. Just ahead, the **Bear Creek Trail** splits off to the left, offering the first of several detour routes to Vermilion Valley Resort, a popular resupply location on the west shore of Lake Thomas Edison (also called Edison Lake), whose waters are dammed as part of a hydroelectric project.

From here, begin the much-dreaded climb up **Bear Ridge**. Aspens pop up alongside pines, and the ground turns soggy in early summer—at times, it feels like you're walking through a mud bath rather than on a trail. However, the dampness encourages wildflower growth—my favorite being the speckled blooms of Kelley's tiger lily. Seasonal water abounds during the first part of the ascent, the first flow arriving via a small two-branch stream ⭘ at 7.4 miles. Just after, three small campsites appear in a row, each about 0.1 mile from the last (**Camp 3**); there are also a few seasonal flows ⭘ in this area.

R & R AT VVR

You'll find several ways to access **Vermilion Valley Resort** (VVR) if you're hoping for some resupply and relaxation. You can depart via the Bear Creek Trail, eventually turning right onto the **Bear Creek Cutoff Trail** to end up on **Kaiser Pass Road** 10.2 miles from the PCT; make a right onto the road, then walk across the dam and follow obvious tire tracks to the resort. You can also hop on the Bear Ridge Trail, which descends 5.7 miles to the spillway. A third option is the Edison Lake Trail, which traverses the water's north shore to reach VVR 4.8 miles later. Finally, you can catch a seasonal ferry across the lake itself; call ahead or look for a sign on the trail to find cost and schedule information. No matter how you get there, VVR offers a rustic experience, with an oddball assortment of trailers, cabins, and campsites dotting the lakeside resort. Recreation opportunities abound, and you can do laundry, shower, shop in a small convenience store, and gobble down tasty pie in the café. The resort also coordinates resupply packages for hikers—visit their website or call for more information.

Continue up through mixed forest, including a smattering of pretty red firs, to reach a junction with the **Bear Ridge Trail** at 8.9 miles, which offers another route to VVR. If you have cell reception here, call the resort to inquire about their seasonal ferry service across Edison Lake, which offers another way to reach fresh food and flush toilets. The trail then mellows out as you contour along forested slopes, until beginning a lengthy switchback descent on the north side of Bear Ridge. This segment can feel maddeningly long, especially if you're already indulging in pre-resupply food fantasies—my buddy and I spent at least a half hour here ranking our favorite potato products. I chose crinkle-cut fries.

Even if you're not dreaming of fried delights, a distraction arrives in the form of views directly north to the striking **Vermilion Cliffs**. Finally, descend into a moist forest filled with ferns, cottonwoods, and other delightful greenery, then cross a few streams 🌊 to reach a wood and steel bridge above beautiful **Mono Creek** 🌊 at 13.1 miles. Wave goodbye to Bear Ridge, cross the span, then decide whether you want to continue on the PCT (turn right) or head toward VVR (stay straight on the **Edison Lake Trail**).

Continuing on, ascend through mixed conifers to reach the **North Fork Mono Creek** 🌊 at 13.8 miles; a few campsites sit hidden in the trees (**Camp 4**). Sometimes it's possible to cross

just upstream on large boulders, but it may be safer to just wade. Head uphill with more gusto, weaving around manzanita and boulders to find another campsite on the right at 14.4 miles (**Camp 5**), with creek 🌊 access. At 0.1 mile later, pass the **Mono Pass Trail** on your right, which leads to the Mosquito Flat Trailhead just under 16 miles east.

Forest cover reappears for a while, and the scenery becomes prettier as the North Fork cascades down past **Pocket Meadow** just over 1 mile ahead, where it's possible to find a few campsites (**Pocket Camp**) and water access 🌊. Not 0.5 mile ahead, reach a junction with the **Mott Lake Trail**, which angles up sharply to your right. Face a second ford of **North Fork Mono Creek** 🌊, rowdier than the first—wade or cross carefully on large boulders upstream.

It's time now to head straight up the cliffs in front of you via an impressive (and impressively steep) segment of trail. Quickly meet up with a waterfall created by **Silver Pass Creek** 🌊 at 16.1 miles, the latter continuing down the sheer cliff just below—carefully navigate this precipitous crossing, which may be possible along a line of rocks. The terrain mellows as you near the top of the climb, wandering through meadow-fringed forest to reach a second crossing of **Silver Pass Creek** 🌊 less than 1 mile past the first. Dance across boulders to find a few campsites shortly thereafter (**Camp 6**).

The canyon narrows as you ascend then widens as you close in on Silver Pass. Tree cover disappears as alpine meadows take over, and these provide a few seasonal stream **O** crossings before you venture past **Silver Pass Lake** on the left and a small tarn on the right. Reach **Silver Pass** itself at 19.3 miles; the view here is not as breathtaking as some of the other Sierra passes, but it improves as you continue the ascent—yes, I'm sorry to say, there's more uphill to start the next leg!

CAMP-TO-CAMP MILEAGE

Selden Pass to West Fork Camp	2.6
West Fork Camp to Camp 2	2.7
Camp 2 to Bear Camp	1.4
Bear Camp to Camp 3	0.8
Camp 3 to Camp 4	6.3
Camp 4 to Camp 5	0.6
Camp 5 to Pocket Camp	1.1
Pocket Camp to Camp 6	1.7

3 SILVER PASS TO DUCK PASS TRAIL

DISTANCE 10.8 miles

ELEVATION GAIN/LOSS
+2470/-3080 feet

HIGH POINT 10,938 feet

CONNECTING TRAILS
Goodale Pass Trail, Fish Creek Trail, McGee Pass Trail, Purple Lake Trail, Duck Pass Trail

ON THE TRAIL

Generally, the upward struggle toward a pass means you're rewarded with some glorious descent directly afterward. Not so with **Silver Pass**, since the trail builders decided to taunt hikers with a bit more uphill after the gap. This part is over quickly as you finally head down a set of tiny zigzags that unveil the lake-filled surrounds. Spy **Warrior Lake** to the right, then **Chief Lake** down to the left as

you pop over a ridgeline; a use trail descends to the latter around 0.8 mile.

Continue along granite slabs and talus to reach a junction with the **Goodale Pass Trail** just over 1 mile in. This route heads over its namesake pass, then descends to reach the Edison Lake Trail (described in the previous leg), offering an alternate access point to VVR. Otherwise, stay straight to wander through meadowy bliss, eventually descending toward beautiful **Squaw Lake O**, a sparkling, cliff-ringed gem filled by the outflow from Warrior Lake. Reach its outlet at 1.6 miles and make a long traverse via a series of well-placed rocks. Idyllic campsites are located on the far side, although it's important to camp well away from the water itself (**Squaw Camp**).

Leaving the alpine wonder behind, slip down into the trees via a set of switchbacks. A subpar campsite (**Camp 7**) appears in a small clearing on the left at 2.3 miles, but better (and bigger)

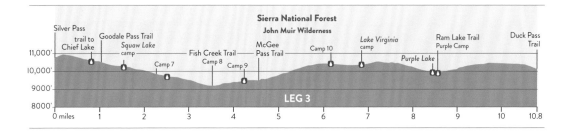

Stay the night near Purple Lake to discover how it earned its name.

spots await. Waltz over a small wooden footbridge spanning a stream ◐ 0.3 mile ahead, with several more small wades to follow. These waters, created by the outflow from both Squaw Lake and Lake of the Lone Indian, drain into much larger Fish Creek. Before reaching the latter, pass the **Fish Creek Trail** junction (signed for Cascade Valley) at 3.6 miles—stay right toward Tully Hole. Just afterward, look to the left to find a few sandy campsites (**Camp 8**). Another good-sized clearing appears on the left just ahead, after you cross a seasonal flow ◐.

The downhill reverie ends as your quads are called to duty, but a quick distraction arrives when Fish Creek roars into view 1 mile past the junction as you cross via a large steel bridge. The water tumbles down canyon with power and grace, creating an impressive waterfall effect; photo-taking resistance is futile. Once you've memorialized its majesty, begin hiking along **Fish Creek** ◐ itself. Small swimming holes occasionally reveal themselves, but campsites are much harder to come by in the narrow canyon; a decent spot appears at 4.3 miles (**Camp 9**).

Reach a junction with the **McGee Pass Trail** 0.3 mile ahead; this departs right toward the McGee Creek trailhead 15 miles away. Now

the creekside stroll turns into an uphill grind as you ascend a steep, wildflower-dotted slope along tightly placed switchbacks, revealing a few seasonal flows along the way. The upside to this slog is that it offers incredible vistas over

MAMMOTH LAKES

The Duck Pass Trail offers the first of several options to detour into the resort town of Mammoth Lakes. This is one of my favorite non-PCT hikes in the area since it winds past the otherworldly blue waters of **Duck Lake** ◐ before popping through Duck Pass on the Mammoth Crest, which offers a jaw-dropping perch over the basin below, filled with more gemstone lakes. Once you drag yourself away from the beauty, descend to the Duck Pass Trailhead at the south end of **Coldwater Campground** (itself located at the southeastern tip of Lake Mary), where it's just a short drive or hitch into town. There, you'll find multiple lodging options, grocery stores, restaurants, a post office, and several outfitters as well as a popular brewery. Bottoms up!

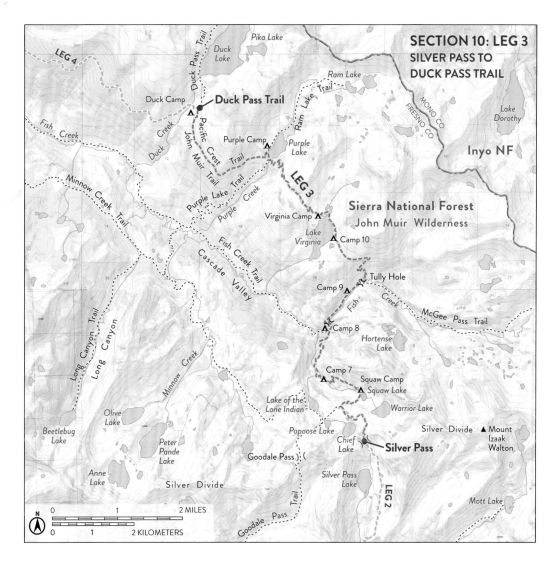

the snowcapped Silver Divide and back down to lush **Tully Hole**, the latter dubbed in honor of a Forest Service ranger named Gene Tully who enjoyed relaxing in this grassy little paradise with his livestock.

The hard work is over as you land in relatively flat terrain offering a few campsites scattered around large boulders and shady stands of hemlock and lodgepole; the best sites are located on your left at 6.2 miles (**Camp 10**), situated between a small pothole lake and much larger, beautiful **Lake Virginia ◐**. It's possible to pop over to either from

your perch. Walk along the lakeshore, gawking at the deep blue waters, then cross its picturesque inlet at 6.7 miles. Look for a use trail less than 0.25 mile ahead on the left if you want to stay and swoon a while (**Virginia Camp**). While the sites themselves are tucked into the trees high above the lake, it's easy enough to find your way down to the shore for a dip.

The rollercoaster ride continues as you head up for a bit, and you then descend past an obvious deposit of avalanche debris. Trekking poles come in handy as you stumble around on ankle-rolling rocks, especially when **Purple Lake** ⚫ comes into view and threatens to steal your attention. Reach a small wooden bridge that spans its outlet at 8.6 miles; camping is not allowed within 300 feet. The **Purple Lake Trail** banks left just ahead to connect with the Fish Creek Trail in Cascade Valley; instead, stay right and leave the lakeshore all too soon to intersect the **Ram Lake Trail** 0.1 mile past the outlet. If you want to stay and see why Purple Lake earns its name (hint: early bird gets the worm), find some mediocre spots just below the junction and better ones if you head toward Ram Lake and explore south of the trail (**Purple Camp**).

If you're not a morning person, continue left to begin a gradual uphill contour around an unnamed high point, enjoying views into Cascade Valley far below, the distant burbling of Fish Creek echoing through the canyon. An eventual descent leads into a side canyon, where you reach the **Duck Pass Trail** (signed for Duck Lake) and this leg's end at 10.8 miles. In early summer, the headwaters of Duck Creek spill over the valley walls; you'll cross it during the next leg. Until then, decide whether you want to continue north on the PCT or detour toward Duck Lake, Duck Pass, and the ski town of Mammoth Lakes.

CAMP-TO-CAMP MILEAGE

Silver Pass to Squaw Camp 1.6
Squaw Camp to Camp 7. . . . . 0.7
Camp 7 to Camp 8 . . . . 1.3
Camp 8 to Camp 9 . . . . 0.7
Camp 9 to Camp 10 . . . . 1.9
Camp 10 to Virginia Camp 0.7
Virginia Camp to Purple Camp. 1.8

4 DUCK PASS TRAIL TO REDS MEADOW

DISTANCE 11 miles

ELEVATION GAIN/LOSS
+780/-3220 feet

HIGH POINT 10,220 feet

CONNECTING TRAILS
Duck Pass Trail, Crater Meadow Trail

ON THE TRAIL

Begin at the PCT's junction with the **Duck Pass Trail**, a gorgeous hike on its own. Duck Creek, the outflow from Duck Lake, spills down the canyon wall, creating a beautiful cascade in early summer. Descend toward the sound of rushing water to reach a small campsite on the left shortly before crossing **Duck Creek** ⚫ on a simple log bridge; intrepid campers can scout around to find a few more hidden spots in the area (**Duck Camp**). Tank up here since the next opportunity is over 5 miles ahead at Deer Creek.

The scenery won't change much over those miles, so the novelty will wane, but for now, it's impressive to walk high above Cascade Valley. Open slopes also offer lingering views of the Silver Divide, whose imposing crest you breached at Silver Pass on the last leg. Tree cover becomes thicker as you undulate along, with lodgepole pines eventually obscuring all but brief glimpses at the tall peaks. The forest is beautiful enough, though, if a bit uninspiring after all of that granite excitement. Speaking of rocks, you'll notice some very different ones lining the trail a few miles in— these pink stones are actually pumice deposits, a portent of volcanic magic ahead. Patience, patience.

The topography eventually mellows as you stroll through fragrant pines, many of them scattered on the ground like dropped matchsticks. While it might look like an epic bowling match

Red Cones offer a tantalizing glimpse of volcanic history.

happened in the vicinity, this is actually the result of the 2011 Devils Windstorm, which leveled an unthinkable number of trees with hurricane force. The effects become more pronounced as you near Reds Meadow at the end of this leg, where things turn downright apocalyptic for a bit—avoid pitching your tent underneath snags (aka "dead tree death traps"). Until then, the scenery pretties up as you descend to the swampy, lupine-filled meadows surrounding **Deer Creek** **0**, crossing it on a two-log bridge at 5.3 miles. There's ample opportunity for camping on either

GATHER, YE GEOLOGY FREAKS

Geology fans will be hard-pressed to move fast through this segment of trail since the greater Mammoth Lakes area is the result of both seismic and volcanic forces. Mammoth Mountain sits along the southwestern edge of what's known as the Long Valley Caldera, formed over 700,000 years ago when a violent eruption partially drained a massive magma chamber, causing it to collapse upon itself. The mountain itself is actually a volcanic dome; while it hasn't erupted in thousands of years, it still emits dangerously high concentrations of carbon dioxide gas derived from pressurized magma far below. A visit to nearby Horseshoe Lake demonstrates the obvious effects of the CO_2 emissions, which have killed off a large number of trees in the area. Skiers and snowshoers are warned to be particularly careful that they don't end up headfirst in a tree well, where gases can collect in lethal doses.

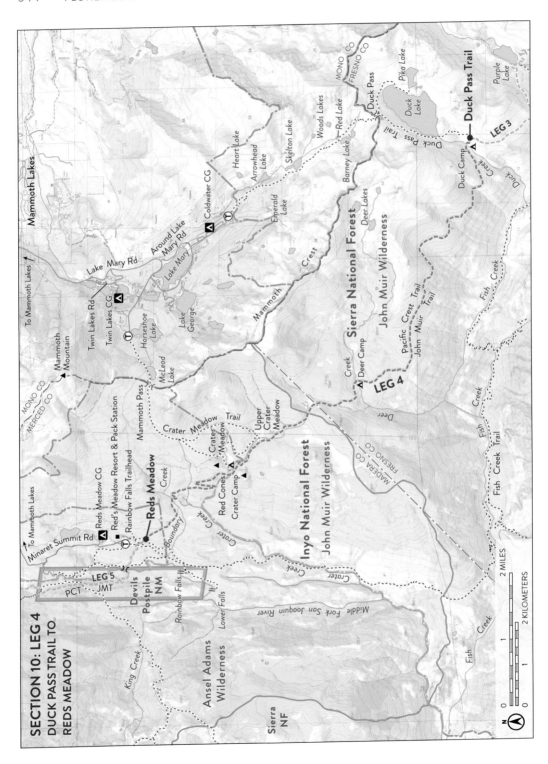

SECTION 10: LEG 4
**DUCK PASS TRAIL TO
REDS MEADOW**

A DEVILISH WIND

The Devils Windstorm raged between November 30 and December 1, 2011, its high velocity winds uprooting tens of thousands of trees throughout the Eastern Sierra. Perhaps nowhere shows the effects more than the denuded Reds Meadow Valley and Devils Postpile area, which previously sustained severe damage when the Rainbow Fire raged through in 1992. The effects of the windstorm (and fire) are still seen today, with snags and downed trees littering a wide swath of land. The Agnew Meadows Campground, toward the end of the next leg, was closed after the windstorm due to severe damage and has not reopened as of this writing—check with the Forest Service for updates.

side (**Deer Camp**)—and you'll be sharing all of that space with about a thousand other people, from fellow PCT hikers, to John Muir Trail travelers, to weekend backpackers who made the short trip from Reds Meadow or the Duck Pass Trail. I wrestled myself asleep to the sounds of a fellow camper's pan flute reverie; don't come here looking for peace and quiet.

Top off your water supply before leaving the hordes—the rest of the sources before Reds Meadow tend to be somewhat ephemeral, disappearing as summer progresses. Cross the first stream **O** at 6 miles, then a pair of smaller ones less than 1 mile ahead. A slightly better source is a branch of **Crater Creek O**, which you'll first cross on a

small wooden bridge at 7.2 miles. Cross again 0.3 mile ahead in **Upper Crater Meadow O**, then stay left at a junction with the **Crater Meadow Trail** (signed for Horseshoe Lake), which offers alternate access to Mammoth Lakes over Mammoth Pass. A third creek crossing **O** brings you to a gentle rise that offers a somewhat startling view of a giant red hill directly ahead along with another to the left. If you think these look like rusty volcanoes, you're not too far off—they're actually a pair of cinder cones (named, unsurprisingly, **Red Cones**) formed by ancient eruptions. From this vantage point, you also see the summit of Mammoth Mountain (and its resident ski machinery) just to the northeast; in winter, this massive peak is covered in snow and adrenaline junkies. Your perch also offers sightlines west to the jagged Minarets in the Ritter Range and down to lush Crater Meadow just below.

REDS MEADOW

Red's Meadow Resort & Pack Station is a rustic Sierra gem and a must-visit for most hikers passing through the area whether or not they're renting a cabin. While it's possible to send a resupply package here, you can also shop the small market, rifle through the hiker bin, or even grab a bite at the Mule House Café, which offers a limited, but tasty menu. On top of that, you'll find laundry facilities, showers, flush toilets, and other basic amenities. If you want to stake down a tent, head north through the resort to the **Reds Meadow Campground** (fee required).

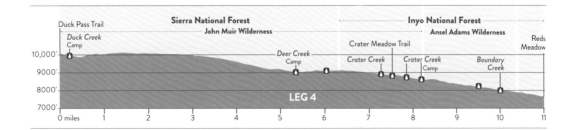

A snapshot of the destruction caused by the Devils Windstorm in 2011

Descend to reach a final crossing of **Crater Creek ⓞ** at 8.2 miles, with a camping area on the near side (**Crater Camp**). Just afterward, pass a connector on your right that meets up with the Crater Meadow Trail to Mammoth Pass and Horseshoe Lake. Ascend a small rise to score even better views of the Ritter Range, with the expansive **Reds Meadow Valley** opening up below, littered with thousands of wind-felled trees. Head down through lodgepole pine and red fir, then pass a spray of bright wildflowers and mosses that guard a spring-fed stream ⓞ at 9.5 miles. Tree cover thins and eventually disappears as you carve a path through massive amounts of downed trees. A chest-high fern jungle obscures a crossing with seasonal **Boundary Creek ⓞ**, adding to the strangeness of the surroundings. Reach the edge of the destruction—and this leg's end—at a junction with a side trail to **Red's Meadow Resort & Pack Station** at 11 miles. The PCT continues down to the left (not a hard left, however, which descends to Rainbow Falls), but you can head straight here to grab a shower, pick up your resupply, or enjoy a cold beer under the fragrant shade of real, live standing trees.

CAMP-TO-CAMP MILEAGE

Duck Pass Trail to Duck Camp 0.2
Duck Camp to Deer Camp 5.1
Deer Camp to Crater Camp 2.9
**Crater Camp to Reds Meadow
    Campground** 2.8

5 REDS MEADOW TO AGNEW MEADOWS

DISTANCE 8.1 miles

ELEVATION GAIN/LOSS
+1730/-1130 feet

HIGH POINT 8333 feet

CONNECTING TRAILS AND ROADS
Reds Meadow Trail, Devils Postpile Trail,
John Muir Trail, Upper Soda Springs
Campground Trail, Agnew Meadows Road

ON THE TRAIL

The biggest challenge of this leg might be moti-
vating yourself to keep walking, since there are
countless diversions along the way. Take it easy
and enjoy the distractions—it's a short segment,
so bounce off on as many side trips as you want!

As many great adventures do, this one begins
at a fork in the trail. The path straight ahead
is signed for **Red's Meadow Resort & Pack
Station 0** (detailed in the previous leg), a worthy detour for those dreaming of sleep, showers,
and burgers. A sharp left marks the first of several spurs that join to create the **Rainbow Falls
Trail**. Head left here for a scenic 1-mile side trip
to upper Rainbow Falls; add another 0.8 mile
if dropping down to the lower falls. Like many
detours in the area, this one is well worth it:
the snowmelt-swollen Middle Fork San Joaquin
River makes a dramatic drop of over 100 feet, the
resulting spray playing host to colorful prisms on a
sunny morning.

If you're a hydrophobic party pooper, make a
soft left onto a trail marked "PCT JMT North."
While the devastation from the Rainbow Fire and
Devils Windstorm is mostly over at this point,
you'll still find felled trees and debris scattered
throughout the forest all the way to this leg's
endpoint. Gawk at The Buttresses rising across
the valley, one of the area's numerous volcanic
formations spit from the earth's core many years
ago, then duck under the welcome shade of lodgepole pines. Reach a second Rainbow Falls Trail
junction 0.1 mile in, then a third just after that.
With all of these, a hard left heads to the falls, a
right to **Reds Meadow**, and the well-signed PCT

ALTERNATE ACCESS

Multiple entry points exist for this leg. The
seasonal Reds Meadow Shuttle offers a
number of stops between Reds Meadow
and Agnew Meadows, and you can drive
down Minaret Summit Road outside of the
shuttle's operating hours (it typically runs
during extended business hours) and operating season (typically between Memorial
Day weekend and early September) until
the road is closed by snowfall. A fee is
required whether you ride the shuttle or
drive your car. If you choose to begin the
leg at Red's Meadow Resort & Pack Station,
head south across the parking lot toward
the corral, passing a unique sign, then look
for a path pointing toward the PCT.

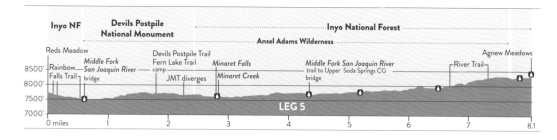

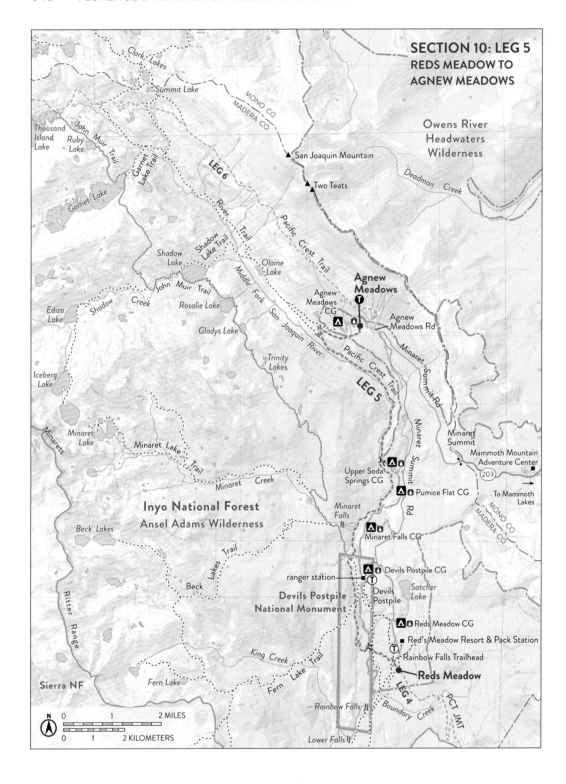

SECTION 10: LEG 5
REDS MEADOW TO
AGNEW MEADOWS

Owens River
Headwaters
Wilderness

Clark Lakes

Summit Lake

MONO CO
MADERA CO

San Joaquin Mountain

Two Teats

Deadman Creek

Thousand
Island
Lake

John
Muir
Trail

Ruby
Lake

LEG 6

Garnet
Lake Trail

Garnet Lake

River
Trail

Pacific Crest Trail

Shadow
Lake

Shadow
Lake Trail

Olaine
Lake

Agnew
Meadows

Agnew
Meadows
CG

Agnew
Meadows Rd

John Muir Trail

Ediza
Lake

Shadow Creek

Rosalie Lake

Middle Fork San Joaquin River

Pacific Crest Trail

LEG 5

Minaret Summit Rd

Gladys Lake

Iceberg
Lake

Trinity
Lakes

Minaret
Summit
Rd

Minaret
Summit

Mammoth Mountain
Adventure Center

Minarets

Minaret
Lake

Minaret Lake Trail

203

To Mammoth
Lakes

MONO CO
MADERA CO

Minaret Creek

Upper Soda
Springs CG

Pumice Flat CG

Inyo National Forest
Ansel Adams Wilderness

Beck Lakes

Minaret
Falls

Minaret Falls CG

Lakes Trail

Beck

Ritter Range

Devils Postpile
National Monument

ranger station

Devils
Postpile

Devils Postpile CG

Satcher
Lake

Reds Meadow CG

Red's Meadow Resort & Pack Station

King Creek

Rainbow Falls Trailhead

Sierra NF

Fern Lake Trail

Fern Lake

Reds Meadow

LEG 4

Boundary Creek

PCT JMT

Rainbow Falls

N

0   1   2 MILES

0   1   2 KILOMETERS

Lower Falls

DEVILS MAGIC

There is perhaps no more stunning geologic formation than the spookily geometric Devils Postpile. Its basalt stacks formed around 82,000 years ago, after a lava flow washed down and pooled in the area. The cooling process was rapid and uniform, resulting in the fractured hexagonal columns we see today. Although you have excellent views of the formation from the PCT, it's worth the side trip to stand at its base and truly feel the scope—and strangeness—of Mother Nature's magic. Hike to the top of the columns for a completely different take on the geologic phenomenon: over many years, glacial activity polished the rock smooth enough that it now looks like a beautifully crafted tile floor.

continues straight ahead. A final junction occurs just over 0.5 mile in; here, the right option is marked for Devils Postpile, but there's easier access ahead.

Pass into **Devils Postpile National Monument**, a thin rectangular preserve designated in 1911 to protect the Middle Fork San Joaquin River's watershed and the park's namesake geologic wonder, which we'll get to soon enough. In the meantime, let the sound of rustling aspens and rushing water guide you to a bridge over the **Middle Fork San Joaquin River ◐**. From here, ascend from shady flats to sparsely forested hillsides strewn with bouldery pumice deposits. A glance backward exposes Mammoth Mountain, whose curves offer kicks to summertime mountain bikers, and whose wintry slopes transform into one of California's most popular ski and snowboard destinations. Imagine that cool air as you continue sweating upward through mule-churned dust, eventually earning views down to the spectacular hexagonal columns of the **Devils Postpile** formation.

A four-way junction at 1.8 miles marks the **Fern Lake Trail** toward King Creek and Fern Lake, with a right-side spur toward Devils Postpile. It's worth the short 0.5-mile roundtrip to get up close and personal with the freaky formation. From there, it's a short walk to a ranger station, where you'll find flush toilets, garbage receptacles, and running water ⦾ during the operating season. There is also a campground (**Devils Postpile Campground**) and access to the seasonal shuttle.

Head straight to continue along the dusty slopes, reaching another junction at 2.3 miles. If you've been hiking with any **John Muir Trail** (JMT) travelers, now is the time to bid adieu—the two paths temporarily diverge (in a wood, technically), with your JMT buddies scooting uphill (signed for Minaret Lake, Shadow Lake, and Beck Lakes), and you continuing straight toward Minaret Falls. A right turn takes you back to Devils Postpile. None of the signs actually *say* JMT or PCT, but trust me on this one.

Drop back into thicker forest cover, heading outside Devils Postpile National Monument but staying within the **Ansel Adams Wilderness**, named for the famous landscape photographer. As promised on the last cluster of signs, the spidery flow of **Minaret Falls** ⦾ waits ahead; you'll hear it before you see it around 2.9 miles. Use trails lead to a small pool, which you'll likely share with any

number of human, canine, and mosquito friends. If you skip the side trip, there's still an opportunity to collect water when crossing the trickling remnants of cascade-creating **Minaret Creek** ⦾. If you come through in fall, it's likely that the whole area will have dried up, so time your visit for summertime if possible.

Red firs mingle with pines as you continue a gentle meander along the Middle Fork San Joaquin River. Cross the flow a final time via a concrete and wood bridge at 4.3 miles, offering the opportunity to carefully pick your way down its banks to tank up ⦾. The PCT continues to the left (toward Shadow Lake and Agnew Meadows) at the far end of the bridge, but an alternate path heads right to the **Upper Soda Springs Campground**, with typical campground amenities including water ⦾ plus access to the Reds Meadow Shuttle.

Continue strolling along the beautiful, crystalline Middle Fork, perhaps passing anglers teasing trout out of the water or bathers relaxing in swimming holes created as the river bends; it's easy enough to join them via multiple use trails. Cross a side stream ⦾ just under 1 mile from the junction, beginning a slight uphill trend, moving away from the water and along the steep canyon wall above. Don't feel too sad, though, as you now find company with a vibrant mix of pine, aspen, sagebrush, and early summer wildflowers. Cross a small seasonal flow ⦾ at 6.5 miles, then reach a junction 0.2 mile ahead—the left fork (signed for Shadow Lake) leads to the River Trail (another route to Thousand Island Lake), but you bank right toward Agnew Meadows. Ascend manzanita-cloaked slopes, whose sparseness offers beautiful views up canyon and even back to Mammoth Mountain once you begin up a series of short switchbacks.

Finish the upward wiggle at 7.3 miles at a junction with the **River Trail**; head right on gentler ground, shortly passing a sign marking the Ansel Adams Wilderness boundary. Here, you might also notice a faint, unmarked trail ascending to the left—this is an old access path to the **Agnew Meadows Campground**, which has been closed since the Devils Windstorm exacted

ALTERNATE ROUTE

If you can't bear to leave behind your trail buddies, it's possible to stay on the JMT until the two paths rejoin near Thousand Island Lake's outlet. This side trip is 14.1 miles (compared to the PCT's 13.9 miles between these two points), with plenty of spectacular beauty to steal your breath along the way. Camping is available near many of the lakes you encounter, except within 0.25 mile of the outlets for Garnet Lake and Thousand Island Lakes, within 300 feet of Shadow Lake, and anywhere along Shadow Creek.

Bathers enjoy the brisk waters of the Middle Fork San Joaquin River.

its toll in 2011. Every time I inquire with rangers, I'm told that it's supposed to open "next year," but several "next years" have come and gone. Still, I'm told that it should be up and running sometime in 2017—check with Inyo National Forest's Mammoth Lakes Ranger District before trying your luck.

Amble along a wide, dusty path to cross a small flow ⓞ at 7.8 miles. Although still in tree cover, over to your left sits the marshy, seasonally green expanse of **Agnew Meadows** itself. Look for mule deer and black bears as you wander alongside the grasses and spring wildflowers. Cross one last tiny flow ahead to reach the Agnew Meadows Trailhead and this leg's end at 8.1 miles, where you'll find parking, vault toilets, garbage receptacles,

bear boxes, and a water spigot ⓞ. If the campground is still closed and you need a spot to rest your head, either continue 5.1 miles into the next leg to find a few small clearings to the left of the trail or follow unpaved **Agnew Meadows Road** under 0.5 mile to reach paved Minaret Summit Road, where you'll catch the seasonal shuttle down to various campgrounds or up to the resort town of Mammoth Lakes, where lodging (and relative luxury) abounds.

CAMP-TO-CAMP MILEAGE

6 AGNEW MEADOWS TO DONOHUE PASS

DISTANCE 14.7 miles

ELEVATION GAIN/LOSS
+4260/-1500 feet

HIGH POINT 11,076 feet

CONNECTING TRAILS AND ROADS
Agnew Meadows Road, River Trail, John
Muir Trail, Rush Creek Trail

you *won't* see are John Muir Trail (JMT) trekkers, since your paths diverged a while back. However, don't be surprised to encounter other backpackers, especially on a summer weekend—Thousand Island Lake is a very popular destination.

Enter the signed **Ansel Adams Wilderness** at the 0.5-mile point, switchbacking up through lodgepole pines. Your calves rejoice once things level out and you begin a long northwestern traverse. In early summer, a healthy dose of vibrant

ON THE TRAIL

Agnew Meadows provides one of the only direct trailheads for the PCT in the Eastern Sierra—you can arrive here by hiking or horse (of course), but also via seasonal shuttle or automobile. You'll find typical trailhead amenities here—garbage receptacles, bear box, vault toilets, picnic table, and water spigot ⬭. When ready to boogie, look for the PCT sign pointing toward Thousand Island Lake and head northeast. Meander through one last bit of meadow and cross gravelly **Agnew Meadows Road** to reach the **High Trail** trailhead at 0.2 mile; this is the continuation of the PCT. You have one last opportunity to commune with a vault toilet, then begin zigzagging up the slope above, quickly crossing a tiny stream ⬭ on a wooden footbridge.

The High Trail earns its name as you climb up above the Middle Fork San Joaquin River drainage, sounds from the nearby pack station fading in the wind—although you may encounter the clacking hooves of a mule train along your route. What

TRANSPORTATION

Shuttle service is available for a small fee from Mammoth Mountain Adventure Center to not just Agnew Meadows (well, to Agnew Meadows Road, 0.3 mile from the trailhead) but also the general Devils Postpile National Monument area. It's required in summer months, typically between Memorial Day weekend and early September, unless you drive down before 7:00 AM or after 7:00 PM or have a campground reservation in the Reds Meadow Valley. If heading to Mammoth Lakes for rest or refueling, catch a shuttle ride out, connecting to public transportation at Mammoth Mountain Adventure Center. Minaret Summit Road usually closes by mid-October; snowshoes are required footwear not too long thereafter.

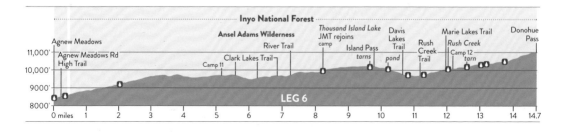

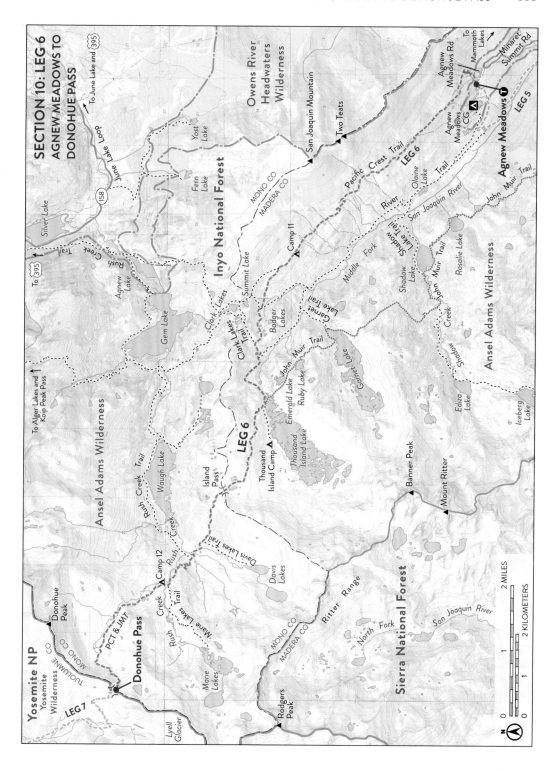

SECTION 10: LEG 6
AGNEW MEADOWS TO
DONOHUE PASS

Island Pass makes for a picturesque rest stop.

wildflowers (and accompanying winged pests) mingle with fragrant sage; you might spot lupine, penstemon, paintbrush, swamp onion, and beautiful Kelley's tiger lilies. The elevated path also offers big views back south toward Reds Meadow and Devils Postpile and across the way to the Ritter Range.

Although I suggest beginning this leg by tanking up at the trailhead spigot, you might be able to top off at any number of seasonal flows along the traverse. Around 2 miles, cross a more noticeable flow **O**, then squiggle around under tree cover for a bit before popping back out to enjoy more magnificent views. A use trail to your left at 5.1 miles leads to a few small campsites (**Camp 11**), which make for a nice sunset perch.

Continue through intermittent tree cover, meeting the first of three spur trails that lead to Clark Lakes at 5.6 miles; stay straight. Begin to lose elevation after this, looking down on a verdant meadow that swirls around Badger Lakes; keep your eyes peeled for mule deer and black bears noshing on the lush surrounds. Crank back uphill to another junction at 6.3 miles; the path on the left drops down to connect with the River Trail, and the one to your right heads toward Clark Lakes. Stay straight. After a bit more grunt work, enter a meadow and pass near some of the smaller **Badger Lakes**, then the last of the Clark Lakes spur trails on your right 0.6 mile ahead. Hit yet another junction just ahead at 7.2 miles—this time with the **River Trail** itself, which offers a route back to Agnew Meadows.

It's a bit startling when Banner Peak and Mount Ritter suddenly come into the picture—these twin hulks guard Thousand Island Lake's southwestern shore, so you know you're getting close. Pass a few small ponds along the Middle Fork, finally reaching **Thousand Island Lake's** ◯ northeastern shore at 8.1 miles; if this beautiful place doesn't inspire your inner Ansel Adams to fire off at least a few shots, I don't know what will.

Thousand Island Lake is one of my favorite Sierra locations—and it's popular with a lot of other people, as well. As such, it's important to minimize your impact on this fragile environment. A sign near the trail junction shows a no-camping zone about 0.25 mile around the outlet; this translates to waiting to throw down your tent until after you pass the first island on your left while walking the lake's use trail. From here, walk ahead a bit and look high to find plentiful (and plenty overused) spots (**Thousand Island Camp**). Be exceptionally cautious to avoid walking on the delicate ground cover, using established dirt and rock paths to reach the water itself, and know that campfires aren't allowed in this area.

From here, the PCT and **JMT** reconnect, now making tracks toward Island Pass. If you weren't sure why the lake earned its name when standing down below, you'll have a better idea once you spot all of the tiny islands speckling its surface. Ascend to more spectacular views, spotting the dark hued Minarets to the south, as well as the slightly reddish San Joaquin Mountain and the Two Teats back to the east.

Compared to the effort required to traverse most Sierra passes, **Island Pass** is a breeze, although the area is quite stunning. Reach it at 9.8 miles, just after strolling between two small tarns; you'll have missed it once you start heading downhill on granite steps. Focus on your feet to avoid tripping on tree roots and rocks underfoot, and make your way down. Pass a pond ◯ on the right at 10.2 miles; this can dry up to a puddle near the end of summer, but there's better water ahead.

You'll encounter several trail junctions in this area, the first being the **Davis Lakes Trail** at 10.8 miles. In short order, cross a multistrand stream ◯, then reach the **Rush Creek Trail** at 11.1 miles. The next stream ◯ crossing comes 0.1 mile later, usually possible on a combination of rocks and logs. It's back to the quad grinding after this, although the sight of giant Waugh Lake below is enjoyable. Ascend to reach the

RUSH CREEK TRAIL

The Rush Creek Trail provides alternate access to this portion of the PCT via a lengthy (but scenic) 9.1-mile route that begins at Silver Lake and weaves along—wait for it—Rush Creek to pass Agnew Lake, Gem Lake, and Waugh Lake before ending at the PCT.

Marie Lakes Trail junction at 12.1, and a wide crossing of **Rush Creek** ◯ shortly thereafter; look for a log to make this easier in times of high water.

Spot some clearings tucked away to the right just after the crossing that make for a fine camp (**Camp 12**). Otherwise, continue regaining all of that elevation you just lost. If thirsty, it's possible to grab water from a small tarn ◯ on the left at 12.6 miles, but there are more streams ahead. Continue through chunks of granite strewn around whitebark pine, lupine, white heather, red mountain heather, and manzanita. Pika and ground squirrels abound, especially cute when they stand like tiny meerkats to chew on blades of grass—and there's plenty of the green stuff around since the area is laced with streams ◯. Cross one at 13.1 miles, another 0.1 mile ahead, then a final one at 13.8 miles.

Continuing on, it's obvious where the trail is headed, although you can't yet see the pass. Leaving the last greenery behind, climb up a seemingly endless (but mellow) series of granite steps and slabs, looking back to score one last view across the Ansel Adams Wilderness—once you hit **Donohue Pass** at 14.7 miles, you're leaving it behind for the **Yosemite Wilderness**—and **Yosemite National Park**! There's one final (mostly downhill) leg left to traverse to reach its namesake meadow and this section's end.

CAMP-TO-CAMP MILEAGE

Agnew Meadows to Camp 11 . . . . 5.1
Camp 11 to Thousand Island Camp 3.0
Thousand Island Camp to Camp 12 . . . . 4.0

7 DONOHUE PASS TO TUOLUMNE MEADOWS

DISTANCE 13 miles

ELEVATION GAIN/LOSS
+470/-2950 feet

HIGH POINT 11,076 feet

CONNECTING TRAILS AND ROADS
Tuolumne Meadows Campground Trail,
Gaylor Lakes Trail, Tuolumne Meadows
Lodge Trail, Tuolumne Meadows Lodge
Road, State Highway 120

ON THE TRAIL

From atop spacious **Donohue Pass**, step into **Yosemite National Park** as you head north toward flat, lush Lyell Canyon, which carves a green swath far below. Almost immediately pass near a bright blue tarn **◑**, a good place to tank up or go for a quick dip if you want to play polar bear. Once you've hiked far enough past the water, consider donning some form of synthetic or natural armor against the multitudes of mosquitos you will likely encounter down the way.

This last leg is mostly downhill, a reward for all the hard work you've put in—or torture if you possess a pair of angry knees. Descend across rock-lined granite slabs and steps, watching the route unfold in front of you. Pass a small bivy spot at 0.7 mile on your right (**Camp 13**), then head down toward a small lake whose startling color is owed to deposits from the Lyell Glacier,

its icy flanks worn like a skirt by Mount Lyell above. Cross a pair of small flows, then carefully traverse the unnamed lake's outlet **◑** 1 mile in. The stunning color may tempt a swim, but the temperature will make you jump right back out.

Head slightly uphill onto a steep slope dotted with red mountain heather, corn lilies, and manzanita, then slosh through the wet trail to make several potentially tricky stream **◑** crossings, the most notable at 1.5 miles. Even during dry summers, this is a raging waterfall that gushes over the trail itself. Even if you find exposed rocks to cross on here, they'll be slippery—take your time and mind your feet, lest you catch a free ride to the bottom.

The widest crossing on this leg is just ahead at 1.7 miles at the **Lyell Fork ◑**, where you can hop across on rocks when the water is low. Find a well-loved campsite (**Lyell Fork Camp**) along an obvious use trail across the way, with a few more campsites just ahead under a cluster of trees. From here, the descent steepens as you move down into hemlock and lodgepole pines, stumbling over ball-bearing rocks and tree roots underfoot, Clark's nutcrackers squawking all around like seagulls of the forest. Perhaps it was just my imagination, but I felt like they were taunting me.

Cross a pair of tiny streams **◑** at 2.2 miles, then look to the right to spot a use trail leading to a small campsite (**Camp 14**) under trees, a nice alternative if the previous camp is crowded. Reach more camping just ahead at 2.6 miles, on either side of a low, wooden bridge over the **Lyell Fork ◑** (**Lyell Bridge Camp**). This area is quite

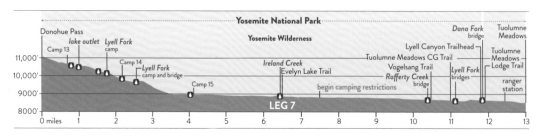

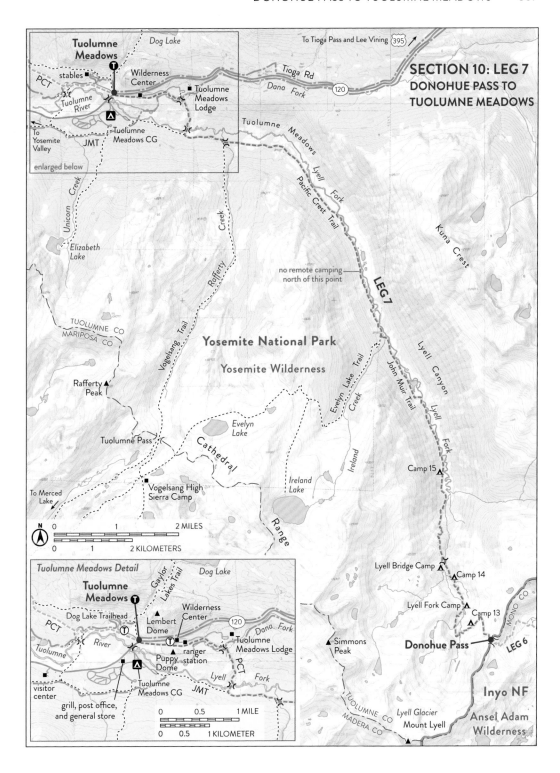

SECTION 10: LEG 7
DONOHUE PASS TO TUOLUMNE MEADOWS

Rise early for a peaceful morning walk across the Lyell Fork bridge in Tuolumne Meadows.

peaceful—the quiet before the tourist storm, which you'll encounter at this leg's endpoint. But forget about all of that and continue advancing toward the floor of **Lyell Canyon**. The route steepens once more for one final plunge toward the green ribbon below, where the trail flattens and widens into a beautiful, pine-fringed meadow filled with mule deer quietly snacking on the verdant bounty. It's only logical that you'll pass a number of seasonal flows feeding into the meadow in early summer, but the first reliable stream **◐** in this area is at 4.1 miles. Look to the left just after crossing to spot a clearing under the pines, which makes for a lovely camp (**Camp 15**)—your last one before reaching Tuolumne Meadows.

Savor the relative quiet in this canyon, looking back toward the Lyell Glacier, Mount Lyell, and Donohue Pass. Wandering along, you'll eventually encounter more people, whether SoBo John Muir Trail hikers, other backpackers, or day hikers out for a stroll. Lyell Fork continues to meander through the meadows to your right, but

avoid temptation to carve your own path to the water in this area—the meadows are incredibly fragile. There are plenty of opportunities ahead to tank up, including a crossing of **Ireland Creek ◐** at 6.5 miles, navigable over rocks or via a downed log in wetter times. Just 0.1 mile ahead, reach a junction with the **Evelyn Lake Trail**, signed not just for Evelyn Lake itself, but also offering detours to Ireland Lake, Vogelsang High Sierra Camp, Merced Lake, and the famous Yosemite Valley, 27 long miles away. Continue straight and note that there's an invisible boundary at the 7.5-mile mark, after which you can't camp outside of Yosemite's developed campgrounds.

Your path moves into thicker tree cover, obscuring meadow views—of course, you'll see another one soon enough. But first, cross a bridge spanning **Rafferty Creek ◐** at 10.6 miles, then reach a junction with the **Vogelsang Trail** 0.1 mile later. The water crossings and trail junctions come fast and furious now as you move into **Tuolumne Meadows**. Next up is a meeting with

TUOLUMNE MEADOWS

The Tuolumne Meadows area offers many services. To access them, continue west on a footpath alongside Tioga Road. You'll first reach a paved road on the left announcing the entrance to the **Tuolumne Meadows Campground.** Spots fill up quickly here, reserved months in advance, but if you hold a wilderness permit, you can stay for one night in the backpacker's campground before or after your trip for a small fee.

Beyond that, you'll next encounter the seasonal **Tuolumne Meadows Store ⦾**, grill, and post office just ahead to your right. Farther up you'll find the visitor center and even more wonderful views of the granite domes towering over the bright green meadows. A shuttle bus offers rides throughout the area, usually between mid-June and Labor Day weekend; you may also consider taking a bus down to Yosemite Valley or perhaps even out to Mammoth Lakes.

the **Tuolumne Meadows Campground Trail** at 11.3 miles; while this takes you to camping, you can also arrive there with a short walk at the end of this leg, so continue straight. Another 0.1 mile later, cross the **Lyell Fork ⦾** on a pair of bridges that makes a worthy place to stop and take in the view.

Reach the **Yosemite Wilderness** boundary just shy of 12 miles in at the **Lyell Canyon trailhead**, right before crossing a bridge over the **Dana Fork ⦾**. A path on the right is signed for Gaylor Lakes, Mono Pass, and Parker Pass, but you head left toward Tuolumne and High Sierra Camp. I had a good laugh here while reading an informational sign that indicated that the "high country" sees almost no rain between May and September—complete lies, considering I spent ten straight days dodging relentless monsoonal thunderstorms en route to this point!

After crossing the bridge, things might seem confusing. The route to your right is marked for Tuolumne Meadows High Sierra Camp (also known as the Tuolumne Meadows Lodge Trail), but you hang a left toward the Ranger Station and Glen Aulin. From here, you're abruptly thrust back into civilization as cars whiz above on **Tuolumne Meadows Lodge Road**, accessed via several spurs to the right. Hang onto your forested dirt path for as long as possible, enjoying the sound of Dana Fork burbling below.

Several tent cabins and the **Tuolumne Meadows Ranger Station** come into view across the road, but focus on the outline of Lembert Dome poking through the trees to provide large, granite comfort in the midst of all of this man-made intrusion.

Stay to the left to skirt another parking area unless you want to pop over and toss something in the garbage or make an early exit. Eventually, the sound of traffic wins out over nature as you near **State Highway 120** (Tioga Road), which you reach at 13 miles—congratulations, you did it! Ignore the multitudes of cars zipping past and focus instead on the **Tuolumne River** snaking through open meadows to your left, while impressive **Lembert Dome** towers to the right. Consider spending some time here once you arrive—head up the road to grab some ice cream and a celebratory beverage, then wander area trails (if your feet haven't gone to pasture) to discover why this area is one of the true gems of **Yosemite National Park**.

CAMP-TO-CAMP MILEAGE

Donohue Pass to Camp 13 . . . . 0.7
Camp 13 to Lyell Fork Camp 1.0
Lyell Fork Camp to Camp 14 . . . . 0.5
Camp 14 to Lyell Bridge Camp 0.4
Lyell Bridge Camp to Camp 15 . . . . 1.5
**Camp 15 to Tuolumne Meadows
    Campground** 7.2

APPENDIX 1

RESOURCES FOR SOUTHERN CALIFORNIA'S PCT

GENERAL

Pacific Crest Trail Association
www.pcta.org

MAPS

Guthook's apps
www.atlasguides.com

Halfmile's maps and apps
www.pctmap.net

US Forest Service maps
www.fs.usda.gov/main/pct/maps-publications

US Geological Survey topographic maps
www.nationalmap.gov/ustopo

PASSES, PERMITS, REGULATIONS

Angeles National Forest
www.fs.usda.gov/detail/angeles/passes-permits

California Department of Fish and Wildlife
www.ca.wildlifelicense.com/InternetSales/Home
/LicensingAndFees

California Fire Permit
www.preventwildfireca.org/Campfire-Permit

Inyo National Forest
www.fs.usda.gov/main/inyo/passes-permits
/recreation

Mount San Jacinto State Park and Wilderness
www.parks.ca.gov/?page_id=636

Pacific Crest Trail Association
www.pcta.org/discover-the-trail/permits

San Bernardino National Forest
www.fs.usda.gov/main/sbnf/passes-permits

Sequoia–Kings Canyon National Parks
www.nps.gov/seki/planyourvisit/wilderness
_permits.htm

Sequoia National Forest
www.fs.usda.gov/detail/sequoia/passes-permits
/recreation

Sierra National Forest
www.fs.usda.gov/detail/sierra/passes-permits

Yosemite National Park
www.nps.gov/yose/planyourvisit/wildpermits.htm

LAND MANAGERS

ANGELES NATIONAL FOREST
www.fs.usda.gov/main/angeles/home

Headquarters
701 N. Santa Anita Avenue
Arcadia, CA 91006
626-574-1613

Santa Clara/Mojave Rivers Ranger District
33708 Crown Valley Road
Acton, CA 93510
661-269-2808

ANZA-BORREGO DESERT STATE PARK
www.parks.ca.gov/?page_id=638

Headquarters
200 Palm Canyon Drive
Borrego Springs, CA 92004
760-767-4205

BUREAU OF LAND MANAGEMENT
www.blm.gov/california

El Centro Field Office
1661 S. 4th Street
El Centro, CA 92243
760-337-4400

Palm Springs–South Coast Field Office
1201 Bird Center Drive
Palm Springs, CA 92262
760-833-7100

Ridgecrest Field Office
300 S. Richmond Road
Ridgecrest, CA 93555
760-384-5400

CLEVELAND NATIONAL FOREST
www.fs.usda.gov/cleveland

Headquarters
10845 Rancho Bernardo Road, Suite 200
San Diego, CA 92127
858-673-6180

Descanso Ranger District
3348 Alpine Boulevard
Alpine, CA 91901
619-445-6235

DEVILS POSTPILE NATIONAL MONUMENT
www.nps.gov/depo/index.htm

Ranger Station
Devils Postpile Access Road
Mammoth Lakes, CA 93546
760-934-2289

INYO NATIONAL FOREST
www.fs.usda.gov/inyo

Headquarters
351 Pacu Lane, Suite 200
Bishop, CA 93514
760-873-2400

Mammoth Ranger District
2500 Highway 203
Mammoth Lakes, CA 93545
760-924-5500

Mono Lake Ranger District
P.O. Box 429
Lee Vining, CA 93541
760-647-3044

Tiny Caribou Creek carves a green path through the trees in the San Bernardino Mountains.

Mt. Whitney Ranger District
640 S. Main Street
Lone Pine, CA 93545
760-876-6200

LAKE MORENA COUNTY PARK

www.sandiegocounty.gov/parks/Camping/lake
_morena.html

Headquarters
2550 Lake Morena Drive
Campo, CA 91906
619-579-4101

MOUNT SAN JACINTO STATE PARK

www.parks.ca.gov/?page_id=636

Headquarters
1 Tram Way
Palm Springs, CA 92262
951-659-2607

SAN BERNARDINO NATIONAL FOREST

www.fs.usda.gov/main/sbnf/about-forest/districts

Headquarters
602 S. Tippecanoe Avenue
San Bernardino, CA 92408
909-382-2600

Mountaintop Ranger District
Big Bear Ranger Station & Discovery Center
41374 North Shore Drive, Highway 38
Fawnskin, CA 92333
909-382-2790

San Jacinto Ranger District
Idyllwild Ranger Station (District Office)
54270 Pinecrest
Idyllwild, CA 92549
909-382-2921

SAN GABRIEL MOUNTAINS NATIONAL MONUMENT

www.fs.fed.us/visit/san-gabriel-mountains
 -national-monument

Jointly administered by Angeles National Forest and San Bernardino National Forest

SAND TO SNOW NATIONAL MONUMENT

www.fs.fed.us/visit/sand-to-snow-national
 -monument

www.blm.gov/nlcs_web/sites/ca/st/en/prog/nlcs
 /Sand-to-Snow.html

Jointly administered by San Bernardino National Forest and Bureau of Land Management

SANTA ROSA AND SAN JACINTO MOUNTAINS NATIONAL MONUMENT

www.blm.gov/nlcs_web/sites/ca/st/en/prog/nlcs
 /SantaRosa_SanJacintoMtns_NM.html

www.fs.usda.gov/detail/sbnf/about-forest
 /districts/?cid=fsbdev7_007801

Jointly administered by San Bernardino National Forest and Bureau of Land Management

Santa Rosa & San Jacinto Mountains National Monument Visitor Center
51500 Highway 74
Palm Desert, CA 92260
760-862-9984

SEQUOIA–KINGS CANYON NATIONAL PARKS

www.nps.gov/seki/index.htm

Headquarters
47050 Generals Highway
Three Rivers, CA 93271
559-565-3341

SEQUOIA NATIONAL FOREST

www.fs.usda.gov/sequoia/

Headquarters
1839 S. Newcomb Street
Porterville, CA 93257
559-784-1500

**Kern River Ranger District
Kernville Office**
105 Whitney Road
Kernville, CA 93238
760-376-3781

**Kern River Ranger District
Lake Isabella Office**
4875 Ponderosa Drive
Lake Isabella, CA 93240
760-379-5646

SIERRA NATIONAL FOREST

www.fs.usda.gov/sierra/

Headquarters
1600 Tollhouse Road
Clovis, CA 93611
559-297-0706

High Sierra Ranger District
29688 Auberry Road
Prather, CA 93651
559-855-5355

VASQUEZ ROCKS NATURAL AREA PARK

parks.lacounty.gov/wps/portal/dpr/Parks/Vasquez
 _Rocks_Natural_Area

Headquarters
10700 W. Escondido Canyon Road
Agua Dulce, CA 91350
661-268-0840

YOSEMITE NATIONAL PARK

www.nps.gov/yose/index.htm

Public Information Office
P.O. Box 577
Yosemite, CA 95389
209-372-0200

TRAIL TOWNS AND SERVICES
(SOUTH TO NORTH)

Here's a list of some of the most popular stops and resupply locations along and near the Pacific Crest Trail between Campo and Tuolumne Meadows. This is not meant to be an exhaustive list but rather a bit of inspiration to help you begin planning. Of course, businesses close, new ones open, and services and hours change—it's best to check websites and call ahead before hitting the trail.

If mailing a package to any post office (aside from the Tuolumne Meadows location), address it using the format below. Zip codes and phone numbers are included in parentheses where post offices are mentioned in this appendix.

Your Name
PCT Hiker, ETA: mm/dd/yy
c/o General Delivery
City, CA Zip Code

CAMPO

The Pacific Crest Trail's southern terminus sits on the fringes of tiny **Campo**, a quiet, pastoral community full of Border Patrol employees and horses. There's not much here aside from several historic museums, a gas station, a small market, and two restaurants, so it's best to arrive fully stocked and ready to roll.

Information

Contact or visit the Bureau of Land Management's **El Centro Field Office** (www.blm.gov/california, 760-337-4400) and/or Cleveland National Forest's **Descanso Ranger District Office** in Alpine (www .fs.usda.gov/cleveland, 619-445-6235).

Transportation

Although it's not possible to take public transportation all the way to the southern terminus, San Diego's **Metropolitan Transit System** (www.sdmts

.com, 619-233-3004) takes you pretty close since Route 894 (Morena Village–El Cajon) stops at the intersection of State Highway 94 and Forest Gate Road in Campo. The bus runs on weekdays only, and the schedule is fairly limited—reservations are recommended at least a day in advance (800-858-0291).

Lodging

There is no lodging available in Campo—your nearest option is the campground at **Lake Morena County Park** (www.sdparks.org, 619-478-5473), 20 miles north on the trail. Chain hotels and small motels can be found in both directions along nearby Interstate 8, although all of them are a bit of a drive from Campo.

Resupply

The **Campo Post Office** (91906, 619-478-5466) is open weekdays during business hours and Saturday mornings. The **Campo Green Store** (619-478-5494), also known as the Trading Post, offers a small selection of groceries.

MOUNT LAGUNA

Mount Laguna is a pine-scented mountain hamlet that serves as the weekend retreat for nature-seeking San Diegans and the first official town (and mountain) stop for northbound PCT hikers. While it doesn't boast a ton of restaurants or services, it has enough to keep you comfortable as you pass through the area.

Information

Cleveland National Forest's **Laguna Mountain Visitor Center** is located in town (lmva.net, 619-473-8547); the volunteer-staffed center's hours are extremely limited, but the public bathrooms remain open even when the main building is closed. **Laguna Mountain Lodge & Store** (www.lagunamountain.com, 619-473-8533) also offers area information, plus they sell maps and Adventure Passes; they're open on weekdays during business hours.

Transportation

Wright Trammel Transportation (www.shuttlesd .com, 760-789-7252) is an on-call service that offers transportation in the general area; reservations are required.

Lodging

Laguna Mountain Lodge & Store offers rustic cabins at reasonable rates. For more savings, stay at **Laguna Campground** or **Burnt Rancheria Campground** on either end of town (www.recreation.gov); the latter closes in the winter months.

Resupply

The **Mount Laguna Post Office** (91948, 619-473-8341) is open weekday afternoons and Saturday mornings. **Laguna Mountain Sport & Supply** (619-473-0450) is a classic outdoor outfitter with a twist—they offer overburdened hikers a complete pack shakedown to see if there's a way to lighten the load. Finally, your old pal Laguna Mountain Lodge & Store offers a small grocery (and limitless tchotchkes), plus they accept hiker packages via UPS and USPS for a small fee—mail to:

    (USPS)
    Your Name
    PCT Hiker, ETA: mm/dd/yy
    c/o Laguna Mountain Lodge
    PO Box 146
    Mount Laguna, CA 91948

    (UPS)
    Your Name
    PCT Hiker, ETA: mm/dd/yy
    c/o Laguna Mountain Lodge
    10678 Sunrise Highway
    Mount Laguna, CA 91948

JULIAN

If we're playing word association games, I say "**Julian**," and you say "Apple pie." While this adorable orchard-filled outpost isn't exactly *on* the PCT (it's about 12 miles west of the trail at Scissors Crossing via Highway 78), many hikers head there for its hospitality and famous desserts.

Transportation

Wright Trammel Transportation operates in this area (see Mount Laguna listing).

Lodging

Prepare to fight the tourist throngs for the town's limited rooms, mostly a quaint assortment of bed and breakfasts and small inns that are nearly always unavailable. The **Julian Lodge** (www .julianlodge.com, 800-542-1420) is fairly hiker friendly, although possibly not budget friendly if yours is tight.

Resupply

The **Julian Post Office** (92036, 760-765-3648) is open weekdays during limited business hours and Saturday mornings. There are two small groceries in town, **Julian Market & Deli** (760-765-2606) and **Jack's Grocery** (760-765-3200), both with deli counters. But let's be real: you're just going to stuff your backpack full of tasty pastries from hiker-friendly **Mom's Pie House** or **Julian Pie Company**.

WARNER SPRINGS

Once a bustling spa getaway for Hollywood types, the small residential ranching community of **Warner Springs** has grown much quieter in recent years. However, that's likely to change as the historic Warner Springs Ranch Resort continues to be revitalized and is in the process of being fully reopened to the public.

Information

The Cleveland National Forest's **Palomar Ranger District Office** is located in Ramona (www .fs.usda.gov/cleveland, 760-788-0250). The **Anza-Borrego Desert State Park Visitor Center** (www.parks.ca.gov, 760-767-4205) in Borrego Springs is open during business hours on weekends and holidays.

Transportation

Wright Trammel Transportation operates in this area (see Mount Laguna listing).

Lodging

The **Warner Springs Ranch Resort** www.warner springsranchresort.com, 760-782-4200) is the only game in town—or *will* be, once its hotel reopens in 2017. Hikers will most likely continue to instead rely on the generosity of the friendly volunteers at the **Warner Springs Community Resource Center** (warnerspringscenter.org, 760-782-0670), who typically allow hikers to sleep on their lawn during the thru-hiking season in late spring. The two nearest campgrounds are the Cleveland National Forest's **Indian Flats Campground** (typically open June through March) and **Oak Grove Campground** (open year-round). Both are first come, first served, although only the latter offers running water.

Resupply

The **Warner Springs Post Office** (92086, 760-782-3166) is open weekdays during limited business hours and Saturday mornings. During the thru-hiking season, the Warner Springs Community Resource Center offers a small seasonal store stocked with portable food and trail-related sundries.

IDYLLWILD

The artsy mountain hamlet of **Idyllwild** is a popular layover for hikers—you can practically smell the relaxation (or is it the hikers?) in the air. It's small, but still manages quite a selection of shops, restaurants, and lodging.

Information

The San Bernardino National Forest's **San Jacinto Ranger District Office** (www.fs.usda .gov/sbnf, 909-382-2921) and **Mount San Jacinto State Park**'s headquarters (www.parks.ca.gov /?page_id=636, 951-659-2607) are both located in Idyllwild.

Lodging

Camping is available in town at Mount San Jacinto State Park. The conveniently located **Idyllwild Inn** (idyllwildinn.com, 888-659-2552) is hiker friendly, offering a PCT discount, trailhead transport, laundry, and package holding. If they're full, there are plenty of other options in town, mostly small inns and private cabin rentals.

Resupply

There are two small grocery stores in town: **Village Market** (951-659-3800) and **Fairway Market** (951-659-2737); the latter typically has a much larger selection. **Nomad Ventures** (www .nomadventures.com, 951-659-4853) is a small but well-stocked outdoor outfitter. The **Idyllwild Post Office** (92549, 951-659-1969) is open weekdays during business hours. The Idyllwild Inn offers package storage for guests—mail to:

Your Name
PCT Hiker, ETA: mm/dd/yy
c/o Idyllwild Inn
PO Box 515
Idyllwild, CA 92549

SAN GORGONIO PASS AND ENVIRONS

There are no services at **San Gorgonio Pass** itself, so some hikers head to **Cabazon**, about 6 miles west, to handle resupply. Be sure to channel your inner Pee-Wee Herman and visit the famous **Cabazon Dinosaurs** if you venture this way.

Information

The **Whitewater Preserve** Ranger Station (www .wildlandsconservancy.org, 760-325-7222) is open daily during business hours.

Transportation

Amtrak (www.amtrak.com, 800-872-7245) offers a combination train/bus service from Los Angeles with a stop at the **Morongo Casino Resort & Spa** in Cabazon, but you'll still need to figure out how to get to the trailhead from there, and you cannot purchase tickets at the stop itself.

Lodging

Whitewater Preserve offers free camping, though donations are appreciated (pay it forward!);

reservations are required for groups of ten or more. Down the road in Cabazon, the Morongo Casino Resort & Spa (www.morongocasinoresort.com, 800-252-4499) caters to those with deeper pockets (or those who dream of them).

Resupply
The nearest post office is in Cabazon (92230, 888-275-8777). It's open during limited business hours on weekdays. There's not much in the way of groceries around here, although you can pick up a few things (including hot food) at the **Main Country Liquor & Deli** (951-849-6422) just around the corner. If it's gear you require, check out the massive **Desert Hills Premium Outlets** just a few minutes west on Interstate 10, with a few outdoor clothing companies tucked around the fancier stuff.

BIG BEAR
Most people use "Big Bear" to encompass the twin burgs of **Big Bear Lake** and **Big Bear City**. The former is a resort town, the latter more residential. Both offer options for hungry, sleepy hikers, although Big Bear Lake has a bit more in the way of tourist attractions—namely, lake access, ski runs, a quaint shopping area, and my favorite breakfast joint, the **Grizzly Manor Café**.

Information
San Bernardino National Forest's **Mountaintop Ranger District Office** is located in the **Big Bear Discovery Center** in Fawnskin (www.fs.usda.gov /sbnf, 909-382-2790), which is closed on Tuesday and Wednesday.

Transportation
Mountain Transit (mountaintransit.org, 909-878-5200) runs several bus lines in the general Big Bear area as well as a weekend trolley service in Big Bear Lake. None of these stop at any of the area trailheads, but they're useful once you're in town.

Lodging
San Bernardino National Forest hosts a number of campgrounds scattered around Big Bear Lake— some of these may be booked at www.recreation .gov. Although there are several chain hotels in

the Big Bear area, I've found the local offerings to be much more attractive (and attractively priced). My favorite is **Sleepy Forest Cottages** and its sister property, **Cathy's Cottages** (www.sleepyforest .com, 909-866-7444); they offer a hiker discount and their properties are unique. Many hikers also love the economical **Big Bear Hostel** (www .bigbearhostel.com, 909-866-8900); they also offer a discount plus package holding.

Resupply
The two biggest grocery stores in the area, **Vons** (909-866-6027) and **Stater Bros.** (909-866-5211), are both in Big Bear Lake. **Big Bear Sporting Goods** (bigbearlakesportinggoods.com, 909-866-3222) is the place to go for basic gear needs. The post office in **Big Bear City** (92314, 909-585-7132) is open limited business hours weekdays, and the one in **Big Bear Lake** (92315, 909-866-1035) is open business hours weekdays and Saturday mornings. Be sure you know which one you sent your package to, since they're 5 miles apart! The Big Bear Hostel also accepts packages for its guests only (via UPS or USPS); mail them to:

(USPS)
Your Name
PCT Hiker, ETA: mm/dd/yy
c/o Big Bear Hostel
PO Box 1951
Big Bear Lake, CA 92315-1951

(UPS)
Your Name
PCT Hiker, ETA: mm/dd/yy
c/o Big Bear Hostel
541 Knickerbocker Road
Big Bear Lake, CA 92315

CAJON PASS AND ENVIRONS
Most hikers know **Cajon Pass** for its nearly trailside **McDonald's**, the Golden Arches acting as an emotional guiding light for hungry trekkers. Sadly, the Blue Cut Fire ravaged the area in 2016, but fire crews were able to save many local businesses that have long been welcoming to hikers—show them that kindness in return by spending money in the area as everyone works to recover.

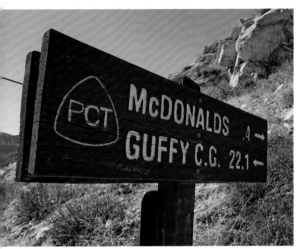

Find the most famous trail sign on the PCT near Cajon Pass.

Information

Silverwood Lake State Recreation Area's park office is located in Hesperia (www.parks.ca.gov, 760-389-2281), a short walk from the trail. San Bernardino National Forest's **Front Country Ranger District Office** is in Lytle Creek (www .fs.usda.gov/sbnf, 909-382-2851).

Lodging

The **Best Western** in Phelan (www.bestwestern .com, 760-249-6777) is exceptionally hiker friendly and located within walking distance of the trail. Camping is also available at Silverwood Lake State Recreation Area.

Resupply

The Best Western holds packages for guests; send packages to:

> Your Name
> PCT Hiker, ETA: mm/dd/yy
> c/o Best Western Cajon Pass
> 8317 CA Highway 138
> Phelan, CA 92371

WRIGHTWOOD

Many hikers detour to **Wrightwood** via the Acorn Trail after the long, hot, dry climb from Cajon Pass. The forested ski town is small but equipped to handle a multitude of needs—and the locals are extremely friendly to PCT hikers.

Information

Angeles National Forest's **Grassy Hollow Visitor Center** (www.fs.usda.gov/angeles, 626-821-6737) is located next to the trail. The Forest's **Big Pines Information Station** (www.fs.usda.gov/angeles, 760-249-3504) is located in Wrightwood; it was closed as of this writing, but is slated to reopen in the future—call before visiting.

Transportation

Victor Valley Transit Authority (vvta.org, 760-948-3030) operates a bus line (Route 20) from nearby Phelan with a stop at the Wrightwood Community Center—not terribly useful unless you're traveling between the two towns or connecting from other routes in the nearby communities of Hesperia, Apple Valley, or Victorville.

Lodging

The **Cedar Lodge Motel** (www.cedarlodgewright woodca.com, 760-249-5062) and **Canyon Creek Inn** (www.canyoncreekinn.com, 760-249-4800) are both small but reasonably priced. Like Idyllwild, Wrightwood also features an assortment of private cabins for rent.

Resupply

Jensen's Fine Foods (760-249-3322) is a well-stocked, large grocery store complete with deli. The **Wrightwood Post Office** (92397, 760-249-8882) is open during business hours weekdays. The town's **Mountain Hardware** store (mtn hardware.com, 760-249-3653) is legendary for its hiker friendliness. The store not only accepts packages but also maintains a list of local trail angels and carries a few camping essentials. They're open during business hours every day. Send packages to:

> (USPS)
> Your Name
> PCT Hiker, ETA: mm/dd/yy
> c/o Mountain Hardware
> PO Box 398
> Wrightwood, CA 92397

(UPS)
Your Name
PCT Hiker, ETA: mm/dd/yy
c/o Mountain Hardware
1390 Highway 2
Wrightwood, CA 92397

ACTON

Acton, a former mining and railroad hub, is one of the quieter towns near the PCT in Southern California. Most hikers only go as far as the KOA Campground just off-trail, but there are opportunities for resupply slightly further afield.

Information
Angeles National Forest's **Santa Clara/Mojave Rivers Ranger District** (www.fs.usda.gov/angeles, 661-269-2808) is just off of State Highway 14 in Acton.

Transportation
Metrolink (www.metrolinktrains.com, 800-371-5465) offers train service on the Antelope Valley Line between Los Angeles and Lancaster, including a stop in Acton; the station is about 10.5 miles northeast of the PCT crossing in Soledad Canyon. The Los Angeles County **Department of Public Works** (dpw.lacounty.gov/pdd/transit, 818-504-7270) operates a limited bus shuttle (Monday, Wednesday, and Saturday) connecting Acton, Agua Dulce, Santa Clarita, and Newhall. The Acton stop is near the Santa Clara/Mojave Rivers Ranger District Office at the intersection of Sierra Highway and Crown Valley Road.

Lodging
The **Acton and Los Angeles North KOA Campground** (koacom, 661-268-1214) is a large, amenity-filled commercial campground located a few minutes' walk from the trail crossing at Soledad Canyon Road. Although it's popular with the RV crowd, there's plenty of space for tent camping, and the management is very welcoming of PCT hikers.

Resupply
The **Acton Post Office** (93510, 661-269-8618) is open limited business hours weekdays. The KOA features a small convenience store, but there are also two groceries in the area. The larger of the two is the slightly more upscale **Acton Market Country Store** (661-269-1522), which offers an extensive bakery and deli, and the slightly smaller is the competitively named **The Original Acton Market** (theoriginalactonmarket.com, 661-441-0455). To make your decision more difficult, both offer fresh pizza.

AGUA DULCE

You don't have to detour off-trail to visit charming, pastoral **Agua Dulce**—the PCT runs straight through town! Although lodging is hard to come by in this area, it's at least worth a stop to stock up at the grocery store and sit down for a non-freeze-dried meal at one of the restaurants.

Information
Vasquez Rocks Natural Area Park (parks.lacounty.gov, 661-268-0840) has an impressive interpretive center that is open daily (except Monday) during business hours.

Transportation
The limited **Department of Public Works** shuttle bus stops adjacent to the trail near the Agua Dulce Women's Club on Agua Dulce Canyon Road just north of Bedworth Road; see the Acton listing for more information.

Lodging
Vasquez Rocks Natural Area Park offers group camping, although it can sometimes accommodate solo backpackers if the group site isn't reserved—inquire at the visitor center during business hours.

Resupply
Sweetwater Farms (www.sweetwaterfarmsmarket.com, 661-268-0700) is a mid-sized grocery with deli counter. There is no post office in the Agua Dulce area, so most hikers rely on the kindness of legendary long-time trail angels Donna ("L-Rod") and Jeff Saufley of **Hiker Heaven** (hikerheaven.com) to help with packages. Check their website before mailing anything to ensure that they are still accepting hiker mail (typically only during the thru-hiker seasons of late spring and early fall).

TEHACHAPI PASS AND ENVIRONS

At Tehachapi Pass, hikers have the option to decamp to **Tehachapi** or **Mojave**, small cities nearly equidistant from the trail. Ask any past hiker and they'll chime in with a favorite, but both offer a multitude of options for rest and resupply. My two cents: Tehachapi has more ambiance, but everything is a bit more spread out.

Transportation

Kern Transit (kerntransit.org, 800-323-2396) offers a Bakersfield to Lancaster line (Route 100) that stops at Tehachapi Pass by request—you must call ahead for a pickup. There are also several stops in both Tehachapi and Mojave. They also offer a Dial-A-Ride service in both cities; one-day notice is required to schedule pickups. **Eastern Sierra Transit** (www.estransit.com, 800-922-1930) operates a limited bus service (once daily in each direction on Monday, Wednesday, and Friday) between Lancaster and Mammoth Lakes that stops in Mojave in front of the Carl's Jr.—reservation is required at least a day prior to travel.

Lodging

Both cities offer several chain hotels. For something a bit different, the **Tehachapi Municipal Airport** (661-822-2220) offers a cheap alternative—camping on the lawn at its Aviator Park (just be sure to move your tent before the sprinklers turn on in the morning unless you're testing its waterproofing). The nearest traditional campgrounds are at **Tehachapi Mountain Park** (www.co.kern.ca.us/parks, 661-822-4632), part of Kern County's Department of Parks and Recreation, and **Brite Lake Aquatic Recreation Area** (www.tvrpd.org, 661-822-3228), part of the Tehachapi Valley Recreation and Park District. The latter is fairly small, and camping is first-come, first-served; the former is much larger and reservations are recommended.

Resupply

The **Tehachapi Post Office** (93561, 661-822-0279) is open business hours on weekdays and limited hours midday on Saturday. The **Mojave Post Office** (93501, 661-824-3502) is open limited business hours weekdays. Both towns offer large chain grocery stores—there's a **Stater Bros.** (661-824-2719) in Mojave and an **Albertsons** (661-823-7090) in Tehachapi. Stick with the latter for general gear needs since there's a **Big 5 Sporting Goods** (661-822-4197) in town.

WALKER PASS AND ENVIRONS

The big question at **Walker Pass** is "Do I head west or east?" To the west is blink-and-you'll-miss-it Onyx and the larger resort town of Lake Isabella. To the east (and much lower in elevation) is blink-*twice*-and-you'll-miss-it Inyokern and the larger military outpost of Ridgecrest. Lake Isabella and Ridgecrest are the most common choices for stopovers, although both are quite a distance from the trail.

Information

Sequoia National Forest's **Kern River Ranger District Office** is located in Kernville (www.fs.usda.gov/sequoia, 760-376-3781).

Transportation

Kern Transit offers a Lake Isabella to Ridgecrest line (Route 227) that stops at Walker Pass by request—you must call ahead for a pickup. There are also several stops in both Onyx and Inyokern. They also offer a limited Dial-A-Ride service in Onyx and Lake Isabella; one-day notice is required to schedule pickups. See Tehachapi Pass and Environs listing for more info.

Lodging

The nearest lodging is the **Walker Pass Campground**, a no-frills BLM site located a few minutes west of Walker Pass itself, accessible from the trail. Aside from a spring down the road, there is no running water here, but there's also no fee (although donations are appreciated). For a stay with a few more creature comforts, hotels abound in Lake Isabella and Ridgecrest. In the former, try the **Lake Isabella Motel** (760-379-2800). For the latter, chain hotels are a dime a dozen due to the nearby Naval Air Weapons Station at China Lake.

Resupply

The **Onyx Post Office** (93255, 760-378-2121) is open limited business hours weekdays. The **Lake Isabella Post Office** (93240, 760-379-1326) is open limited business hours weekdays. The **Inyokern Post Office** (93527, 760-377-5125) is open limited hours weekdays. The **Ridgecrest Post Office** (93555, 760-375-1939) is open limited business hours weekdays and midday hours on Saturday. Your best bet for groceries is to hit the **Vons** (760-379-4461) in Lake Isabella or one of the multiple chain grocery stores in Ridgecrest. You can also find basic camping gear in the latter at **Big 5 Sporting Goods** (760-384-4582).

KENNEDY MEADOWS

Surely no other place glows in the heart of northbound PCT hikers like **Kennedy Meadows**, "Gateway to the Sierra" and erstwhile Land of Plenty. Many hikers stay planted on the expansive deck at the popular Kennedy Meadows General Store for far longer than they anticipate—the lure of cold beer, the taste of hot hamburgers, and the camaraderie with fellow hikers are difficult to resist.

Lodging

The **Kennedy Meadows General Store** (559-850-5647) typically allows PCT hikers to camp in a designated area for free. Since this can turn into a bit of a party scene during the height of thru-hiker season, you might consider the quieter surrounds of the **Kennedy Meadows Campground** just up Kennedy Meadows Road, directly on the trail. Campground management was transferred to Inyo National Forest in 2016, and its amenities and fees may change in the future. As of my last visit in summer 2016, piped water was no longer available (although the South Fork Kern River runs nearby), and campsite fee payment was on the honor system at the General Store.

Resupply

Although there is no post office in Kennedy Meadows, the Kennedy Meadows General Store accepts packages for hikers for a small fee (UPS and USPS), has a small selection of groceries and

Poppies and lupine decorate the trail in spring.

camping gear, and offers bear canisters for rent. Their hours are limited outside of the summer season, so call ahead before planning a mail drop or visit. Mail packages to:

Your Name
PCT Hiker, ETA: mm/dd/yy
c/o Kennedy Meadows General Store
96740 Beach Meadows Road
Inyokern, CA 93527

COTTONWOOD PASS AND ENVIRONS

While you won't find anything at **Cottonwood Pass** other than fantastic views, thin air, and possible cell reception, it's common to hike down to the Horseshoe Meadow Recreation Area (aka "Horseshoe Meadows") to score a ride down the hill to **Lone Pine**, a classic hiker hamlet tucked into the hot Owens Valley far below. Since it serves as launchpad for Mount Whitney climbers, the town knows how to cater to trekkers—and does it well.

Information

Inyo National Forest's **Eastern Sierra Interagency Visitor Center** is located in Lone Pine (www .fs.usda.gov/inyo, 760-876-6200); if you stop here, take a moment to appreciate the epic views of Mount Whitney and the spectacular Sierra Crest to the west.

Transportation

Eastern Sierra Transit (www.estransit.com, 800-922-1930) operates limited local and regional bus services in the area. The Lone Pine to Reno route picks up at the McDonald's in Lone Pine, making stops in Independence, Bishop, Mammoth Lakes, and Lee Vining, among other places (once daily in each direction, Monday, Tuesday, Thursday, and Friday); reservation required at least one day in advance. The Lone Pine Express line runs three times per weekday and includes stops in Independence and Bishop. In addition to public transit, several more expensive private shuttle services operate in the area—**East Side Sierra Shuttle** (www.eastsidesierrashuttle.com, 760-878-8047) hits every major trailhead in the Eastern Sierra.

Lodging

Inyo National Forest's **Cottonwood Pass** and **Cottonwood Lakes Trailhead Campgrounds** are located in the Horseshoe Meadow Recreation Area below the pass. Sites are firstcome, first-served, and a cash payment is required at the iron ranger located in each campground. Down in Lone Pine, quite a few hotels serve the large tourist population. I've had great experiences at both the **Whitney Portal Hostel** (www.mountwhitneyportal.com, 760-876-0030) and **Dow Villa Motel** (www .dowvillamotel.com, 800-824-9317). Fair warning—both seem to have paper-thin walls, but the latter has a pool and hot tub, which earns it a few bonus points.

Resupply

Joseph's Bi-Rite Market (760-876-4378) is a small grocery store with a decent selection. While a few stores in town sell basic camping supplies, **Elevation** (www.sierraelevation.com,

760-876-4560) is packed to the gills with actual backpacking gear. The **Lone Pine Post Office** (93545, 760-876-5681) is open limited business hours weekdays. The Whitney Portal Hostel also accepts packages (UPS or FedEx)—send them to:

Your Name
PCT Hiker, ETA: mm/dd/yy
c/o Whitney Portal Hostel
238 S. Main St
Lone Pine, CA 93545

INDEPENDENCE

Located about 13 miles below the popular Onion Valley trailhead (the gateway to Kearsarge Pass), historic **Independence** has an impressive wealth of services for a town its (tiny) size. Many hikers head down the hill to take care of all of their business in town while some hitch or bus farther north to Bishop for more variety in lodging and food.

Transportation

Eastern Sierra Transit Authority and **East Side Sierra Shuttle** both operate in the area; see Cottonwood Pass and Environs listing for info.

Lodging

While there are several motels available in town, the most popular is **Mt. Williamson Motel and Base Camp** (mtwilliamsonmotel.com, 760-878-2121) due to its fantastic treatment of hikers—no surprise, since owner Cris "Strider" Chater is a trail legend herself. Camping is available near town at Inyo County's **Independence Creek Campground** (www.inyocountycamping.com, 760-873-5564), and up the hill at Inyo National Forest's **Onion Valley Campground** (www.fs.usda.gov/inyo), the trailhead for a trip over Kearsarge Pass back to the trail—reservations are recommended at the latter since it's one of the most popular trailheads in the Eastern Sierra.

Resupply

The **Independence Post Office** (93526, 760-878-2210) is open limited business hours weekdays. The Mt. Williamson Motel and Base Camp offers a trail-famous resupply package—visit the website for details. In the past, you could only buy food at the gas stations in town, but now there's the **Owens Valley Growers Co-Op** (owens valleygrowerscooperative.com, 760-915-0091). Its stock is fairly slim, but it offers an impressive selection of organic and health-conscious choices for being located in such a small town; there's also a café on site.

BISHOP

While it's still small, **Bishop** is the largest of the three Owens Valley towns frequented by hikers. Here, you'll find a mix of boutique and big box stores along with a wealth of fellow outdoorspeople and an opportunity to engage in major carbloading at the famous **Erick Schat's Bakkerÿ**. There's no shame in taking an entire loaf of bread back on the trail with you.

Information

Inyo National Forest's **White Mountain Public Lands Information Center** (www.fs.usda.gov/inyo, 760-873-2500) is located in downtown Bishop.

Transportation

Eastern Sierra Transit Authority and **East Side Sierra Shuttle** both operate in the area; see Cottonwood Pass and Environs listing for info. The former also offers an express service between Bishop and Mammoth Lakes.

Lodging

The Hostel California (www.thehostelcalifornia.com, 760-399-6316), cheekily abbreviated as "THC," is the choice for most budget-conscious (or fun-seeking) hikers passing through town, although plenty of chain motels sprinkle the main drag.

Resupply

The **Bishop Post Office** (93514, 760-873-3526) is open limited business hours weekdays and mornings on Saturday. There are several small markets in town, but you'll find the best selection at **Vons** (760-872-9811). Two outdoor shops compete for your gear dollars here—**Eastside Sports** (eastsidesports.com, 760-873-7520) and **Sage To Summit** (www.sagetosummit.com, 760-872-1756); the latter caters to lightweight backpackers.

FLORENCE LAKE TRAIL AND ENVIRONS

The **Florence Lake Trail** leads straight to **Muir Trail Ranch** (MTR), a rustic outpost that offers a spectacular backcountry experience for paid guests and a simple resupply opportunity for (also paying) hikers. About 20 miles north on the PCT, **Vermilion Valley Resort** (VVR) offers a very different experience; no reservations required (although a resupply fee *is*). I feasted like a somewhat feral queen at MTR's generous hiker buckets after grabbing my resupply, and I lounged around VVR for an entire lazy day with beer perpetually in hand; there are positives and negatives to both places.

Information

Sierra National Forest's **High Sierra Ranger District** is located outside the Forest on State Highway 168 in Prather (www.fs.usda.gov/sierra, 559-855-5355).

Lodging

The nearest campground is Sierra National Forest's **Jackass Meadow Campground**, a seasonal first come, first served location near Florence Lake. For a more luxurious option, make a reservation at the full-service Muir Trail Ranch (www.muirtrailranch.com, no phone—instead, email howdy@muirtrailranch.com); be quick as the limited spots are usually snapped up well before summer begins. The vibe is significantly more laid back at VVR (www.edisonlake.com, 559-259-4000), with grassy camping, old school RVs, and rustic rooms for rent.

Resupply

Muir Trail Ranch offers a resupply service for hikers during the summer months. It's very expensive (given the price of transporting and storing packages in such a remote location) and the directions are *very* specific—it's best to head to the website to ensure you follow procedure correctly. VVR also offers a seasonal resupply service; it's less expensive than MTR's, but you also have to travel a lot farther to receive your package. Again, visit the website for specifics.

Glen Pass offers a dazzling view of Rae Lakes waiting below.

MAMMOTH LAKES AND ENVIRONS

Some hikers choose to resupply and relax at Red's Meadow Resort in Reds Meadow Valley for its proximity to trail and its low-key ambiance. Some hikers elect to hop on the Reds Meadow Shuttle and head up to **Mammoth Lakes**, a somewhat upscale year-round resort town that offers ample shopping, eating, and lodging opportunities along with the very popular **Mammoth Brewing Company**.

Information

Inyo National Forest's **Mammoth Lakes Welcome Center** (www.fs.usda.gov/inyo, 760-924-5500) is on par with the Eastern Sierra Interagency Center as one of the best visitor centers I've ever . . . visited. **Devils Postpile National Monument**'s tiny Ranger Station (www.nps.gov/depo) is located just off Minaret Vista Road in the monument.

Transportation

Eastern Sierra Transit Authority and **East Side Sierra Shuttle** both operate in the area,

with the former offering express service between Mammoth Lakes and Bishop as well as local service within Mammoth Lakes; see Cottonwood Pass and Environs listing for info. **YARTS** (yarts .com, 877-989-2787) offers seasonal bus service connecting Mammoth Lakes, Tuolumne Meadows, and Yosemite Valley. Finally, the seasonal **Reds Meadow Shuttle** (operated by Eastern Sierra Transit Authority) connects The Village in Mammoth Lake with the Adventure Center at Mammoth Mountain and multiple trail-adjacent stops in the Reds Meadow Valley.

Lodging

Plenty of camping options exist in and around town—I tend to stay at Inyo National Forest's **Old Shady Rest Campground** (www.fs.usda .gov/inyo) whenever I need a cheap place to lay my head, although far more scenic options abound near Twin Lakes and Lake Mary. There is no shortage of walled accommodations available, ranging from upscale ski lodges to chain motels to hostels—I've heard from many hikers that the **Shilo Inn** (shiloinns.com, 800-222-2244) is the place to go if you're on a budget and don't want to stay at a hostel, but haven't been there myself.

Resupply

The **Mammoth Lakes Post Office** (93546, 760-934-2205) is open limited business hours weekdays. Much closer to trail, **Red's Meadow Resort** also offers seasonal package services; visit the website for mailing specifics. The resort has a small convenience store on site; for more variety, head into Mammoth Lakes, where you'll find a much larger grocery selection at **Vons** (760-934-4536). There are a lot of gear shops in town, most of them catering to snow sports—start with **Mammoth Mountaineering Supply** (mammoth gear.com, 888-395-3951) for a good selection of hiking gear.

TUOLUMNE MEADOWS

Tuolumne Meadows is one of the most iconic locations in **Yosemite National Park**. Climbers frequent its granite domes, and animals frequent its lush meadows. PCT and JMT hikers converge at the Tuolumne Meadows Store (and Grill and post office) to eat, drink, and be hairy. Don't be offended when fascinated tourists stare at your bedraggled form. Remember, sometimes the best things in life are only temporary—the entire Tuolumne Meadows area operates on a seasonal basis, so once snow closes Tioga Road (usually by early November), the magic is gone until the following summer.

Information

If requesting a wilderness permit, contact or visit **Yosemite National Park's Tuolumne Meadows Wilderness Center** (www.nps.gov/yose, 209-372-0740). For other inquiries, contact or visit the **Tuolumne Meadows Ranger Station** (209-372-0309).

Transportation

All transportation services that go through Tuolumne Meadows are seasonal. **YARTS** offers bus service connecting Tuolumne Meadows with both Mammoth Lakes and Yosemite Valley; see Mammoth Lakes and Environs listing for info. The Park Service offers the **Tuolumne Meadows Shuttle Bus** (www.nps.gov/yose, 209-372-0200) that makes stops between Tuolumne Meadows Lodge and Olmsted Point. Yosemite concessionaire Aramark (www.travelyosemite.com, 888-413-8869) offers a "hikers bus" that makes several stops between Tuolumne Meadows and Yosemite Valley. There is also **Amtrak** bus service to Tuolumne Meadows; you must purchase outgoing tickets in advance.

Lodging

Only the fortunate will snag a coveted reservation at the park's seasonal **Tuolumne Meadows Campground**—plan ahead to grab a spot or come armed with your permit and prepare to spend a night at the cash-only, walk-up backpacker's site. If you want something slightly nicer, try your luck with the equally difficult-to-reserve **Tuolumne Meadows Lodge** (actually a small village of "tent cabins") just down the road; both places are within walking distance of the trail.

Resupply

The **Tuolumne Meadows Store** (209-372-8428) is a fairly large convenience store, offering food, beverages, tchotchkes, and firewood. The **Tuolumne Meadows Post Office** (209-372-8236), located next to the store, is open business hours weekdays and Saturday mornings. Mail packages to:

Your Name
PCT Hiker, ETA: mm/dd/yy
c/o General Delivery
Tuolumne Meadows
Yosemite National Park, CA 95389

INDEX

ABOUT THE AUTHOR

SHAWNTÉ SALABERT is a Los Angeles–based outdoor enthusiast and curiosity seeker on a never-ending mission to cram as much California sunshine into her life as possible. When she's not wandering the desert, tucked beside alpine lakes, or dangling from precipitous rock climbing routes, Shawnté serves as a trip leader and Wilderness Travel Course instructor for the Angeles Chapter of the Sierra Club, and also volunteers with local trail crews and other outdoor organizations.

Off-trail, Shawnté is the senior writer for California's premier outdoor adventure website, Modern Hiker. Her words have also appeared on the pixels and pages of *Outside Online, Backpacker, Adventure Journal, REI Co-op Journal, Land+People*, and other fine outlets. When not scribbling away, she enjoys eating enchiladas, hanging with her pal Eddie Cat Halen, and working to "earn" a series of badges featured in the 1947 edition of the *Girl Scout Handbook*. For more information, or to drop her a line, please visit www.shawntesalabert.com.

MICHAEL LEMMON

ABOUT THE SERIES

The Pacific Crest National Scenic Trail meanders north from California's border with Mexico to the entrance of Manning Provincial Park in British Columbia, on the Washington State–Canada border. This rigorous trail has evolved since its earliest envisioning in 1926 to encompass approximately 2650 miles, traveling through some of the West Coast's most stunning country. Now with the new series **Hiking the Pacific Crest Trail** hikers and other adventurers can enjoy beautiful, full-color guides to section hiking the entire trail.

- All new guides, focused on section hiking the PCT
- Each volume researched and created by an experienced hiker and backpacker
- Inspirational full-color guides with more than 150 photographs
- Section-by-section routes for day hikers, backpackers, and thru-hikers
- Four volumes in series: Washington, Oregon, Northern California, and Southern California

MOUNTAINEERS BOOKS

SKIPSTONE BRAIDED RIVER

recreation · lifestyle · conservation

MOUNTAINEERS BOOKS is a leading publisher of mountaineering literature and guides—including our flagship title, *Mountaineering: The Freedom of the Hills*—as well as adventure narratives, natural history, and general outdoor recreation. Through our two imprints, Skipstone and Braided River, we also publish titles on sustainability and conservation. We are committed to supporting the environmental and educational goals of our organization by providing expert information on human-powered adventure, sustainable practices at home and on the trail, and preservation of wilderness.

The Mountaineers, founded in 1906, is a 501(c)(3) nonprofit outdoor recreation and conservation organization whose mission is to enrich lives and communities by helping people "explore, conserve, learn about, and enjoy the lands and waters of the Pacific Northwest and beyond." One of the largest such organizations in the United States, it sponsors classes and year-round outdoor activities throughout the Pacific Northwest, including climbing, hiking, backcountry skiing, snowshoeing, camping, kayaking, sailing, and more. The Mountaineers also supports its mission through its publishing division, Mountaineers Books, and promotes environmental education and citizen engagement. For more information, visit The Mountaineers Program Center, 7700 Sand Point Way NE, Seattle, WA 98115-3996; phone 206-521-6001; www.mountaineers.org; or email info@mountaineers.org.

Our publications are made possible through the generosity of donors and through sales of more than 800 titles on outdoor recreation, sustainable lifestyle, and conservation. To donate, purchase books, or learn more, visit us online.

OTHER MOUNTAINEERS BOOKS TITLES YOU MAY ENJOY!

Mountaineers Books is proud to be a corporate sponsor of the Leave No Trace Center for Outdoor Ethics, whose mission is to promote and inspire responsible outdoor recreation through education, research, and partnerships. • The Leave No Trace program is focused specifically on human-powered (nonmotorized) recreation. • Leave No Trace strives to educate visitors about the nature of their recreational impacts and offers techniques to prevent and minimize such impacts. • Leave No Trace is best understood as an educational and ethical program, not as a set of rules and regulations. • For more information, visit www.lnt.org or call 800-332-4100.